The Multiply Handicapped
Hearing Impaired Child

The Multiply Handicapped Hearing Impaired Child

Edited by

George T. Mencher, Ph.D.

Director, Nova Scotia Hearing and Speech Clinic
Professor of Audiology
Dalhousie University
School of Human Communication Disorders
Halifax, Nova Scotia, Canada

Sanford E. Gerber, Ph.D.

Professor and Chairman
Department of Speech
University of California
Santa Barbara, California

(G&S)

Grune & Stratton

A Subsidiary of Harcourt Brace Jovanovich, Publishers
New York   London
Paris   San Diego   San Francisco   São Paulo
Sydney   Tokyo   Toronto

Grune & Stratton, Inc.
111 Fifth Avenue
New York, New York 10003

Distributed in the United Kingdom by
Grune & Stratton, Inc. (London) Ltd.
24/28 Oval Road, London NW 1

Library of Congress Catalog Number 83-12826
International Standard Book Number 0-8089-1618-1

Printed in the United States of America

This book is dedicated to our children
Erika and Jordan
Michael, Howard, Naomi, and Sharon
With love and respect for all they have taught us

Contents

Foreword   xi

Preface   xiii

Contributors   xv

Position Statement: The Multiply Handicapped
Hearing Impaired Child   1

Hearing Loss and Multiple Handicaps: Occurrence
and Effects   5
George T. Mencher

The Educator–Therapist and Deaf, Multiply Disabled
Children: Some Essential Criteria   13
Kevin Murphy

Prospective Identification of Infants with Hearing Loss
and Multiple Handicaps: The Role of the Neonatal
Follow-up Clinic   27
Charlene Robertson, Lillian Whyte

Habilitation Facilities at the Glenrose School Hospital   45
Robert Shea

The Otological Perspective   51
Irwin F. Stewart

Multiple Handicaps and Ear Malformations in Hearing
Impaired Preschool Children   67
Gunnar Liden, Aira Kankkunen, Andre Tjellström

Early Intervention: The Prevention of Multiple Handicaps   83
Hilde S. Schlesinger

Assessment and Intervention from a Developmental
Perspective   117
Arthur Boothroyd

The Child Neurologist's Contribution to the Care of
Children with Hearing Loss   139
Isabelle Rapin

Manual Aids: A Must for the Psychotic Deaf and a
Fail-Safe Measure for Other Deaf Children   155
Olivier Perier, Anne Bochner-Wuidar

Considerations for Evaluating Hearing   171
Arthur J. Dahle, Faye P. McCollister

Mobile Audiometry for the Multiply Handicapped
Hospitalized Child from Birth to Six Years   207
Martha Rubin, Gene Kunreuther, Neil Lombardi

Selective Impairment of Late Vertex and Middle Latency
Auditory Evoked Responses   233
Paul Kileny, David A. Berry

Hearing Impairment in Down's Syndrome Children   259
Wesley R. Wilson, Richard C. Folsom, Judith E. Widen

Is There Hearing Help for Down's Syndrome?   301
Marion P. Downs

Language Disorders in Neonatally Asphyxiated
Congenitally Deaf Children   317
Sanford E. Gerber, Carol A. Prutting, Elizabeth Wile

Developing Preparatory Skills for Using Augmentative
Communication Aids   333
Elaine M. Heaton, Barbara L. Strohbach

Selection of Optimal Modalities as Avenues of Learning in
Deaf, Blind, Multiply Disabled Children   355
Kevin Murphy, David J. Byrne

The California School for the Deaf: Special Unit Program   397
Eugene LaCosse

Working with Parents toward Acceptance and Beyond   409
Sara C. McClain

Bibliography   421

Index   455

Foreword

In 1965 a special committee of the Benevolent and Protective Order of the Elks of Canada and their auxiliary, the Order of the Royal Purple, met in Edmonton to consider ideas for the expansion of a program known as the Elks Purple Cross Fund. This fund and its associated program, which were established in 1956 to provide care for any handicapped child in need, had reached a point where the interest of our membership needed revitalizing. To do so required the creation of new goals and objectives. The special committee suggested to the membership that they establish a program "to speak for those who could not speak for themselves." This led to a further committee recommendation to establish what is now known as the Elks Purple Cross Deaf Detection and Development Program.

In October of 1972 during the joint meeting in Calgary of the Speech and Hearing Association of Alberta and the Canadian Speech and Hearing Association, I had the good fortune to meet Dr. Mencher. He had recently moved to Halifax and was interested in establishing a program for the early identification of hearing impaired Canadian children. He and I met again in December in Halifax to plan a special international conference to study methods for the earliest possible identification of hearing loss in newborns. This conference would incorporate the study and propositions of the United States Joint Committee on Infant Hearing, then chaired by Professor Marion Downs.

We held the conference in Halifax in September 1974. It was fully funded by the Elks and their auxiliary, and it brought together professionals from seven countries who, after three days of intensive effort, produced a series of guidelines for the early identification of hearing loss. The recommendations from that meeting, now known as the Nova Scotia Conference, have become some of the most important contributions to the field of early identification.

Many of the programs in use today are based on the information provided through that meeting.

As a result of the Nova Scotia conference, Dr. Mencher, Dr. Gerber (then the new chairman of the Joint Committee on Infant Hearing), and I met to plan ways of preparing and funding a second meeting, this one to study methods for the early diagnosis of hearing loss in the infant population. This conference was held in Saskatoon, Saskatchewan, in May 1978. Again, professionals from five countries met to share their ideas and develop clinical guidelines. These results, published under the authorship of Drs. Mencher and Gerber, have also made a significant contribution to the literature concerning hearing loss in infancy.

It seemed most appropriate, therefore, that a third meeting should be held. This conference, perhaps the most important one, was organized for the purpose of studying early management of hearing loss. Held in May 1980 in Winnipeg, Manitoba, that conference brought together again those who could share ideas and develop recommendations. At that time, we met with scientists from five other countries. This successful conference was also followed by publication.

The Elks and their auxiliary are proud of our contribution through the Purple Cross Deaf Detection and Development Fund. We can point with great pride and satisfaction to the trilogy "Early Identification, Early Diagnosis, and Early Management of Hearing Loss" and know that our organizations have, in a significant way, helped further the care of hearing impaired children.

It was only fitting, then, that we met again in Edmonton for further study and discussion. This conference brought together a group of the most competent and dedicated professionals with whom I have had the pleasure of working. We all shared a common interest: the problems of identification, diagnosis, and management of the multiply handicapped, hearing impaired child. These areas desperately need more attention. The Elks Purple Cross Deaf Detection and Development Fund is proud to have been able to assist in directing that attention and contributing in some small way to the improvement of the care of the multiply handicapped hearing impaired child.

Robert K. Coulling, P.G.E.R.
Elks Purple Cross Deaf Detection and Development
Program
Regina, Saskatchewan

Preface

The Purple Cross Fund of the Benevolent and Protective Order of Elks and their auxiliary, the Order of the Royal Purple, was established in 1968 to provide support for clinical services to communicatively impaired children in Canada and to assist professional agencies in research. The series of Elks International Conferences represent a major contribution to research endeavors in Canada. The conference reported in this volume is the fourth in a series which cumulatively has had 118 participants from 13 different countries. It has been a delight and an honor for us to chair these conferences.

During the Edmonton conference, we congratulated each other on our success with these programs and endeavored to understand why they succeeded. We came to the conclusion that our specific success was due to inviting the best possible people to participate. The leading scholars and scientists from several related disciplines attended each of these conferences. Each participant came with respect for the others and with a wish to present the best possible show. Each came with an open mind and overt willingness to share ideas with respected colleagues from all over the world, and each came to present his or her best work. We are all—the editors, the readers, and the children we serve—beneficiaries of that attitude.

The multiply handicapped hearing impaired child represents one of our most painful and perplexing clinical problems. What is the primary handicap? How is it influenced by the other handicaps? Are we, for example, dealing with a hearing impaired child who happens to be retarded or a retarded child who has a hearing impairment? These are not trivial questions, and we believe they are addressed as clearly as possible in this volume.

Issues of interpersonal communication between child and family, child and teacher–therapist, and clinicians and family are considered. The ongoing effort to establish realistic goals for the multiply handicapped child is discussed. These goals are not just therapeutic but aid in life planning as well. Issues such as family counselling, education, behavior modification, medical diagnosis and care, early intervention, and amplification are presented. We believe the position statement and the various papers that evolved from this conference address the perplexity, complexity, joy, and challenge of the multiply handicapped hearing impaired child.

Thanks are due to special people and institutions for special efforts. Glenrose Hospital and its staff did so much for us that we cannot list their contributions without adding another entire section to this volume. To Paul Kileny, Barbara Strohbach, Dr. McPhail, and all the speech pathology and audiology staff, we offer genuine thanks. There is one person at Glenrose who needs special attention, and she is Elaine Heaton. She made all the arrangements at the hospital, hotel, and airport, held a reception at her home, registered visitors, ran errands, and generally wore herself to a frazzle on our behalf. If this volume helps one clinician help one child, Elaine deserves a large share of the credit.

The Board of Directors and staff of the Nova Scotia Hearing and Speech Clinic also deserve a special comment. They were extremely helpful, tolerant, cooperative, and generous with their time, energies, and efforts as this volume was prepared. We are genuinely appreciative of that committment. One person at the clinic worked diligently with us during the entire preparation of this volume despite serious personal discomfort. She has earned a special place in our hearts. To Joan H. (whose name we are forbidden to mention), we offer a silver rose.

Again and ever again, we must express our great appreciation to Robert K. Coulling, whose efforts on behalf of these children are reflected in the international conferences. Mr. Coulling, Executive Director of the Elks Purple Cross Fund, works tirelessly on behalf of the hearing impaired. His uncanny ability to support and sustain these international conferences merits the gratitude of all of us who work for the benefit of the hearing impaired child. The children and we are forever indebted to him and the organizations he represents—The Benevolent and Protective Order of Elks and the Order of the Royal Purple.

George T. Mencher
Sanford E. Gerber

Contributors

David A. Berry, M.D.
Chief Resident
Department of Pediatrics
University of Alberta Hospital
Edmonton, Alberta, Canada

Anne Bochner-Wuidar, M.D.
Centre Comprendre et Parler
Bruxelles, Belgium

Arthur Boothroyd, Ph.D.
Professor
Doctoral Program in Speech and
Hearing Sciences
City University
New York, New York

David J. Byrne, M.Ed.
Director, Niagra Research Unit
Mary Sheridan Unit
Royal Berkshire Hospital
Reading, England

Arthur J. Dahle, Ph.D.
Director, Division of Speech and
Hearing
Center for Developmental and
Learning Disorders
University of Alabama
Birmingham, Alabama

Marion P. Downs, M.A., D.P.H.
Professor Emerita
Department of Otolaryngology
University of Colorado
Denver, Colorado

Richard C. Folsom, Ph.D.
Associate Professor
Department of Speech and
Hearing Sciences
University of Washington
Seattle, Washington

Sanford E. Gerber, Ph.D.
Professor and Chairman
Department of Speech
University of California
Santa Barbara, California

Elaine M. Heaton, M.A.
Director, Department of Speech
Pathology
Glenrose Hospital
Edmonton, Alberta, Canada

Aira Kankkunen, M.A.
Head Audiologist
Pediatric Audiology Section
University of Göteborg
Göteborg, Sweden

Paul Kileny, Ph.D.
Director, Department of Audiology
Glenrose Hospital
Edmonton, Alberta, Canada

Gene Kunreuther, M.S.
Chief, Speech-Language
Department
St. Mary's Hospital for Children
Bayside, New York

Eugene LaCosse, M.Ed.
Special Unit Principal
California School for the Deaf
Fremont, California

Gunnar Liden, M.D., Ph.D.
Director of Audiology
Associate Surgeon and Professor
Departments of Audiology and
Otolaryngology
Sahlgren's Hospital
University of Göteborg
Göteborg, Sweden

Neil Lombardi, M.D.
Director of Developmental
Disabilities Center
St. Mary's Hospital for Children
Bayside, New York

Sara C. McClain, M.A.
Supervisor, Preschool Program for
the Hearing Impaired
Glenrose Hospital
Edmonton, Alberta, Canada

Faye P. McCollister, M.A.
Center for Developmental and
Learning Disorders
University of Alabama
Birmingham, Alabama

George T. Mencher, Ph.D.
Director, Nova Scotia Hearing and
Speech Clinic
Professor of Audiology
Dalhousie University School of
Human Communication Disorders
Halifax, Nova Scotia, Canada

Kevin Murphy, Ph.D.
Audiology Unit
Royal Berkshire Hospital
Reading, England

Olivier Perier, M.D.
Director, Centre Comprendre et
Parler
Bruxelles, Belgium

Carol A. Prutting, Ph.D.
Associate Professor of Speech
Pathology
University of California
Santa Barbara, California

Isabelle Rapin, M.D.
Professor, Neurology and
Pediatrics
Albert Einstein College of
Medicine of Yeshiva University
New York, New York

Charlene Robertson, M.D.,
F.R.C.P. (C)
Department of Pediatrics
Neonatal Follow-up Clinic
Glenrose Hospital
Edmonton, Alberta, Canada

Martha Rubin,.Ed.D.
Director, Lexington Hearing and
Speech Center
Lexington School for the Deaf
Jackson Heights, New York

Hilde S. Schlesinger, M.D.
Director, Center on Deafness
Training and Mental Health
Services
San Francisco, California

Robert Shea, M.D.
Department of Pediatrics
Glenrose Hospital
Edmonton, Alberta, Canada

Irwin F. Stewart, M.D.,
F.R.C.S. (C)
Clinical Associate Professor
University of British Columbia
Head, Department of
Otolaryngology
St. Mary's Hospital
New Westminster, British
Columbia, Canada

Barbara L. Strohbach, D.S.P.
Supervisor, Speech Pathology
Department
Glenrose Hospital
Edmonton, Alberta, Canada

Andre Tjellström, M.D., Ph.D.
Assistant Professor
Director of Audiology and
Associate Surgeon
University of Göteborg
Göteborg, Sweden

Lillian Whyte, Ph.D.
Professor of Special Education
Department of Educational
Psychology
University of Alberta
Edmonton, Alberta, Canada

Judith E. Widen
Department of Speech and
Hearing Sciences
University of Washington
Seattle, Washington

Elizabeth Wile, B.A.
Department of Speech
University of California
Santa Barbara, California

Wesley R. Wilson, Ph.D.
Professor
Department of Speech and
Hearing Sciences
University of Washington
Seattle, Washington

POSITION STATEMENT: THE MULTIPLY HANDICAPPED
HEARING IMPAIRED CHILD

The Population and Nature of Multiple Handicap

There are many children with a hearing loss of sufficient magnitude to interfere with development. Our emphasis here is a subgroup of those children - those for whom identification, diagnosis and management are complicated by the simultaneous existence of one or more additional problems. These include, but are not necessarily limited to:

- disruption in central auditory processing;

- disruption in peripheral and/or central visual function;

- disorders of motor function;

- disorders of sensory and sensory motor integration;

- disorders of affective and intellectual function;

- speech, language, cognitive, social and emotional deficits secondary to a long-standing peripheral hearing loss;

- an environment which fails to promote optimal, reciprocal communication.

From earliest infancy, there is a mutual exchange between the child and his/her care-givers, usually the parents. The baby's response to stimulation encourages further stimulation, in a continuing and growth fostering process. The infant and parents are partners in this exchange, which, under normal conditions, leads to language development and linguistic communication. Disruption in this reciprocity by the infant, parent, or, of course, by the environment, will thwart this delicate and important process. Sensory deficits disrupt and, as such, can have a profound, immediate effect on the language development of the infant and, in turn, a further influence on cognitive and affective growth.

The special nature of multiple handicaps is such that their effects are not simply additive, but rather they interact with each other in ways not thoroughly understood to

1

create a complex array of secondary consequences. These
present enormous problems in assessment and intervention.
While the focus in this text is on hearing loss in multiply
handicapped children, the concepts discussed and all their
implications have applicability to any multiply disabled child
whether or not there is hearing impairment present.

Assessment

Whatever the child's presenting symptoms, the presence
of additional handicaps should always be considered. Hearing
impairment is often overlooked. Therefore, in addition to
those generally considered at risk for hearing loss, detection
and diagnosis of an auditory deficit must be vigorously
pursued with all appropriate methods in all handicapped
children.

Every child deserves a multi-disciplinary evaluation at
the time of detection, its primary goal being the provision
of a working diagnosis which includes:

1. identification of the primary handicap;

2. genetic counselling;

3. emotional support for the family;

4. advice regarding habilitation; and,

5. an answer to questions concerning management,
    education, availability of resources, and probable
    outcome.

A considerable period of diagnostic intervention is often
required for the multiply involved individual before diagnosis
is reached. Thus, evaluation of these children should be an
ongoing process requiring frequent re-assessment of the
various areas of dysfunction and strength, and of the efficacy
and impact of the intervention program.

Intervention

Management begins with the identification of assets. In multiply disabled children, such identifications need to be accurate, though cautious, and must recognize that the capacity of the child to respond to certain forms of sensory stimulation will not emerge without training and experience. Furthermore, peripheral sensory sensitivity may well be a poor guide to the potential capacity of the child to communicate by speech or, indeed, by gesture.

Interpersonal communication for the multiply disabled child is more vulnerable than for the child with a single disability. Besides the barriers to communication arising directly from the child's handicaps, his parents and family may be subject to more stress than are those of other children. The multiply disabled child needs therapy from a wide variety of agencies, not all of which may see that communication as a primary component in that therapy. Adequate provisions should be available to inform parents of immediate therapeutic requirements which may represent only the first step in both clinical and educative-therapeutic management. Though the first steps in therapy may not necessarily be medical-surgical, it is essential that such facilities be available at the commencement of and throughout the therapeutic regime.

Management must be collaborative and interdisciplinary, utilizing every available sensory mode and all relevant habilitative methods, regardless of individual management philosophies. The primary vehicle for management is the family. Programming and decision-making must include them as equals. Sensitivity to individual differences, emotional, social, cultural and economic, is essential. Parents must be helped to understand that diagnostic therapy may well lead to modified diagnoses and, hence, to changes in patterns of therapy and care. Long-term and short-term goals must be specified and clearly understood by all involved. Long-term goals should include helping families face life planning for their multiply handicapped child. Periodic measures of progress and accountability are fundamental aspects of programming.

HEARING LOSS AND MULTIPLE HANDICAPS: OCCURRENCE AND EFFECTS

George T. Mencher
Nova Scotia Hearing and Speech Clinic, Halifax, Nova Scotia

Welcome to the Fourth International Elks Symposium, this one entitled "The Multiply Handicapped Hearing Impaired Child", certainly the ultimate challenge to clinical ingenuity. We are, here, focusing on a subset of a subset of a subset of the population; that is, first and foremost the child; second, the child with a hearing impairment; and third, the child with a hearing impairment who also has another major handicap.

According to Statistics Canada, the 6,369,000 children in this country under 16 years of age last year comprised 26.2% of the total population. Utilizing statistics from the "Report on Childhood Deafness in the European Community (1977)", which included a comprehensive evaluation of 9 major western European countries, we can project that just over 16,000 of those 6,000,000+ children (.9/1000) were born with a hearing loss of 50 dB or more in the better ear. Further, based on those same European figures which indicated that 28.8% of those born with a hearing impairment will have an additional major problem (usually mental retardation, blind, or cerebral palsy), we can say that in 1981 there were approximately 1,750 children under 16 years of age living in Canada, who were born hearing impaired and multiply disordered. These figures, of course, say nothing of those adventitiously impaired through accident, injury, or disease. So to include them, we would have to say that, scattered throughout the large geographical area of Canada, there are fewer than 2,500 children with multiple disorders as diverse in type and degree of severity as the children themselves. Such a vast geographical region as Canada with its multiplicity of educational and health models, coupled with the relatively small number of these children, makes programming "difficult" to say the least, and provides us with that "ultimate challenge". In the U.S., the number should be approximately 10 times greater, 25,000 children, but then the problems will also be 10 times greater.

Keet (1982) recently described a group of children from the 1974 Rubella epidemic in the Maritimes. One child, whose initial presentation in the newborn period was cardiovascular, required surgery in addition to conservative management. He was typical of that group. Ophthalmological deficits and sensorineural hearing loss were later diagnosed. Surgery for cataracts, audiological testing, and the fitting of hearing aids followed. Then a conductive hearing loss due to otitis media required myringotomy and tubes. By 1 year of age, because of developmental delay, pediatric neurology became involved. Now, at 7 years of age and classed as deaf, blind, and moderately retarded, this child is no longer able to live at home but rather, resides in a special resource center unit for Rubella children. One of his playmates went through the same course of events, plus orthopedic surgery for malformed hip joints, while another is severely cerebral palsied. This is the group for discussion here, not the "normal" healthy deaf or hearing impaired child.

Programs for the handicapped begin with prevention and progress through surveillance, identification, diagnosis, treatment and management. We like to provide ourselves with the self-delusion that these programs are usually initiated as a result of our advocacy. Perhaps that is true for a number of programs, but it seems to me that Lis (1970) was more than correct when he suggested that the most significant force behind the development of special programs is not people, but rather "dollars" - cost effectiveness. That is, prevention becomes a priority if it leads to a lesser financial outlay in the future.

Consider, for example, that Rubella epidemic in the Maritimes. Immunization programs were not actively pursued because they were too costly. Four years and two-score multiply handicapped children later, an intensive immunization scheme was initiated with great haste, and ultimately with such great success and thoroughness that one of the Maritime Provinces can now clearly demonstrate the lowest incidence of Rubella pregnancies in North America. Their prevention program is a model for the rest of the world. But what did it cost to achieve that goal?

In still another location, inadequate funding resulted in at least a 2 year delay in educational programming for a similar group of multiply disabled children. When it became evident to the legislators of that government that, as a result of their delays even greater funding would be required to provide for the now compounded educational deficits of these children, and that future expenditures would escalate as educational deficits compounded, money suddenly became available.

When funding is available (notice I didn't say adequate funding - few of us, if any, have ever achieved that ultimate state of nirvana), the progress of the children is often impeded by a lack of professional co-operation. Multi-disciplinary committees and approaches are essential. Often, however, a multi-disciplinary team is a group of individual specialists who may never actually physically meet together to consider the child or to agree on a course of action. Professionals are often blind to disorders other than their own speciality, or even worse yet, they may fail to see that there is more to the child than a cataract, a spastic adductor or an undescended testicle. Often, one member of the professional team considers his specialty paramount, and ignores the implications for others. Cleft palate teams are notorious in this regard. Plastic surgeons often disagree with otolaryngologists and prosthodontists often disagree with both. Hearing impaired children often become the victims of professional disagreements among deaf educators, audiologists, and speech pathologists.

Sometimes professional disagreements are compounded by parents who are confused, emotionally distraught, and as a normal part of their adjustment to the situation, travel from Specialist A to Specialist B to hear the answer they want to hear. Some parents are not easily able to recognize that their children are most susceptible to complicating diseases or disorders, or that "silent" secondary disorders may appear later in life. They may not have the ability to carry out the recommendations of the professionals for financial, intellectual, social, or emotional reasons. The professional can heap on the guilt for inaction. The parent with limited parenting skills to begin with, who may just get by under normal conditions, may find himself pitted against the

professionals and his own multiply handicapped child. Child
dependency, abuse, and discipline become even more sensitive
issues. There are many families in which the birth of a
multiply handicapped baby has led to long-standing conflict
between partners, guilt, financial hardship, and perhaps,
even eventually, divorce.

Fortunately, "Not all parents and their handicapped
children are tragic figures" (Lis, 1970). However, happiness,
love, coping, adjustment, expectations, self-image, and all
those "nice terms" and what they represent, if not recognized
and accepted for what they are, can be distorted and, thus,
lead to "those tragic parents with their tragic child".

Our subject population at this meeting is one which, to
paraphrase Meier (1973), consists of those individuals likely
to sink when they can be taught to swim in our complex world
or, if not to swim, at least to properly protect themselves
from that fatal immersion and be able to crawl or walk or run
on land. More specifically, I suggest to you THAT OUR PURPOSE
IS TO DISCUSS THOSE CHILDREN WHO HAVE A HEARING LOSS OF 50 dB
OR MORE, OR OF SUCH A DEGREE AND NATURE THAT IT INTERFERES
WITH THE INITIATION AND DEVELOPMENT OF COMMUNICATION AND/OR
ITS ONGOING PROCESS, PLUS THEY HAVE OTHER MEASURABLE AND/OR
SCIENTIFICALLY DIAGNOSABLE CONDITIONS LIKELY TO PREVENT
OPTIMAL GROWTH AND DEVELOPMENT IN THE SOCIAL, EMOTIONAL,
INTELLECTUAL, LINGUISTIC OR PHYSICAL REALM, EITHER CONSIDERED
SINGLY OR IN COMBINATION.

Unfortunately, such a definition, while fine for text
books and perhaps even considered excellent by some for legal
purposes, says little about individual beings; about children,
parents, siblings, teachers, legislators, aunts and uncles,
clinicians, etc., all affected by long hours of waiting,
working, and worrying at doctors' offices, hospitals, classrooms, clinics, schools, bus stops, budget meetings, parent
groups, etc. It says nothing about the incredible variability
of expression associated with multiple handicaps, or the
shock of latent onset, or the painful recognition, "I have a
multiply disabled child". In spite of all these short-
comings, however, it is a definition we can use for these
discussions, provided that we keep all those limitations in
mind.

You will note that the terms *handicapped* and *disordered* have been utilized so far, along with the more currently in-vogue *disabled*. The dictionary (American Heritage, 1971) defines *disability* with such terms as *incapacity*, and *handicap*, and it defines *disabled* as "to weaken or destroy the normal physical or mental abilities...". These are most unsatisfactory definitions. One of the sub-definitions of *disordered* (as in the disordered child), is "...an upset of health or functioning". This is close, but still not exactly correct. A *handicap* is defined as a "deficiency that prevents or restricts <u>normal</u> achievement". Obviously, that is not true for all of these children and, thus, to me at least, seems even less satisfactory a definition. Terms such as *impediment* (a hindrance), *special* (aren't all of us special?), and *unique* (different), are even less meaningful, more distressing and perhaps, even further afield from the truth. What, then, can we call these children who most likely will require more help than their friends and playmates to achieve their full potential as human beings?

Interestingly enough, the primary dictionary defintion of *handicapped* does not relate to a disability, but is based on the infinitive *to handicap*; that is, a situation in which advantages or compensation are given to equalize the chances of winning. I would suggest that our entire educational, health, and social system - our human services - are predi-cated on giving everyone an equal chance to succeed in life, not by impeding the best, but rather by providing extra opportunities to those who need or want that help. With that in mind, I would consider the term *handicapped child* as used here as meaning a child given that support necessary to equal his or her chances of success in life. Those advantages may be educational, medical, social, and/or psychological, and are entirely dependent on the nature of the child and the extent of his or her needs. In that sense, *handicapped* is not a negative term. One could say, then, that this confer-ence is concerned with the identification of those children who will require a handicap. The diagnostic process deter-mines how much of a handicap they will require and the manage-ment process determines the best method for providing it. We hope that we can learn <u>to</u> handicap children, as opposed to being a handicap to them. Dr. Shea, in his paper, offers a further discussion regarding the definition of our subject population. His definitions are based on correct educational thinking and probably offer more applicable definitions. The reader is urged to consider them.

Preparing a conference on the child with a multiple handicap, including hearing impairment, is not an easy task. For example, one question we discussed at great length was how to divide the topics. One approach could have been a review of each of the major disorders most often accompanying hearing loss. That is, a presentation on mental retardation, on cerebral dysfunction, and on blindness. Another approach was to consider each discipline providing support to the hearing impaired multiply handicapped child, for example, Medicine, Audiology, Speech Pathology, Education, Psychology, etc. Still another approach would have been a consideration of the stages in programming, for example, surveillance, prevention, identification, diagnosis, management, etc. Our choice was to do some of all of these. That is, to integrate disorders, disciplines, and stages, and to use our material to weave a blanket which, although admittedly thin, provides what we hope will be reasonable coverage of this rather enormous topic. We know that we are only touching the surface, but perhaps we can also touch the essence of the problem.

There is no question but that time helps to heal, in both the figurative and literal sense of the word. Tissue changes, surgical alteration, normal growth and development, adjustment, coping, will make their contribution with, we hope, each of us adding a little something along the way. Eventually, most of these children will become productive, vital members of society, primarily because of their own hard work, the intensive efforts of their parents, and, if not in spite of us, because of the supplements we provide. We hope these proceedings can, in some small fashion, help that productivity come about and help us to help them when they need help, not to do so when they don't, and to know the difference.

If I were looking for an ideal person to talk to us about multiply handicapped, I would choose someone from within that group. Unfortunately, that's not completely possible. There is an alternative, however, someone who has been there and returned. Dr. Kevin Murphy is such an individual. Severely injured during a plane crash, he spent a brief portion of his life as a deaf, blind, completely paralyzed human being. His knowledge of our topic is deep, real, and very personal. No doubt his interest, achievements and success in working with the multiply handicapped are based on that rather unique experience. Dr. Murphy was born in Ireland and trained at the Doctoral level in England by the Ewings at Manchester.

Although he now has a background in criminology, sociology, educational psychology, clinical psychology, deaf education, and audiology, he began his work as a remedial therapist.

His work in early identification of hearing loss with the infant cradle, his published works considering the hierarchy of sensory function, and his previous efforts at the Winnipeg conference on the Early Management of Hearing Loss are well known to you all. Suffice it to say, he is known for his professional accomplishments, but those pale when compared to his sense of humor, his reputation as a genuine caring human being, his dedication to his work, and his commitment to the children he serves. For these reasons, we have asked Dr. Kevin Murphy to prepare the Keynote chapter for this book.

References

Lis, E.F., "Implications of Screening Techniques for Comprehensive Care," Proceedings Bi-Regional Institute on Earlier Recognition of Handicapping Conditions in Childhood (Berkeley: University of California School of Public Health), Oglesby, A., and Sterling, H. (Eds.), 1970.

Martin, J.A.M., and Moore, W.J. (Eds.), Childhood Deafness in the European Community (Luxembourg: Office for Official Publications of the European Communities), 1979.

Meier, J., Screening and Assessment of Young Children at Developmental Risk (Washington, D.C.: DHEW Publication #05-73-90), Produced by The President's Committee on Mental Retardation, 1973.

THE EDUCATOR–THERAPIST AND DEAF, MULTIPLY DISAB
CHILDREN: SOME ESSENTIAL CRITERIA

Kevin Murphy

Royal Berkshire Hospital, Berkshire, England

Deaf multiply disabled children pose a series o:
to which the teacher-therapist is forced to respond.
relationship between the adult and the child in most
situations may be predicated, and the patterns of mu
learning have been amply described. However, multip.
abled children may be seen as gross contaminants in
psycho-social situation which is fundamental to harm
development. The feelings of despair, inadequacy an
which one commonly meets in the parents, teachers an
therapists of these children make considerable deman
confidence and equanimity of the persons involved.
turn, leads to a reduction in the quality of the emo
relationships which are essential to progress and ed
growth.

Two major population categories may be consider
review the problems of the deaf, multiply disabled,
mentally retarded children. These are:

1. Those children who suffer congenital disabi
    but, apart from severe failure to learn, do
    present any disruptive behaviour patterns;

2. Those children who, besides their congenita
    disabilities, have acquired a series of dis
    behaviours ranging from hyperkinesis to gro
    self-mutilation. That range includes prone
    to violent outbursts, severe tantrums, dest
    iveness and uncontrolled aggressions to adu
    peers, and/or small animals.

When Peppard Trust established its first Resea1
at the Mary Sheridan Educational Unit in Berkshire,
one of its goals was to identify how an unskilled bu
thetic staff could be encouraged to acquire skills ɛ
to the well being of the children in its care. In 1

the students in training, it became clear that the work with
severely damaged children demanded certain qualities without
which progress was well-nigh impossible. Such skills may be
summarized as follows:

1. Basic professional competence;

2. Belief that change is possible;

3. Faith in one's ability to promote such change.

Basic Professional Competence

This term is used to identify those persons who, by
training and experience, have acquired the skills to identify
a child's needs and potential; who are consequently able to
predict optimal intervention programs and also able to
refrain from using irrelevant or potentially disturbing ones.
Both these elements are essential to progress. Enthusiastic
prosecution of an irrelevant program can be as dangerously
inappropriate as the absence of any program. Multiply disabled children have the same rights as children not so
afflicted, hence experimentation must be based on sound ethics
and a clear understanding of the likely outcome of such
approaches. Competence should naturally generate confidence,
but it is also based on a capacity to restrain such confidence
where caution and diagnostic therapy are needed.

The teacher, one of the trained people to whom parents
and society have delegated responsibility for education and
therapy, is seen as performing a function which, in more
primitive communities, would be the responsibility of the
parents. As parental delegates, we are not parental sub-
stitutes. Parents do not delegate their rights to us. They
delegate a limited degree of responsibility for the care of
those aspects of their child's condition for which, through
lack of training, time, or personal motivation, they feel help
is required. We, as educator-therapists, should not assume a
degree of control or responsibility which undermines parental
rights or excludes them from our concern.

Consideration of parental rights is, in this paper,
placed before the child's rights simply and solely because our
contact with the child in diagnosis and in therapy begins

from, and operates through, the parents. When David Byrne
and I wrote our last contribution to this series (Mencher &
Gerber, 1981), we stressed the idea that long before a child
comes to diagnosis, social disruption will have created
modifications in family cohesion and that, since the family
is seen as the epi-centre of diagnosis and therapy, it is
essential that our concern for the client begin with the
parents and family. Basic professional competence, then, is
not solely a capacity to diagnose hearing impairment, or to
perscribe suitable amplification, or to initiate relevant
medico-surgical intervention, or to commence auditory and
communication training. Let me hasten to say that all of the
above have their place in the competencies we all seek, but
primacy must be given to the capacity to identify and empa-
thize with parental needs, to recognize and respect parental
rights, and to co-operate with parents in the realization of
their ambitions for their child.

At this point, I suspect you are likely to feel more
than a little mutinous. We all know that parental expectations can be, and often are, grossly over-optimistic and that,
as time goes on, they may well veer to the opposite extreme –
acute pessimism. How, then, are we to co-operate with such
shifting targets and emphases? At the heart of any definition
of *Education* is the notion of the development of a child into
an harmonious congruence of emotional, social, intellectual
and spiritual factors which will facilitate a way of life
conducive to the well being of the individual and his community. The educator-therapist must be able to see the extent to
which those elements within the child, crucial to the above
aims, can be identified and presented to the parents in such
a way that the well being of the child is maximized. It
should be clear that one major component of professional
competence lies in the experience acquired by working successfully with parents and children.

Hopefully, you will not feel me too harsh if I beg leave
to doubt the complete professional competence of our newly
qualified colleagues. Wisdom is difficult to define, but
experience, patience, insight and empathy are at least as
important as sagacity in the alchemy of that precious
commodity. Many of our newly qualified colleagues are
personally bright, excellent students of excellent training

centers, who, molded in the furnace of experience, will become ideally qualified as educator-therapists. The furnace of experience to which I refer will, hopefully, develop the relevant insights and capacity to listen, and to:

1. identify parent and child needs;

2. avoid classification and judgmental postures; and,

3. educe from all concerned those positive components which will encourage all involved in the pursuit of progress.

My reason for stressing experience and wisdom stems from my conviction that the wise and experienced therapist can identify, at the heart of parental concern, their hopes and aspirations for their child's complete well being within the community. That therapist also knows that mutual co-operation between the parent and himself will lead to a search for the child's assets and trainable capacities conducive to the development of realistic parental ambitions. This is not to say that the teacher-therapist has the right or responsibility to convince parents that their ambitions are preposterous!

When I began work in Reading 26 years ago, it was the custom to place all Down's Syndrome infants in a local long-stay mental subnormality hospital. Parents, and some teachers, insisted that the "experts" were wrong in this. Eventually, children were kept at home in spite of all the gloomy prognostications. Today, who would deny the successes of many of these youngsters. We all know that the range of intellectual capacity and the potential for learning varies widely amongst multiply disabled children and that, therefore, our approach to parental ambition must take into account that the majority of parents know their children much better than do the majority of therapists. Hence, until there are realistic indices of current skills and we have an intimate knowledge of the capacity of the family to support, stimulate and encourage their child, we must exercise extreme caution when approaching parental ambition, particularly if we plan to cast any doubts on its validity.

Having said this, it must be recognized that the therapist has a responsibility to give parents a realistic view of the general limitations imposed by a multiple disability.

Probably all of us are aware of profoundly prelingually deaf
doctors, lawyers, architects (or in my recent experience,
musicians!). We are all aware of the achievements of Helen
Keller or the successes of some persons born with spina
bifida. Many parents, too, rapidly become expert in the
bibliography of disability. The biographies of such people
teach that progress was often a result of the fortunate combination of parental and therapist-teacher dedication. So
much of the early work with such people was devised, as it
were, en route. Skilled improvization, allied to tenacity of
purpose and an almost fanatical resolve on the part of all
concerned, seem to have been the common criteria.

Biographies and autobiographies have stressed the early
confusion of parents, their search for guidance and help,
their commitment and dedication, and one cannot help surmis-
ing, their suppression of so many more tender attributes in
their determination, which often borders on the fanaticism I
mentioned earlier. But not all parents are educated, middle
class, and monied. The progress described by the late Christy
Brown, in which parental support was confined to a resigned
but over-flowing affection, may well be uniquely dependent on
the personality and inherent capacities of that writer. However, the parents he describes must represent a large proportion of those with whom we come in contact. These are impov-
erished people, full of affection but lacking any educational
or therapeutic skills, burdened by the need to keep their
family clothed and fed, resigned to what they described as
the "Will of God", haphazard in their approach to and co-
operation with therapy; the kind of people that officialdom
finds it all too easy to criticize.

We know that there are uniquely gifted people within all
areas of ability and disability. If we have been privileged
to work with such people, we recognize that they are rare
indeed, and that the majority of patients, pupils, and clients
in our care will never gain such heights. We must, therefore,
be realistic, recognize the dangers of facile optimism and
the stultifying effects of impossible goals. We must
refrain from encouraging parents to goals which our experience tells us are almost certainly beyond the competence of
their child. How best are we to balance honest appraisal and
optimism; the need for accurate prognosis on the one hand,

and parental encouragement and support on the other? In my
own experience, this is best done at each step of therapeutic
progress by emphasizing, within a grand strategy, the relevance of the "here and now". Taking parents into our confidence and sharing goals relevant to current and future
activity, and discussing mutual descriptions of their child's
responses to learning experiences, is a powerful method.
"Taking each day as it comes" used to be a gangplank of
therapy. Within limits, such a therapeutic approach may well
commend itself with multiply disabled children. As diagnosti-
cians, therapists and educators, however, we must be aware
that such approaches may, rightly or wrongly, be seen by
parents as uncharted drifting through some therapeutic regime.
As such, the relevance of daily routines is not always
immediately clear to them.

Belief That Change is Possible

     Throughout this paper, I have stressed the value of
experience. My main purpose in so doing is based on the
knowledge that, in any carefully charted account of therapy
and education, it is clear that some children have made progress at a rate and to an extent that had not been expected.
Careful analysis of such progress may have provided clues to
new or alternative strategies which work well for some children. New equipment may have been devised which benefitted a
large proportion of the children in our care. New philosophies may have been found helpful in approaching some parents.
All of these may have been combined to provide a formidable
educational and therapeutic armamentum. But all of these will
fade into irrelevance unless they are fuelled by a conviction
based on prior experience that change is possible.

     The first parental response to multiple disability cannot
but contain shock, grief, bewilderment, some anger, resentment
and despair. These are often dangerously productive of a
lethargic, fatalistic conviction that progress is unlikely.
Almost defiantly, parents tell us "We love him for what he is,
not for what he may or may not be". This may be used to
excuse a drift into a permanent infantilization of the child.
Attempts to introduce a more practical therapeutic approach
may be seen as heartless. Potential progress, as described

by the clinician or teacher, may be seen as so minimal as to
be irrelevant, insignificant, or certainly not worth all the
striving to which the family is being exhorted. Fathers may
opt for a role in which new ambitions and career strivings
are justified - their child's future is going to need financial support. They may see this kind of extra-familial concern as an acceptable alternative to the satisfaction of the
child's own immediate needs.

Given early guidance and support, these kinds of reactions can be channeled more productively. The energy released
will provide additional impetus to the therapeutic drive.
During this initial period, the teacher-therapist may find
progress to be almost entirely dependent on non-familial
effort. The experienced worker will take this role for
granted, but the less experienced person may be led into a
false judgmental stance and a mistaken evaluation of the permanence of the situation. All too often, one sees therapists
slowly assuming a quality of possession of the child which is
dangerously close to excluding the parent, belittling their
contribution, and/or deriding the quality of their involvement. The experienced worker knows only too well that progress can only occur when the whole therapeutic team is
united in its aims, agreed on methods, and convinced of
eventual success.

For the majority of parents, multiple disability is a
unique catastrophe. They have no prior experience with it,
are unprepared for its demands, and are bewildered by its
unexpected complications. Recognition of the gravity of
their child's problems may take many years to develop. A
realistic appraisal of assets and deficits will occur only
in collaboration with those involved in diagnostic therapy.

From the beginning of diagnosis, the emphasis must always
be on the child's positive aspects. Diagnostic therapy,
which should begin as early as possible, should include a
search for assets and concentrate on their consolidation and
preservation. Even during the early days of therapy, when
the full extent and range of sensory residua is not completely
identified, the importance of some sensory information must
be recognized. This is necessary for the development of
cognitive structures, interest in events, introspection, and

for a reduction in self-stimulation. The capacity to learn is
a skill based on regular, consistent information, cognition,
self-directed activity, self-monitoring, and the process of
ratiocination. This latter identifies the relationship
between cause and effect as a basis for future self-directed
activity in the meeting of needs.

Even the recognition of needs requires learning. For
instance, the identity of hunger and thirst may begin at that
primitive level of discomfort which is assuaged by food or
drink. This permits the idea of the need for food or the
need for drink to emerge as separate entities. The process
goes something like this:

1. The child may indicate discomfort by crying;

2. Parental reaction confirms the signal quality of the
    cry;

3. Partial satisfaction of the need or continued dis-
    comfort lead to a recognition of the specificity of
    that need; thus,

4. The concept of need, the existence and role of others,
    the purpose of signalling, and the ultimate satis-
    faction of needs begin to emerge.

Even the most rudimentary intellectual function can begin this
process. Planned consistency of parental response can be a
potent factor in its continuance. Once the ability to
identify emerges, even at the most primitive level, the existence of other persons as separate from self and as sources of
comfort and satisfaction appear. The capacity to seek others,
to identify by touch and smell, can be encouraged, and a
pattern of early training encouraging primitive exploration,
curiosity, the search for satisfaction and the recognition of
modes of rudimentary communication can begin. Such simple
patterns of information gathering and interchange, when
identified by the therapist, can encourage parents to identify
the slow but positive emergence of cognitive skill upon which
other and more complex learning can be based.

At our last meeting in Winnipeg, we were all agreed on the need for early diagnosis and therapy. In the short time since that meeting, I have become even more and more convinced that the most urgent need in early diagnosis is the establishment of early consistency in care. Based on the functioning senses, a foundation for development of increased skill and use of sensory residua in deficit areas can be created.

For the above and many other reasons, my second criterion of therapy is presented. The skilled educator-therapist recognizes that change can and will occur. The urgency for early therapy lies in the recognition that without intervention, such changes may be degenerative. We recognize that the capacity to explore, the development of simple curiosity (the very emergence of simple learning) can be fatally stultified without proper help. Delayed intervention leads to an almost insuperable task in trying to shift the child's focus of attention away from himself to the events of the world around him. I am convinced that one element of the stereotypic behaviour so frequently seen in these children relates to the development of self-exploration and manipulation in the absence of extra-personal stimulation consequent to multiple sensory deprivation. This is especially true where intellectual deficits preclude the spontaneous emergence of environmental exploration and curiosity. Change will occur immutably. Our challenge is to prevent degeneration and to lay down the foundations of learning. Then we must encourage the application of those learning skills to the development of improved cognitive functions. These are, of course, primary aims. The organization of information from the sensory residua will be impossible without the satisfactory implementation of these aims.

This point is made to stress that, although the audiologist may identify the amount of amplification which is likely to be necessary for optimising auditory sensitivity, the presence or absence of such amplification in a multiply disabled child may well prove irrelevant unless that child and family have begun to establish the bases of learning. At its simplest, we may say that learning through the ears or eyes cannot begin unless and until the multiply disabled child learns to learn. The fierce conviction that change is possible demands confidence on the part of parents and educators that such simple foundations can be created.

There is a tendency in meetings concerned with specific disability to elevate that disability and its amelioration to a central significance. In the past 5 years, we have attended meetings of workers in the areas of blindness, physiotherapy, occupational therapy, speech pathology, and grief and deprivation therapy. It has been interesting to see how each group sees its role as the natural leader in a team approach to multiple disability. Each seems to be at least as concerned with their primacy in the team as in the need for a collaborative professional approach to those aspects of the child's condition which precede specific therapy. These latter, as progress occurs, demand close consultation, understanding of joint responsibility, and the capacity to see that other professionals will have valuable suggestions for enhancing sensory stimulation and sensory-motor behaviour.

Just as there are very few therapeutic methods applicable to all children, so there are few, if any, educators who can hope to carry the total burden of educating a multiply disabled child. Leadership roles are essential, but effective leadership never occurs through imposition. The leader will be the person who can identify potential, plan a pattern of care with the family and fellow professionals, identify progress as it emerges, and use such progress to encourage all involved in that joint enterprise. The educator-therapist who is convinced that progress can be made is in a good position to join fellow professionals of similar conviction or, where necessary, to provide a lead to those professionals which will encourage them to that conviction.

Faith in One's Own Ability to
Promote Such Changes

The promotion of change in children with multiple disabilities involves a much wider spectrum of society than the immediate professional or familial team. Hence, promotion of change in the child can be a sterile exercise unless such changes are recognized and accepted by the general community. The growth of personal skill can lead to increased frustration

on the part of the disabled individual and his family, as
well as to a loss to the community if that skill is not
allowed to flower as a full extension of the individual's
life style. The effect of such social restriction can be
catastrophic for educator-therapist as well. We all take
legitimate pride in the progress of our patients, pupils and
clients until we see that the skills and intellectual functions we have labored so hard to produce are either unused
by the community, or resented by it for requiring adaptations
in attitudes and patterns of care for which the community is
unprepared. For example, the therapeutic and educational
staffs of one special school found that when children were
moved from child care to adult care, the self-help skills of
the children posed problems for adult care workers to which
they were unaccustomed. Careful programming was necessary, as
there was danger of restriction of the use of such skills.
Simultaneously, the original educators and therapists lost
heart and asked, quite legitimately, what was the point of
developing such skills and producing independence and pride
if there was not a continuum of care in which these assets
would be used and, equally important, continue to develop.

The time scale for development of multiply disabled
children is necessarily prolonged. Faith in one's own ability
to promote change demands access to assurance that changes
will be maintained and enhanced over time, and that, in particular, growth in self-regard and independence will be
fostered throughout life.

Recently, I received some cartoons which raise other
important issues related to this. The first depicts a blind
man with his dog and their joint collision with a lamppost.
This is followed by another sketch in which the dog is now
fitted with spectacles and provided with his own guide in
the shape of a cat! Where do we fit in the sequence? Do we
see ourselves as the dog or the cat? How often have special
centers been approached by parents who have recently left
other special centers in a search for an alternative "method"
applicable to their child? Practically every second opinion
referred to the Unit in which I work at the Royal Berkshire
Hospital in Reading seeks new or different approaches. Rarely
do they wish to be told that they were in good hands where
they were, and that progress is more likely to stem from a
personal involvement on their part than from a restless search
for some panacea.

Parents are right to seek the best they can for their child. There may well be times when they find themselves at odds with individual therapists. We are human and the children we are considering are potent sources of stress. We too often find ourselves tired and vulnerable so that disagreements can arise. The team approach should take this into account and, in doing so, arrange the rotation of responsibilities such that, although the therapeutic theme is maintained consistently, there is a constant injection of renewed interest and enthusiasm. By doing so, it should be more feasible for parents to discuss their areas of concern as widely as possible, and to discern the underlying strategies to which the team is committed. Faith in progress and in one's capacity to promote it is not, therefore, a simple faith in one's methodological skills. It demands a conviction that what we are trying to do is right for the child and family, and will be accepted and extended by the community.

The second cartoon I received illustrates the potential for hurt or humiliation in a therapeutic situation, primarily through community attitudes. In it, a blind man with his guide dog is seen enquiring his way from an official wearing a uniform cap. The drawing shows the official on one knee pointing out the directions to the dog! How often have you found yourself in the company of a deaf friend who, when making enquiries, finds himself by-passed by the respondent who insists on addressing his remarks to you? One of my blind friends takes a mischievous delight in teasing people who insist on addressing their remarks to his companions as though blindness implies deafness or mental incapacity.

I find myself irresistibly reminded of an occasion when my father went with me to be measured for my first hand-made suit. The tailor was a courteous old gentleman who asked my father "What would the young gentleman require?" My father went up several notches in my esteem by replying equally courteously, "If you wish him to remain a young gentleman, you'd better consult him yourself!"

The last cartoon I have draws together the many themes I have tried to introduce. In it, the disabled client is seen standing with his therapist, who is harnessed on his knees as a guide dog. The client holds a stick in front of the therapist's nose from which a bone labelled "fulfillment" dangles. A bitter cartoon, this one reminds us that in the approach to therapy, the goal of fulfillment is not merely client oriented. We must always be aware of to what extent our efforts to enhance the life style of those in our educational or therapeutic care stem more from our needs, than from those of our client populations. Few advertisements for educators, therapists, or child care personnel avoid the cliche description of "challenging position". At interview, such personnel are commonly asked if they face such a challenge with equanimity. It is true, of course, that such positions are immensely challenging and also immensely rewarding. Both the challenge and the rewards, however, should primarily stem from the needs and ultimate progress of the client population and not from the needs of the employee.

The personality, energy and drive of the educator-therapist are all deeply relevant to progress. More relevant, however, than these is the capacity to judge that aims for therapy are derived from the needs of child and family. Those aims must never be a mere response to a challenge in which methodology is paramount, success is a source of self-congratulations and progress is measured more in completion of a set schemata than in measurable increments in the child's information and skill. Whose fulfillment are we seeking? The answer can only be "That of the child". As the child's skills emerge and family stability is achieved, there is a sure basis for emotional strength and contentment. When these goals have been achieved, we, too, can claim fulfillment. Let us hope, for the sake of the children in our care, that such fulfillment becomes a regular and frequent event.

References

Brown, C., My Left Foot (London: Pan), 1972.

Eppstein, J., No Music By Request (Melbourne: Collins), 1979.

Hetherington, J., Uncommon Men (Melbourne: Cheshire), 1965.

Murphy, K.P., and Byrne, D., "The Deaf-Blind Multiply Disabled Infant," Early Management of Hearing Loss (New York: Grune & Stratton, Inc.), Mencher, G.T. & Gerber, S.E. (Eds.), 1980.

Schoenberg, B., "Loss and Grief," Psychological Management in Medical Practice (New York: Columbia University Press), Schoenberg, B. (Ed.), 1970.

Wright, D., Deafness - A Personal Account (New York: Penguin Press), 1969.

PROSPECTIVE IDENTIFICATION OF INFANTS
WITH HEARING LOSS AND MULTIPLE HANDICAPS:
THE ROLE OF THE NEONATAL FOLLOW-UP CLINIC

Charlene Robertson
Lillian Whyte
University of Alberta, Edmonton, Alberta

The concept of the early identification of conditions in infants thought to be "at risk" for various types of handicaps is becoming universal. This chapter describes the organization of our identification program for multiple handicaps through the follow-up of ill neonates. In addition to some background information about our Neonatal Follow-up Clinic and its functions, we have included some preliminary results from our program to date, specifically about 1084 children now 3 1/2 to 5 1/2 years old. Please keep in mind that the analysis of the 3 1/2 year old data is not complete and only one half of the children have reached 5 1/2 years of age. Therefore, while these are the most recent statistics available, they are subject to alteration.

Background Information: Neonatal Follow-up Clinic

The Neonatal Follow-up Clinic, Glenrose School Hospital, Edmonton, was established in 1974 as part of the Northern and Central Alberta Perinatal Program. The overall program represents the co-operative efforts of the Ministry of Health of the Government of Alberta, the University of Alberta Medical School, the Royal Alexandra, University of Alberta, and Glenrose Provincial Hospitals. The program consists of two neonatal intensive care units providing tertiary care for critically ill newborns, two perinatal obstetrical units providing tertiary care for high risk mothers, and the neonatal follow-up clinic providing continuing care for selected high risk neonates discharged from the two intensive care units.

The neonatal follow-up clinic has two populations of children. The first is the longitudinal on-going follow-up of 1084 children to 8 years of age, where the children were born from August 1, 1974, to March 31, 1979. The second population includes 672 children born after that time, who are to be followed to 2 years of age and then discharged if no major handicap is found. The documentation of handicap in a neonatal clinic population is more meaningful with background statistics.

TABLE I: Background Statistics.

Year	Provincial Births	Northern Alberta & Central Alberta Births (estimates)	Tertiary Neonatal Intensive Care Admissions*
1975	31,998	19,167	900
1979	37,524	22,477	1,509

* Just under 5% to just over 6% of our births received tertiary neonatal intensive care.

The children selected within the first 28 days of life for the longitudinal program included surviving neonatal intensive care graduates in the following classification groups (see Figure 1), with approximately the same number of children in each group.

Objectives

The primary objective of the neonatal follow-up clinic is the evaluation of neonatal intensive care in this region through documentation of the quality of the cognitive, behavioural, and motor performance of the survivors.   A

FIGURE 1:   Classification groups.

(1)   1500 grams birthweight or less

(2)   Over 1500 grams birthweight with central nervous sytem
      conditions complicating their course. These conditions
      include: meningitis; suspected or known intracranial
      hemorrhage; convulsions; hypoxic-ischemic encephalopathy
      or other evidence of asphyxia; head trauma requiring
      neonatal intensive care treatment; recurrent apnea
      requiring ventilation; and apnea or cyanosis thought to
      be on a central nervous system basis.

(3)   Over 1500 grams birthweight without any complications
      under (2) above, but requiring ventilation or ventila-
      tory aids.

(4)   Over 1500 grams birthweight without any complications
      under (2) or (3) above, and including a random sample
      population of those children not included under (1),
      (2), or (3) above.

---

specific goal includes a detailed evaluation of the school
performance of the children at age 8 to determine which of
the graduates are "at risk" for future developmental problems.
The clinic is also assisting in answering questions concerning the length of follow-up required to predict accurate
neonatal outcome data.

The intensive care graduates included in the follow-up
study are assumed to have been children with potential for
normal development, and the study is concerned with whether
the complications of illnesses in the perinatal period have
caused permanent damage.

Organization

The clinic combines service with research. The Glenrose Hospital is the major center for assessment and treatment of children with handicapping conditions in Northern
Alberta. It provides access to all modern treatment facilities and personnel, should they be required by neonatal
intensive care graduates. A child is first diagnosed in the
neonatal clinic and then transferred to the appropriate
department or program within the Glenrose for therapy.
Handicapped children return to the long-term follow-up clinic
at regular intervals, as do the other graduates. Should a
neonatal intensive care graduate not be seen in the follow-
up clinic, but have a significant handicap, cross-checking
within the total Glenrose Hospital program provides outcome
information.

The approach used by the clinic is an interdisciplinary
evaluation providing regular assessments of growth, motor
and sensory development, and psychomotor, cognitive, and
educational performance. The team specialists include a
pediatrician with special interest in developmental medicine,
a nurse, occupational therapist, physiotherapist, psychologist, audiologist, speech pathologist, and an educator. An
ophthalmologist examines all children of 1500 grams birthweight or less. Consultation has been available with social
work, physiatry, psychiatry, otolaryngology, research design
specialists, and statisticians. Every effort is made to
determine the status/outcome of the child, should that child
not be available for complete assessment. Assessments are
done 6 to 9 times during the 8 years of the study, with more
frequent examinations being completed on the small, pre-term
infants, and if a handicapping condition is expected.

Assessments involve the use of standard testing procedures, appropriate for the age of the child. A *Neonatal
Follow-up Study Data Collection and Coding Manual* published
in 1980, provides a detailed description of the instruments
used in this study, references, and instructions for its own
use. Intelligence testing is reported in groups defined by
the American Association for Mental Deficiency. The term
"visual impairment" refers to a best corrected vision of
20/60 or less, while blindness refers to legal blindness and

to light perception only. Speech and language delays are
grouped as mild, moderate, and severe. A detailed description
of these groupings is available through the Department of
Speech Pathology at the Glenrose School Hospital.

Children attending the neonatal follow-up clinic are
routinely seen by the audiologist at 6 months adjusted age,
2 years, and 3 1/2 or 5 1/2 years of age. Recall examinations
are done if the routine procedures are not satisfactory.
Standard testing for infants includes startle response to
speech and noise, sound field responses, speech awareness
responses to warbled pure tones, visual reinforcement audiometry, and impedance testing including acoustic reflexes.
Each examination requires 20 to 30 minutes. If deafness is
suspected, serial testing is completed. Hearing loss is
categorized as Group I (unilateral), Group II (mild to moderate), and Group III (severe to profound). A hearing loss of
greater than 70 dB in the better ear would place the child
into Group III.

Preliminary Results:
1084 Neonatal Intensive Care Graduates

This information concerns 1084 neonatal intensive care
graduates now between 3 1/2 and 5 1/2 years of age. For the
purpose of outcome statistics, handicapping conditions have
been defined as cerebral palsy, visual impairment or blindness, trainable or severe mental retardation, convulsive
disorders (excluding febrile seizures), neurosensory (or
mixed) hearing loss, and severe psychiatric disturbance.
Speech, language, and lesser emotional disturbances (not
requiring psychiatric care) have not been included in this
handicapped group. At this time, 160 of the 1084 (14.7%)
graduates have one or more of the above handicapping conditions. Of the 160, 11 have died as a complication of their
handicap. None of the 11 was thought to have bilateral
hearing loss. There is no information concerning the presence or absence of a unilateral hearing loss in the 11
handicapped and 3 non-handicapped children who died before
the age of 3 1/2 years.

The total remaining living children at 3 1/2 years was
1070. Assessment information for age 3 1/2 years is available
on 904 of the original 1084 children, or 83.4% follow-up at
3 1/2 years. There is detailed statistical analysis of the
first 619 children reaching 3 1/2 years of age.

Sensorineural or Mixed Hearing Loss

    To date, 27 of the 1070 children have a diagnosed
sensorineural or mixed hearing loss. As indicated earlier,
the pattern of the hearing loss has been categorized as either
unilateral (regardless of severity), mild/moderate bilateral,
or severe/profound bilateral. Twenty-seven children represents
2.5% of the total group.

TABLE II: Known sensorineural or mixed hearing loss of 1070
           children at 3 1/2 to 5 1/2 years.

	Number	%
Unilateral	5	.4
Mild/moderate bilateral	12	1.12
Severe/profound bilateral	10	.93
Total	27	2.5

    Hearing losses were found in the original neonatal
classification groups as seen in Table III.

TABLE III: Distribution of known sensorineural or mixed
            hearing loss.

Classifica-tion Group*	Unilateral Loss	Mild/Moderate Bilat. Loss	Severe/Profound Bilat. Loss	Total Number
1	0	4	2	6
2	4	7	7	18
3	0	1	1	2
4	1	0	0	1
Total	5	12	10	27

*See Figure 1.

In our neonatal intensive care population, excluding
those disorders known to be associated with deafness, 24 of
the 27 children were found in classification Groups I or II;
that is, less than 1500 grams at birth, or neonatal problems
associated with the central nervous system. None had a
family history of hearing loss, although in one child with
moderate, bilateral sensorineural loss there are some family
members with manifestations of Waardenburg's Syndrome.

From the more formal analysis of the 619 children 3 1/2
years old, 16 were diagnosed with sensorineural or mixed
hearing loss: 4 unilateral; 5 bilateral mild to moderate;
and 7 bilateral severe to profound.

When the central nervous system factors and sensorineural or mixed hearing loss are compared by Chi square
analysis for the 619 children, 5 factors have significant
values:
> neonatal meningitis ($p=0.0114$)
> abnormal neurological and developmental examination
>   on discharge from hospital ($p=0.0115$)
> hypoxic-ischemic encephalopathy ($p=0.0118$)
> hydrocephaly ($p=0.0212$)
> bilirubin encephalopathy ($p=0.0604$)

Ten of the 16 children with sensorineural or mixed hearing loss have 1 or more deficits in articulation, receptive
and expressive language, vocabulary, and/or deviant function
of the oral mechanism. No child with a unilateral loss has
any language deficit. Three of 5 children with bilateral
mild to moderate loss have language deficit(s), and 7 of 7
(100%) with severe/profound loss have language deficits. Six
of the 10 with language deficit(s) also have I.Q. scores
below 85.

Multiple Handicapped and Sensorineural
or Mixed Hearing Loss

Seven (26%) of the 27 children with some sensorineural
hearing loss have at least 1 major handicap, including
cerebral palsy, trainable or severe retardation, visual
impairment or blindness, or convulsions. Of these 7 children, 3 were 1500 grams or less at birth, and 4 had central

nervous system problems in hospital. No child was found in
the other 2 classification Groups seen in Figure 1.

A detailed clinical description of the handicaps of
these 7 children is given in Appendix A. The handicapping
conditions include visual impairment or blindness in all of
the children, cerebral palsy in 2 children, and convulsions
in 1 child. Utilizing the intelligence groupings provided
by the American Association of Mental Deficiency, individual
intelligence as determined by the best measure or estimate
possible, varied from trainable to superior.

A review of some of the neonatal factors of the children
is given in Appendix B. Complications of prematurity and
known asphyxia or intracranial bleed were causes as would be
expected. One child with congenital bowel malrotation
requiring intravenous Amphotericin B for fungemia, had
multiple handicaps and hearing loss. The sex distribution
shows 3 boys and 4 girls. The average scores for other
variables were:
            maternal age - 19.6 years
            1-minute Apgar score - 4.8
            5-minute Apgar score - 6.6
            gestation - 34.1 weeks
            highest total bilirubin - 11.1 mgs%
            days duration of administration of intravenous
                aminoglycosides - 17.0 days
Five of the 7 children required ventilation.

Multiple Handicap - Sensorineural
or Mixed Hearing Loss at 3 1/2 Years

Six Hundred nineteen (619) of the 1084 children we are
following are now 3 1/2 years of age. Of those, 7 (1.1%)
have sensorineural or mixed hearing loss in the severe/
profound range. All are in classification Group II (Figure
1), that is, neonatal problems related to the central nervous
system. Hearing loss occurred as a single major handicap for
5 of the 7, and as a multiple handicap with visual loss and
low I.Q. (less than 52) for 2 of the 7 children.

Known Conductive Hearing Loss
at 3 1/2 Years

From the more detailed analysis of the 619 children, we
found that 64 (10.3%) had conductive hearing loss without
sensorineural involvement at the time of the 3 1/2 year old
assessment. Twenty (3.2%) had unilateral loss and 44 (7.1%)
had mild to moderate bilateral loss. The neonatal central
nervous system factors (under classification Group II) which
had significant values (Chi square analysis) when compared to
conductive hearing loss were:
        apnea requiring ventilation (p=0.004)
        apnea on a central nervous system basis (p=0.0223)
        treatment for head trauma (p=0.0483)

Of the 619 children, 403 (65.1%) were born into homes
where there was smoking by mother or other family member(s).
Any amount of smoking was considered to be "smoking in the
home". The Chi square value, when this smoking was compared
to conductive hearing loss, was also significant (p=0.0525).
Where there was smoking in the home, 4.5% of the children had
unilateral conductive loss. Only 2.3% of the children had
unilateral conductive hearing loss when there was no smoking
in the home. When there was smoking in the home, 7.7% of the
children had bilateral conductive hearing loss. When there
was no smoking in the home, only 3.7% of the children had
bilateral conductive hearing loss. In this neonatal intensive care graduate population of 619 children, with 64
children with conductive hearing loss, smoking in the home
appears to have doubled the incidence.

Twenty-six (40.6%) of the children with conductive loss
(based on N=619), had one or more areas of language deficit:
6 of 20 (30%) of the children with unilateral loss had
language deficit(s), while 20 of 44 (45.5%) children had
bilateral mild/moderate hearing loss and language deficits.
I.Q. scores were less than 85 for 13 of the 20 children
(52.8%) with language deficits.

Ten children with some degree of conductive hearing loss
also had one or more major handicaps.

Comparison of Children with Conductive
and Sensorineural or Mixed Hearing Loss

When children with conductive loss at age 3 1/2 years
are compared with children with sensorineural or mixed hearing loss, significant Chi square values were found for 4
neonatal variables:
>   administration of intravenous Kanamycin given in
>   days duration (p=0.006)
>   presence of hypoxic-ischemic encephalopathy (p=0.03)
>   abnormal neurological and developmental examination
>   on discharge from the neonatal intensive care
>   unit (p=0.03)
>   by classification Group as seen in Figure 1 (p=0.03)

For each variable, more children with sensorineural or
mixed hearing loss than children with conductive loss were
involved. For example, significantly more sensorineural
hearing loss children had an abnormal neurological examination on discharge and were in classification Group II
(Figure 1) than the children with conductive hearing loss
only.

Multiple Handicap and Bilateral
Conductive Hearing Loss

For the purpose of this review, conductive loss was not
considered unless it was bilateral, at least moderate in
severity at 3 1/2 years, and present, continuously or fluctu-
ating, prior to that time. With these restrictions, 20 of
the surviving handicapped children, excluding those with
sensorineural mixed hearing loss, had conductive loss.
Table IV indicates that 18 of these children were found
within classification Groups I and II.

A detailed description of the handicaps of the 20 children can be found in Appendix C. Nine of the 20 children have
cerebral palsy, and 8 of the 20 have impaired vision or
blindness. Intellectually, the range is from average I.Q.
to severe retardation.

The presence of conductive hearing loss complicates the
progress of learning for these multiply handicapped children
and is a component of their handicap which could, theoretically, be eliminated. To date, 10 of the 20 children have

received surgical treatment for their conductive disorder.
Four of the 10 had their initial myringotomies after their
3 1/2 year old neonatal clinic assessment. A number of the
children had some investigation for allergies, and all had
some recurrent medical treatment.

TABLE IV: KNOWN MULTIPLE HANDICAPS AND CHRONIC BILATERAL
            CONDUCTIVE HEARING LOSS

Classification Group	Multiple Handicaps With Conductive Loss
1	11
2	7
3	1
4	1
Total	20

    Appendix D outlines the neonatal data of these 20 child-
ren and the presumed cause of the handicapping condition.
Complications of prematurity account for 16 of the 20 children. Sixteen of the 20 children had smoking in their home
environment from birth to 3 1/2 years.

    The sex distribution shows 12 boys and 8 girls.   The
average scores for other variables were:
        maternal age - 25.3 years
        1-minute Apgar score - 4.2
        5-minute Apgar score - 6.7
        gestation - 32.6 weeks
        highest total bilirubin - 7.3 mgs%
        days duration of administration of intravenous
            aminoglycosides - 18.4 days
Sixteen of the 20 children required ventilation.

In summary, of our long-term follow-up population, 160 of the 1084 children had one or more handicapping conditions. Seven children had handicaps with sensorineural or mixed hearing loss, and 20 had handicaps with chronic conductive hearing loss. The total number of children with multiple handicaps with hearing loss equalled 27, or 16.8% of the handicapped group.

Second Population: Neonatal Follow-up Clinic
(672 Children to Date)

As part of an ongoing program, a second group of children is under investigation. These youngsters, not included in our long-term cohort, receive the same interdisciplinary assessments as the previous group. However, if no handicap is diagnosed by 2 years of age, the child is discharged from follow-up. The nurse-clinical specialist, audiologist, physiotherapist, occupational therapist, and speech pathologist are available to the tertiary neonatal intensive care units for consultation. We now attempt to do Auditory Brainstem Evoked Response testing in the neonatal period on all children who will subsequently come to the follow-up clinic. The children now coming to the clinic are from the classification groups we previously found to be at highest risk:

1. 1250 grams birthweight and less;

2. Over 1250 grams birthweight with central nervous system problems.

Of the 672 children, 12 have sensorineural hearing loss. Six of these (.89% of 672) have multiple handicaps: 3 with spastic quadraplegia (1 blind); and 3 with significant retardation and delayed development.

Our ongoing neonatal follow-up is becoming increasingly service oriented. Information from our initial pilot cohort of 1084 children helped us to know which of the neonatal intensive care graduates was at-risk for handicapping conditions. This assisted in our selection of children for follow-up.

Discussion

We have presented information on the organization of our neonatal follow-up clinic which assists us in the identification of those children with handicapping conditions, and in determining which are the risk factors for handicapping conditions. Preliminary information suggests that multiply handicapped children with sensorineural or mixed hearing loss occur relatively infrequently in a neonatal intensive care graduate population, where the specific syndromes known to be associated with hearing loss are excluded. In our first cohort of 1084, we found 7 such children, and in the second cohort of 672, there were 6 multiply handicapped children with sensorineural hearing loss. This represents less than 1% of the population screened in each group.

It appears from our study of our pilot cohort that neonates at greatest risk for multiple handicaps and hearing loss (as well as sensorineural hearing loss alone) appear to be those with a very low birthweight or those with manifestations of central nervous system disease secondary to perinatal and neonatal complications. We now recommend Auditory Brainstem Evoked Response testing for such children in the neonatal period.

Significant conductive hearing loss occurs in those neonates, handicapped or not, with predisposing factors such as prolonged ventilation, chronic lung disease and environmental irritants such as smoking in the home. Although we do not yet have the statistics for the mode and age of treatment of conductive hearing pathology for our total cohort population to compare with the multiply handicapped group, there is a suggestion that the treatment in the multiple handicapped group may be less vigorous. In view of the importance of minimizing handicapping conditions as much as possible, we would like to underline the importance of vigorous treatment for conductive hearing pathology. As these multiply handicapped children are usually under close surveillance by therapists and educators, it would be possible to ensure that they are screened regularly and treated for this portion of their handicapping condition.

One of the difficulties we face in the prospective
identification of infants with hearing loss and multiple
handicaps in our neonatal clinic population is a lack of
predictability of the extent of the handicap. For children
with specific syndromes (such as Down's Syndrome), one often
can be much more accurate in giving a prognosis at a much
earlier age. In children with perinatal insults, there frequently are unexpected components to the overall handicapping
condition, and there may be major strengths in the child's
profile as well. We strongly recommend frequent interdisciplinary assessments of the handicapped child to ensure that
other possible associated handicaps are identified early.
The early initial and ongoing identification of the strengths
and weaknesses of these children is a great challenge for the
interdisciplinary team approach and for neonatal follow-up
clinics.

Discussion

S. GERBER
    In your last group – those with conductive hearing
impairments and other handicaps, what proportion had additional handicap in the form of a cranio-facial anomaly?

C. ROBERTSON
    None. That's the point I tried to make. Every child
with anomalies which could be defined and associated with
handicap had been eliminated. If they were not eliminated in
the newborn period, I eliminated them by age 3 1/2 years. We
may have seen them, but they are not in the statistical
analysis. So, these are children I have assumed would have
been normal without perinatal insult. The only exception
might have been a hearing loss, because there might have been
some familial instance not related to the perinatal insult
which I wouldn't have known about.

M. DOWNS
    Thank you again for a beautiful study. You always do
such a magnificent job of giving us beautiful statistics.
In regard to Dr. Gerber's question, too, I am not surprised
that you're seeing a large number of conductive hearing losses
in this particular group. Recall that Berman and Balkany

found that 100% of intubated babies suffered otitis media
during their stay in the newborn nursery. These are the
children, then, who are at risk for recurrent otitis media.
I would suggest that a proper concern is to begin to look at
high risk for another type of hearing problem, the conductive
hearing loss.

G. MENCHER
    Do you have any indication as to an average age for
identification of the multiple handicap of a child?

C. ROBERTSON
    We have been doing this now for 8 years and, in my
opinion, most of the children with multiple handicaps can be
defined in the newborn period. I do that by criteria which I
have outlined. I have a data collection and coding manual,
and they're listed there. We use that examination of the
children on discharge and very, very good physical examinations up to 6 months. I don't try to make the diagnosis
before 6 months, but I almost always can make it by 6 months.
I don't want to mislead anyone, so I'm very cautions under
6 months. We have brainstem audiologic evoked response
testing on all children who fall into the high risk categories,
plus, of course, other children where there is a syndrome
which would indicate neurosensory hearing loss. This is in
addition to neonatal follow-up screening.

APPENDIX A
Clinical Description
Neurosensory or Mixed Hearing Loss - Multiple Handicaps

Child	Hearing Loss	Speech	Intelligence	Vision	Motor	Other
1	severe-bilateral high frequency	moderate delay	slow learner	impaired (R.L.F.)	delayed	active
2	mild-unilateral	normal	superior	impaired (R.L.F.)	poor quality	
3	profound-bilateral	severe delay	slow learner	blind (cataracts and R.L.F.)	delayed	active
4	moderate-bilateral mixed	severe delay	educable	normal	cerebral palsy	
5	severe-unilateral mixed	normal	average	impaired (amblyopia)	delayed	hydro-cephalus (shunted)
6	severe-bilateral	severe delay	educable	impaired (macula + cornea damage)	delayed	
7	severe-bilateral high frequency	severe delay	trainable retardation	impaired (optic atrophy)	cerebral palsy	convul-sions

APPENDIX B
Neonatal Data
Neurosensory or Mixed Hearing Loss - Multiple Handicapped

Child	Sex	Mom's Age	Smoking in home	Apgar	Gesta-tion	Birth Weight	Ventila-tion	Highest Bilirubin	Amino-glyco-sides (days)	Presumed cause of handicap
1	M	21	no	5-8	25	870	yes	11.0	47	prematurity chronic lung disease
2	F	21	no	6-8	32	1680	yes	11.7	11	prematurity I.C.B.
3	F	17	no	3-6	29	880	yes	15.0	14	prematurity asphyxia
4	F	17	no	0-5	32	1340	yes	13.0	21	prematurity asphyxia
5	M	18	no	9-9	40	3680	no	7.0	7	birth trauma I.C.B./hydro-cephalus
6	M	17	yes	8-9	42	2630	no	18.3	10	bowel mal-rotation-fungemia
7	F	26	no	3-1	39	2353	yes	2.0	9	placental insufficiency/birth asphyxia

HABILITATION FACILITIES AT THE GLENROSE SCHOOL HOSPITAL

Robert Shea
Glenrose Hospital, Edmonton, Alberta

"Deaf people with good ability have been misdiagnosed as mentally retarded; some with poor balance in childhood have been labelled as having cerebral palsy. Many of those with additional medical labels function very well. The challenge is not to reject the label, but to understand what the child can and cannot do, and then to see what can be achieved under the best possible circumstances." (Freeman, Carbin & Boese, "Can't Your Child Hear?").

In the previous paper in this text, Dr. Robertson's statistics demonstrate that approximately 5% of all pregnancies in Alberta result in infants requiring admission to a Neonatal Intensive Care Unit (N.I.C.U.). It is mainly that group of infants for whom intensive screening and follow-up facilities have been structured. Dr. Robertson has also demonstrated that for the 95% of infants who do not require a N.I.C.U. setting at birth, or for those within the 5% for whom such a setting is not available because of distance, weather, or whatever circumstance, appropriate assessment facilities should also be in place to determine not only impairments of hearing, vision, motor development, or cognition, but also to define specific abilities on which habilitation strategies, if needed, can be based.

Assessment

Locally, follow-up of N.I.C.U. infants is done by the Glenrose Neonatal Follow-up Clinic which functions as described by Dr. Robertson. Children who at birth may not have been deemed to require an N.I.C.U., but about whom there are later concerns regarding hearing, vision, motor development or cognitive delays, are usually referred to Glenrose. There they are evaluated in the Physically Handicapped Children's Unit by an interdisciplinary assessment team whose function is to delineate the above impairments as well as specific areas of intact function. Through this assessment procedure, problems are listed, recommendations derived, and habilitative programs instituted.

The determination of hearing loss can be made very early if the "at risk" criteria are applied and the appropriate audiological investigations done to determine the presence and degree of hearing loss. One of the old maxims in Pediatrics is, "When abnormality occurs, there is a high likelihood of additional or associated abnormality". It is imperative that this be considered in the presence of any abnormality. It is reasonable to assume that whatever insult caused one abnormality might well have provoked a deficit in another organ system at the same time. Such deficits can impair other sensory organs, motor co-ordination, speech, and/or intellect. The combinations can be devastating. Statistically, depending on the survey, type of deafness and severity of secondary involvement, it has been reported that 11% to 40% of hearing impaired children will have an additional impairment (Budden et al., 1974; Rawlings & Gentile, 1970; Schein, 1974).

In the recent book *Can't Your Child Hear* (Freeman, Carbin & Boese, 1981), distinctions among the terms *impairment, disability,* and *handicap* are made as follows:

1. An impairment refers to the actual physical or structural deviation from normal. It may have great, little, or no practical consequence. People who wear prescription glasses have visual impairment. A mild hearing loss correctable by means of a hearing aid may result in an impairment with few limitations.

2. A disability refers to loss of an important function in spite of any aids or treatment. Everyone who is disabled has an impairment, but not everyone with an impairment is disabled. If a hearing aid cannot correct for a hearing impairment, then the person cannot perform an important function. This may be considered a disability.

3. A handicap refers to attitudes, feelings and barriers which increase the effect of the disability, turn it into a problem of living, and put a person at a disadvantage. For example, a qualified deaf person who cannot obtain a job because of employer attitude or lack of a communication device on the telephone is handicapped.

Common Associated Impairments

The type of additional impairment depends partly upon the cause of the deafness. Among these, associated visual deficit is prominent. Depending on the type of test and definition of hearing and visual involvement utilized, between 8% and 50% of all hearing impaired children will have some associated visual problem (Hicks & Pfau, 1979). The 50% figure would include patients with a simple refractive error. Usher's Syndrome, a recessively acquired degenerative retinopathy, accounts for one-half of all deaf-blind adults. Three to 6% of congenitally deaf infants will be involved with this Syndrome (Freeman et al., 1981). Rubella deaf children have additional impairments in 13% to 60% of cases (Chess, Korn & Fernandez, 1971; Peckham et al., 1979). These usually involve the heart, the eye, and/or intellect. When meningitis results in deafness, 15% of the children will also be retarded. Rh incompatibility resulting in jaundice and deafness is associated with other physical impairments, usually the athetoid form of cerebral palsy, in 75% of the children (Freeman et al., 1981).

Eight to 12% of hearing impaired children are retarded, as compared to 3% in the general population (Freeman et al., 1981). Much of the determination of retardation or developmental delay in the infant is based upon the maturation of the central nervous system and the age at which the child

learned to sit, stand, walk, and communicate. Mental retardation should be suspect when there is delayed motor progress or
when communication is slower than expected.

For a more complete catalogue of conditions associated
with deafness, the reader is referred to the chapters on
ophthalmology and neurology in *Hearing Loss in Children*,
(Jaffe, 1977).

Habilitation Programs at Glenrose

Admission to the habilitation program at Glenrose follows
assessment by either the Neonatal Clinic or the Physically
Handicapped Children's Unit. The *Preschool Program for the
Hearing Impaired* (PPHI) which is staffed by educators of the
hearing impaired, speech pathology, audiology, psychology,
social service, and medicine, functions in 2 sections. It is
a parent/infant program for those identified in infancy and
goes until approximately age 3 years. It serves hearing
impaired children as well as hearing impaired multiply handicapped. The other section serves children 3 to 6 years of age
with both individual and group therapy in classes having a
maximum number of 7. The approach is auditory/oral, although
some children require manual communication assistance.

The *Infant Intervention Program* provides ongoing assess-
ment/treatment for developmentally delayed children aged 0 to
2. It is a stimulation program in which parent training in
age-appropriate cognitive stimulation techniques is employed.
There are half-day sessions held twice a week for a block of
3 months, with 3 or 4 children seen in each treatment block.
The program is operated by the Psychology Department with
assistance from the Departments of Occupational Therapy,
Speech Pathology, Physiotherapy and Medicine.

Junior Nursery is a group setting for severely disabled
2 to 3 year olds. There are 3 three-month sessions per year
with approximately 18 children seen. The program runs one-
half day per week and is staffed by occupational therapy,
speech pathology, physiotherapy, and social service. Children
from this program proceed into the *General Nursery* setting or
are placed in alternative community programs.

The *General Nursery* serves children from 3 to 5 who have
physical disabilities or language and motor delays. It is a
setting where children explore and learn in group and play
situations. The focus is on development of physical, cognitive, social, emotional, and communication skills. The
emphasis is on parental involvement, support, and education.
The program is served by occupational therapy, speech pathology, medicine, social service, psychology, and physiotherapy.
Children from this program progress into the kindergarten,
Glenrose Language Program, or to alternate programs in the
city.

Summary

The goal of each program is to habilitate, to bring the
child to the point where integration can occur into an appropriate community facility geared to the child's level of
ability; a place where facilities and personnel are available
to foster further progress through ongoing therapies.

Program development for multi-sensory disabled children
requires early identification, parental involvement, and an
individualized, developmentally based, optimistic approach
which utilizes the co-operation of several disciplines and
incorporates support and relief systems for parents (Klein,
1978). We feel this has been achieved, in part, at Glenrose.

References

Budden, S.S., Robinson, G.C., MacLean, C.D., and Cambon, K.G.,
    "Deafness in Infants and Preschool Children: An Analysis
    of Etiology and Associated Handicaps," American Annals of
    the Deaf 119:387-395, 1974.

Chess, S., Korn, S., and Fernandez, P., Psychiatric Disorders
    of Children with Congenital Rubella (New York: Brunner/
    Mazel, Inc.), 1971.

Freeman, R.D., Carbin, C.F., and Boese, R.J., Can't Your
    Child Hear? - A Guide for Those Who Care About Deaf Child-
    ren (Baltimore: University Park Press), 1981.

Hicks, W.M., and Pfau, G.S., "Deaf-Visually Impaired
    Persons: Incidence and Services," American Annals of the
    Deaf 124:76-92, 1979.

Jaffe, B.F. (Ed.), Hearing Loss in Children (Baltimore:
    University Park Press), 1977.

Klein, C., "Variables to Consider in Developing and Selecting
    Services for Deaf-Blind Children, Part 2," American Annals
    of the Deaf 123:430-433, 1978.

Peckham, C.S., Martin, J.A.M., Marshall, W.C., and Dudgeon,
    J.A., "Congenital Rubella Deafness: A Preventable
    Disease," Lancet Vol 1, 1:258-261, 1979.

Rawlings, B., and Gentile, A., Additional Handicapping
    Conditions, Age at Onset of Hearing Loss, and Other
    Characteristics of Hearing Impaired Students, United
    States: 1968-69 (Washington, D.C.: Office of Demographic
    Studies, Gallaudet College), 1970.

Schein, J.D. (Ed.), Education and Rehabilitation of Deaf
    Persons with other Disabilities (New York: Deafness
    Research and Training Center, New York University), 1974.

THE OTOLOGICAL PERSPECTIVE

Irwin F. Stewart
University of British Columbia, Vancouver, British Columbia

It is traditionally a joyous time for the new mother in the delivery room when she is able to check out the physical features of her newborn baby. There is usually a good deal of concern if the baby is flaccid, blue, or does not breathe well. There is usually a good deal of shock if there is some obvious physical abnormality. There is further shock when a silent handicap such as deafness or mental retardation is demonstrated. Indeed, the shock and concern associated with more obvious or immediate problems may shunt aside one's concentration when searching for additional silent handicaps.

It is a medical tragedy that, even in this modern world of medicine, the silent handicaps which frequently co-exist with physical handicaps are often very delayed in diagnosis. This situation is compounded in later years by the reticence of many physicians to aggressively diagnose, treat, and follow the hearing handicapped child with multi-handicaps. In part, this stems from a lack of understanding of studies which have demonstrated severe developmental delays associated with even mild hearing losses (Balkany et al., 1979; Downs, 1977; Holm & Kunze, 1969).

The diagnosis of hearing loss in a newborn has always been a challenge to the otologist. The challenge is made more difficult when the multi-handicapped, deaf child has no obvious physical abnormalities, but deafness is combined with such problems as brain damage, mental retardation, or autism. There is still considerable debate over what type of routine screening for hearing loss is the most cost effective. There is no question, however, that the establishment of High Risk Registers has given the practicing physician the most effective warning about impending birth defects, particularly with respect to hearing.

Incidence

An estimate of the number of babies born with multiple
malformations has been placed at about 0.7% (Smith, 1976).
This rate of 7:1000 live births compares with the rate of
1:1000 live births of hearing impairment due to embryologic
related, genetic, or congenital acquired diseases (Sarno &
Clemis, 1980; Stewart, 1977; Northern & Downs, 1974). The
multiple malformation rate of 7:1000 probably indicates a
higher rate of multiple "handicap" because, in many cases, a
silent handicap such as deafness might go undetected unless
it occurred within a recognized syndrome (e.g. Waardenburg's
or Usher's Syndrome). It is also likely that account would
not be taken of progressive deafness which may be genetic
(Paparella, 1978), or non-genetic through viremia or other
infective factors (Davis, 1979). The difficulty inherent in
reaching accurate figures on prevalence was reflected in a
U.S. Report which studied the hearing impaired - developmentally disabled population (Stewart, 1978). Children who were
either autistic, cerebral palsied, epileptic, or mentally
retarded, and hearing impaired were included. The study
concluded that about 0.5%, or 1 million, in these various
categories were present in the 1977 United States population.

The prevalence of hearing impaired children with additional handicaps may be considered from another perspective,
as was demonstrated by the Gallaudet College, Canadian
Survey, reported in 1981 (Karchmer et al., 1981). This
survey indicated that 30% of hearing impaired children had
additional handicaps. Non-physical handicaps were found to
be more common than physical ones, with emotional-behavioural
problems, mental retardation, and specific learning disabilities the most frequently encountered. Of the organic handicaps, visual difficulties and cerebral palsy were the most
frequent, followed by brain damage, epilepsy, orthopedic, and
cardiac abnormalities.

Today physicians may succeed in preventing the birth of
a multiply handicapped child because of early warning signals.
Genetic counselling may lead to amniocentesis, fetoscopy, or
intra-uterine audiology. The use of ultra-sound is commonplace in most hospitals.

Routine rubella vaccine has been made available, although the duration of immunity has been questioned (Vernon, 1982). Antibiotics have reduced the severity of the scourge of meningitis.

While medicine, through prevention, is contributing to some reduction in the number of multiply handicapped, deaf children, it is, at the same time, contributing to an increase in that population. Reduction in infant mortality, improved prenatal care, and improved identification and diagnostic procedures have resulted in increased numbers surviving for longer periods of time (Flathouse, 1979). In addition to these factors which tend to prolong the life of borderline newborns, a number of newly recognized diseases are emerging to produce multiply handicapped children. The cytomegalovirus (CMV) for example, may produce a spectrum extending from severe central nervous system destruction with multi-handicaps, to asymptomatic viruria (Davis, 1979). Children with this simple viruria have a high incidence of unsuspected hearing loss. The CMV has now also been shown to be the cause of unsuspected learning and speech disorders, infantile spasms, and hearing loss (Hanshaw, 1976; Kumar & Nankeruis, 1973).

Transplacental infection with CMV of the fetus in an asymptomatic mother can result in cytomegalic inclusion disease in the neonate with low birthweight, hepatospleno- megaly, jaundice, petechiae, and purpura. This pattern is common to several agents causing congenital infection - toxoplasmosis, rubella, cytomegalovirus, herpes simplex virus and syphilis. The group has been referred to by the acronym TORCH(S) to describe the common presenting signs and symptoms of congenital infection.

While rubella may, in the future, be controlled through the use of a vaccine, there is increasing cause for concern that the viruses and organisms making up the TORCH(S) group are increasing in the general population.

The herpes simplex virus has been implicated as a cause of the increasing prevalence of deafness combined with other handicaps, particularly cerebral palsy and mental retarda- tion. With an increase in sexually transmitted disease, it is now estimated that 25% of the population is infected with herpes simplex in the genital tract (Medical World News, 1980).

Evaluation

Differentiation between conductive, sensorineural and/or
mixed hearing loss can usually be made through a very complete
otolaryngological and general history. Special emphasis
should be placed on intra-uterine and peri-partum history and
intellectual and speech development. The history must be
followed by a complete head and neck examination, with
emphasis on visual inspection of the auricle, external
auditory canal, and tympanic membrane. General examination
must include careful review of the integumental, cardiovascular, genito-urinary, occular, musculo-skeletal, and endocrine
systems, as well as a complete neurological examination.

After the history and physical examination, audiological
investigation of the hearing loss with special site of lesion
tests and the vestibular battery should be obtained. Follow-
up tests must be modified, depending on the clinician situation, but most protocols indicate certain studies to be
essential and others to be done selectively (Meyerhoff, 1978).

The multiply handicapped deaf child must have mastoid
and internal auditory canal films carried out, together with
polytomography of the labyrinth and CT Scan of the temporal
bones. All of the infants require a cardiac evaluation, as
well as hematological and coagulation factor analysis. In
addition, renal function should be studied through routine
urinalysis and creatinin clearance evaluation. It is mandatory to carry out VDRL and FTA-ABS (Flourescent treponema
antibody) tests. It is optional to carry out sweat tests,
fasting blood sugar, serum electrophoresis, and thyroid and
liver function studies. While it has been considered
optional to do viral studies, a recent report suggests that
a greater effort be made in the natal period to diagnosis
viral causative agents (Pappas & Mundy, 1982). That study
advocates carrying out at least the simple and inexpensive
screening procedures IgM and RF (Rheumatoid Factor). Where a
syndrome complex is suspected but not obvious, an electro-
cardiagram may demonstrate a Jervell and Lange-Nielsen
Syndrome, a Pendred's Syndrome, or an Alport's Syndrome.
Finally, it may be necessary to carry out exploratory tympanometry when a spontaneous rupture of the round window or other
middle ear pathology is suspected.

Diagnosis and Management

Conductive, sensorineural and mixed types of hearing loss
may be congenital or delayed, genetic or non-genetic, and
progressive or stable (Meyerhoff, 1978).

Congenital Conductive and Mixed
Hearing Loss

Hearing loss often occurs in association with one of
many syndromes, and treatment is surgical when possible.
Early auditory habilitation, genetic counselling, and epidemiological studies are indicated. Medical treatment is of
little value.

Genetic: Such syndromes include the dominant syndromes
of Treacher-Collins (external auditory canal atresia, middle
ear anomalies, downward slanting eyes, lower lid coloboma,
flat malar eminence, micrognathia), Apert (frontal bossing,
exophthalmos, hyperplastic maxilla, syndactyly), and Pierre-
Robin (glassoptosis, micrognathia and cleft palate). It also
includes the recessive syndromes such as Möbius which is
characterized by a facial diplegia, ophthalmoplegia, external
ear malformations, and tongue paralysis (see Figure 1).

FIGURE 1: Möbius Syndrome.

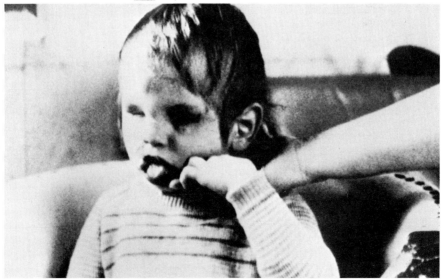

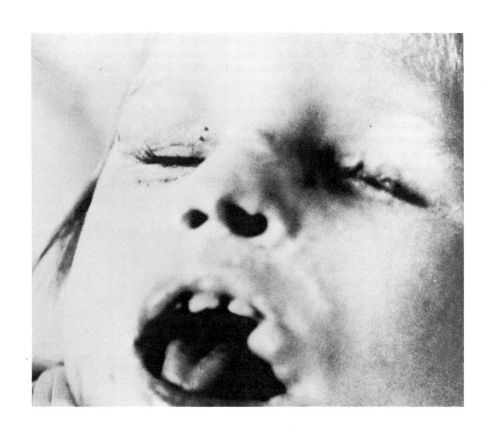

Non-Genetic: This grouping includes intra-uterine
infection with a virus such as rubella or cytomegalovirus
(growth deficiency, mental deficiency, deafness, cataracts,
and septal defect), ototoxic drugs, and/or metabolic disorders.

Delayed Conductive and Mixed Hearing Loss

Treatment of a hearing loss of this type is usually
surgical, although some patients respond to medical treatment, auditory rehabilitation and counselling.

Genetic: Aside from otosclerosis, which is not usually
associated with multiple handicaps, this group includes
osteogenesis imperfecta (fragile bones, large skull, blue
sclera, triangular facies, hemorrhagic tendencies, stapes
fixation), Paget's Disease, Albers-Schönberg Disease (osteopetrosis, dense fragile bone, cranial nerve compression, and
bone marrow compression), and Hurler's Syndrome (abnormal
disposition of mucopolysaccharides, frontal bossing, and
mental retardation).

Non-Genetic: Otitis media and serous otitis media are
the usual causes, secondary to Eustachian tube dysfunction.
This is a problem seen frequently among retarded children and
thus, requires more attention than usual from the Otologist.
Eustachian tube dysfunction is usually associated with
allergy, rhinitis, and adenoid infection, immunoglobulin
deficiency, metabolic disturbance, and adenoid obstruction.
Recently, Down's Syndrome studies have indicated an anatomical
problem in the nasopharynx leading to poor ventilation of the
Eustachian tube (Strome, 1981).

Congenital Sensorineural Hearing Loss

These hearing losses, when occurring with a multiple
symptom complex, rarely improve with medical therapy. Treatment is directed toward habilitation, genetic and social
counselling, and epidemiological studies (Meyerhoff, 1978).

Genetic: The classic temporal bone deformities include
the total aplasia of Michel and the partial aplasias of
Mondini, Scheibe, and Alexander. These congenital anomalies
may occur alone or as part of Syndromes such as Pendred's
(abnormal iodine metabolism), Jervell and Lange-Nielsen

(prolonged Q-T interval on electrocardiogram), Waardenburg's
(white forelock, sensorineural hearing loss and hypoplasia of
the nasal alae), and Usher's (retinitis pigmentosa and
sensorineural loss of hearing).

Non-Genetic: Sensorineural hearing loss may present with
other multihandicaps from such environmental factors as
hypoxia at birth, erythroblastosis fetalis, metabolic disorders, intra-uterine infection, and irradiation. Hypoxia at
birth has contributed significantly to that large group of
children with cerebral palsy and sensorineural hearing impairment. The example illustrated demonstrates a 5 year old with
cerebral palsy, strabismus and a unilateral, sensorineural
hearing loss (see Figure 2). He wears leg braces, uses a
pusher, attends a regular school, and participates in class
activity. His audiological status is monitored carefully and
regularly.

Delayed Onset of Sensorineural Hearing Loss

Generally, this category, with a few exceptions, is not
amenable to medical therapy. Since the socioeconomic considerations of this disability are immense, it is essential that
best efforts be directed to group rehabiliation, epidemiologic
study and genetic and social counselling (Meyerhoff, 1978).

Genetic: Alport's Syndrome is characterized by progressive, sensorineural loss and glomerulonephritis and neither
are responsive to treatment. The hearing loss usually becomes
demonstrable by 10 years of age. Alstrom's Syndrome demonstrates retinal degeneration at 1 year of age and progressive
hearing loss at adolescence. Friedreich's Ataxia is characterized by optic atrophy, ataxia and hearing loss. The progressive hearing loss of Von Recklinghausen's Syndrome
secondary to acoustic neuroma is accompanied by ataxia and
cafe-au-lait spots.

Non-Genetic: Bacterial infections, particularly meningococcal meningitis, have been a major cause of brain injury,
retardation, and irreversible sensorineural hearing loss. In
addition, any virus which may produce a viral meningo-
encephalitis is capable of producing a multihandicapped child
with a sensorineural hearing loss. Measles, mumps, adenovirus
type III, and herpes zoster have been implicated.

FIGURE 2: A 5 year old child with Cerebral Palsy resulting from hypoxia.

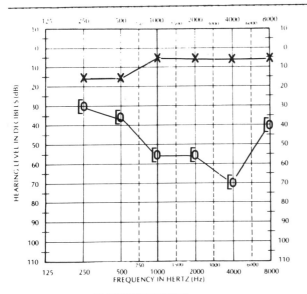

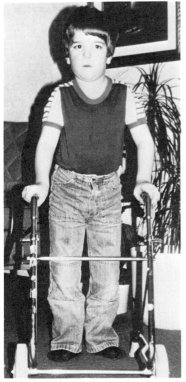

Finally, there are a number of multiply handicapped children who are difficult to classify and who lend credence to the observation that the majority of handicapped children are multiply handicapped (Woods, 1979). The example illustrated is a child who has defied genetic classification at this time (see Figure 3). He demonstrates multiple palatal, facial and pinna deformities, partial left facial paresis, low-slung ears, congenital deformity of both middle ears, and Eustachian tube dysfunction with repeated otitis media. He also proved to have a bilateral, sensorineural hearing loss and a central nervous system disorder, leaving him unable to suck or swallow. Despite such handicaps, he is now almost 5 and thriving. Because of the magnitude of the related anomalies in such children, the question of hearing loss is sometimes overlooked. Fortunately, the establishment of the high risk register has tended to alert physicians and expedite referrals. In fact, the otologist must request early referral and be prepared to treat vigorously and aggressively.

FIGURE 3: A multiply handicapped child - genetic classification unknown.

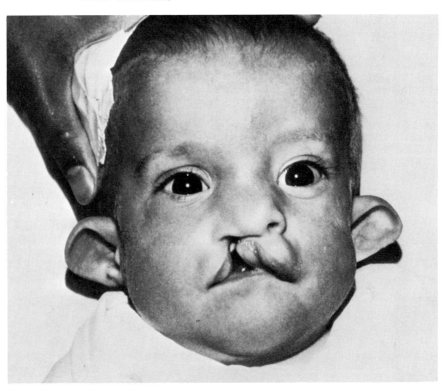

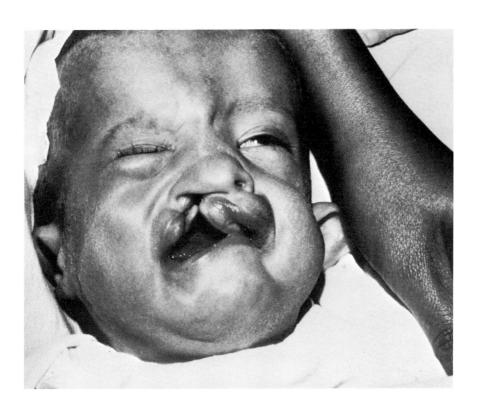

We have noted that among hearing impaired children with
additional handicaps, non-physical handicaps are the more
frequent (Karchmer et al., 1981). We are also aware that
hearing impairment results in sensory deprivation and that
the sensory deprivation model is the basis for the "critical
period hypothesis of language acquisition" (Sarno & Clemis,
1980). It has been suggested that the situation is even
worse than that for the hearing impaired child with a non-
physical handicap such as mental retardation. It has been
described as producing a devastating downward spiral wherein
the child has a more difficult time learning because of
hearing loss, and this reduced ability to use auditory input
increases the retardation (Stewart, 1978). Thus, the effect
of hearing loss plus a developmental disability such as
mental retardation, is one of multiplication - not addition.

In this circumstance, therefore, the otologist must
strive to see that the presence or absence of hearing impairment is determined while the child is still in the hospital
intensive care nursery. Suspect babies must be identified
for testing through application of a high risk register,
and this should be supplemented by behavioural screening.
With the use of brainstem electric response audiometry (BERA)
electrophysiological conformation of hearing loss is now
available to many of our patients. It is no longer appropriate for the otologist to tell parents of a multiply
handicapped child to wait until the child grows older.
Testing can and should be done at the earliest possible
time.

Finally, the otologist must avoid concentration on the
more outstanding physical or mental defects of the child
and organize a diagnostic and management treatment plan to
reduce as completely as possible, the sensory deprivation
accompanying the deafness.

Conclusion

The presence or absence of hearing impairment can be
determined while the child is still in the hospital's newborn nursery - it is no longer appropriate to tell parents
to wait until the child gets older.

The establishment of a high risk register has been
instrumental in raising the physician's "index of suspicion".
An extremely thorough history with acute awareness of the
high risk register and a careful physical examination is
still a cornerstone of diagnosis. This may now be supplemented by sophisticated polytomography and CT Scan. The
work-up may involve an extensive neurological examination,
including electroencephalogram as well as a battery of
laboratory tests (e.g. thyroid and sweat tests). Careful
and deliberate auditory evaluation must be arranged because
it is the responsibility of the physician to detect a hearing loss if one is present.

The percentage of hearing impaired students suffering
from additional handicaps is approximately 30%, according to
a recent survey. Non-physical handicaps are more common
than physical ones, with emotional behaviour problems and
learning disabilities the most frequently encountered. The
diagnosis of hearing loss in the newborn has always been a
challenge to the otologist. That challenge is made more
difficult when the multihandicapped, deaf child has no
obvious physical abnormalities.

Discussion

I. RAPIN
    In your manuscript, you indicate that mental retardation,
autism and learning disability are not organic disorders. I'm
sure you didn't mean that - you meant to say somatic disorders.
Any thought that these are not organic disorders, of course,
is abhorrent to a neurologist, who believes that one reads
and does all these things with one's nervous system.

I. STEWART
    I agree with you. However, this was taken from the
Gallaudet College survey and I used their language.

References

Anonymous, "Beyond V.D.," Medical World News 21:56-63, 1980.

Balkany, T.J., Downs, M.P., Jafek, B.W., and Krajicek, M.J., "Hearing Loss in Down's Syndrome," Clinical Pediatrics 18:116-118, 1979.

Davis, G.L., "Clinical Cytomegalovirus and Hearing Loss: Clinical and Experimental Observations," Laryngoscope 89:1681-1688, 1979.

Downs, M.P., "The Expanding Imperative of Early Identification," Childhood Deafness: Causation, Assessment and Management (New York: Grune & Stratton), Bess, F.H. (Ed.), 1977.

Flathouse, V.E., "Multiply Handicapped Deaf Children and Public Law 94-142," Exceptional Children 45:560-565, 1979.

Hanshaw, J.B., "School Failure and Deafness After 'Silent' Congenital Cytomegalovirus Infection," New England Journal of Medicine 295:468-470, 1976.

Holm, V., and Kunze, L., "Effects of Chronic Otitis Media On Language and Speech Development," Pediatrics 43:833-838, 1969.

Karchmer, M.A., Petersen, L.M., Allen, T.E., and Osborn, T.I., Highlights of the Canadian Survey of Hearing Impaired Children and Youth (Washington, D.C.: Gallaudet College), Office of Demographic Studies, Spring, 1979.

Kumar, K.L., and Nankeruis, G.A., "Inapparent Congenital Cytomegalovirus Infection," New England Journal of Medicine 288:1370-1372, 1973.

Meyerhoff, W.L., "Medical Management of Hearing Loss - The Otolaryngologist's Responsibility," Laryngoscope 88:960-973, 1978.

Northern, J.L., and Downs, M.P., Hearing in Children (Baltimore: Williams and Wilkins), 1974.

Paparella, M.M., "Differential Diagnosis of Hearing Loss - The Otolaryngologist's Responsibility," Laryngoscope 88:952-959, 1978.

Pappas, D.G., and Mundy, M.R., "Sensorineural Hearing Loss: Infectious Agents," Laryngoscope 92:752-753, 1982.

Sarno, C.N., and Clemis, J.D., "A Workable Approach to the Identification of Neonatal Hearing Impairment," Laryngoscope 90:1313-1320, 1980.

Smith, D.W., "Recognizable Patterns of Human Malformation: Genetic, Embryologic and Clinical Aspects," Major Problems in Clinical Pediatrics - Volume 7 (New York: A.J. Saunders Co.), A. J. Schaffer (Consulting Ed.), 1976.

Stewart, I.F., "Newborn Infant Hearing Screening - A Five Year Pilot Project," Journal of Otolaryngology 6:477-481, 1977.

Stewart, L.G., "Hearing Impaired/Developmentally Disabled Persons in the United States: Definitions, Causes, Effects, and Prevalence Estimates," The American Annals of the Deaf 123:488-498, 1978.

Strome, M., "Down's Syndrome: A Modern Otorhinolaryngological Perspective," Laryngoscope 91:752-753, 1982.

Woods, G.E., "Visual Problems in the Handicapped Child," Child: Care, Health and Development 5:303-322, 1979.

Vernon, M., and Klein, N., "Hearing Impairment in the 1980's," Hearing Aid Journal 35:17-20, 1982.

MULTIPLE HANDICAPS AND EAR MALFORMATIONS IN HEARING IMPAIRED PRESCHOOL CHILDREN

Gunnar Liden
Aira Kankkunen
Andre Tjellström
University of Göteborg, Göteborg, Sweden

According to Hammarstedt and Amcoff (1979), 2.1% of the 1,033,932 pupils in the 9 year comprehensive compulsory schools in Sweden are hearing impaired. About 10% of those are described as having an additional handicap. Cerebral palsy, including some malformations such as cleft palate, amounted to 3.5%, visual disorder represented 1.6%, while mental retardation including brain lesions appeared in 1.4% of the children.

In Göteborg, a joint program for the early identification of hearing impaired and deaf children has been in operation between pediatricians and the Audiological and Otolaryngological Departments at Sahlgren's Hospital since 1970. One of the aims of that team work has been to analyze our efficiency in detecting and tracing hearing impaired preschool children (Kankkunen & Liden, 1982; Liden & Kankkunen, 1982). We also compared our results with those of an earlier period (1964-1969) when no special measures were adopted for identifying hearing impaired children (Kankkunen, 1983).

The purpose of this paper is two-fold. First, to analyze the types and frequency of associated handicaps, including malformation of ears, in preschool children with hearing impairment born between 1964 and 1979. Second, we shall discuss some new techniques in the management of ear malformations including:

1. a new bone-conduction hearing aid anchored in the bone; and,

2. a bone-anchored auricular episthesis for patients with aplasia of the pinna.

67

Associated Handicaps

Subjects and Methods

Two hundred and sixty-four hearing impaired children
born between 1964-1979 were analyzed with regard to frequency
and type of multiple handicaps, as well as ear malformations.
Figure 1 illustrates the sample population. The children are
divided into 3 Groups according to age and periods of
investigation.

During the 10 years, 1970-1980, 179 children out of
57,172 live births were diagnosed in Göteborg as hard-of-
hearing or deaf (Group 1). The children were referred to us
from the maternity hospital (the high risk register), the
well baby clinics, the Children's Hospital, the otolaryngologists, the speech pathologists, and the parents.

Group 2 consisting of 85 five year olds born between
1964-1969, has been compared with an age matched group of
130 hearing impaired children born between 1970-1975 and
selected from Group 1.

Depending on the age of the child, the hearing assessment was based on the following methods:

1. newborn to 5 mos.   – respiration audiometry
                           (Kankkunen & Liden, 1977)
2. newborn to 9 mos.   – observation audiometry
3. 10 mos. to 2 1/2 yrs.– visual reinforcement audio-
                           metry (Liden & Kankkunen,
                           1969)
4. 2 1/2 yrs. to 6 yrs. – play audiometry (Barr, 1955).

All children with unclear syndromes and symptoms were
referred to and investigated by both a neuropediatrician and
a psychologist.

Results

The causes of hearing impairment in the 179 children in
Group 1 (1970-1980) are shown in Table I. As can be seen,
genetic factors were dominant and present in 55%. Non-
hereditary causes amounted to 29%, while unknown causes
accounted for 16%.

FIGURE 1: Multiple handicaps and ear malformations in hearing impaired preschool children.

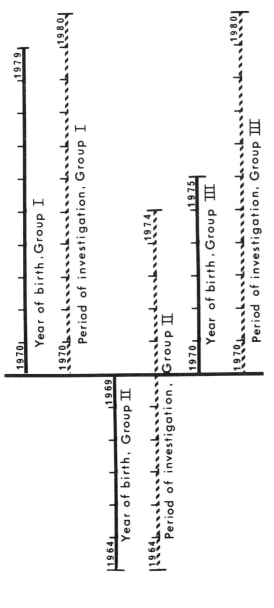

TABLE I: Causes of hearing impairment in 179 children born
           1970-1979 (after Kankkunen, 1983).

	Number		Per Cent
Heredity	75		
		99	55%
Heredity and other causes	24		
Other causes		51	29%
Unknown		29	16%
		179	100%

An additional handicap was found in 7.8% of the hearing
impaired children (Table II). Mental retardation (including
Down's Syndrome) amounted to 3.9%. Cerebral palsy (CP) and
CP with mental retardation counted for 3.4%. The degree of
hearing loss was mostly mild to moderate. Only one was
totally deaf and one had unilateral deafness.

Different malformations in the hearing impaired children
are listed in Table III. As can be seen, they were rather
common in that group, 23 of 179 (12.8%).

In relation to the total number of live births (57,172)
in the same period, the frequency amounted to .04%. If we
include ear malformations as additional to the handicaps
shown in Table II, we reach a figure of 20.6%. Some aspects
of the management of these malformations will be discussed in
a later section.

The degree of hearing loss and the frequency of hearing
impairment in children born between 1964-1974 were investigated through 85 five year olds born 1964-1969 (Group 2).
The frequency of hearing impairment amounted to 2.08% out of
40,963 live births (Table IV). Twenty of these children

TABLE II: Associated handicaps of 14 of 179 hearing impaired preschool children (1970-1979)

Case	Assoc.Hdcp.	Etiology of Disorder	Cause of Hrng.Imp.	BW in gms.	Type	PTA R/L in dB
1.	MR	heredity	heredity	3,050	SN	30/30
2.	MR	unknown	heredity	3,200	SN	35/35
3.	MR	heredity	heredity + mal.ext.ear	3,480	SN	35/35
4.	Down's	–	S O M*	2,800	Cond	30-60 range
5.	Down's	–	S O M	3,010	Cond	30-60 range
6.	Down's	–	S O M	2,570	Cond	30-60 range
7.	Down's	–	S O M	3,300	Cond	30-60 range
8.	CP + MR	heredity	unknown	3,000	SN	25/30
9.	CP + MR	CMV	heredity	4,050	SN	deaf/deaf
10.	CP + MR	anoxia	S O M	2,110	Mixed	35/35
11.	CP + MR	anoxia	heredity	3,300	SN	65/65
12.	CP	immaturity	meningitis	1,940	SN	28/26
13.	CP + unilat. blindness	prematurity	unknown	1,000	SN	25/25
14.	Marfan Synd. + vis.hand.	heredity	heredity	3,350	SN	15/deaf

* S O M = serous otitis media.

appeared to have an associated handicap (Table V). Mental
retardation was present in 11.7%. CP alone or combined with
mental retardation appeared in 7.1%. Only 2 children from
this Group had malformed ears (2.3%).

TABLE III: Type of malformations in 23 of 179 hearing
             impaired children born 1970-1979 (after
             Kankkunen, 1983).

	Number
Bilateral microtia and meatal atresia + Robin Syndrome	1
Bilateral meatal atresia + unilateral malformation of inner ear	1
Unilateral microtia and meatal atresia	8
Unilateral partial malformation of the pinna and middle ear	2
Preauricular pits + partial malformation of the pinna and the meatus + unilateral deafness	1
Malformation of the pinna + unilateral malformation of inner ear + malformation of face + skeletal defects	1
Treacher-Collins Syndrome	2
Preauricular pits + unilateral deafness	1
Hemifacial microsomia	4
Cheilo-palatoschisis	1
Oculo-auriculo vertebral dysplasia (Goldenhar Syndrome)	1
	23

     The degree of hearing loss and the frequency of hearing
impairment in the first period of the study (1970-1980) were
investigated through 130 five year olds born 1970-1975 (Group
3) in relation to 36,855 live births in Göteborg during the
same period (Table IV).

TABLE IV: Degree and frequency of hearing impairment pre-
            sented as pure tone average in Group 2 (85 child-
            ren) and in Group 3 (130 children) in relation to
            total number of live births in Göteborg during
            same period (after Kankkunen, 1982).

Hearing Loss	Group 2 - % out of 49,963	Group 3 - % out of 36,855
25 dB HL	0.20	0.16
25 - 40 dB HL	0.51	1.38
41 - 60 dB HL	0.34	0.40
61 - 99 dB HL	0.51	0.46
100 dB HL	0.20	0.16
Deafness	0.17	0.05
Monaural Hearing Loss	0.10	0.30
Monaural Deafness	0.05	0.60
Total	2.08%	3.51%

The frequency of hearing impairment amounted to 3.5%.
The investigation also showed that .2% were ranked as deaf,
1.1% had an average (0.5-2.0 KHz) hearing loss worse than
40 dB HL, and 2.4% had a mild hearing loss (e.g. equal to or
less than 40 dB HL in the best ear, or monaural hearing loss
or monaural deafness).

TABLE V: Comparison of frequency of associated multiple
           handicaps in 5 year olds born 1964-1969 and 1970-
           1975, respectively.

	Group 2 1964-1969		Group 3 1970-1975	
Live births	N	40,963	N	36,885
Hearing impairment	85	2.1%	130	3.5%
Associated handicaps	18 (21%)	0.44%	9 (7%)	0.24%
Malformations	2 (2%)	0.05%	14 (11%)	0.38%

A comparison between the two groups of 5 year olds born
1970-1975 (Group 3) and 1964-1969 (Group 2) showed a higher
incidence of hearing impairment in Group 3. After a closer
analysis, the difference appeared to be due to a greater
number of mild losses and monaural deafnesses being diagnosed
during 1970-1975. On the other hand, multiple handicaps
diminished considerably during that time (Table V). Only 9
of the 130 hearing impaired 5 year olds (7%) in Group 3
showed an associated handicap, while the corresponding figure
in Group 2 was 21%. This favourable development was mainly
due to a lower incidence of Rubella in the '70s. The frequency of hearing impaired children with malformations (not
necessarily handicaps) on the other hand, increased during
the 1970-1975 period, and was present in 14 of the 130 five
year olds (11%). In Group 2 (1964-1969), ear malformations
were only present in 2 of 85 five year olds (2%).

The reason for this discrepancy is only a matter of
speculation. There might be factors in the environment of
the pregnant women, such as insecticides and other poisons,
polluting the air which might have contributed to the
increase in malformations in the last period (Group 3).

During the last decade, children with minimal brain
dysfunction (MBD) have contracted considerable attention.
Special tests are required for diagnosing that dysfunction.
The children have perceptual, motor and attentional deficits
and have reduced concentration ability. In most cases,
these deficits give rise to very disturbing hearing disabilities and psychical difficulties. According to
Rasmussen (1982), severe MBD is present in 1.2% of the 6-7
year olds in Göteborg. The milder forms can be diagnosed in
an additional 3-6%. It is highly probable that children with
MBD will also be found among the hearing impaired. In our
study, however, we have not had the opportunity to include
special tests for diagnosing these children.

Some Aspects of the Management
of Malformed Ears

The frequency of congenital, isolated external ear
defects amounted to 0.92 per 10,000 live births in 1980,
according to Swedish Board of Welfare statistics. Including

children with such other defects as Treacher-Collins and
similar syndromes, the yearly incidence of congenital ear
defects amounts to approximately 0.2%. For some unknown
reason, we found the actual incidence during 1970-1979
twice as large.

During the habilitation of any hearing impaired child,
the simultaneous presence of ear malformations creates
special problems for the child and the family. Children
with bilateral congenital meatal atresia usually have a
hearing loss of at least 50-60 dB. From early infancy, they
have to use a bone conduction hearing aid attached with an
elastic band. Later on, to avoid delayed speech development,
the aid is attached via a steel spring over the head. Within
a few years, in school, when the child starts to be aware of
any auricular malformations, this creates psychological problems which also have to be treated.

The surgical treatment of bilateral congenital meatal
atresia is not the topic here. Suffice it to say, inspite of
some promising operating room results, there will still be a
need for hearing aids for these children. Very often the ear
starts to discharge as soon as the new auditory canal is
blocked by an ear mold. Thus, a bone conduction oscillator
has to be applied to the skin over the mastoid process by
means of a steel spring over the head. The same is true for
children with chronic ear conditions who cannot use air
conduction hearing aids for long periods without developing
an acute and recurrent middle ear effusion.

Further, patients with bone conduction hearing aids
often complain about the pressure with which the transducer
must be applied. Such pressure can cause pain and can give
rise to a reddening and irritation of the skin. The position
of the transducer must often be adjusted to remain comfortable while still providing for good hearing. This may be due
to an uneven bone surface under the skin. Many patients also
complain about the poor sound quality of this type of aid.
Esthetic problems with a steel spring obviously placed over
the head to hold the hearing aid oscillator in position are
very evident during the teen age period. For these reasons,
then, there has been a need for the development of a bone
conduction hearing aid which minimizes these drawbacks and
maximizes amplification.

Bone Anchored Hearing Aids

     Due to the pioneering work of Branemark et al., (1969,
1977) on osseointegrated implants, and Tjellström et al.,
(1980, 1982a) on osseointegrated titanium screw implants in
the temporal bone, a new approach to the wearing of bone conduction hearing aids has been developed. Fourteen patients
not satisfied with their own bone conduction hearing aids
were selected for trial with the new procedure (Tjellström
et al., 1981a). Fitting of the device is performed in two
stages. At the first stage, a hole is prepared in the mastoid
process utilizing a gentle technique described by Lindström
et al., (1981). The hole is threaded and a titanium screw is
inserted. The system is left unloaded for 3 to 4 months,
during which time the implant will become integrated within
the bone tissue. In other words, an osseointegration is
established. At the second stage, a skin penetrating titanium
device is put on top of the screw. This device contains the
connecting mechanism for the hearing aid (Figure 2). The
whole arrangement reaches about 2 mm. above skin level and is
about 8 mm. in diameter. To avoid any soft tissue reaction
around the skin penetrating abutment, a subcutaneous skin
reduction is performed at the second seance to ensure that
the soft tissues do not move in relation to the abutment.
Bone anchored fixtures have now been functioning and stable
for about 5 years, with only slight skin irritations in 2 of
14 patients.

FIGURE 2: The coupling mechanism for the bone anchored
           hearing aid.

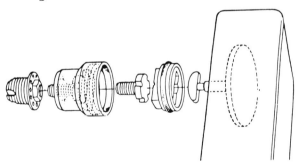

During the first years, patients used the same transducer attached to the bone anchored screw as they had previously worn directly on the skin. However, the impedance of the skull has been found to be considerably larger by 10 to 25 dB, compared to the skin and subcutaneous tissue (Tjellström et al., 1980).

Because of this mismatch, it was necessary to construct a new transducer which optimizes listening (Hakansson et al., 1983) (Figure 3). Ten of the patients have been equipped with the new impedance matched hearing aids. Hearing has been measured with the hearing aid on the titanium screw and with the aid directly on the skin. The differences are presented in Table VI. Around 500 Hz, there is no great difference between the two test situations. This could be expected as the skin in this frequency range could be regarded as rather stiff. A pronounced peak can be seen in most patients around 750 Hz, as the transducer has a less damped resonance in this area.

FIGURE 3:   Schematic drawing of the skin penetrating coupling device for the bone anchored aid, and with the aid in place.

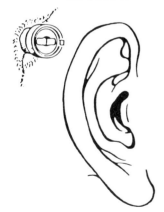
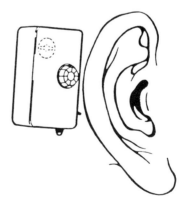

TABLE VI: Improvement of bone conduction thresholds with the
            bone anchored hearing aid as compared to the con-
            ventional bone conduction hearing aid in dB.

Frequency/Intensity

Patient	500	750	1000	2000	4000
M.L.	4	22	6	16	25
S.S.	9	10	9	15	6
J-M.A.	6	21	20	0	15
J-L.M.	-4	12	7	7	20
B.J.	-1	25	17	16	14
H.G.	-5	18	10	15	20
M.A.	-5	23	14	17	15
R.A.	10	28	14	24	24
M.W.	6	17	23	15	23
G.S.	4	23	11	11	12

Speech discrimination has also been tested, but no significant differences have been noted. It is our experience that
it is very hard to find any substantial improvement in intelligibility. However, in a questionnaire filled out by our
patients, they have all expressed satisfaction with the new
aid, specifically concerning the perception of speech. The
sound is softer, more comfortable, and "better". One explanation for this may be that the lower signal level required by
the device means less distortion. A detailed report and
evaluation on the hearing of our patients is in preparation
(Hakansson et al., 1983). However, preliminary findings indicate that when tested in traffic noise with a signal/noise
ratio of 50/40, the impedance matched transducer results in a
significantly higher discrimination score compared to a non-
matched but bone anchored aid.

Of the 14 patients who have obtained a bone anchored
hearing aid, one is 12 and another is 15 years of age. However, based on our present experiences, we are now going to
recommend a bone anchored aid for school children with
malformations.

Bone Anchored Auricular Episthesis

Microtia or malformations in connection with congenital
meatal atresia have considerable psychological impact on the
patient and his/her family. Similar auricular defects can
appear post-traumatically or following tumor surgery.
Plastic surgery procedures are generally not very successful
and some sort of episthesis is preferred by many. The
attachment of an episthesis is, however, often a problem.
Tjellström et al., (1981b, 1982b) have reported 7 patients
who had a silicon episthesis fixated to an osseointegrated
titanium screw implanted into the temporal bone above and
behind the external meatus. The implantation technique is
similar to that described above concerning bone anchored
hearing aids (Figure 4). These patients have been followed
post-operatively for more than 2 years. No problems concerning bone anchorage or skin penetration have been reported.
Because of these favourable experiences with adults, we are
now using this procedure as the method of choice for children
with malformed ears.

FIGURE 4:   Schematic drawing of the auricular episthesis and
             its attachment.

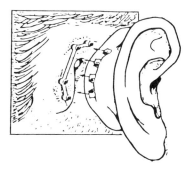

80   Liden, Kankkunen, and Tjellström

Discussion

M. RUBIN
   Is there a possibility that during 1970-1975, more
children were saved who were premature or of low birthweight
than in your previous data?

G. LIDEN
   No. My co-worker is going to present the data in Acta
Otolaryngologica where all the details of the material will
be described. But no, that was not the case.

References

Barr, B., "Pure Tone Audiometry for Preschool Children,"
   Acta Otolaryngologica (Stockholm), Supplement #121, 1955.

Branemark, P-I., Breine, U., Adell, R., Hansson, B.D.,
   Lindstrom, J., and Ohlsson, A., "Intraosseous Anchorage
   of Dental Prosthesis: I. Experimental Studies,"
   Scandinavian Journal of Plastic and Reconstructive Surgery
   3:81-100, 1969.

Branemark, P-I., Hansson, B-O., Adell, R., Breine, U.,
   Lindstrom, J., Hallen, O., and Ohman, A., "Osseointegrated
   Implants in the Treatment of the Edentulous Jaw,"
   Scandinavian Journal of Plastic and Reconstructive Surgery
   (Volume 11, Supplement #16), 1977.

Hammarstedt, B., and Amcoff, S., Integration of Hearing
   Impaired Children in Comprehensive School (In Swedish)
   (Uppsala: Pedagogic Institution, Uppsala University), 1979.

Hakansson, B., Tjellstrom, A., and Rosenhall, U., "Psychoacoustic Measurements with the Bone-Anchored Hearing Aid,"
   In Preparation, 1983.

Kankkunen, A., "Preschool Children with Impaired Hearing,"
   Acta Otolaryngologica (Stockholm) Supplement # 391, 1982.

Kankkunen, A., and Liden, G., "Respiration Audiometry,"
   Scandinavian Audiology 6:81-86, 1977.

Kankkunen, A., and Liden, G., "Early Identification of Hearing Handicapped Children," Acta Otolaryngologica (Stockholm) Supplement #386, 1982.

Liden, G., and Kankkunen, A., "Visual Reinforcement Audiometry," Acta Otolaryngologica (Stockholm) 67:281-292, 1969.

Liden, G., and Kankkunen, A., "Methods of Early Identification of Hearing Impaired Children," Proceedings of the First Otolaryngology Congress of the South-East Asian Federation, Thailand (Basel, Switzerland: Karger), 1982.

Lindstrom, J., Branemark, P-I., and Albrektsson, T., "Mandibular Reconstruction Using Preformed Autologous Bone Graft," Scandinavian Journal of Reconstructive Surgery 15:29-39, 1981.

Rasmussen, P., "Neuropediatric Aspects of Seven-Year-Old Children with Perceptual, Motor and Attentional Deficits," In Preparation, 1982.

Tjellstrom, A., Hakansson, B., Lindstrom, J., Branemark, P-I., Hallen, O., Rosenhall, U., and Leijon, A., "Analysis of the Mechanical Impedance of Bone-Anchored Hearing Aids," Acta Otolaryngologica (Stockholm) 89:85-92, 1980.

Tjellstrom, A., Lindstrom, J., Hallen, O., Albrektsson, T., Branemark, P-I., "Osseointegrated Titanium Implants in the Temporal Bone," American Journal of Otology 2:304-310, 1981a.

Tjellstrom, A., Lindstrom, J., Nylen, O., Albrektsson, T., Branemark, P-I., Birgersson, B., Nero, H., and Sylven, C., "The Bone-Anchored Auricular Episthesis," The Laryngoscope 91:811-815, 1981b.

Tjellstrom, A., Lindstrom, J., Hallen, O., Albrektsson, T., and Branemark, P-I., "Direct Bone Anchorage of External Hearing Aids," In Preparation, 1982a.

Tjellstrom, A., Lindstrom, J., Nylen, O., Albrektsson, T., and Branemark, P-I., "Direct Bone-Anchored Implants for Fixation of Aural Episthesis," In Preparation, 1982b.

EARLY INTERVENTION: THE PREVENTION OF
MULTIPLE HANDICAPS

Hilde S. Schlesinger
Center on Deafness, San Francisco, California

"There is nothing inherent in a hearing deficit that should create additional social or psychological problems" (Meadow, 1980). This modern view gains credence as it is backed by more and more research data; however, it has had a long and not always peaceful history. As Moores (1978) in a brief historical review pointed out, "Every issue presently facing those concerned with the optimum development of the deaf was also addressed by our predecessors...". Such issues include:

The relation of language to thought, 'natural' vs. 'grammatical' approaches to language development, segretated education vs. mainstreaming, the early teaching of reading, the development of speech by elemental vs. syntactic means, early home education, auditory training, sense training, and information processing via auditory and visual channels (Moores, 1978, p. 46).

Despite a fervent interest in deafness and vigorous attempts to provide education to that population, dating from Biblical and Socratic times, and Spain in the 1570s, successful education of the deaf remains problematical. In spite of normal intellectual potential, the deaf continue to be characterized, to a disturbing degree, by cognitive/educational retardation and psychological maladaptations (Vernon, 1969).

Deafness itself may present a disability, but it appears increasingly clear that the cognitive retardation and psychological maladaptations so frequently found among the deaf represent a superimposed and preventable handicap.

It is said that one-third of deaf youths who leave
school each year do not possess the qualifications to continue their education or to become employed. The characteristics of these young adults, categorized as multihandicapped
or low-achieving (one important aspect of our superimposed
disability), were presented by Rice (1973) as: (a) severely
limited communication skills; (b) low academic achievement
levels; (c) emotional immaturity; (d) secondary disabilities; and, (e) poor vocational preparation. The superimposed disability goes back to unmet preschool needs
(Stewart, 1971). It is now argued that meeting the linguistic, psychological, and cognitive needs of the deaf infant
will, to a large extent, prevent the maladaptive concomitants
of deafness.

Deaf individuals have difficulties with speaking, speech
reading, and reading and writing English. Two large-scale
reading studies conducted almost 10 years apart indicate that
not much progress has been made (Wrightstone, Aronow &
Moskowitz, 1963; Gentile & DiFrancesca, 1972; Trybus, Buchanen
& DiFrancesca, 1973), and that Furth's 1966 interpretation
still holds true: by age 11, only 1% of the deaf children
are functionally literate (reading scores of grade 4.9 or
better), and by age 16, only 12% of the deaf children reach
this level. Furth also indicates that the advance between
11 and 16 years is only .8 of a grade. Other achievement
scores, such as arithmetic, are somewhat less depressed.
Despite these deficiencies, however, there is an increasing
body of evidence suggesting that non-linguistic cognitive
tasks are performed at age level (Furth, 1970).

Psychologically, the most frequently stated generalization about deaf individuals is that they seem to reflect a
high degree of "emotional immaturity". Levine (1956) describes this in terms of a pronounced underdevelopment in
conceptual forms of activity, an emotional underdevelopment,
a substantial lag in understanding the dynamics of interpersonal relationships and those of the world in general, a
highly egocentric life perspective, a markedly constricted
life area, and a rigid adherence to the book-of-etiquette
code rather than use of an inner sensibility as a standard
for behaving, and even for feeling. Myklebust (1960) finds

that the deaf are immature in "caring for others". Altshuler (1964) characterizes the deaf as showing egocentricity, lacking empathy, displaying gross coercive dependency, being impulsive, and not practicing thoughtful introspection. A more recent cross-cultural (American-Yugoslav) study of impulsivity indicates that in both countries, deaf individuals were considerably more impulsive than their hearing counterparts (Altshuler et al., 1976).

These differences start early. The typical deaf preschooler appears to be less competent in many of the areas leading to later achievement and maturity. Imaginary play may be reduced (Heider & Heider, 1941). Compared to hearing children, deaf preschoolers in this study had fewer social interactions, especially in the categories of verbal interchange and mutual attention. However, they had more physical contact, requests for approval, and negative interactions. Deaf children spent more time in parallel play than did hearing children (Van Lieshout, 1973). Deaf children's interactions tended to be less highly organized and showed less continuity of structure. Without adequate language, they tended to provoke either aggression or withdrawal from their peers in order to gain control of the situation (Heider, 1948). Social maturity has been seen as low in a number of studies; furthermore, the gap seems to increase with age (Myklebust, 1960; Burchard & Myklebust, 1942). The deaf preschooler has been described as immature, impulsive, and showing a lower level of autonomy, even in areas where the skills were available (Chess, Korn & Fernandez, 1971).

The language deficits of the young deaf child are universally lamented but subject to relatively little research. The hearing child at age 5 years is said to know at least 2,000 words; a deaf child is said to be unusual if he knows about 200 (Hodgson, 1953). Without language teaching, the deaf child may be expected to know fewer than 25 words (DiCarlo, 1964). More recently, studies have appeared focusing on spoken, manual and gesture language acquisition. Goldin-Meadow (1975) investigated the use of gestures by deaf children of hearing parents. The author felt that gestures are linguistic and that they parallel the acquisition of semantic functions in other languages. Similarly, results of a number of studies which examined the spoken

language of hearing impaired children exposed to oral language learning, indicated that the youngsters acquire semantic
and syntactic structures in the same sequence, although at a
delayed rate, as hearing youngsters (Juenke, 1971; Hess,
1972). Collins-Ahlgren (1974, 1975) studied sign language
acquisition and described "baby signs" with similar features
to "baby words" and similar patterns in vocabulary acquisition, semantic intent, and the functions of language as are
seen in normally hearing children.

Schlesinger and Meadow (1972) collected language data
from 40 deaf and 20 hearing preschoolers, and found that 75%
of the deaf (mean age: 44 months) had a language level of
28 months or less. All the hearing children scored at the
expected age level. An English study (Gregory, 1976), cutting
across all degrees of hearing impairment in 5 year olds,
indicated that 56% knew how to use sentences, 29% used
slightly more than 6 words, 12% used fewer than 5 words, and
3% used zero words. Receptively, the situation was not much
better; 50% understood anyone, 32% understood only friends
and relatives, and 17% understood only mother.

Research in deafness has been characteristically
reported with an omission of certain variables. The onset
of deafness, the amount of residual hearing, the audiometric
shape of the hearing loss, the absence or presence of other
handicaps, and the hearing status of the parents, all
crucially affect the early parent-child interaction/communi-
cation, which leads to optimal development. Thus, there are
identifiable deaf individuals who present a more felicitous
outcome of deafness.

Deafness Without Superimposed
Disability

Some deaf individuals as youngsters, have had the opportunity to establish an early, largely meaningful, reciprocal,
and enjoyable language interchange with their parents. This
can happen when the hearing loss occurs after language
acquisition, when the residual hearing is extensive, when the
curve of the hearing loss is propitious, and/or when early,
appropriate and consistent amplification is provided. All of

the above increase the auditory contact with the environment and, thus, enable the infant to acquire the basic linguistic tools at the usual time and through the usual auditory route. Deaf children of deaf parents can also usually establish successful communication at an appropriate age through the visual modality of sign language. Without this early linguistic interchange, through either auditory-vocal or visual-motor modalities (or both) the deaf child suffers a cumulative linguistic deficit which, in turn, affects most areas of life.

There have been a number of studies, summarized by Meadow (1980), indicating that deaf children of deaf parents have significantly better scores on reading and written language, with no difference on tests of speech and lip reading skills. These youngsters also have a more optimal adjustment in terms of maturity, responsibility, independence, popularity, and adjustment to deafness. Brasel and Quigley (1977) found that the children of deaf parents who used manual communication, especially manual communication closely approximating English, consistently out-scored youngsters whose parents did not use any form of manual communication. This was true even when the parents expended large amounts of time, effort, and money in obtaining early, intensive and continuous oral training for their children, and worked intensively with them at home during the preschool years. Harris (1978) also compared deaf children of deaf parents with deaf children of hearing parents, controlling for age, socio-economic status, and I.Q. test scores. Deaf children of deaf parents consistently had scores reflecting greater impulse control than did the deaf children of hearing parents. Harris indicates that this may result from the early use of manual communication, which may have provided the child with a tool for monitoring impulses.

Poverty and Deafness

There are some striking and haunting parallels between seriously disadvantaged populations and the large segment of the deaf population described as multihandicapped. The state of being disadvantaged is not defined by class or ethnicity or minority group membership. However, the risk of

being a member of the so-called disadvantaged community is
greatly increased if one is also a member of a minority group.
Although in recent years there have been reservations about
psychological characterizations of socioeconomic or disabled
groups, it remains clear that a disproportionately large
number of individuals within these groups demonstrate academic retardation and psychological adaptations which
approach maladaptation. The following list of characterizations of disadvantaged persons, found in a report of psychiatry in the urban setting (Sadock et al., 1975) can apply
equally well to a large segment of deaf individuals.

> They are visual, rather than aural
> They are externally oriented, rather than introspective.
> They are content centered, rather than form centered,
>   problem centered rather than abstract centered,
>   spatial, rather than temporal.
> They are impulsive.
> They are oriented to the present, with failure to
>   learn delay of gratification.
> They show a restricted vocational picture.
> They are more direct in aggression and less in self
>   blame.   (p. 2503)

It has been suggested that when social scientists report
on the poor (and possibly on the deaf), "...it seems reasonable to believe that they describe the psychological consequences of powerlessness" (Haggstrom, 1964). Power is a
central component of several of the major criteria of mental
health, particularly mastery of the environment, autonomy,
and self-esteem as delineated by Coopersmith (1967).

What contributes to powerlessness? The powerless are
accustomed to being treated as objects in contradistinction
to acting like subjects. The powerless have a long experience of being acted upon, over-looked, derogated, and left
out of decision making. For the powerless, education is a
passive event, a receptacle being filled, instead of a
mutual learning effort.

Poverty can be described in terms of four characteristics: "...being poor, despised, incompetent, and powerless"
(Gladwin, 1967). The steps leading to the powerlessness

experienced by the poor may be obvious. A large segment of
the poor lives from cirsis to crisis, they are perpetually
attempting to procure the basic necessities of life - money,
food, housing, medical care, and jobs - or are passively
resigned to their status. They frequently incorporate the
disdain shown to them by the majority culture and its professionals. A paraprofessional describing his work with
members of the underclass stated that his task was to:

> ...prepare people for the real world, concentrat-
> ing on the development of social skills and work
> habits among a group of people who often operate
> outside society, who have often lost self-
> confidence, have frequently grown up with few
> positive role models, have scant exposure to the
> world of work, have low frustration thresholds,
> and are generally unacquainted with being on time,
> following orders, saying 'Thank you' and 'Please'
> (Auletta, 1981).

This segment of the poor see themselves as victims and as
not contributing to their fate.

Parents of the Hearing Impaired
and Powerlessness

There may be a subtle, yet forceful relationship
between parental feelings of powerless, linguistic stances
towards their children, especially at toddler age, and the
subsequent cognitive/motivational and affective stances of
their growing youngsters. Parents of deaf children frequently present with feelings of powerlessness and/or incompetence. Although the origin of the feelings springs from
different crises and they are usually not the result of
poverty or disadvantaged situations, the feelings are
similar. The grieving process described by many authors
(Schlesinger & Meadow, 1972; Ross, 1964) and most recently
so sensitively discussed by Moses and Hecke-Wulatin (1980),
contributes pervasively, especially when not initially
resolved. A lack of support by professionals during the
diagnostic crisis, followed later by "professional" advice
which is seen as overwhelming, conflicting, or incompatible,
and which frequently revives sorrow and fear, or seems to

usurp the parents' right to know or to decide, can all contribute to stress and often lead to crises in parenting
(Schlesinger & Meadow, 1976). Some features of their deaf
child's lack of responsiveness to sound or lack of understanding may revive some potent ghosts from the nursery.
These may be seen as rejection, exclusion, gossiped secrets,
or simply as not being understood, and thus, contribute to
parental perplexity. Having born a deaf infant may tug at a
parent's self-esteem for many years.

Language Environment

    Plumer (1970) has proposed a negative circle for des-
cribing the plight of the children and adults of poverty (see
Figure 1). This circular representation recommends itself
because it invites multiple solutions, and because it reasonably represents the magnitude of the problem. Most significantly from the view of our concerns, each point along the
circle can be elaborated upon and measured in terms of
deafness.

FIGURE 1: Circle of poverty

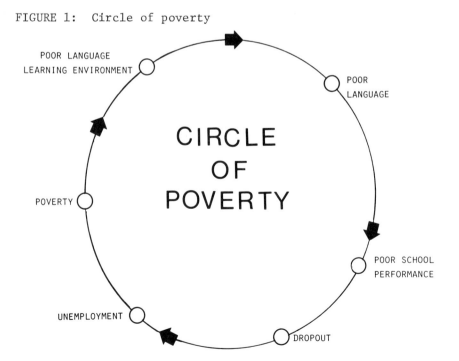

A poor language learning environment, one of the marking posts on the circle, includes the relative inaccessibility of those linguistic building blocks associated with taboos or prejudices toward either the visual or auditory components, as well as some others to be described later. The concept of a "poor language environment" for poverty children has had a long and vitriolic history. The heredity-environment and deficit-difference controversies have flourished among professionals and disciplines. The most commonly held view today, and one shared by this author, is that the disadvantaged child attains language competence, as does the advantaged child. Disagreement remains as to the performance evaluation of the disadvantaged child (i.e. is the competence in a different language altogether, or does the performance of the majority language depend on more vulnerable contexts for the disadvantaged child?)

With impressive consistency, the language environment of the child has been found to be the major factor distinguishing the early home environments of disadvantaged and advantaged children. Some investigators have found social class differences as early as 11 months of age (Wachs, Uzgiris & Hunt, 1971). Others indicate that the class differences emerge between 18 and 36 months (Golden et al., 1971). Most investigators stress some specific aspect of language and communication as yielding demonstrable social class differences. Schoggen and Schoggen (1976) describe message exchange through the verbal medium as one of the main factors producing differences between social classes. Tulkin and Kagan (1972) concur, describing significantly greater verbal productivity from middle class mothers when interacting with their 10 month olds, although no differences have been found in physical contact. In addition, observational studies of early home influences on child development have consistently reported the verbal environment as the key factor of competence, regardless of social class. The quantity of mother talk with 9 to 18 month olds has a significant effect on the child's development, specifically on linguistic performance (Clarke-Stewart, 1973). Maternal verbal responsiveness to children age 2 was found to be significantly correlated with cognitive performance at age 4 (Bradley & Caldwell, 1976). Well developing 1 and 2 year olds have been shown to have more life talk directed toward them (White et al., 1977).

Schachter (1979) studied 24,192 speech acts in 30
mother-toddler dyads, 10 in each of 3 groups: black disadvantaged, black advantaged, and white advantaged. She
studied the verbal environment of toddlers because of the
postulated importance of verbal environment, as described
above. She observed the toddlers in the home because several
researchers have indicated th ˇ the data collected in the
laboratory may be influenced negutively because lower class
subjects are likely to feel alienated and uncomfortable in
unfamiliar surroundings (Baratz & Baratz, 1970; Labov, 1970;
Sroufe, 1970). She studied the toddler because, although
some investigators feel that social class differences occur
very early, results below toddler age have been inconsistent.
Social class differences in developmental assessments do
emerge consistently between 18 and 36 months (Golden et al.,
1971). She studied three different socioeconomic groups in
order to elucidate the contribution of class vs. race. There
were no differences between black and white advantaged
mothers. There were significant differences between the
advantaged and disadvantaged mothers' talk to their toddlers.

Advantaged mothers were found to talk twice as much as
disadvantaged mothers; however, there was no difference
between the two groups in the amount of spontaneous talk, only
in the amount of talk responsive to the child's communications.
Advantaged mothers showed a three-fold increment in responsive
speech.

A significantly larger proportion of advantaged
mothers' speech consists of responses to the two
main types of child communication, desire requests
and reports. These mothers explicate and fulfill
their children's desires, helping them to attain
the goals that the children have set for themselves. They also explicate and confirm the
children's reports, providing consensual validation for the child's own observations and experiences. Additionally, advantaged mothers are more
likely to express pride in their child's actions,
and less likely to prohibit them. They minimize
"don'ts" and when they do inhibit the child, they
feel the need to justify the prohibition with an
explanation or to suggest a substitute for the
prohibited action. When they refuse the child,
they suggest a substitute means of gratification
at the same time. Finally, when advantaged mothers
teach, they do so responsively when their children

are already engaged in communication with them,
often at their own initiative -- rather than at
a moment of the mother's choosing (Schachter,
1979, p. 156).

Schachter's findings do not support the concept of early
cognitive deprivation in the disadvantaged environment.
Indeed, mothers of toddlers, disadvantaged or not, devote
about 10% of their speech to teaching new knowledge. Techniques and communication strategies are similar in both
groups. The content of the teaching activity appears identical, except for a significantly higher focus on teaching
numbers and letters on the part of the disadvantaged mothers.
Parents of deaf children seem to spend a disproportionate
amount of time teaching colours. Although the proportion of
spontaneous teaching is similar for both groups of mothers,
the advantaged mothers are significantly more likely to inter-
polate their teaching speech acts into a series of responses
to the child. Although Schachter noted that disadvantaged
mothers were not found to be deficient in their mastery of
Baby-Talk code, she also found that they use a higher percentage of exact self-repetitions. Advantaged mothers are
more apt to repeat the child's utterances, to make sure that
the child's meaning is clearly understood, and to confirm the
validity of the message.

Schachter concluded that "... a single unifying theme
seems to integrate all of the findings: advantaged mothers,
both black and white, appear to support and facilitate the
actions of their toddlers". This, in turn, has a significant
positive impact on the child's self-confidence and feelings
of mastery and power, which is bound to affect the child's
performance in linguistic and cognitive tasks. "A self-
motivated, inquisitive, self-confident child arrives at
school prepared to learn and perform effectively, at the
level of his/her potential" (Schachter, 1979, p. 157).

It may well be that the Circle of Poverty (Figure 1) is
also crucially influenced by other features of middle class
linguistic input, specifically what Schachter calls the
cognitive/affective/motivational theory and linguistic stance
of the toddler's parents. Bernstein (1967, 1971) has frequently postulated that the culture of poverty is transmitted
not through a genetic code, but through a specific linguistic
system. He initially referred to this as public vs. formal

language, and later as the restrictive vs. the elaborative
code. Williams and Naremore (1969) have postulated that the
content and meaning of a message, rather than its structural
features, are responsible for differences. What are those
differences? Middle class mothers emphasize the use of
language for socializing and disciplining their children when
teaching them moral standards, and when communicating feelings
and emotions. The restricted language code of the lower class
mother, however, tends to limit use of messages primarily for
denoting things and action. Lower class communication codes
tend to emphasize the concrete rather than the abstract, the
substance rather than the elaboration of a thought, the here-
and-now, rather than the explanation of motive and intentions.
Youngsters socialized with these linguistic codes tend to be
closely tied to a given context.

If we look at Bernstein's work as interpreted by Robinson
and Rackstraw (1967), we also note that, relative to the poor
class, middle class mothers are more likely to answer questions. The information given will be more accurate, and there
will be more of it. The information will be embedded in a
less noisy linguistic context. When the modes of answers to
why questions are categorized, it is found that middle class
mothers are more likely to use compound arguments, to give
analogies, to provide a greater variety of purposive answers,
and are less likely to repeat the question as an answer.

The stance towards school is also different. Hess and
Shipman (1965) found that, when preparing children to go to
school, middle class mothers were more likely to encourage
them to learn as much as possible and to ask their teacher
questions whenever things were unclear; while lower class
mothers were more likely to tell their children to be obedient
and to stay out of trouble (Heider, 1948; Cazden, 1972).

These early middle-class linguistic features appear to
have a direct impact on future reading ability. Recent
research in the United States and in England notes that there
is a complex relationship between early language interchange
and future reading success. Loban (1963) failed to find any
relationship between the complexity of children's language
and success in reading at the first-grade level. However, he
found an increasingly significant relationship in the next 4
grades. Other researchers (Pringle, 1965; Milner, 1951) point
out that the quality of the child's early verbal interactions

in the home - the reading of stories, active dialogue, etc. -
correlate highly with good reading skills. Finally, and
interestingly enough, Whiteman (1967) found that simple
family activities, as warm and pleasant as they may be, do
not correlate highly with the later reading skills, while
activities requiring discussion and some explanation do highly
correlate.

Cognitive/Affective/Motivational
Theory

Schachter (1979) described one of the most important
contributions to both optimal and less than optimal parental
actions as follows:

> ...our educated mothers adjust their communica-
> tions to the child's affective development,
> particularly to the early development of the ego.
> Since the toddler stage is the time of emerging
> autonomy, the time of 'psychological birth'
> (Mahler, Pine & Berman, 1975), it seems essential
> to support the child's budding individuality. Our
> educated mothers tend to provide this support.
> Failure to do so is likely to produce problems in
> asserting autonomy with potentially dire conse-
> quences for the child's later school performance.
> The child may not acquire the confidence necessary
> for sustained goal-directed activity, or may remain
> enmeshed in a perpetual power struggle with adult
> care providers in an attempt to regain his or her
> psychological birthright. Evidence based on
> observations in inner city classrooms (Silverstein
> & Krate, 1975) suggests that these problems may be
> the major obstacle to effective school performance
> among disadvantaged children. Indeed, ego theory
> could explain why social class differences in
> cognitive performance emerge at toddler age, as
> children begin to assert their power. How can the
> powerless support the power strivings of their
> children? (p. 160).

Others (e.g. Zigler & Trickett, 1978) have also stressed
the role of such motivational factors as distrust of adults,
a lack of self-confidence, a feeling of powerlessness, low
effectance, and low self-image in the cognitive performance
of disadvantaged children. Fisher (1981) indicated that
"Anomie" contributes to failure to close the academic achievement gap between black and white students. Anomie is defined
by the dictionary as an "anxious awareness that the prevailing values of society have little or no personal relevance to
one's condition".

Linguists agree that the disadvantaged show linguistic
competence. Educators note that, despite linguistic competence, disadvantaged youngsters are at odds with the school
environment. They have difficulty following directions, par-
ticipating in discussions, comparing two objects, classifying,
drawing inferences, and using rules efficiently. They show a
vagueness of reference, a communicational egocentrism. They
are less active in verbal initiative and have less ability to
use the teacher as a resource. Their lexical items may be
limited to objects at home or school, and they have very
dramatic reading difficulties (Lavatelli, 1974).

The Language Interactions of
Disadvantaged Children

Beyond the motivational and affective factors mentioned
above, results of another important study found that language
differences occur during 3 year olds' speech acts with one
another. Tough (1977) conducted a very interesting study
comparing advantaged and disadvantaged children's language as
used between peers. Disadvantaged children scored less well
than the children in the advantaged group on measures of
linguistic structure. They used explicitness or elaboration
less frequently, pronouns instead of nouns more frequently,
and adjectives and extensions of verbs to future, conditional
and past tenses less frequently than the advantaged groups.
There was no evidence, however, that the disadvantaged children did not have those structures within their repertoire,
nor was it felt that their use of fewer complex utterances
was due to an inability to make complex utterances. All the
children in the disadvantaged groups showed that they had an
adequate vocabulary and knowledge of linguistic structures

which, when pressed or when their own need to be explicit made it essential, they were able to draw out (Tough, 1977). The major difference between children in the advantaged and disadvantaged groups was in the disposition to use language for particular purposes.

At age 3, children in the disadvantaged group were not using spontaneous language for purposes which were already evident in the speech of the children of the advantaged group. The disadvantaged group showed little evidence of the use of language for:

1. Recalling and giving detail of past experiences;

2. Reasoning about present and recalled experiences;

3. Anticipating future events and predicting the outcome;

4. Recognizing and offering solutions to problems;

5. Planning and surveying alternatives for possible courses of action;

6. Projecting in to the experiences and feelings of other people;

7. Using the imagination to build scenes through the use of language for their play.
(Tough, 1977, p. 169).

Later (ages 5 and 7 1/2), when presented with pictures to elicit language, these same youngsters continued to show marked differences. The disadvantaged youngsters continued to rely heavily on a labelling strategy, enumerating single objects. The advantaged youngsters gave more elaboration and were more frequently able to describe a central meaning. Furthermore, they were more disposed to provide causal and dependent relationships, to forecast more, and to use justification for events.

The Language Environment of the
Deaf Children

How does advantaged vs. disadvantaged relate to deafness? Hearing parents of deaf children often resemble
parents of poverty children in their feelings of powerlessness. Furthermore, the frequent absence of a joint symbolic
system forces parents to resort to nonresponsive, nonrecipro-
cal stances, similar to those seen in disadvantaged mothers
(Schachter, 1979). The children, in turn, resemble children
of poverty in their academic retardation, especially reading
and motivational deficits in school.

Deafness appears to linguistically transcend socioeconomic class, as can be seen by well spoken mothers of
deaf children who resort to restricted messages to their
language-delayed children. When lexical items are not known,
not understood, or cannot be pointed to, the message tends to
be short and concrete or long and largely unintelligible.
There may be avoidance of the labelling of causality, of
temporal relationships, or of feelings, all difficult to
express without a visual referent. Mothers of deaf children
with residual hearing can continue to use their normal
messages; mothers who use sign language effectively and
early can also do so.

The optimal linguistic environment for the hearing
impaired is replete with many variables, including prompt
diagnosis, amount of residual hearing, early, appropriate,
and consistent amplification, and finally, the interpersonal
aspects of the language environment.

Study of the optimal language learning environment for
the infant is still in its own infancy. We are presently
engaged in studying deaf infants with their parents - hearing
and deaf - to determine the special features of the antecedents of communication: "motherese" and baby talk (Snow,
1977), turn-taking (Kaye, 1977), imitation (Pawlby, 1977),
and others. Bruner, in a delightful quote whose origin
eludes me, indicated that joint attention, joint focus,
joint action, and joint enjoyment lead the child into
language. We hope to have more information on this exciting
topic in the near future.

One longitudinal study which focused on the genesis of communicative competence is nearly finished (Schlesinger, in preparation). An infant diagnosed at 5 months as profoundly deaf, was immediately provided with appropriate amplification and a bimodal linguistic input (English via signs and spoken words). Our research, thus far, indicates an acceleration of language acquisition -- 35 signs at 13 months, 107 signs at 17 months, and 226 signs at 21 months. Although initially the signs were not entirely adult in character, they remarkably approximated adult versions. Spoken words followed signs within a few months. This youngster's behaviour corroborates some earlier findings:

> ...bimodal language acquisition shares many of
> the known characteristics of spoken language
> acquisition. Bimodal language acquisition
> proceeds from holophrasis to two-sign utterances
> expressing semantic intent, to sentences. Bi-
> modal language acquisition appears to help, not
> hinder, spoken language acquisition (Schlesinger,
> 1978).

To repeat: there are haunting parallels between the development of "poor" children and that of deaf children, as well as haunting parallels in the eventual outcome in terms of educability, psychopathology, and work potential. The common denominator may be the functional components of language use, rather than the structural ones. After all, structural components are known to the developing disadvantaged child, whereas most deaf toddlers show a massive delay of language acquisition at the same age. As we shall try to demonstrate, in some very crucial ways the parental messages are similar.

Delayed language acquisition may tie the deaf child to the here and now, as Bernstein (1967) postulated for poor children. A comparison of deaf and hearing preschoolers during a 7 minute segment of mother-child interaction indicated that 95% of the deaf children and their mothers limited communication to topics with a visual reference. On the other hand, 45% of the hearing group made at least a passing comment concerned with a nonvisual reference, while 15% had a prolonged conversation about some topic without

any visual reference (Schlesinger, 1972). This inability to
communicate without visual reference has also been noted by
Blank (1974) and has been demonstrated in older school
children by Hoemann (1972).

Our longitudinal study can now be interpreted in a new
light. The study has usually been summarized as follows.
Forty deaf youngsters have been involved in a longitudinal
study for more than 10 years. When first seen, they were
between the ages of 2 1/2 and 4. They are now between 13
and 15 years, and are being seen for the fifth time. All of
the children had an onset of deafness prior to 16 months,
and all but 6 were known or suspected to be deaf at birth.
All had a hearing loss of more than 80 dB in the better ear,
and all had hearing parents. These youngsters were studied
with their mothers and compared with hearing children and
their hearing mothers.

As a group, the mothers of deaf children were less
flexible, permissive, encouraging, and creative; they were
more frequently didactic and intrusive. There is repeated
evidence in other studies that hearing mothers of deaf children are more intrusive and less responsive in their communicative acts (Schlesinger & Meadow, 1972; Collins, 1969; Goss,
1970; Greenberg, 1980).

As a group, the deaf children were less buoyant, less
compliant, showed less enjoyment of their mothers, and less
pride in their achievement. However, within the group of
deaf children, one subset revealed more successful, meaningful, and gratifying communication with their mothers. These
understanding and understood youngsters had a higher level
of communicative competence and more closely resembled their
hearing peers.

As we followed all the children for the first 5 years,
we noted that as communication skills improved, mothers'
behaviour increasingly began to resemble that of mothers of
hearing children, and the deaf youngsters increasingly
resembled their hearing peers. For those whose communication
continued to be poor, the gap between them and their hearing
peers grew wider as they grew older. They were seen as
enjoying the interaction even less, as being less independent,
creative, and happy, and as exhibiting even less pride in
mastery.

Youngsters who were described as possessing a high level of communicative competence also demonstrated significant increases in nonverbal I.Q. scores. Clearly, communicative competence is related to buoyancy, pride in mastery, cognitive task performance, and enjoyment of interactions with parents. Within the context of this discussion, then, it might be said that parents of deaf children with successful communication feel more powerful, have a greater sense of mastery, and are able to pursue optimal linguistic stances with their children thus, in turn, fostering the child's sense of autonomy and motivational stances.

What are the psychological concomitants of this early language acquisition? If we look at early competencies, we note that all the social competencies (e.g. maturity, buoyance) are more easily fostered by parents and blossom in children when mutual understanding and enjoyment are available. Similarly, we feel that verbal mediation fosters cognitive structuring of the environment (e.g. observations of similarities and differences, plans for the future, memories of the past and their retrieval of absent objects). The ability to put oneself in the place of another, the antecedent of empathy, may be more easily fostered when the feelings of both the mother and the child can be clearly labelled and can be related to differences. Furthermore, parents can more easily monitor their child's understanding, thus avoiding an unintelligible barrage or short concrete sentences. Parents will be reinforced by early linguistic feedback, and will, thus, attempt to promote communication more frequently. Child and parent will have some of the tools and skills which permit and encourage reciprocity and responsiveness. Increased communication skills are also postulated to foster communicative confidence and the ability to communicate more freely with peers and other adults.

Bilingualism and the Conflict of
Value Systems

One major aspect of language remains to be considered in the cognitive/affective/motivational theory of language differences: bilingualism and the extant attitudes towards bilingualism.

A large number of disadvantaged individuals are bilingual, primarily English/Black English and English/Spanish.
Deaf individuals have been found to use sign language primarily with their deaf friends. Many deaf persons can thus be
described as living in a bilingual environment in which
parents, teachers and society generally stress spoken English,
while peers stress sign language. As in many bilingual
situations, one of the languages is frequently devalued and
stigmatized.

Traditionally, although Europeans have valued multiple
language acquisition, Americans have tended to feel that
bilingualism is "bad -- that is, may have deleterious effects
on personal and intellectual development" (Lambert & Peal,
1962). This view is, however, being treated more and more as
an unfounded ethnocentrism. For example, Diebold (1966)
found that cases of genuine bilingual pathology were related
to a crisis in personal and social identity symbolized by
negative attitudes towards the second language. These attitudes usually occur in a monolingual society where there are
antagonistic pressures for linguistic acculturation, and
where minority language is stigmatized as socially inferior.

More recently, bilingualism has been encouraged vigorously in America. It may be that the pendulum has swung to
the other extreme, where English is devalued. The entire
bilingual movement in the United States has been based, in
part, on the assumption that respect for the original language is a necessity. It is interesting to note that
Schachter (1979) contents that the respect for the other
language is related to social class. For example, affluent
English speaking children suffer no special academic problems
when transferred to French speaking schools in Quebec. Also,
in Israel where few immigrant children arrive at school
speaking Hebrew, it is only those from educationally disadvantaged backgrounds who have special academic problems.

Labov (1967) has suggested that antagonistic attitudes
towards a second communicative system create major obstacles
to successful dialect switching. Bernstein (1961) agrees,
arguing that a "public language" must be freely accepted if
the "formal language" is to be learned successfully. All
these authors see the possible cognitive advantages of bilingualism given an atmosphere of acceptance and an opportunity

for utilization. Such benevolence is not frequently found in
Anglo-Saxon countries, particularly if one of the languages
uses body motion in the elaboration of its symbols.

An ethnocentric bias also exists within the population
primarily using sign language. Our center has frequently
suspected a stigma toward the spoken language among deaf
adults, possibly created by onerous years of arduous language
learning. Among adolescents, it may even be responsible for
the frequent occurrence of stigmatization of speech when,
after years of Sign language taboo, they suddenly discover
its potentialities. This, we feel, would not and should not
occur if both speech and sign language were on an equal foot-
ing from early childhood. We have noted that youngsters with
early bimodal input, that is to say, with positive attitudes
toward speech and signs, have reached adolescence with equal
verve towards signs and words.

One addendum from studies of later development may add
to these conceptualizations. It has been frequently stated
that there appears to be little improvement in the specific
language skills, reading, and language arts of deaf children
through the school years. Al Pimentel, the Executive Secretary of the National Association of the Deaf, has stated that
a number of deaf individuals make "spurts in language" after
leaving the school environment (personal communication).
Boothe, Lasky and Kricos (1981) have provided some research
evidence to support this interesting speculation. Specific
comprehension and production of syntactic structures in
English, said to be markedly delayed in deaf individuals
(e.g. negation, 'who' question formation, and passivization),
all of which had shown only minor changes throughout the
school years, improved markedly <u>after</u> the school years. The
authors speculate that this may have taken place because
adults are "...involved in more frequent, more spontaneous,
and often more demanding communication-interactions than those
usually found in classrooms". Lengthy communications are
daily occurrences and the information exchanges often have
critical, personal consequences. It may be that adult subjects away from a situation burdened by the frequently
didactic, non-responsive stances of the school environment
and their own motivational stances towards learning, are free
to engage in autonomous and responsive communicative acts
leading to linguistic spurts.

Early Intervention

Both deaf children and disadvantaged children need early
intervention, and so do their parents, particularly in the
verbal environment. Professionals can sensitively "support
and facilitate the actions" of parents, thus helping them to
gain a sense of mastery, a sense of competence, a sense of
autonomy, which in turn, will lead to mastery, competence and
autonomy in their youngsters. Fraiberg (1980) describes how
even the most disadvantaged parents can be helped to be responsive to their children. Lillie, Goin and Trohanis (1976)
describe a series of responsive parent-centered programs.
Positive attitudes towards bilingualism can be encouraged.

"Surprising as it may seem, many adults need help in
learning how to talk to children in productive ways" (Cazden
et al., 1971). What are the productive ways? Here we touch
upon a controversy. There are two approaches to early intervention, the didactic or behaviouristic approach (Bereiter &
Englemann, 1966), and the child development approach (Biber,
1977; Kamil, 1972). These two approaches present radically
divergent views of the caregiver's role in fostering the
child's development. They have a different concept of child
development, of the contribution of socioeconomic status, and
of the role of language.

In didactic programs, the focus is on structured lessions
aimed primarily at developing specific linguistic or cognitive
skills believed to be "non-existent" among the disadvantaged.
Early intervention programs were designed to compensate for
"environmental deprivation". The primary linguistic focus is
on correct syntax and semantics, and on the correct use of
the grammar of standard English. The child development
approach, on the other hand, relies on Piagentian theory.
Followers believe that children actively propel their own
development, and that the acquisition of linguistic and
cognitive competence occurs throughout the day in the course
of those daily complex interactions between social and emotional factors (themselves extrinsic to questions of competence). Development is seen as a progression of qualita-
tively different stages, universal among disadvantaged and
advantaged children. The importance of language is viewed
in relation to the use of the speech act, utterance, intentions, purposes, or motives of a speaker, rather than the use

of his/her syntax or semantics. In this approach, the focus
is upon the social use of language rather than its form (Dore,
1975; Halliday, 1973).

Schachter (1979) indicates "...educated mothers are
Deweyites or Piagetians". She has designed a curriculum to
foster the motivation for active learning in children and to
enhance their self-confidence, sense of power and feeling of
mastery over the environment. In general, the curriculum is
designed to help disadvantaged mothers and teachers of
toddlers understand those principles leading to the cognitive
and affective stances which make for educability. Those
principles are:

1. The principle of active learning;

2. The principle of interaction between language and
    cognitive development on the one hand, and social
    and emotional development on the other;

3. The principle of developmental stages.

Teachers need to be involved in early intervention, for
they, too, frequently develop a sense of incompetence vis-a-
vis deaf children which leads to a didactic intrusive stance.
Supervisors can, in turn, support and facilitate the actions
of teachers. All of us can successfully find ways to talk
more joyfully <u>with</u> the deaf child, rather than didactically
<u>at</u> the deaf child.

Discussion

S. GERBER
     Several of you may have read the proceedings of an Elks
Conference held in Winnipeg, a volume called *Early Management
of Hearing Loss*. I suggest that you do, so that you will
believe what I am about to tell you. These are comments to
underline this business of powerlessness and how we behave
toward the hearing impaired population. In a paper at the
Winnipeg Conference by my colleague, Prof. Carol Prutting,
there is reference to a man, a product of an oral school,
saying that even as an adult, he associated the use of Signs
with the smell or urine. That was because, as students in an

oral school, the only place they could sign was the toilet.
My second comment is to remind you that one of the leading
scholars in our profession at that Conference said that we
should no more ask the deaf how they wish to be educated
than we should ask that question of the mentally retarded.

H. SCHLESINGER
     I'm glad that I have had some experiences like those
deaf individuals sometimes receive, but not as frequently as
they receive it. For example, when I became a citizen of the
United States, a Daughter of the American Revolution handed
me my papers and said, "Now you're almost as good as we are."
I remember how that one event made me angry. You would be
surprised how often deaf individuals encounter similar events,
daily.

A. DAHLE
     I attended, recently, a conference on Developmentally
Disabled Deaf. One of the speakers had a pretty nice study
showing that children raised with at least one deaf parent or
who have some ties to a deaf relative, have much better
emotional adjustment and fewer behavioural problems than those
children who don't. Have you seen that in your experience?
Secondly, in my experience with the multiply handicapped deaf,
I have noted very few have ties to the deaf community. Is
that generally true? Could this be one of the reasons why
multiply handicapped deaf do have more emotional types of
problems?

H. SCHLESINGER
     Deaf children of deaf parents do tend to do better than
deaf children of hearing parents. When they don't, they're
really problems. Usually they are better off, both academic-
ally and psychologically. As far as the other question is
concerned, I think that the deaf community is just reaching
its own as a "respectable community with a respectable
language" after centuries of being told that's not so. I do
feel that because of that, the deaf community has not been
quite as anxious to accept people who have additional problems.
It's a little bit like women professionals wanting to initially
have some pretty, bright, and half-way attractive professionals
while climbing the equality ladder. I think the deaf may feel

the same way for awhile. I also think what happens with
multiply handicapped deaf children is that their parents
feel much more powerless and do a lot more avoidance. For
example, the disabled I work with tell me that people don't
touch them. Out of a feeling of revulsion, they're not
touched - including by their pediatrician. That kind of
powerlessness occurs at a much earlier age than for the deaf
community. The problems really start during infancy, and
should be prevented because, if you let it develop, it costs
a lot in time and money to reverse it.

References

Altshuler, K.Z., "Personality Traits and Depressive Symptoms
    in the Deaf," Recent Advances in Biological Psychiatry
    Volume VI (New York: Plenum Press), Wurtis, J. (Ed.),
    1964.

Altshuler, K.Z., Deming, W.E., Vollenweider, J., Rainer, J.D.,
    and Tendler, R., "Impulsivity and Profound Early Deafness:
    A Cross Cultural Inquiry," American Annals of the Deaf
    121:331-345, 1976.

Auletta, K., "A Reporter at Large - The Underclass," New
    Yorker, Nov. 16, 23, 30, 1981.

Baratz, S.S., and Baratz, J.C., "Early Childhood Intervention:
    The Social Science Base of Institutional Racism," Harvard
    Educational Review 40:29-50, 1970.

Bereiter, C., and Engleman, S., Teaching Disadvantaged
    Children in Preschool (Englewood Cliffs, New Jersey:
    Prentice-Hall), 1966.

Bernstein, B., "Social Structure, Language, and Learning,"
    The Psychology of Language, Thought and Instruction (New
    York: Holt, Rinehart & Winston), DeCecco, J.P. (Ed.),
    1967.

Bernstein, B., (Ed.), Class, Codes and Control: Vol. 1,
    Theoretical Studies Towards a Sociology of Language (London:
    Routledge & Kegan), 1971.

Biber, B., "A Developmental-Interaction Approach: Bank Street College of Education," The Preschool in Action: Exploring Early Childhood Programs (Boston: Allyn & Bacon), Day, M.C., & Parker, T.K. (Eds.), 1977.

Blank, M., "Cognitive Functions of Language in the Preschool Years," Developmental Psychology 10:229-245, 1974.

Boothe, L.L., Lasky, E.Z., and Kricos, P.B., "Comparison of the Language Abilities of Deaf Children and Young Deaf Adults," American Annals of the Deaf 15:10-16, 1981.

Bradley, R.H., and Caldwell, B.M., "The Relation of Infants' Home Environments to Mental Test Performance at Fifty-Four Months: A Follow-up Study," Child Development 47:81-94, 1976.

Basel, K.E., and Quigley, S.P., "Influence of Certain Language and Communication Environments in Early Childhood on the Development of Language in Deaf Individuals," Journal of Speech and Hearing Research 20:81-94, 1977.

Burchard, E.M., and Myklebust, H.R., "A Comparison of Congenital and Adventitious Deafness with Respect to its Effect on Intelligence, Personality, and Social Maturity," American Annals of the Deaf 87:140-154, 342-360, 1942.

Cazden, C., Child Language and Education (New York: Rinehart & Winston), 1972.

Cazden, C.B., Baratz, J.C., Labov, W., and Palmer, F.H., "Language Development in Day Care Programs," Day Care: Resources for Decisions (Washington, D.C.: Office of Economic Opportunity, Government Printing Office) Grotberg, E.H. (Ed.), 1971.

Chess, S., Korn, S.J., and Fernandez, P.B., Psychiatric Disorders of Children with Congenital Rubella (New York: Brunner/Mazel), 1971.

Collins-Ahlgren, M., "Teaching English as a Second Language to Young Deaf Children," Journal of Speech and Hearing Disorders 39:486-500, 1974.

Collins-Ahlgren, M., "Language Development of Two Deaf Children," American Annals of the Deaf 120:524-539, 1975.

Clarke-Stewart, K.A., "Interactions Between Mothers and Their Young Children: Characteristics and Consequences," Monographs of the Society for Research in Child Development 38 (6-7, Serial No. 153), 1973.

Collins, J.L., Communication Between Deaf Children of Pre-School Age and Their Mothers (Unpublished Ph.D. dissertation, University of Pittsburgh), 1969.

Coopersmith, S., The Antecedents of Self-Esteem (San Francisco: W.H. Freeman), 1967.

DiCarlo, L.M., The Deaf (Englewood Cliffs, New Jersey: Prentice-Hall), 1964.

Diebold, A.R., Jr., "The Consequences of Early Bilingualism in Cognitive Development and Personality Formation," Paper prepared for the Symposium, The Study of Personality: An Interdisciplinary Appraisal (Rice University, Houston, Texas), 1966.

DiFrancesca, S., Academic Achievement Test Results of a National Testing Program for Hearing Impaired Students, United States: Spring, 1971 - Series D, Number 9 (Washington, D.C.: Office of Demographic Studies, Gallaudet College), 1972.

DiFrancesca, S., and Carey, S., Item Analysis of an Achievement Testing Program for Hearing Impaired Students, United States: Spring, 1971 - Series D, Number 8 (Washington, D.C.: Office of Demographic Studies, Gallaudet College), 1972.

Dore, J., "A Pragmatic Description of Early Language Development," Journal of Psycholinguistic Research 4:343-351, 1974.

Fraiberg, S., Clinical Studies in Infant Mental Health: The First Year of Life (New York: Basic Books, Inc.), 1980.

Furth, H.G., "A Comparison of Reading Test Norms of Deaf and Hearing Children," American Annals of the Deaf 111:461-462, 1966.

Furth, H.G., "A Review and Perspective on the Thinking of
    Deaf People," Cognitive Studies (New York: Bruner/Mazel),
    Hellmuth, J. (Ed.), 1970.

Gentile, A., and DiFrancesca, S., Academic Achievement Test
    Performance of Hearing Impaired Students, United States:
    Spring, 1969 (Washington, D.C.: Office of Demographic
    Studies, Gallaudet College), 1969.

Gladwin, T., Poverty U.S.A. (Boston: Little, Brown & Co.),
    1967.

Golden, M., Birns, B., Bridger, W., and Moss, A., "Social-
    Class Differentiation in Cognitive Development Among Black
    Preschool Children," Child Development 42:37-45, 1971.

Goldin-Meadow, S., The Representation of Semantic Relations
    in a Manual Language Created by Deaf Children of Hearing
    Parents: A Language You Can't Dismiss Out of Hand
    (Unpublished Doctoral Dissertation, University of Pennsyl-
    vania, College Park, Pennsylvania), 1975.

Goss, R.N., "Language Used by Mothers of Deaf Children and
    Mothers of Hearing Children," American Annals of the Deaf
    115:93-96, 1970.

Greenberg, M., "Social Interaction Between Deaf Preschoolers
    and their Mothers," Developmental Psychology 16:465-474,
    1980.

Gregory, S., The Deaf Child and His Family (London: George
    Allen & Urwin), 1976.

Haggstrom, W.C., "The Power of the Poor," Mental Health of
    Poor (New York: Free Press), Riessman, F., Cohen, J., &
    Pearl, A. (Eds.), 1964.

Halliday, M.A., Exploration in the Functions of Grammar
    (London: Arnold Publishing), 1973.

Harris, R.I., "Impulse Control in Deaf Children: Research
    and Clinical Issues," Deaf Children: Developmental Per-
    spectives (New York: Academic Press), Liben, L.D. (Ed.),
    1978.

Heider, F., and Heider, G.M., "Studies in the Psychology of the Deaf," Psychological Monographs, Volume 53, No. 242, 1941.

Heider, G.M., "Adjustment Problems of the Deaf Child," Nervous Child 7:38-44, 1948.

Hess, R.D., and Shipman, V.C., "Early Experience on the Socialization of Cognitive Modes in Children," Child Development 34:869-886, 1965.

Hodgson, K.W., The Deaf and Their Problems, A Study in Special Education (London: C.A. Watts & Company, Ltd.), 1953.

Hoemann, H., "The Development of Communication Skills in Deaf and Hearing Children," Child Development 43:990-1003, 1972.

Juenke, D., An Application of a Generative-Transformational Model of Linguistic Description of Hearing Impaired Subjects in the Generation and Expansion Stages of Language Development (Unpublished Master's Thesis, University of Cincinnati, Cincinnati, Ohio), 1971.

Kamil, C.K., "An Application of Paiget's Theory to the Conceptualization of a Preschool Curriculum," The Preschool in Action: Exploring Early Childhood Programs (Boston: Allyn & Bacon), Parker, R.K. (Ed.), 1972.

Kaye, K., "Toward the Origin of Dialogue," Studies in Mother-Infant Interaction (New York: Academic Press), Schaffer, H.R. (Ed.), 1977.

Labov, W., "Some Sources of Reading Problems for Negro Speakers of Nonstandard English," New Directions in Elementary English (Champaign, Illinois: National Council of Teachers of English), Frazlea, A. (Ed.), 1967.

Lambert, W.E., and Peal, E., "The Relation of Bilingualism to Intelligence," Psychological Monographs, Number 76, 1962.

Lavatelli, C. (Ed.), Language Training in Early Childhood Education (Urbana, Illinois: University of Illinois Press), 1974.

Levine, E.S., Youth in a Soundless World, A Search for Personality (New York: New York University Press), 1956.

Lillie, D.L., Trohanis, P.L., and Goin, K.W. (Eds.), Teaching Parents to Teach (New York: Walker & Co.), 1976.

Loban, W., The Language of Elementary School Children: Research Report No. 1 (Champaign, Illinois: National Council of Teachers of English), 1963.

Meadow, K.P., Deafness and Child Development (Berkeley: University of California Press), 1980.

Milner, E., "A Study of the Relationship Between Reading Readiness in Grade One School Children and Patterns of Parent-Child Interaction," Child Development 22:95-112, 1951.

Moores, D.F., Educating the Deaf: Psychology, Principles and Practices (Boston: Houghton Mifflin Co.), 1978.

Moses, K., and Hecke-Wulatin, M.V., "The Socio-Emotional Impact of Infant Deafness: A Counselling Model," Early Management of Hearing Loss (New York: Grune & Stratton, Inc.), Mencher, G.T. & Gerber, S.E. (Eds.), 1981.

Mykelbust, H., The Psychology of Deafness: Sensory Deprivation, Learning, and Adjustment (New York: Grune & Stratton Inc.), 1960.

Pawlby, S.J., "Initiative Interaction," Studies in Mother-Infant Interaction (London: Academic Press), Schaffer, H.R. (Ed.), 1977.

Plumer, D., "A Summary of Environmentalist Views and Some Educational Implications," Language and Poverty (Chicago: Rand McNally Publishing), Williams, F. (Ed.), 1970.

Pringle, M.L.K., Deprivation and Education (London: Longman's Green), 1965.

Rice, B., A Comprehensive Facility Program for Multiply Handicapped Deaf Adults (Fayetteville: Arkansas Rehabilitation Research and Training Center), 1973.

Robinson, W.P., and Rackstraw, S.J., "Variations in Mothers' Answers to Children's Questions as a Function of Social Class, Verbal Intelligence Test Scores, and Sex," Sociology 1:259-265, 1967.

Ross, A.E., The Exceptional Child and the Family (New York: Grune & Stratton, Inc.), 1964.

Sadock, B.J., "Psychiatry and the Urban Setting," Comprehensive Text Book of Psychiatry (Baltimore: Williams & Wilkins), Sadock, B.J., Kaplan, H.I., Freedman, A.M., Suffman, N. (Eds.), 1975.

Schachter, F.F., Everyday Mother-Talk to Toddlers: Early Intervention (New York: Academic Press), 1979.

Schlesinger, H.S., "Meaning and Enjoyment: Language Acquisition of Deaf Children," Psycholinguistics and Total Communication: The State of the Art (Washington, D.C.: American Annals of the Deaf) O'Rourke, T.J. (Ed.), 1972.

Schlesinger, H.S., Early Words Manuscript In Preparation, #1, 1981.

Schlesinger, H.S., Untitled Manuscript In Preparation, #2, 1981.

Schlesinger, H.S., and Meadow, K.P., Sound and Sign: Childhood Deafness and Mental Health (Berkeley: University of California Press), 1972.

Schlesinger, H.S., and Meadow, K.P., Studies of Family Interaction, Language Acquisition and Deafness. Final report to the Office of Maternal and Child Health, Grant MC-R-060160 (San Francisco: Langley Porter Neuropsychiatric Institute), 1976.

Schoggen, M., and Schoggen, P., "Environmental Forces in the Home Lives of Three-Year-Old Children in Three Population Subgroups," JSAS Catalog of Selected Documents in Psychology (No. 1178), 1976.

Snow, C.E., "Mother's Speech Research: From Input to Interaction," Talking to Children: Language Input and Acquisition (Cambridge: Cambridge University Press), Snow, C.E. and Ferguson, C.A. (Eds.), 1977.

114 Hilde S. Schlesinger

Stewart, L., "Problems of Severely Handicapped Deaf:
Implications for Educational Programs," American Annals
of the Deaf 116:362-368, 1971.

Tough, J., The Development of Meaning: A Study of Children's
Use of Language (New York: John Wiley), 1977.

Trybus, R., Buchanan, C., and DiFrancesco, S., Studies in
Achievement Testing, United States: Spring, 1971, Series
D, Number 11 (Washington, D.C.: Office of Demographic
Studies, Gallaudet College), 1973.

Tulkin, S.R., and Kagan, T., "Mother-Child Interaction in
the First Year of Life," Child Development 43:31-41, 1972.

Van Lieshout, C.F.M., "The Assessment of Stability and Change
in Peer Interaction of Normal Hearing and Deaf Preschool
Children," Paper presented at the 1973 biennial meeting of
the International Society for the Study of Behavioural
Development, Ann Arbor, Michigan, August 21-25, 1973.

Vernon, M., "Sociological and Psychological Factors
Associated with Hearing Loss," Journal of Speech and
Hearing Research 12:541-563, 1969.

Wachs, T., Uzgiris, I., and Hunt, J.McV., "Cognitive Develop-
ment in Infants of Different Age Levels and from Different
Environmental Backgrounds: An Exploratory Investigation,"
Merrill-Palmer Quarterly 17:283-317, 1971.

Williams, R., and Naremore, R., "Social Class Differences in
Children's Syntactic Performance: A Quantitative Analysis
of Field Study Data," Journal of Speech and Hearing
Research 12:778-793, 1969.

White, B.L., Kaban, B., Shapiro, B., and Attanucci, J.,
"Competence and Experience," The Structuring of Experience
(New York: Plenum Press), Uzgiris, I.C., & Weizmann F.
(Eds.), 1967.

Wrightstone, J.W., Aronow, M.S., and Moskowitz, S.,
"Developing Reading Test Norms for Deaf Children," American
Annals of the Deaf 108:311-316, 1963.

Yamamoto, K., "Bilingualism: A Brief Review," Mental Hygiene 48:468-477, 1964.

Zigler, E., and Trickett, P.K., "I.Q., Social Competence and Evaluation of Early Childhood Intervention Programs," American Psychologist 33:789-798, 1978.

ASSESSMENT AND INTERVENTION
FROM A DEVELOPMENTAL PERSPECTIVE

Arthur Boothroyd
City University, New York, New York

The causes, characteristics and consequences of sensory (i.e. cochlear) hearing loss have been studied and analyzed in depth. Educators may disagree on some of the goals of intervention and on the most suitable way of meeting those goals, but at least the issues involved are fairly well understood. Formal methods exist for assessing the various parameters of the primary impairment, such as degree of hearing loss, as well as for parameters of the more obvious secondary impairments, such as vocabulary size. Various philosophies of intervention have been translated into recognizable methods. There is, in short, a general sense that cochlear hearing impairment in an otherwise intact child is a problem whose boundaries are definable, whose effects are both predictable and measurable, and whose long-term consequences ought to be preventable (Boothroyd, 1982).

No such sense exists for the hearing impaired child with serious additional sensory, motor or neurological deficits. If the additional problems are of such a nature as to resist definition, measurement or remediation, the presence of a hearing loss serves to make the situation even more complicated. Even when the additional impairments are less severe, their interactions with the hearing loss and with its secondary consequences serve to multiply the effects of both. Consider, for example, the challenge facing a child who is trying to master spoken language without the benefits of audition. The task becomes infinitely more difficult if there are additional primary impairments of cognitive or sensory-motor capacity. Conversely, the language deficit caused by the hearing loss may render assessment and treatment of the additional disorder even more difficult than it would otherwise have been.

A developmental approach to assessment is one that
focuses less on the identification and quantification of
impairments, and more on the nature of their separate and
joint interactions with the process of development. Armed
with an understanding of the processes at work within and
between the child and the environment, interventionists have
the task of modifying that environment in order to redirect
development along some more appropriate course.

This approach to assessment and intervention has been
discussed by several writers in connection with the uncomplicated hearing impaired child. For example, models of normal
cognitive development (Piaget & Inhelder, 1969), language
development (Bloom, 1970; Chomsky, 1968; Dore, 1974; Gleason
& Weintraub, 1976), attachment (Bowlby, 1969), and the
development of personality (Erikson, 1963) have been used to
provide a framework for discussion of the nature of deafness
and, in some cases, have served as the rationale for particular methods of intervention. See Blackwell et al., (1978),
Corsaro (1981), Furth (1973), Greenberg and Marvin (1979),
Kretschmer and Kretschmer (1978), Litoff and Feldman (1981),
Simmons-Martin (1978), and Sisco et al., (1979), for
examples.

One of the inherent difficulties with the developmental
approach is that the models on which it is based are often
incomplete, either because of insufficient knowledge, or
because of the particular interest and orientation of their
originator. Failure to recognize this limitation has led to
many unfortunate examples of over-generalization in both
regular and special educational practice. Nevertheless, so
pervasive are interactive effects in the development of the
hearing impaired child with additional handicaps, that a
developmental approach seems essential. The purpose of this
paper is to outline a comprehensive model of development and
to discuss some of the general issues involved in its application to assessment and intervention with these complex
children.

Development

A Model

Figure 1 illustrates a comprehensive model of the normal
developmental process. This model is based on the research
and writings of numerous authors and on the writer's own

clinical experiences, and is intended to embody several basic
principles:

1. Two actors and reactors are involved in the develop-
    mental process, the child and the world.

2. The child does not have direct access to the world,
    but must interact with it through sensory and motor
    systems. Basically, the world acts on the child
    through the sense organs and the child acts on the
    world by movement.

3. The world has the following components:

    a) the dimensions of space and time in which it
        exists;

    b) its content, consisting of objects (e.g. water,
        chairs, cats and people) that become involved in
        events (e.g. boiling, falling, running and
        talking);

    c) attributes of space, time, objects and events
        (e.g. distance, duration, color and rate);

    d) evidence that serves as stimuli for the child's
        sense organs (e.g. light reflected by objects,
        sound produced by events, chemical traces
        released from objects, and forces generated
        either by gravity or by contact between objects);

    e) rules that govern the behaviour of the world
        (e.g. mathematical rules of space and time,
        physical and chemical laws of the inanimate
        world, biological laws of the animate world,
        social rules of people-objects, and the linguis-
        tic rules of language-events);

4. The child has the following components:

    a) sense organs and their associated neural
        systems;

    b) skeletal and muscular structures and their
        associated neural systems;

FIGURE 1:   The process of development.   In response to
extrinsic demands, inner drives and basic capacities, the
child explores his environment and organizes the information
provided by his senses.   The result is a "world model" that
represents the child's inferences about the real world.   At
first, this is a world of sensations and impressions.   Then
the sensations are interpreted in terms of objects and events.
Next, the objects and events are interpreted in terms of
underlying rules, roles and relationships.   Finally, the child
acquires a system of symbols to represent categories within
his world model.   The world model can be accessed directly by
sensory input (for example, seeing a cat) or indirectly via
receptive language (for example, hearing the word "cat").
Similarly, the child can influence the physical world by
direct movement and the social world by expressive language.
Because of complex interdependencies, primary impairment of
one function causes secondary impairment of other functions.

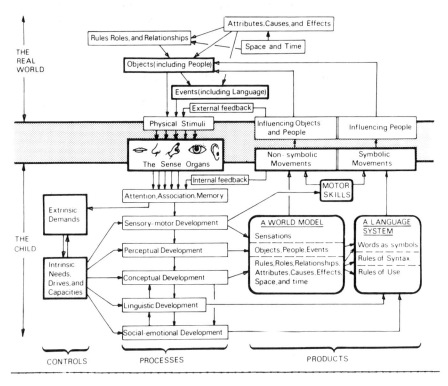

Arthur Boothroyd, *Hearing Impairments in Young Children*, 1982.
Reprinted by permission of Prentice-Hall, Inc., Englewood
Cliffs, New Jersey.

    c) neurological mechanisms for perceptual, conceptual, and symbolic organization;

    d) drives that stimulate and guide development.

5. The child's sense organs convert world evidence into sensory evidence, much of it being self-generated by motor activities which are, at first, reflexive and later exploratory.

6. One of the child's first tasks is to learn how to manage the sensory and motor systems, mastering, in the process, such abilities as gaze direction and focus, sensory-motor association, sensory-sensory association, selection and attention, and memory.

7. Armed with these abilities, the child attempts to explain sensory and motor evidence by constructing an inner model of reality - a world model.

8. Cognitive development involves the passage of the child's world model through several stages, reflecting at each stage reality as the child currently knows it.

9. These stages are characterized by re-organizations of the world model, beginning with a "sensory-motor model" of sensations and movements, progressing to a "perceptual model" of objects and events existing in time and space, and eventually to a "conceptual model" in which the world's content and dimensions are governed by rules.

10. Central to the child's development is the separation of self from other world content and recognition of people as a special class of objects governed by special rules. Progress in this area represents social-emotional development and the development of social cognition.

11. Central to the child's understanding of the world of people is the discovery that they are influenced not only by the direct movements (e.g. biting and pushing), but also by symbolic movements (e.g. smiling, pointing and talking), of the individual.

12.   Out of a drive to communicate with people, the
      child develops a language system which provides
      access, both expressively and receptively, to his
      or her world model.

13.   This language system has the following components:

      a)   a lexicon or set of word symbols that refer to
           objects and classes of objects (nouns), events
           and classes of events (verbs), attributes
           (adjectives and adverbs), and relationships
           (prepositions and function words);

      b)   a grammar or set of rules that permits general
           symbols to be selected, modified and combined
           in sentences which have specific meanings
           derived from the child's world model;

      c)   rules of use which express the child's know-
           ledge of language as a vehicle for social
           interactions.

14.   Once sufficient competence has been gained, language
      becomes a principal medium for further social,
      emotional and conceptual development.

15.   The process of development just outlined is not
      simply one in which the child responds to internal
      drives and external pressures. It involves inter-
      actions between the child and the world. In par-
      ticular, the child's family has its own drives and
      needs and must react to the child's behaviours.

Developmental Stages

    Development is frequently described in terms of a
sequence of stages through which the child passes. What
characterizes a transition to a new stage is the appearance
of skills and behaviours not previously observed. It is
misleading, however, to suggest that these behaviours are
entirely new or that they will simply disappear at the beginning of the next stage. The child may be busily acquiring
prerequisite subskills, or "readiness" skills, long before

engaging in a particular overt activity and may, in fact, be observed to be rehearsing the activity in a simpler form. The beginnings of language development, for example, cannot be tied to the appearance of 1- or 2-word utterances. From the moment of birth, the child begins to acquire the prerequisite sensory, motor, and cognitive skills. Much of the early interaction between mother and child can be interpreted as dialogue in its essential form (Bloom, Lifter & Broughton, 1981; Tronick, 1981). Educators concerned with early intervention and hearing impaired children have, in fact, been crying "language development begins at birth" for some time.

A particular aspect of development does not cease at the end of a period of intense activity. For example, the adult who takes tennis lessons is acquiring sensory-motor skills, but vocabulary acquisition does not cease. Furthermore, there are several times in life when progress in the area of social cognition is required, but this does not occur at the cost of cessation of growth in other developmental areas.

The emergence of the child into a new stage is characterized by accelerated development of particular aspects of behaviour. For the first few months of life, for example, the focus is on sensory-motor organization. This focus quickly shifts to perceptual-motor organization as the child discovers the simplifying notion that sensory data originate in a world of permanent objects and predictable events which exist in the dimensions of time and space. Between 1 and 2 years of age, the focus is on conceptual development, leading the way for rapid advances in social cognition, social-emotional function, and language during the 3rd and 4th years. Throughout the school years, the most obvious areas of activity are linguistically mediated conceptual development and an increasing refinement of the ability to operate on the world model independent of concrete evidence. During adolescence, the focus returns to social and emotional issues. Throughout this process, new and higher levels of organization are being overlaid on continuously developing subskills. This makes possible new skills which will, themselves, become subskills for some later purpose.

In the model of development described earlier, this process is implicit in the concept of a world model that is continually being expanded and reorganized.

Developmental Synchrony

The transition from 1 developmental stage to another
requires at least 4 components:

1. Intrinsic drives;

2. Sensory, motor, and neurological capacities;

3. Appropriate input and feedback from the world;

4. Prerequisite subskills.

Furthermore, these 4 components must be present at the
same time. Subskills which may involve developmental areas
other than the one in which accelerated progress is occurring
must be available when needed to satisfy internally and
externally defined needs. Such developmental synchrony
characterizes the normal child in a normal environment.

Developmental asynchrony occurs when the 4 components are
out of step; when, for example, the necessary subskills are
not yet developed by the time the drives emerge, or when the
child's development fails to keep pace with the needs of the
parents. Such asychrony is one of the more serious problems
facing the handicapped child and family.

Critical Age

The concept of developmental synchrony can be related to
the issue of critical age. It has been suggested that rapid
acceleration of development in particular skill areas
requires the maturation of neurological systems which render
an organism receptive to certain kinds of input at a given
time, but unreceptive at some later time. An implication of
this "hard" view of critical age is that it can become too
late for the development of the skills in question. This
view is unpalatable to many educators.

A less extreme or "soft" view of critical age can
explain reduced receptivity to learning without invoking a
neurological parking meter. If, because of developmental
asychrony, internally or externally defined needs emerge in
the absence of the necessary capacities or subskills, the

child is obliged to meet those needs in inappropriate ways, inappropriate in the sense that they will interfere with subsequent developmental progress. Consider, for example, the child who, lacking language as a means to negotiate issues of control, resorts to tantrums and ritual. Once established, these behaviours may be difficult to displace in favor of more constructive ones.

The distinction between a neurological and a developmental explanation is hazy at best. The practical difference between the two views is that one suggests it can become impossible for certain skills to be acquired after the optimal time has passed, whereas the other simply suggests that it becomes increasingly difficult. As with most aspects of human behaviour, the truth probably lies in a combination of neurological and developmental explanations.

Primary and Secondary Impairments

So complex are the developmental interactions within and between inner drives, basic capacities, and external demands, that a single primary impairment quickly produces multiple secondary impairments. A sensory hearing loss, for example, interferes with the development of language. The language delay causes a reduction in quality and quantity of parental interaction, which undermines social-emotional development, and so on. Even when the primary impairment is as simple as a loss of one sensory channel, it need only exist for 1 or 2 years before being overtaken in severity and intractability by its secondary consequences.

I am using the term "primary" in this context to refer not just to the original source of the child's difficulties, but to all non-remediable impairments. If a secondary impairment persists so long that it becomes non-remediable, the fact that it was caused by something else is irrelevant from a practical point of view - it then becomes a primary impairment. Such a situation might occur as a result of sensory deprivation, the passage of a neurologically determined critical age, or the establishment of maladaptive behaviours in response to developmental asychrony. For example, the hearing impaired child who goes without amplification for 3 or 4 years will have a primary impairment of the neural mechanisms of hearing. Similarly, the otherwise normal child who

suffers repeated ear infections during the first 2 or 3 years
of life may develop a secondary impairment in auditory attention which may eventually become non-remediable and, therefore, present as a primary impairment.

The use of remediability as a criterion for distinguishing primary from secondary impairments offers the opportunity
for operational definitions based on the results of diagnostic intervention. By the same token, however, it introduces
the risk of misdiagnosis if the assumption of non-remediabil-
ity is based on the results of poor teaching.

Assessment

Goals

The problem of the multiply handicapped child has just
been described in terms of:

1. Primary impairments which are non-remediable and
   which directly interfere with development in particular aspects of function;

2. Secondary impairments caused directly by a primary
   impairment, or indirectly through a breakdown of
   developmental synchrony;

3. The eventual transformation of secondary into primary impairments because of the passage of a neurologically or developmentally determined critical age;

4. Interactions between and among primary and secondary
   impairments which produce even more impairments.

Faced with a child in whom development has gone so awry,
the goal of assessment becomes less one of identification and
quantification, and more one of description and explanation.
The components of a complete description must include both
the child and the environment with which the child interacts.
The description of the child must take into account:

1. The existence and quality of basic drives (e.g. for avoidance of discomfort, for exploration, for control, and for communication);

2. The existence and quality of sensory and motor mechanisms, both peripheral and central;

3. The integrity of the neurological mechanisms needed for sensory-sensory and sensory-motor association;

4. The existence and quality of the neurological mechanisms needed for perceptual, conceptual, and symbolic organization;

5. Current motor, perceptual, cognitive, linguistic, social and emotional status.

The description of the child's environment must take account of:

1. Its physical characteristics (e.g. play materials, experiential variety and predictability, and opportunities for exploration and problem solving);

2. Its social characteristics - primarily the parents' physical, social, and linguistic interactions with, and their emotional reactions to the child, the major focus being on the mother or other primary care giver.

Above all, the description must account for the mechanisms of interaction within and between the child and the environment, so as to provide an understanding of the processes which have led to the present status, as well as the processes currently at work. A particular goal of this aspect of description is to differentiate primary from secondary impairments.

In summary, descriptive assessment should include the drives, capacities, and performance of the child, the physical and social characteristics of his or her environment, and the processes of interaction among them. The separation of primary (i.e. non-remediable) from secondary (i.e. remediable) impairments is also important.

Assessment Tools

The information needed to develop a complete description
of the multiply handicapped child can be acquired in 3 ways —
by observation, by formal testing, and by diagnostic
intervention.

The astute clinician can learn much about the child and
his environment from careful observation. The child's interactions with play materials, approaches to new and challenging situations, the parents' verbal and non-verbal interactions with the child and with each other about the child,
all provide raw material for working hypotheses about
strengths, weaknesses, and cause-effect relationships.

Formal tests also have a role to play in assessment,
but the interpretation of results must be approached with
caution and skepticism. Standardization will most likely
have been carried out with normal children, or with children
exhibiting only one primary impairment. Even the instructions for test administration may carry implicit assumptions
about the child's abilities which are not valid for the
multiply handicapped. To take a simple example, the use of
visual reinforcement audiometry to test the hearing of
infants presupposes the existence not only of sufficient
visual acuity, but also of adequate motor skill, attention,
memory, space perception, and conditionability. Failure to
respond to such testing should not be interpreted as evidence
of a primary auditory impairment unless it has been demonstrated that these aspects of function are intact. Even
physiological techniques such as brainstem audiometry may
give misleading results when applied to a neurological system
structurally or organizationally abnormal.

Rigid adherence to standardized procedures and instructions for the interpretation of results is counterproductive
when dealing with children who have confirmed or suspected
multiple handicaps. Informed flexibility and cautious
adaptability are the keys to the effective use of formal
tests with this population.

The third and most powerful component of assessment is
diagnostic intervention. It is only through the child's
responses to intervention that initial hypotheses can be
refined or revised, that the full extent of capacities can be
revealed, and that the distinction between primary and secondary impairments can be established.

The kind of assessment just outlined cannot be accomplished in a few short sessions of clinical evaluation. Assessment of the multiply handicapped child is an ongoing process in which one must continuously be ready to revise or abandon earlier conclusions as the combined effects of learning, maturation, and development reveal the inadequacies of those conclusions.

Personnel

Just as assessment for the multiply handicapped child resists temporal boundaries, so it resists disciplinary boundaries. A complete description may require input from several specialists. Each must be prepared to consider the interactions between those aspects of function in which he or she has special expertise and other aspects. Consideration must also be given to the mechanisms of interaction among the specialists; that is, to the use of a structured assessment team. A team is more than a collection of individuals, just as a multiply handicapped child is more than a collection of impairments. Not until the members of an assessment team can interact with each other at least as effectively as do the child's impairments, can a complete and meaningful description be approached.

Intervention

Goals

Armed with a working description of the child, the environment and their interactions, it is appropriate to consider intervening in the developmental process. The intervener, or "teacher-therapist", modifies the child's physical and social environment either directly, by becoming part of it, or indirectly, through parent counselling and education. Changes are introduced in the stimuli impinging upon the child, in the reactions contingent upon behaviour, and in the expectations placed upon the child.

The long-term goal of intervention is, or <u>should</u> be, realization of the child's maximum capacity for independence and self-fulfillment. The short-term goals of particular intervention procedures can be of several types.

Diagnosis

Diagnostic intervention is intended to test working hypotheses and to contribute to an emerging description of the child. In a sense, all intervention with handicapped children should be considered as having diagnosis as one of its goals.

Correction

Corrective intervention is aimed at eliminating or reducing a primary impairment. Examples are the surgical treatment of middle ear infections, the fitting of hearing aids, parent counselling, and certain kinds of drug therapy.

Prevention

Preventive intervention is the most powerful tool at the disposal of the teacher-therapist. Its purpose is to prevent the emergence of secondary impairments. It must, therefore, begin before secondary impairments have had a chance to appear. A major hindrance to effective prevention is the fact that secondary impairments are often the impetus for evaluation and identification, as in the case of the child who is not brought to a clinic until it becomes apparent that he or she is not learning to talk. One of the keys to successful prevention is the avoidance of developmental asynchrony. Two complementary approaches are possible. One is to accelerate the development of readiness skills, either by compensation or by circumvention, so that they will be available to meet emerging environmental demands. The other is to delay the emergence of environmental demands so that the child will have more time to develop the prerequisite subskills. This second can be accomplished by suitable structure of educational programs and through parent education and counselling. The appropriate balance between these two approaches depends on the drives and capacities of the individual child.

Compensation

Compensatory intervention involves making up for a weakness by providing enrichment. The reduction of auditory experience caused by a hearing loss, for example, may be offset by enriching the acoustic environment. Similarly, the reduction of linguistic input caused by the same loss may be compensated for by enrichment of the linguistic environment (e.g. when the parents of hearing impaired children are encouraged to "talk, talk, talk" to their offspring). There are, however, serious limitations to the concept of compensatory intervention. If the primary impairment is too severe, no amount of environmental enrichment can provide adequate compensation. Talking more to a totally deaf child does not enrich the auditory experience. Note also that compensation for a deficit at one stage of development by enrichment at a later stage may be of limited benefit because of problems of developmental asynchrony. It is doubtful that acoustic enrichment with a 6 year old hearing impaired child can ever fully compensate for the absence of auditory experience during the first few years of life.

Circumvention

When a need emerges, either internally or externally defined, for which the prerequisite subskills are lacking, alternative methods of meeting that need must be found. Examples of circumventive intervention include the use of vision and touch to provide access to speech information which is not accessible via the defective ear, and the use of sign language to meet the child's emerging needs for symbolic communication. The essential difference between compensatory and circumventive intervention, as defined here, is that the former teaches to the child's weaknesses, while the latter teaches to strengths.

Remediation

Remedial intervention focuses on the elimination or minimization of secondary impairments. The aim is to turn back the clock and to give the child a chance to develop those skills that did not develop spontaneously. Both compensatory and circumventive techniques may be used. Once

again, the need for the maintenance of developmental synchrony dictates that remediation begin as early as possible,
lest the secondary impairments become so well entrenched
that they are non-remediable and, therefore, primary.

The foregoing classification of intervention goals is
illustrated below:

Types of Intervention

Diagnostic

  Corrective

    Preventive   INTERVENTION

      Compensatory

        Circumventive

          Remedial

Alternatives

In the opening paragraphs of this paper, I may have
created the impression that a developmental approach is only
necessary for the multiply handicapped child and that some
other approach is appropriate for the uncomplicated hearing
impaired child. I believe, in fact, that the principles
outlined here are valid for any child, regardless of type,
number, or severity of handicaps. I also believe that good
teacher-therapists have always used a developmental approach
to intervention, either explicitly or implicitly.

But what are the alternatives? If we don't attempt to
understand the child and the family as a dynamic, interactive,
evolving system and seek to operate on that system according
to its own rules, how do we go about intervention? Two
approaches come to mind.

Behaviour Modification

This approach to intervention places less emphasis on
process and more on product. The only process of interest
is that of operant conditioning. Inputs to the child are
made contingent upon behaviours. Those contingencies which

increase the frequency of occurrence of a particular behaviour are operationally defined as *reinforcers*, while those which decrease the frequency of occurrence are operationally defined as *punishers*. The goal is to increase the frequency of occurrence of desirable behaviours and to decrease the frequency of occurrence of undesirable behaviours.

While the principles of operant conditioning have an obvious place in any developmental model and any program of intervention, their uncritical application to the shaping of behaviour carries serious risks. One problem is that the same surface behaviour may result from different underlying processes. By reinforcing a behaviour without considering how it is being attained, we run the risk of also reinforcing processes that may prove counter-productive at some later stage of development. An example that comes to mind is the imitation of single syllables by young deaf children. The student may receive social reinforcement for starting and stopping the breathflow at about the right time. If, however, the control of airflow is being accomplished by valving at the glottis, the teacher is also reinforcing behaviours that will interfere with the later development of smooth, connected speech.

A second problem with the behaviour modification approach arises when behaviours are extinguished without considering the reason for their existence. Consider the case of a girl with severe neurological impairments who, at age 4, was still "putting everything in her mouth". Since this was a clearly identifiable behaviour that was not age-appropriate, it became the obvious target for the behaviourally oriented teacher-therapist who was working with her. Had this attempt at extinction been successful, it could well have deprived the child of her one effective avenue for exploration of the world and development of a world model.

I should stress that the concerns expressed here do not relate to behavioural theories themselves, but to their uncritical and superficial application to problems of intervention.

The Procrustean Approach

The second alternative is that of Procrustes, the
mythical character who stretched or mutilated his guests to
fit his bed. There is an ever-present danger in work with
the handicapped that a particular method of intervention,
once developed, will be applied uniformly to all children of
a certain type, regardless of individual differences. In the
management of hearing impaired children, we have seen the
concept of "best method" surface in many guises. The appeal
of such an approach is its simplicity. The task of assessment is to determine that the child is, indeed, of the right
type (e.g. has a severe or profound hearing loss), and the
task of intervention is to follow the "method". While the
teacher-therapist may make minor adaptations in strategy, the
major responsibility for adaptation rests with the child.
The shortcomings of such an approach, especially with the
multiply handicapped child, are too obvious to bear scrutiny.

While the two approaches just discussed were introduced
as possibel alternatives to a developmental approach, it
should be clear that this writer considers neither of them to
be viable.

Personnel

The application of a developmental approach to intervention presupposes the availability of teacher-therapists with
extremely high levels of training and competence. As was the
case with assessment, this training and competence cannot be
confined within the boundaries of traditional disciplines.
Nor can it be provided by a group of individuals representing
different specialities but with no mechanisms for effective
interaction. The issues of personnel preparation and program
organization must be addressed as part of any attempt to
improve the management of multiply handicapped hearing
impaired children.

                         Conclusion

Two fundamental issues underly the ideas presented in
this paper - logic and adaptability. A developmental approach
to assessment and intervention must first be based on the

assumption that the child and family respond as a system with its own inherent logic. No matter how abnormal or bizarre the resulting behaviours, we must believe that they are a logical outcome of the drives, needs, capacities, and mechanisms operating within that system. Our task is to understand each system so that we can deal with it on its own merits, rather than attempt to apply the logic of some other system.

The second issue is adaptability. As humans, we are endowed with a phenomenal capacity for adaptability. Our sensory systems, our neurological mechanisms, our capacity for conceptual thought, our capacity for symbolic communication and our capacity for social organization, all contribute to the ability to adapt to wide variations in the physical and social environment. Impairments, almost by definition, reduce adaptability. A single impairment reduces it considerably; multiple impairments reduce it almost to zero. This simple concept has far-reaching implications for educational-therapeutic management. If the goal is that the environment and the needs of the child shall match, then the responsibility for adaptation shifts from the child to the environment as the impairments become more severe and more numerous. Whereas the normal child can often grow and learn in spite of the short-comings of the social-educational environment, the hearing impaired child is highly dependent upon the quality of that environment, and the multiply handicapped, hearing impaired child is totally dependent. The responsibility for adaptation is ours.

References

Blackwell, P.M., Engen, E., Fischrund, J., and Zarcadoolas, C., Sentences and Other Systems: A Language and Learning Curriculum for Hearing-Impaired Children (Washington, D.C.: A.G. Bell Association), 1978.

Bloom, L., Language Development: Form and Function in Emerging Grammars (Cambridge, Massachusetts: M.I.T. Press), 1970.

Bloom, L., Lifter, K., and Broughton, J., "What Children Say and What They know: Exploring the Relations Between Product and Process in the Development of Early Words and Early Concepts," Language Behaviour in Infancy and Early Childhood (New York: Elsevier North Holland), Stark, R.E. (Ed.), 1981.

Boothroyd, A., Hearing Impairments in Young Children (Englewood Cliffs, New Jersey: Prentice-Hall), 1982.

Bowlby, J., Attachment and Loss: Volume I (Attachment) (New York: Basic Books), 1969.

Chomsky, N., Language and the Mind (New York: Harcourt, Brace, Jovanovich), 1968.

Corsaro, W., "The Development of Social Cognition in Pre-school Children: Implications for Language Learning," Language Disorders 2:77-95, 1981.

Dore, J., "A Pragmatic Description of Early Language Development," Journal of Psycholinguistic Research 3:343-350, 1974.

Erikson, E., Childhood and Society (New York: Norton Press), 1963.

Furth, H., Deafness and Learning: A Psychological Approach (Belmont, California: Wadsworth Press), 1973.

Gleason, J., and Weintraub, S., "The Acquisition of Routines in Child Language," Journal of the Linguistic Society 5:129-136, 1976.

Greenberg, M., and Marvin, R., "Attachment Patterns in Profoundly Deaf Preschool Children," Merrill-Palmer Quarterly 25:265-279, 1979.

Kretschmer, R.R., and Kretschmer, L., Language Development and Intervention with the Hearing-Impaired Child (Baltimore: University Park Press), 1978.

Litoff, S.G., and Feldman, V.J., "Treatment Issues with Deaf Children: An Eriksonian Perspective," Deafness and Mental Health (New York: Grune & Stratton, Inc.), Stein, L., Mindel, E., & Jabaley,T. (Eds.), 1981.

Piaget, J., and Inhelder, B., The Psychology of the Child (New York: Basic Books), 1969.

Schlesinger, H.S., "The Effects of Deafness on Childhood Development: An Eriksonian Perspective," Deaf Children: Developmental Perspectives (New York: Academic Press), Lieben, L.S. (Ed.), 1978.

Simmons-Martin, A., "Early Management Procedures for the Hearing Impaired Child," Pediatric Audiology (Englewood Cliffs, New Jersey: Prentice-Hall), Martin, F.N. (Ed.), 1978.

Sisco, F.H., Krantz, P.L., Lund, N.L., and Schwartz, G.C., "Developmental and Compensatory Play: A Means of Facili-tating Social, Emotional, Cognitive, and Linguistic Growth in Deaf Children," American Annals of the Deaf 124:850-857, 1979.

Tronick, E., "Infant Communicative Intent: The Infant's Reference to Social Situations," Language Behaviour in Infancy and Early Childhood (New York: Elsevier North Holland), Stark, R.E. (Ed.), 1981.

THE CHILD NEUROLOGIST'S CONTRIBUTION
TO THE CARE OF CHILDREN WITH HEARING LOSS

Isabelle Rapin
Albert Einstein College of Medicine, Bronx, New York

Few physicians have a great deal of experience with deaf (or blind) children: These children are not "ill". Since the severely to profoundly hearing impaired number approximately only 1 per 1000, most family physicians and pediatricians will have very few in their practice. Child neurologists and pediatricians specialized in child development and the care of chronically handicapped children are, by training, concerned with medical diagnosis, habilitation and special education. However, with the exception of those who work in speech and hearing centers and those attached to schools for the deaf, they are often inexperienced when it comes to the care of that special population.

All deaf children are seen by otolaryngologists. After an initial diagnostic evaluation and referral to an audiologist for habilitation, however, the otolaryngologist's role is typically limited to checking for middle ear effusion and external otitis, and to reviewing the most recent audiogram for a change in threshold. Parent counselling regarding management and education is often assigned to audiologists, speech pathologists, psychologists, and other non-medical professionals who follow the child in multi-disciplinary clinics or specialized schools. The situation is quite different in some countries in Europe, where audiologists are physicians concerned with all aspects of the management of the deaf.

My own interest in congenitally deaf children grew from the great difficulty I experienced as a resident working with babies in the clinical differential diagnosis between hearing loss and developmental dysphasia or other disorders of communication associated with autism, mental deficiency and other signs of brain dysfunction. The advent of

brainstem and cortical auditory evoked response tests has
changed matters by putting the diagnosis of peripheral hearing
loss on firmer ground; but thus far, those techniques have not
been of great assistance in the differential diagnosis of
other disorders of language processing.

What The Child Neurologist Can Do

The pediatric neurologist's first contribution to the
care of a deaf child is to try to determine whether that
child's clinical picture can be entirely ascribed to hearing
loss, possibly with associated vestibular dysfunction. If
not, then he will attempt to identify and assess the extent
and nature of any neurological deficit and then decide
whether that deficit and hearing loss are: 1) directly
related as integral parts of a common syndrome (e.g. Möbius
Syndrome); 2) separate consequences of a common insult (e.g.
congenital rubella or purulent meningitis), or, 3) whether
they both occurred fortuitously in a particular child. This
is, of course, followed with a decision regarding treatment.

The consequences for brain function of sensory deprivation, notably auditory, have, until recently, received little
attention. Now, they are starting to be evaluated in animal
models (Ruben & Rapin, 1980; Rapin, 1979). Besides the
obvious effects on acquisition of language and, secondarily,
on cognitive competence, the other consequences of deafness
on the brain function of man are essentially unknown.

The effects of congenital vestibular dysfunction on the
acquisition of early motor milestones like head control,
sitting balance, and the maintaining of an upright posture
were described early in the century (Prechechtel, 1925), but
have not attracted adequate attention and are still unknown
to most physicians, physical therapists, and other professionals. Children with impaired vestibular function often,
but not invariably, hold up their head, sit, and walk late,
and may crawl with the head hanging (Rapin, 1974; Kaga
et al., 1981). These signs are regularly ascribed to non-
existent "brain damage" when, in fact, it is cochlear

and vestibular function which are really impaired. For example, these signs may appear in purulent meningitis (Landthaler et al., 1974), congenital rubella (Chess et al., 1971), or Usher's Syndrome (Vernon, 1969). In my role as consultant child neurologist at St. Joseph's School for the Deaf in the Bronx, I often dismiss the complicating diagnosis of brain dysfunction and ask for vestibular tests for children who stumble in the dark and cannot walk on a balance bar. I also frequently dismiss the diagnosis of dysphasia complicating deafness in children who do not learn language as well as their teachers had hoped, and for whom alternate explanations for slow progress can be invoked.

Does the child neurologist have any role in the evaluation of deaf children who have no seizures, no obvious motor deficit, and no other overt evidence of brain dysfunction? In our institution, the majority of young infants with a documented hearing loss are screened by neurology at initial diagnosis, because so many of the causes of adventitious hearing loss (i.e. complications of prematurity, meningitis, and intrauterine infection) may damage both the brain and the ear. While this "extra referral" may seem a luxury, it does have the value of reassuring the parents of infants who are developmentally normal, and inversely, of detecting existing neurological or developmental deficits early so that they may be considered in the habilitation plan.

The contribution of the child neurologist is probably most valuable in somewhat older hearing impaired children whose development is slower than expected, who walk late and are clumsy, and/or whose acquisition of language or scholastic skills lags. Many of these children are erroneously not viewed as multiply handicapped, or else as having central nervous system dysfunction. The child neurologist's broad training enables him to take into account audiograms, evoked response records, vestibular tests, psychological and educational test results, and medical data, in order to arrive at a diagnosis. Keep in mind, however, that a deaf interpreter whom the child knows and trusts is required if an adequate assessment is to be obtained. In my own experience, this interpreter is more often the teacher than the mother. I shall come back to this point later.

The more subtle the suspected neurological deficit, the more important it is to find a child neurologist who has experience with hearing impaired children. Any child neurologist can evaluate and treat a convulsive disorder, but deciding whether or not a deaf child's particular behaviour has neurological implications is not an easy task.

How The Child Neurologist
Conducts An Examination

Since Pediatric Neurology is an unfamiliar field to many of those working with the deaf, describing what the Neurologist does may be the most expeditious way of indicating when this profession may be of service. None of what is done is unique, and some or much of it probably will have been done earlier by other physicians and professionals, but the Neurologists' unique, analytical point of view is their main contribution. Concerned with the integrity of brain function, the Neurologist will attempt to ascribe behavioural deficits to the dysfunction of specific brain systems and, if possible, to a particular etiology, and then consider the therapeutic implications of any findings.

The first step is to obtain the child's medical history including, in particular, details of the pregnancy and delivery, developmental milestones, intercurrent illnesses, and any potentially ototoxic drugs prescribed. The next step is to draw up a family tree, emphasizing consanguinity between the maternal and paternal lines and conditions in other family members which suggest a particular genetic deafness syndrome. For example, these may include a white forelock and irises of different colors (Waardenburg's Syndrome), goiter (Pendred's Syndrome), or sudden death in childhood (Jervell and Lange-Nielsen Syndrome).

The Pediatric Neurologist then performs a physical examination, looking especially carefully at the skin, pinnae, external ear canals, spine, and heart. An examination of the eye is critical, notably of the retina, since either chorioretinitis (which indicates an intra-uterine infection), or retinitis pigmentosa (pointing to Usher's Syndrome), would be a crucial finding for diagnosis. An examination of the genitalia is also important, as the genitourinary system forms approximately at the same time as the ear. In short, the examiner searches for any anomaly which might shed light on the cause of the hearing loss.

In the infant, the neurological examination emphasizes posture and tone, since motor deficits are frequent accompaniments of both brain dysfunction and vestibular lesions. A small baby can be rotated by the examiner who, holding the child up, inclines the infant's head 30°. A lack of nystagmus (rhythmical jerky movements of the eyes) at the end of rotation suggests defective vestibular function. This test is not reliable in older infants in whom visual fixation overrides the effects of vestibular stimulation. This clinical screening test should be supplemented by formal vestibular testing, ideally with a recording of eye movements (electronystagmography) as that provides a permanent record which can be reviewed as needed (Eviatar et al., 1979). A measure of the child's responsiveness to faces, cooing and babbling, smiling, reaching for objects, and localization to such sounds as crumpling paper, a small bell, or other noise makers, are as important as parts of the pediatric neurological evaluation as tapping the reflexes.

In older children, examination of gait, how the child manipulates small objects (i.e. 1" blocks, a pencil and paper), and how a ball is thrown and/or caught, provide more reliable data on the functional integrity of the motor system than manual motor testing and the reflexes. I make a point of having deaf children walk a line (tandem gait), or better still, on a balance bar, in order to assess the integrity of the vestibular system. Those in whom it is impaired have great difficulty with these tasks, as well as standing on one foot. This difficulty becomes insurmountable if one asks the child to close its eyes since, of the three systems required to maintain balance - vision, the vestibule, and sensory information from muscles and joints - two will, thus, be abolished.

The signs of neurological dysfunction are by no means restricted to sensory motor activity. They encompass disorders of higher order functions such as attention, memory,

cognition, language, and affect, and their assessment is part
of any neurological examination. In hearing impaired children, language use and communicative ability are evaluated,
including speech and speech reading, signing, gestures, nonverbal communicative interaction (regard, facial expression,
body language), and reading. I ask the child to copy graded
drawings, to reproduce block patterns, to read aloud with
signing and to read silently. I ask the child questions about
what was read, taking into account the deaf child's usual
difficulty with question forms (Quigley et al., 1974), and
utilizing questions appropriate to the child's level of linguistic development (Hsu, 1977).

I perform most of my neurological assessments of hearing
impaired children at the child's school, where I can take
advantage of the child's teacher as an interpreter and of
that individual's detailed awareness of the pupil's language
skills. Many deaf children of nursery school age experience
examination in school as much less stressful and threatening
than evaluation during a visit to a clinic or office, even
though the mother is rarely present when the child is seen in
school.

Unfortunately, many mothers of the inner city children I
am asked to see do not learn sign language and do not speak
English. Thus, they have only rudimentary language skills in
common with their child. As a result, they are often less
successful than teacher at getting the child to show what he
or she can do.

The next step is to review results of tests which have
already been obtained and to ask for others deemed necessary
(Rapin & Ruben, 1981). In infants, toddlers, and multiply
handicapped children, it should be routine to see brainstem,
and in some cases cortical auditory evoked responses, in
addition to behavioural audiograms and tympanometry. Laboratory tests should include: urinalysis and blood creatinine
to screen for renal disease or a genitourinary malformation;
antibody levels to check for intrauterine infections; an
electrocardiogram to screen for congenital heart disease and
cardiac conduction defects; and, mastoid radiographs to look
for unsuspected mastoiditis or malformation of the bony
labyrinth. We have seen sclerosis of the otic capsule in
some children whose deafness and dead labyrinths we were then
confidently able to ascribe to an earlier meningitic infection.

I have already stressed the importance of tests of vestibular function which should be administered to all children with serious hearing loss. One of our goals is to determine whether intact or impaired vestibular function may be helpful in discriminating amongst deafness syndromes. While some investigators express skepticism, the fact is that too few deaf children have had their vestibular function tested adequately to justify this skepticism.

Except under very special circumstances, tests such as electroencephalograms (EEG), computerized tomography (CT Scans), and laminograms of the temporal bones are not usually obtained. Chromosome tests are normal in children whose impaired hearing is the result of a single gene defect and, in our experience, have rarely been diagnostically useful in children with malformation syndromes affecting the ears (Rapin & Ruben, 1976). In contrast, both groups have such a high incidence of genito-urinary malformations that ultrasound examination of the kidneys should be carried out. In specific children, thyroid function tests and other examinations may be informative.

We make sure that deaf children are referred for an ophthalmological evaluation. Its purpose is two-fold: first, to ensure that the child has no refractive error requiring glasses, particularly because hearing impaired children depend so much on vision; and second, to examine the retina thoroughly for chorioretinitis and pigmentary degeneration, as discussed earlier.

Psychological test scores and, in older children, scholastic achievement scores, should be thoroughly reviewed since they provide a most sensitive assessment of brain function. Any IQ score in a preschool child must be considered nonpredictive, even though it may describe quite accurately the child's current level of function, since the cognitive skills and personality traits that will contribute most to adult intelligence are not yet fully developed. It is important to know if the hearing impaired child was tested by a psychologist with experience evaluating nonverbal children, and with an instrument such as the Wechsler Performance, Leiter, Hiskey-Nebraska, Snidjers/Oomen Nonverbal scales or Raven Matrices. Keep in mind even tests adequately standardized for the deaf assess a narrower range of competencies

than standard batteries with both verbal and nonverbal scales.
This somewhat limits their predictive value (Vernon, 1967;
Rapin, 1979). For any child, the full-scale IQ is not nearly
as informative as subtest scores where patterns yield a
profile of cognitive strengths and weaknesses. The profile
provides useful insights concerning the efficiency of particular brain systems (Rapin, 1982), and furnishes data which
help teachers design individualized teaching strategies to
capitalize on strengths in order to circumvent deficiencies.
The neuropsychological test profiles of the deaf have not
been studied systematically, but one can anticipate that they
will be just as informative as for the normal hearing child
(Wilson et al., 1975).

       Evaluation by a child psychiatrist, data concerning the
child's home circumstances provided by social workers and,
most valuable of all, reports by the child's teachers and
therapists regarding behaviour in the classroom and ability
to profit from various educational inputs and therapies and
to relate to adults and peers, round out the clinical picture.
These social and behavioural data are particularly important
for diagnosis when the child fails to progress as well as
expected, or when behaviour gives cause for concern.

                     Informing The Parents

       Each of the professionals - and there are many - who
interact with the parents of a hearing impaired child will
share with them the data collected. Unfortunately, each
professional speaks from the rather myopic point of view of
one discipline when answering the questions the parents are
bound to ask. While the professional should be on firm
ground in his own speciality, parents' questions do not fit
neatly into these specialities, so that each professional has
to answer broader questions. Those answers are likely to
conflict in some ways, even though perhaps only in wording
or emphasis, with what others have said, with resulting
confusion for the parents. To avoid this, definite statements and detailed recommendations should be deferred until
all the data are collected. This approach will work only
when all investigations are completed within a short time

span. It is good practice to invite both parents (without the child) and, if they wish, other family members, teachers, and therapists working with the child, to an open-ended, mutually informing conference. Remarks should be directed to the parents and not to the professionals, whose evaluations and recommendations should be collated and reconciled before the meeting. At a minimum, the professionals who participate in the conference should include an audiologist and an otologist with particular expertise and interest in childhood deafness, who does not see his role as terminated with the diagnosis of sensorineural hearing loss. In a pinch, the informing conference may be conducted by such a knowledgeable otologist, a child neurologist, or a pediatrician, provided all the data is available and provided that person is a true pro in the management of deaf children.

Physicians are singled out for this role because they can answer those questions which we find all parents ask concerning availability of drugs and surgical intervention, reversal of the hearing loss, its probable course, the interpretation of laboratory tests, and recurrence risks. It should be routine to provide genetic counselling, even in cases where the diagnosis is uncertain and recurrence risks, therefore, can be stated in only the most general way.

In our Center, we also discuss education, recommending the approach to language acquisition which we believe will maximize early progress. This approach is Total Communication in the case of all, or almost all, very young deaf children, especially the multiply handicapped. There are new data that indicate that signs, together with speech, foster linguistic development, assist rather than hinder the emergence of speech, and go a long way toward normalizing the deaf child's life experience at home - provided the parents are motivated to learn signs and use them as they speak to their child (Dee et al., 1982).

At each step in counselling, the parents must be given the opportunity to ask all the questions they may have. They should be provided with a concrete plan for habilitation that meets their needs and those of their child. Arrangements for ongoing and regular medical follow-up should be made, so that further clarification can be provided, since, no doubt, the parents will have absorbed only a part of what was said.

They should be sent a written summary of the conference which
they can review at their leisure. Utilizing all of these
approaches we, in our Center, hope to have achieved the goal
of providing as comprehensive and definitive a diagnosis as
possible from our first contact with the child and his family
and to enable them to move from the stage of query to the
stage of habilitation.

Summary

        A child neurologist's narrow role is to decide whether
a hearing impaired child has signs of brain dysfunction over
and above what can be attributed to the direct and indirect
consequences of hearing loss and, quite often, a parallel
vestibular dysfunction. At least some child neurologists
can play a much broader role because their training enables
them to assess cognitive and affective development and to
interpret the results of all the procedures that a deaf child
may have undergone, from audiometry and evoked responses, to
psychological and neuropsychological tests, to blood and
urine analysis, to radiographs. Because so many neurological
illnesses have a genetic etiology, child neurologists are
usually adept at genetic counselling. Genetic counselling
should always be made available to deaf adolescents and to
the parents of deaf children. In the absence of corroborat-
ing independent evidence, it takes a child neurologist with
considerable experience with deaf children to render an
opinion on whether problems such as lack of progress in
school, inadequate acquisition of language, an attention
deficit, or disordered behaviour should be attributed to
subtle complicating brain dysfunction, or whether they are
explained adequately by hearing loss and the circumstances
of the particular child's life and educational experience.
The child neurologist's greatest challenge is to decide how
much of a multiply handicapped child's atypical behaviour to
attribute to hearing loss and how much to brain dysfunction.
It is usually in the child's best interest for the neurologist
to defer an opinion and observe the child's progress while in
a program for the deaf where Total Communication is the
vernacular. Denial of access to this most specialized of all
interventions on a priori grounds because of neurological,

affective, or cognitive deficits is an error since the key-
stone for all habilitative effort is an effective channel for
communication. Furthermore, there is no way to predict
reliably at the start which of the deaf child's problems are
primary and which are secondary to lack of communication.
One of the surest signs of neurological experience is modesty
about one's ability to predict the future of a nonverbal child
coupled with an interventionistic attitude from the time of
first contact.

Discussion

M. DOWNS
    Do you have any prescription for the kinds of vestibular
tests you recommend, and at what ages?

I. RAPIN
    With the very young infant, that is, soon after birth and
prior to excellent visual fixation, one can screen by rotating
the child while holding the head down 30°. The child faces
you. This test is not valuable once good visual fixation has
been established because visual fixation overrides the effects
of post rotational nystagmus. For older children, we recommend
that electronystagmography be obtained. This has the great
advantage of giving you a permanent record allowing you to go
back and look at it again. One can also determine by looking
at the record whether this was a decent test or not. Sometimes a test is performed and a report is given. In looking
back at it, one realizes that it was really not a satisfactory
test, so we recommend doing electronystagmography in all hearing impaired children and rechecking results.

R. SHEA
    What do you do with the child who has a moderate to
severe hearing loss who, with aiding, is brought into a normal
range, and who still appears to have a problem with auditory
processing? In other words, they continue to have a receptive
and, of course, an expressive language delay.

I. RAPIN
       I think one should immediately dispell the idea that one
can bring any child with a severe hearing loss into the normal
range. It is true that one can amplify to the point that
there is perception of sounds at 10 or 20 or 0 dB, but that
does not mean a restoration of normal hearing. All that has
been done is to bring sounds which were previously below the
threshold of hearing into range. But the new range is
extremely narrow compared to the normal range. I think they
should be treated like severely hearing impaired children.
One of the things that I would recommend for such a child, if
progress is not made, is that Sign language be used with
language. In other words, Total Communication should be used.
I think that the idea that Total Communication is useful only
to the severe to profound hearing impaired child is just not
so. There are many neurologically handicapped children with
normal hearing who benefit greatly from Total Communication.
I don't see why this should not be the case for some children
with less severe hearing losses. I don't mean to say that
one will need Total Communication forever, but there are
children for whom it helps to get them started to use their
hearing in a more meaningful way.

K. MURPHY
       Am I correct in assuming that you would say that all
hearing impaired children should have vestibular testing?
Would it not be restricted to children who are, as it were,
not showing normal neuromotor functioning? Why give it to
children who are not causing distress or showing signs of
anything that would cause you to be suspicious?

I. RAPIN
       Well, for 2 reasons:
       1. When we work with very young children, we cannot
predict who will and who will not have trouble standing
upright or holding the head up. In fact, I have seen a number
of children with vestibular dysfunction who have walked at a
normal age. As a matter of fact, I have 2 siblings who turned
out to have Usher's Syndrome, and 1 walked at 10 months,
despite profound loss of vestibular function. So I think it's
very helpful.

       2. Lack of vestibular function is a strong factor to
make me look very carefully at the retina. It is among this
group that the Usher Syndrome children are found. One needs

to make this diagnosis because it will have very important implications for the entire educational approach, educational counselling, and so on. Vestibular testing is not harmful in any way, and I think one needs to collect data. I also think that it is just as important to know that certain syndromes are not associated with vestibular impairment, as it is to know that there are syndromes that are. I don't recommend that every child with a 30 dB hearing loss be tested, but certainly I would strongly recommend that the severe to profound be evaluated.

G. LIDEN

It is true that very many of the deaf children also have a dead labyrinth and don't have any vestibular function. It is easy to check vestibular function. It is not necessary to do ENG, because that's rather complicated and often you get a very unreadable recording. You can just irrigate with a syringe (100 ml – 30°C) on each side and see if you get a reaction. If you don't get one, you know that the child has bad function.

I. RAPIN

I think that we're talking of doing the same test. In some cases, I think that if one has available the ability to record eye movements, the advantage of having a permanent record is very great. I think one should be cautious, however, in realizing as in every test in medicine, there are both false positives and false negatives, so that if one is uncertain, one should probably repeat the test.

References

Barr, B., Stensland-Junker, K., and Svard, M., "Early Discovery of Hearing Impairment: A Critical Evaluation of the BOEL Test," Audiology 17:62–67, 1978.

Chess, S., Korn, S.J., and Fernandez, P.B., Psychiatric Disorders of Children with Congenital Rubella (New York: Brunner/Mazel), 1971.

Dee, A., Rapin, I., and Ruben, R.J., "Speech and Language
     Development in a Parent-Infant Total Communication Program,"
     Annals of Otology, Rhinology, and Laryngology, In Press.

Eviatar, L., Miranda, S., Eviatar, A., Freeman, K., and
     Borkowski, M., "Development of Nystagmus in Response to
     Vestibular Stimulation in Infants," Annals of Neurology
     5:508-514, 1979.

Hsu, J.R., A Developmental Guide to English Syntax: An Aid
     for Teachers in Facilitating the Acquisition of Linguistic
     Competence by Hearing Impaired Children (New York: St.
     Joseph's School for the Deaf), 1977.

Kaga, K., Suzuki, J., Marsh, R.R., and Tanaka, Y., "Influence
     of Labyrinthine Hypoactivity on Gross Motor Development of
     Infants," Annals of the New York Academy of Science 374:
     412-420, 1981.

Konigsmark, B.W., and Gorlin, R.J., Genetic and Metabolic
     Deafness (Philadelphia: W. B. Saunders), 1976.

Landthaler, G., and Andrieu-Guitrancourt, J., "Contribution
     à l'étude des Ataxies et des Surdités Secondaires aux
     Meningites Purulents de l'Enfant," Annals of Otolaryngology
     (Paris) 91:293-309, 1974.

Prečechtél, A., "Contribution a l'Etude de la Fonction
     Statique dans la Periode Foetale et dans la Première
     Periode de la Vie Extrauterine: Syndrome Typique du
     Défaut Congénital de l'Appareil Otolithique," Acta
     Otolaryngologica 7:206-226, 1925.

Quigley, S.P., Wilbur, R.B., and Montanelli, D.S., "Question
     Formation in the Language of Deaf Students," Journal of
     of Speech and Hearing Research 17:699-713, 1974.

Rapin, I., "Hypoactive Labyrinths and Motor Development,"
     Clinical Pediatrics 13:922-937, 1974.

Rapin, I., "Effects of Early Blindness and Deafness on
     Cognition," Congenital and Acquired Cognitive Disorders
     (New York: Raven Press), Katzman, R. (Ed.), 1979.

Rapin, I., Children with Brain Dysfunction: Neurology,
     Cognition, Language, and Behaviour (New York: Raven Press),
     1982.

Rapin, I., and Ruben, R.J., "Appraisal of Auditory Function in Children," Developmental Disabilities in Preschool Children (New York: S. P. Medical and Scientific Books), Lewis, M., and Taft, L.T. (Eds.), 1981.

Ruben, R.J., and Rapin, I., "Plasticity of the Developing Auditory System," Annals of Otology, Rhinology, and Laryngology 89:303-311, 1980.

Vernon, M., "Relationship of Language to the Thinking Process," Archives of General Psychiatry 16:325-333, 1967.

Vernon, M., "Usher's Syndrome - Deafness and Progressive Blindness: Clinical Cases, Prevention, Theory and Literature Survey," Journal of Chronic Disorders 22:133-151, 1969.

Wilson, J.J., Rapin, I., Wilson, B.C., and VanDenburgh, F.V., "Neuropsychologic Function of Children with Severe Hearing Impairment," Journal of Speech and Hearing Research 18: 634-652, 1975.

MANUAL AIDS: A MUST FOR THE PSYCHOTIC DEAF
AND A FAIL-SAFE MEASURE FOR OTHER DEAF CHILDREN

Olivier Perier
Anne Bochner-Wuidar
Centre Comprendre et Parler, Bruxelles, Belgium

An intensive oral-aural habilitation program has been implemented at the Brussels Centre Comprendre et Parler (CCP) and Integrated School (IS), an educational facility for the deaf which has, since 1961, been closely linked to a school for normal hearing children.

The program includes early intervention, early hearing aid fitting, auditory training, parental support and participation, and the utilization of Guberina's verbo-tonal method (1981) which stresses the importance of the rhythm and prosody of speech for language development. As well as music and body rhythm, the method also places great emphasis on the need to attend to the deaf child's voice quality early in the habilitation process in order to prevent initiation of faulty vocal habits. Exploitation of vibro-tactile perception, another important aspect of the Guberina approach, is widely applied at CCP and IS.

Mainstreaming hearing impaired children who can, with adequate support, hold their own in an ordinary school, has been a prominent feature of the program from the beginning. The results, considered satisfactory when compared to those most often observed in the field of education of the deaf, have been described elsewhere (Perier et al., 1980). All of the moderately deaf (40-70 dB) and a high proportion of the severely deaf (70-90 dB) achieved good speech and language and were being successfully mainstreamed. Among the profoundly deaf, 30% achieved mainstreaming at some stage in the schooling process. The remainder had to pursue education in the special school with partial mainstreaming for some subject matter.

Most of the older students in the study were satisfied with the oral-aural education they had received, and considered that it had been a determining factor in their social integration into the hearing world.

Some of the profoundly deaf students, however, despite intensive habilitation measures, did not develop satisfactory speech and speech reading skills. Their language level, as judged by reading and composition, was direly insufficient. Several expressed resentment at having been kept in ignorance and mistrust of Sign language. This lead us to a reappraisal of the overall results, including those which were considered "good". The conclusion drawn was that even our "good" language level results were not good enough for the profoundly deaf.

Previously, it had been considered unavoidable that the language level of the deaf would be at least somewhat inferior to the average level of the hearing population. In that sense, it can be said that in addition to the primary sensory impairment of deafness, it was accepted that they should have a secondary disability, language deficiency, as a necessary consequence of the first.

During the last 10 years, as our program attracted increasing interest, more and more severely handicapped children requested admission. Among these, several had psychological problems which appeared to be a consequence of the communication difficulties which arise in a family because of a child's hearing impairment.

Paradoxically, the rich, nonverbal communication which normally exists between a baby and its parents is often reduced drastically following diagnosis of hearing impairment. For some children, this disruption takes place at a crucial period in the development of personality, and is liable to be conducive to the evolution of a full-fledged psychosis. For other children, the ultimate consequences are less severe, but they may still provoke such psychotic-like symptoms as massive regression, infolding upon self, depression, severe instability, and impoverishment of motor and cognitive skills.

The psychological disturbances we saw associated with deafness seemed to fall into 2 categories: 1) true psychosis requesting specific psychiatric therapy; and, 2) psychotic-like symptoms which could be alleviated or completely corrected by a restoration of adequate communication. Some of the children in the second category also needed concomitant psychiatric therapy.

In 1980, no specific program was available in Belgium, nor in most European countries, for deaf children with psychiatric problems, most of whom were directed toward schools for the deaf where they were often grouped with the mentally retarded. The children were usually not subjected to any psychiatric investigation or therapy until the beginning of adulthood, by which time they had irreversible personality defects and severe intellectual and academic retardation. The alternative, that of directing psychotic deaf children towards institutions specializing in normally hearing psychotic children, was not satisfactory either since their deafness was not adequately considered and it prevented them from having full access to the therapeutic measures utilized with hearing children.

It should be stressed that this situation was peculiar to the deaf since nearly all normally hearing psychotic children were taken in charge by a pedopsychiatric consultation before entry in primary school. This difference may be due to the absence of involvement by any psychiatrist in the difficult communication problems encountered with deaf children. It may also be the result of poor information provided to teachers of the deaf about the normal development of a child's personality and about the alarm signals which can point to an anomaly in this development. Such signals are obviously more difficult to perceive with a poorly communicating deaf child than with a normally hearing one.

Pressure resulting from our team's helplessness with respect to the specific needs of psychotic deaf children prompted the implementation of a new specific program for them. In addition, our concerns for the non-psychotic deaf child led us to the introduction of supplementary methods of communication in the parental guidance and school programs of CCP and IS. The results of both approaches are quite interesting.

Hearing Impaired Children
(Non-psychotic)

In order to prevent the secondary handicap of language deficiency in addition to deafness, two alternative methods of communication, Cued Speech (Cornett, 1967) and Bimodal Communication (Schlesinger, 1978), were considered and thoroughly discussed.

Cued Speech is a complement to speech reading. Phonemes
which are ambiguous or not visible on the lips are clarified
by manual "cues". This is accomplished through 8 configura-
tions of the fingers placed in 4 different positions of the
hand relative to the speaker's mouth. The finger's configuration provides information about the consonants, while the
hand's position reflects the vowel sounds. Complete information about each phoneme is provided through association of
the combined information provided by the lips and the hand.
Since Cued Speech is essentially a method for the visual
perception of speech, it is the hearing person who makes the
cues when speaking.

Cued Speech provides for a deaf child through the visual
channel, pertinent information about phonemes comparable in
informational capacity to that which the hearing child
receives through the auditory channel. If used consistently,
it can facilitate understanding of spoken language at a
relatively normal pace, and simultaneously, nearly automatically impregnate grammatical structure. A criticism often
levelled at Cued Speech is that it is too difficult for an
infant to master the cues expressively. The deaf child is,
therefore, denied the possibility of early expressive communication, an essential part of the language learning process.
It has been reported, however, that some children have
developed expressive language at a satisfactory rate when
Cued Speech was consistently used as a reinforcement of
spontaneous babbling from a very early age.

In bimodal communication, parents and therapists speak
and sign simultaneously, using Signed English (or in this
case, Signed French) rather than the proper Sign Language of
the Deaf. Bimodal communication allows the prompt installa-
tion of efficient communication with the deaf child, who not
only manages to easily understand what is said and signed,
but also quickly learns to express himself, having no difficulty in reproducing those signs for which meaning has been
grasped. The child is thereby provided at an early age with
a language having the same syntactic structure as spoken
language; a language which can, indeed, be considered a
"mother tongue" presented in two simultaneous modalities,
oral and manual. The child can simultaneously process both
modalities through the visual channel and concomitantly
utilize residual hearing to obtain coherent additional information through the auditory channel.

With both Cued Speech and bimodal communication, the
early, easy acquisition of linguistic structure facilitates
the transition to purely oral modes of comprehension and
expression. These can develop without the inherent stress
and frustration experienced from trying to learn them through
a purely oral-aural methodology which brings incomplete and
insufficient information for acquiring language through a
natural learning process.

For the last few years, all the logopeds, teachers, and
the Medical Director of our Centre, have been trained in Cued
Speech and most of them, plus pertinent personnel, have also
started to learn Signed French in order to practice bimodal
communication.* Parents of children already in the school
have been informed about these two methods and encouraged to
train in at least one of them in order to improve communication with, and improve the language development of their own
deaf child. Several have done so. The majority, however,
had already settled into habits of approximate language
intercourse. This is satisfactory for day-to-day, matter-of-
fact communication and, thus, many parents could not be
motivated to make the effort to acquire and practice the new
skills.

A quite different and much more encouraging situation
prevails with the parents of hearing impaired children
enrolled in the program since June, 1980. In order to enable
them to choose that for which they feel most capable and
motivated, all these parents have been thoroughly informed
about both methods, provided with occasions to witness their
implementation, and given an opportunity to engage in a few
preliminary training sessions. Presently, there are 13 hearing impaired children from 1 to 4 years of age, with whom we
have consistently used one of the supplementary methods for a
minimum of 6 months to a maximum of 2 years. Seven of the
families chose Cued Speech, 3 adopted Signed French, and 2
did not make any choice and did not become seriously involved
in the habilitation process. One family was so intent on
using all the available possibilities to restore communication with their 17 month old boy, Simon, that they were
reluctant to choose any one method. They felt that by so
doing, they could deprive him of something which might be

---

*Thanks to the collaboration of Deaf Sign Teachers, Mr.
& Mrs. M. Rasquinet

useful, and thus fall short of the very best. Of their own
decision, and despite the wariness expressed by CCP's team,
they chose to combine the two methods, the mother specializing
at first in Cued Speech, and the father in Signed French.

Of the 13 youngsters, 1 of the eldest, a child with a
severe hearing loss whose parental participation could not be
obtained, was seriously emotionally disturbed. Another child,
having suffered from serious neonatal pathology with sequelae
of epilepsy, cataract in one eye, and retinopathy in the
other, which lesions resulted in very poor sight, is severely
multiply handicapped. Apart from these 2 children whose
progress has been relatively slow, all the others display much
better communication with parents and logopeds than was previously observed at corresponding ages and after corresponding
periods of habilitation. The language level attained by the 8
children who have benefitted from the new program for 1 year
or more is patently and considerably higher than what was
achieved previously. The best results have been obtained with
those children with whom one or both methods is consistently
used by the parents.

Two of the children who use Cued Speech alone, and little
Simon whose parents decided to combine it with Signed French,
are particularly impressive as far as language comprehension
is concerned. All 3 (age range: 2-6 to 3-3) understand "all
that one says to them", displaying a language comprehension
level at least equal to that of most hearing children of the
same age. All 3 are also using language expressively. The
first 2 on Cued Speech alone, have a definite time lag as
compared to comprehension skills, their present expression
consisting of speech sometimes accompanied by baby cues.
Simon expresses himself alternately or simultaneously with
Signed French, speech, and baby cues. His expressive capacities are on par with his comprehension skills and display a
remarkable mastery of syntax. A few examples are:

  1. When he was less than 3, he had learned the idiom
      expression "tu es casse-pied", "you are a pain in the
      foot". On seeing that Simon's logoped was being
      bothered by the dog, his mother told him "Snoopy est
      casse-pied." Simon corrected her: "Non, pas casse-
      pied, casse-pattes," meaning "paw-breaker".
  2. A little before he was 3, he told his mother about
      his little sister, "Caroline n'entend pas. Tu dois
      lui acheter une petite prosthese." (Caroline was
      cued, the rest signed).

3. Recently (at 3 years-2 months), as Simon was dis-
    playing a wounded knee, the psychologist asked him
    what happened and he answered "Je suis tombe a cause
    Snoopy"   (I fell down because of Snoopy), the a and
    Snoopy being cued, the rest signed.

Simon's parents are now using more and more Cued Speech,
particularly because, with their limited knowledge of Signed
French, they cannot keep pace with Simon's vocabulary
explosion and also because they feel that it is now the best
way to develop his knowledge of spoken language.

It was decided by common assent of all members of the
staff in the Integrated School to utilize Cued Speech in all
primary and secondary grades. It was felt that this method
would permit good communication with correct linguistic
structure which, in turn, would result in a simplification of
teaching procedures and an improvement of the children's
language level.

In the maternal classes, after a brief trial of Cued
Speech alone which was not successful with those children
who had no support from the family, it was decided to use
bimodal communication. Later on, based on the observations
of Simon and his family, we adopted a blend of bimodal communication and Cued Speech. That is, all proper names and
function words for which there is no sign are cued, permitting
the children to progressively absorb the code of Cued Speech.
In addition, when the meaning of a sign has been acquired,
that word is repeated with Cued Speech or first presented in
this manner, then explained or confirmed by its sign.

When Simon's parents started this system on their own,
several members of the staff had strong reservations against
this "hodge-podge", fearing that it might confuse and bewilder
the child. However, observation of Simon's progress and
capacity to sort out cues and signs, as well as further
theoretical reflection, overcame those reservations. Whether
with cues or with signs, it is the same language, French,
which is presented. Since the word is always spoken simultaneously, there is a constant visuo-acoustic image for lip-
reading and residual hearing utilization.

As a neurologist interested in neuropsychology, the
senior author is impressed with the high degree of plasticity
exhibited by a child's brain. It is gifted with unpredictable
capacities for compensation when it is damaged or unable to
function as genetically planned. One should trust it to
accomplish highly elaborate performances, even when it is not
clear through which cognitive processes it does so. All it
seems to require are the necessary "nutrients", that is,
appropriate information channeled through adequate sensory
receptors and neural pathways. The acquisition of language
through hearing for a normally hearing child is, in itself,
a formidable cognitive process which utilizes complicated and
not fully understood strategies. One should not, therefore,
underestimate the brain's capacity to sort out complex information presented to it, or fear that it will become muddled
just because it is not theoretically clear how it is going to
sort things out. It is too early to evaluate the results of
the widespread utilization of these new methods in the school.
However, observations of the language progress of young
children with whom they were used from the beginning of
habilitation, warrant the assumption that their sustained use
will effectively prevent (or at least considerably reduce)
the supplementary language handicaps which beset nearly all
profoundly deaf children.

Furthermore, the use of bimodal communication with those
children already at school who were not making good progress
in oral language and displayed psychotic-like behaviours has
resulted in an important improvement for many of them. This
has been most impressive in those children whose families have
agreed to collaborate and to use bimodal communication with
their child. In several cases, a dramatic improvement in the
inter-familial relationship has resulted, the parents re-
discovering the child they had lost, and the child reacting
by regression of, and sometimes complete suppression of
abnormal behaviours. These observations seem to confirm that
early use of adequate methods of communication with deaf
children prevent the development of supplementary psychological disturbances. These communication methods can, therefore, be considered a means of reducing the number of psychologically involved multihandicapped deaf children.

Hearing Impaired Children (Psychotic)
Centre Lui et Nous (Him and Us)

Without attempting any etiological definition, one may
consider infantile psychosis as a severe disturbance of

personality consisting of a disorder of the organization of
Self and of the relationship between the child and the real
world. Psychosis varies in features and intensity, from
Kanner's autism characterized by a complete lack of contact
with the real world, to some types of psychological dysharmony
allowing for partial adaptation to the environment.

While it seems that the sensory deprivation associated
with deafness can be conducive to psychosis, no clear relationship between these two conditions emerged from the review
of de Ajuriaguerra and Abensur (1972). However, most of the
psychologists and psychiatrists working with the deaf feel
that the proportion of severe emotional disturbances among
deaf children is larger than in the general population
(Schlesinger & Meadow, 1972).

In the evolution of a psychosis in a hearing child, the
onset of language has considerable prognostic value. The
word, through its symbolic function, gives the child a chance
to pull out of his total "subjectivity" and gain access to
other people's "objectivity". The sentence, when it appears,
allows for real communication. It is, therefore, of paramount
importance that an institution designed to treat psychosis
should use a language suitable to children. As soon as any
child becomes ready to accept or request language, he should
have easy access to it. In order to meet this requirement for
hearing autistic children, the use of Sign language has been
advocated by Creedon (1972), Miller and Miller (1973),
Fulwiler and Fouts (1976), and Salvin et al., (1977). In the
case of deaf psychotic children, it seems even more obvious
that the requirement for an easily accessible language can be
satisfied only by some form of Sign language.

During the year prior to the creation of the Centre Lui
et Nous (Him and Us), the team of Centre Comprendre et Parler
tried to do something for a 15 year old psychotic deaf girl.
The work carried out with her provided the team with the
necessary impetus to undertake the creation of the Centre.
The story of this deaf girl well illustrates what had been the
prevailing situation:

Nancy has a profoundly deaf twin sister and 3 elder
brothers and sisters, 1 of whom is also deaf. The
parents noticed a difference in behaviour between
their twin daughters soon after birth. Nancy had
no contact with her surroundings, did not respond
to facial expression, did not smile, and was passive

in her crib. Her motor activity was stereotyped,
and from the age of 2 she became self-aggressive
and violent. At that same age, both twins were
admitted to a day centre for deaf children, where
Nancy showed no response to the speech and hearing
habilitation process. When she was 4, she transferred to a day centre for psychotic children with
normal hearing, which she attended consistently
until the age of 14. Her behaviour was progressively modified, in the sense that she became more
reactive to external stimulation, though remaining
violent and highly vulnerable to the slightest
frustration. Except for a few poor quality signs
developed and exchanged with the family, her
language remained at point zero.

During all these years, the psychiatric team of
that Centre confirmed Nancy's psychotic state,
but denied she was deaf. The parents, however,
with the experience of deafness in their other
children, remained uncertain. Finally they
decided to submit Nancy to electrocochleography.
That procedure confirmed their doubts and the
earlier diagnosis of the Centre Comprendre et
Parler. Nancy was profoundly deaf. Since there
was no available program which could cope with
her double handicap, and since she was more and
more reluctant to attend the Centre for Psychotic
Children, the parents decided to keep her at
home. They asked CCP to provide a logoped
experienced in home training of deaf children
by both the oral-aural methodology and Signed
French. Despite all the difficulties attending
any type of pedagogic action with psychotic
patients, Nancy did eventually acquire a commend-
able sign vocabulary and began to establish a
rich communication with her family and the logoped.
It is widely recognized in the field that if
children with infantile psychosis have not acquired
language by the age of 6 or 7, they rarely develop
it later. In Nancy's case, it is highly probable
that psychiatric treatment had resulted in an
affective and intellectual readiness for language,
but that it had remained inaccessible to her in an
oral modality.

Presently, Nancy is in a recently created psychiatric unit for deaf children near Paris. This
unit, located in a large psychiatric institution,
utilizes Sign language with psychotic and other
physiologically disturbed deaf children, and
applies a jointly therapeutic and pedagogic
program. Close contacts are maintained with her
family, who visit her about once a month and
where she returns for part of the holidays. Her
Sign language communication and behaviour continue to develop and improve.

Nancy's favourable evolution was both an incentive and a
guideline for the creation of Centre Lui et Nous. This program started in September, 1981, with a team consisting of
1 pedo-psychiatrist, psychologist, logoped, psychomotrician,
secretary, and 3 educators, 1 of them being a deaf woman.
Most members of the team had professional experience with
deaf and/or psychotic children. Some of them have a good
command of Signed French, all others are in the process of
training.

The Centre is foremost a place for children to live.
From their arrival in the morning, the day is spent going
through vital activities which are ritualized: greetings;
preparation of the meal; eating the meal; nap for some;
departure. There are also outdoor activities such as swimming
or going shopping. Children who are ready for them, are
offered individual sessions in psychomotricity, logopedics, or
psychotherapy. Pedagogic activities are also proposed as soon
and as often as a child is amenable to them.

The therapeutic approach is based on trying to understand
behaviour, the child's interactions with adults or with peers,
and a group analysis of the therapist's reactions towards
them. This reflexive process is ever present, constitutes the
core of the team work and, in addition, allows each therapist
to pursue his own specific activity.

The permanent presence of an educator who is also deaf
guarantees the use of Signed French between adults as well as
with the children. Moreover, current observations demonstrate
that the "expressive style" of the young woman in our Centre
particularly challenges hearing impaired children. Her nonverbal communication with those children who are most

severely disturbed is of a very different essence than that of
the hearing, non-native, signing members of the team. Sustained therapeutic work with the parents with whom the children continue to live outside the Centre is carried out on an
individual basis along different modalities. For some, the
program consists of frequent (weekly or fortnightly) conversations with the psychiatrist in the Centre; for others, there
are more widely spaced interviews. For others yet, interaction between the team and the parents takes place in the
home. Although work with the parents has been set as a
requisite for the admission of a child into the Centre, it has
seemed best to establish a relationship with them progressively, rather than to impose on them a rigid schedule from the
start. It was originally hoped that would induce in parents
a desire for reflection and dialogue. While certainly a
slower approach to bear fruit, it has seemed to prove to be
more efficient in the long run.

Presently, 5 children ranging in age from 2.5 to 10
years attend the Centre daily and full-time, while 4 more
come to it several times a week on a part-time basis. All of
the children except the 2 youngest ones were attending special
schools prior to their admission and only 1 had attended
institutions or programs for psychotic children. The one exception had attended a centre for normally hearing psychotic
children for 1 year.

After only 10 months of operation, no firm results are
available, but some general ideas emerge concerning the
evolution of Lui et Nous's children.

1. All the children who had been or were in schools
    went through a period of "unconditioning" in respect
    to the habits artificially established in the
    previous school setting. For all of them, this
    period was one of deep anxiety.

2. After this first period, all the children have
    achieved a truer relationship with adults, more
    adequate to their needs, desires and real capacities.

3. Some children have undergone an important evolution
    in language, others have not (the elder profoundly
    psychotic child, 10 years old on admission, has not
    acquired a single sign within these 10 months).

4. In the field of intellectual achievements, all
    children have progressed toward more real
    interests and some demand for organized activities.

A more concrete illustration of the type of evolution
observed is provided by the case study of Marin, a little boy
who was 6 years old on admission in September, 1981.

Marin has a bilateral perceptive hearing loss.
Clinical audiometry could only be performed
recently, and shows a 75 dB mean threshold on
the right, and an 89 dB threshold on the left.
He is, therefore, in the category of severe
auditory deficiency. He is also afflicted with
several congenital malformations: a facio-digito-
vertebro-costal dysmorphic syndrome; an absence of
the right kidney; and valgus flat feet. Psychomotor retardation and a slight bilateral pyramidal
syndrome were observed when he was 2 years. No
data in his familial or personal history was
relevant to any etiological factor for either his
deafness or the malformations.

Marin has benefited from the age of 2 years-9 months
from an early habilitation program for hearing
impaired children. He was admitted to the maternal
section of IS at the age of 3 years-8 months. He
appeared as a very clumsy toddler. During motor
activities, the different parts of his body seemed
completely dissociated. He had no relationship
with his peers except some rare aggressive bouts,
and did not participate in any group activities.
With adults, he adopted a completely regressive
behaviour. There was no evidence of any learning
process, whether in the area of language or of so-
called "awakening" activities aimed at stimulating
the development of cognitive processes. His preferred activity was to play with water. When not
engaged in this, he would spend hours sucking four
fingers of his right hand while profusely drooling
in the process. At the age of 5, since he was
making no progress and considering that this
psychiatric condition was more in need of specific
institutional care than his hearing impairment, the
IS team recommended his transfer to a Centre for
Psychotic Children, the same one that had cared for
Nancy for many years. He attended that Centre for
one year prior to his admission to Lui et Nous at age 6.

On admission to Lui et Nous, he displayed improvement in the extent of his interaction with other
persons, although the interactions oscillated
unwarrantedly between global regression and an
impulsive and indiscriminate aggressivity.
Probably due to 1 year of psychiatric help, Marin
adapted to Lui et Nous faster than the other
children. One month after admission, he was using
his first sign, "to sleep". Shortly thereafter,
he integrated the signs used by adults into his
communication process. In the beginning, he would
ask for them in the setting of stereotyped drawing
activities: the therapist would draw an object,
then show the sign for it. Marin would look at
him or her as if he discovered an extraordinary
link between the symbol and the object. Somewhat
later, he would, himself, designate the drawn
object by its sign. Formerly, Marin would suddenly
fall asleep several times a day. Since the first
time he was able to sign "to sleep", this has not
reoccurred. His acquisition of the signs for
"pipi" and "caca" coincided with the beginning of
toilet training.

Little by little, Marin continues to introduce
appropriate signs into his communication, first
with adults, later with children, sometimes with
animals. He presently understands a little under
100 signs and utilizes about 50 of them. From
the single word sentence, he has progressed to the
understanding of a 4- to 5-signs proposition and
he, himself, uses 2- or 3-word signs in succession.
His vocabulary, as is characteristic of most
psychotic children, consists principally of nouns,
although he does utilize 4 or 5 verbs. He never
signs adjectives or pronouns.

Parallel to his language evolution, his behaviour
has also undergone modifications:

1. His interactions with peers are more frequent
    and richer;

2. He now shows interest in such activities as
    pushing shapes into holes, sorting out similar
    objects, or construction games. These interests
    are new, since previously he even refused to
    look at the materials as if he did not dare to
    involve himself with them.

These encouraging results are probably partly due to the relatively young age of this child, and to the preparatory psychiatric work done by the Centre which he attended during the previous year. However, his evolution since admission to Lui et Nous seems to illustrate what can be hoped for and accomplished with psychotic deaf children, especially when such a program can be started early. Joined with the observations made with the other children who have progressed, although some not as strikingly or in the same manner, Marin's evolution is an incentive for the team of Lui et Nous, and for all of us to pursue action despite all the material difficulties which such an enterprise encounters. We are supported in our determination by the strong personal relationship which several of us have developed with several children, certainly an important factor in their rehumanization, and a true justification for the term "Lui et Nous" (Him and Us).

Acknowledgement

The work reported in this paper is supported by Grant #3.4553.79 from the Belgian Fonds de la Recherche Scientifique Medicale.

References

Ajuriaguerra, J. de., and Abensur, J., "Désordres Psycho-pathologiques Chez l'Enfant Sourd," Psychiatric Enfant, pp. 217-244, 1972.

Cornett, R.O., "Cued Speech," American Annals of the Deaf 112:3-13, 1967.

Creedon, M.P., Appropriate Behaviour Through Communication: A New Program in Simultaneous Language for Non-Verbal Children (Chicago: Dysfunctioning Child Center Publications), 1973.

Fulwiler, R.L., and Fouts, R.S., "Acquisition of American Sign Language by a Noncommunicating Autistic Child," Journal of Autism and Childhood Schizophrenia 6:43-51, 1976.

Guberina, P., and Asp, C., The Verbo-Tonal Method (New York: World Rehabilitation Fund Monographs), 1981.

Miller, A., and Miller, S., "Cognitive-Developmental Training with Elevated Boards and Sign Language," Journal of Autism and Childhood Schizophrenia 3:65-85, 1973.

Perier, O., Capouilliz, J.M., and Paulissen, D., "The Relationship Between the Degree of Auditory Deficiency and the Possibility of Successful Mainstreaming in Schools for Hearing Children," First International Congress of the Hard of Hearing (Hamburg: Deutscher Schwerhorigenbund), Hartmann, H. (Ed.), 1980.

Salvin, A., Routh, D.K., Foster, R.E., Jr., and Lovejoy, K.M., "Acquisition of Modified American Sign Language by a Mute Autistic Child," Journal of Autism and Childhood Schizophrenia 7:359-371, 1977.

Schlesinger, H.S., "The Acquisition of Bimodal Language," Sign Language of the Deaf (New York: Academic Press), Schlesinger, I.M., and Namir, L. (Eds.), 1978.

Schlesinger, H.S., and Meadow, K.P., Sound and Sign (Berkeley: University of California Press), 1972.

CONSIDERATIONS FOR EVALUATING HEARING

Arthur J. Dahle
Faye P. McCollister
University of Alabama in Birmingham, Birmingham, Alabama

Greater numbers of children are being identified who have handicapping conditions in addition to hearing impairment (Moores, 1978). Surveys of educational programs for the hearing impaired, compiled by the Office of Demographic Studies at Gallaudet College, show that the number of multiply handicapped, hearing impaired children enrolled in school programs has grown rapidly since 1968 (Gelatt et al., 1982).

One of the latest reported demographic surveys (Karchmer, Milone & Wolk, 1979) indicated that in 1977-78, 28% of the hearing impaired students had one or more additional handicaps, while approximately 65% of the multiply handicapped, hearing impaired children had a severe-to-profound hearing loss. Analysis of the percent distributions for handicapping conditions indicated that the most frequently occurring associated handicaps were mental retardation (7.8%), visual impairment (7.8%), and emotional/behavioural problems (6.7%). Unfortunately, these impairments often complicate the assessment of hearing sensitivity. For example, the presence of visual problems may preclude the use of visual reinforcement audiometry, while children with mental retardation and/or behavioural disorders are frequently difficult to condition to behavioural procedures.

Although evaluating a multiply handicapped child is not an easy task, there are audiometric procedures and techniques which may be used effectively with this population. Many were, of course, originally developed for testing normal infants. The early studies conducted by Ewing and Ewing (1944), Downs (1947), Hardy, Dougherty and Hardy (1959) and others provided evidence that behavioural responses to sound could be elicited in newborns and young infants. Programs

171

for the identification of hearing impaired infants developed
during the 1960s (DiCarlo & Bradley, 1961; Downs & Sterritt,
1964; Davis, 1965) helped to refine the behavioural observation audiometric procedures which are also applicable to
multiply handicapped children (Lloyd & Frisina, 1965). The
use of novel visual activities in testing young children,
such as those employed in the peep show (Dix & Hallpike, 1947)
and the pup show (Green, 1958), demonstrated that visual
stimuli could serve as an effective reinforcer for eliciting
behavioural responses to sound. Suzuki and Ogiba (1961)
extended the use of visual reinforcement to very young children by using a visual stimulus to reinforce a child's natural
tendency to localize towards a sound source. This procedure,
known as Conditioned Orientation Reflex (COR) audiometry, has
been shown to be useful when testing the mentally retarded
(Fulton & Graham, 1966). A modification of the COR method
has proven effective for assessing hearing in infants (Moore,
Wilson & Thompson, 1977) and low functioning children
(Thompson, Wilson & Moore, 1979).

Much of the work with older multiply handicapped, hearing impaired individuals has involved development of procedures for use with the retarded. The pioneering work by
Kodeman et al., (1958), Schlanger (1962), Lloyd (1965), and
Fulton (1967), pointed toward the development of audiological
procedures useful with this population. Fulton and Lloyd
(1975) present detailed information on behavioural and physiological methods which can be used for evaluating the hearing
of the retarded or other difficult-to-test subjects.

Unfortunately, in spite of the fact that methodologies
are available for testing the hearing of the multiply handicapped, many audiologists are unsure of how to approach the
task of evaluating a child who may have visual, mental, motor,
and/or linguistic impairments. The audiological assessment
of the multiply handicapped requires knowledge of appropriate
procedures, proper structuring of the test environment, perceptive judgment of response behaviour, and most of all,
patience and perserverance. The remainder of this chapter
focuses on the procedures and methodologies found to be useful
in evaluating auditory sensitivity in young, multiply handicapped children.

Asking The Right Questions

A detailed case history should be obtained prior to performing the audiological evaluation. The information will aid in selecting appropriate test procedures and in interpreting the results. Probably the most important question to ask concerns the parents' possible suspicion that their child has a hearing problem. Most parents have a fairly accurate impression of their child's hearing ability and are frequently the first to detect a hearing deficit. However, with multiply handicapped children, it is sometimes difficult to differentiate between a true loss of hearing sensitivity and a generalized lack of attending skills. Questions concerning consistency of response to sound stimulation in comparison to visual and tactile stimulation may provide clues to help clarify the nature of the problem. The parents should be questioned about the presence of congenital high risk factors for hearing impairment (ASHA, 1982), and any illnesses (e.g. bacterial meningitis) which could cause a loss of hearing. A history of congenital rubella or cytomegalovirus (CMV) should alert the clinician to the possibility of progressive hearing impairment (Gerber & Mencher, 1980; Dahle et al., 1979). The case history of a child with a progressive hearing loss may contain conflicting information, especially where it concerns the child's hearing and language development.

Information concerning physical problems should be included so that behavioural patterns may be viewed in relation to the child's general health. Many multiply handicapped children have serious health problems which necessitate being on medication (e.g. seizures and metabolic disorders). The amount and types of medication the child may be receiving should be taken into consideration when evaluating responses to behavioural audiometry. Indications of middle ear problems, allergies, and chronic upper respiratory congestion should also be noted. For example, mentally retarded children often have a high incidence of middle ear disorders and, in particular, children with Down's Syndrome are known to often have chronic middle ear disease (Balkany, 1980).

A detailed developmental history serves an important role in the assessment process. Motor and social development may be utilized to estimate the child's approximate developmental age and to indicate which audiological procedures might be most appropriate. The ability to pre-select the most appropriate procedures provides for more efficient use of the time allotted for testing, and improves the likelihood of obtaining valid responses.

In addition to being skilful in asking the right questions, the audiologist must develop a keen awareness of the physical traits which may be indicators of the genetic syndromes or diseases associated with hearing impairment. Documentation of a specific syndrome aids in establishing the time of onset of a disorder, the nature and probable course of the problem, and the likelihood of having additional handicapping conditions. For example, Campbell et al., (1981) presented evidence to show the importance of identifying visual abnormalities as an aid to determining the cause of congenital hearing impairment. Their records of ophthalmological examinations helped in diagnosing such conditions as Usher's Syndrome, congenital toxoplasmosis, and congenital rubella. They found the results of the visual evaluation to be important in determining the etiology of hearing impairment in 16% of 64 children examined.

It is also helpful to observe the child's play activities and interaction with parents and others prior to audiometric testing. These informal situations may provide an indication of the child's hearing ability and the manner of response to sound. Responses which occur outside the test room can be used as a guide for judging responses to the less familiar test stimuli. For verbal children, the examiner should also attempt to determine the extent of the child's receptive and expressive language skills.

Behavioural Audiometry

Behavioural audiometry is a generic term used to describe a variety of procedures designed to elicit behavioural responses to auditory stimuli. As Lloyd and Dahle (1976) point out, most behavioural audiometric procedures are

designed to bring operant (voluntary) behaviour under stimulus control. Although operant conditioning is sometimes used
in a more restrictive sense to mean utilization of structured
reinforcement schedules, Lloyd (1966) suggests that all
behavioural audiometric tests can be viewed as an operant
procedure. The main exception is the use of behavioural
observation audiometry (BOA) with young infants. In that
case, the child's responses may be largely involuntary or
reflexive, which would be classified as respondent behaviour.

Behavioural Observation
Audiometry

     Behavioural observation audiometry (BOA) refers to the
use of procedures which rely on the observation of overt
behavioural responses to the occurrence of sound (Murphy,
1962; Weber, 1970). Although BOA procedures are not as well
defined as those for visual reinforcement audiometry, the
technique has been shown to produce useful information when
used with young children (Thompson & Weber, 1974) and may be
the only behavioural audiometric method which can be used
with some multiply handicapped children (Sheeley, 1978).

     BOA is generally used when the child's developmental
age or handicapping conditions preclude use of a conditioned
response to sound. Consequently, this procedure is most
often employed with very young infants and older children who
have severe developmental delays, visual impairments or
motor control problems. However, the presence of these other
handicaps necessitates making allowances for physical limitations and level of responsiveness (Tait, 1977; Kent, 1981).
In the simplest form of BOA, various auditory stimuli are
presented through loudspeakers and the examiner observes the
child for any overt change in behaviour.

     Most young children respond best if a parent is present
in the test room. If possible, BOA should be conducted by
two examiners, one in the control room and one in the test
room. The child is allowed to sit on the parent's lap and
engage in quiet play with toys or stuffed animals. The child
should be positioned 45 to 90 degrees from the speaker to
facilitate observation of possible orienting responses.

Although testing is usually conducted in sound field, some
young children can be tested successfully using earphones and
bone conducted stimuli. Additional speakers can be used to
assess the child's developmental level for localization to
sound. The importance of obtaining a baseline of the child's
pre-stimulus activity cannot be overemphasized. The child's
posture, movement level, and focus of attention should be
observed prior to the onset of each stimulus.

The behavioural responses an audiologist may expect to
elicit vary considerably from one child to the next, although
they appear to follow a developmental pattern (Watrous et al.,
1975). A startle response can often be elicited from normal
infants to moderately intense sounds, but many multiply handicapped children fail to startle at any intensity level.
Cessation of ongoing activity is a more typical response,
especially in visually impaired children (Tait, 1977). The
response is often quite subtle and may be accompanied by
slight eye movement toward the sound source. Other behaviours
which may be observed include changes in facial expression,
body movement, and head-turn localization responses. Sucking
behaviour has been demonstrated to vary in response to
auditory stimuli (Eisele, Berry & Shriner, 1975), and it is
frequently helpful to allow the child to suck on a bottle or
pacifier/soother. Some infants will consistently stop sucking momentarily in response to sounds, even at relatively low
intensity levels.

It is important to allow enough time between stimulus
presentations to reduce the potential for response habituation. Alternating between presentation of live voice, pure
tones, narrow band noise and noisemakers is also helpful in
maintaining a high level of response. The most frequent
error made by inexperienced clinicians is to present signals
in rapid succession without allowing the child to return to
a pre-stimulus state. It takes time to adequately assess
young children with BOA procedures. The examiner must follow
a pace that is appropriate for each child. Attempting to
rush through the procedure will, in most cases, compromise
the test results.

Northern and Downs (1978) present norms for BOA which
can be used in interpreting the responses of children ranging
in age from birth through 24 months. We have found their
norms to be useful in making a tentative judgment concerning

hearing sensitivity in young children. However, it appears
that a child's performance is dependent more on developmental
age than on chronological age. This is particularly true in
the case of premature infants. Longitudinal data collected
on 148 premature children at the University of Alabama in
Birmingham has shown that a correction factor for prematurity
is necessary when comparing their performance to expected
chronological age norms.

Since BOA procedures rely on eliciting very subtle overt
behaviours, the infant's general state should be noted and
considered in interpreting the results. Children who are
restless, sleepy, or heavily medicated, may respond at intensity levels much higher than they would under more ideal
conditions. If possible, children should be evaluated when
they are likely to be most alert. If there is any question
concerning the validity of the results, additional testing
should be performed.

Visual Reinforcement Audiometry

As previously indicated, several audiological assessment
techniques have been developed which employ visual stimuli.
The goal is to increase a child's responses to auditory signals by reinforcing correct responses with interesting visual
presentations. Fulton and Lloyd (1975) grouped these visual
stimuli into 5 areas: pictures; minature scenes; animated
toy animals or puppets; toy trains; and other mechanical toys.
Generally, visual reinforcement is presented on a continuous
(100%) schedule, along with periodic verbal praise or nonverbal signs of approval.

The conditioned response to auditory stimuli may vary
from pushing a button to head turn localization. The latter
method is sometimes referred to as Conditioned Orientation
Reflex (COR) audiometry. Suzuki and Ogiba (1961) developed
this procedure for use with children and found it effective
with infants as young as 1 year of age. Although the original
COR procedure relied on a "reflexive" orienting response, the
method is probably more accurately described as an operant
procedure, at least when used with older subjects. For this
reason, the procedure is often referred to as Conditioned
Orientation Response audiometry (Lloyd & Dahle, 1976).
Visual Reinforcement Audiometry (VRA) (Liden & Kankkunan,
1969), is usually used to mean any procedure employing head

turn or alerting response to sound coupled with visual
reinforcement. More recent applications of this procedure
have shown that it is effective with normal infants as young
as 5 months (Moore, Wilson & Thompson, 1977), and with
retarded and low functioning children having a developmental
age of 10 months or higher (Thompson, Wilson & Moore, 1979).
Although VRA has been used primarily for assessing hearing
sensitivity, a modification of the approach has also been
used for measuring speech sound discrimination ability in
low functioning children (Thompson, Wilson & Moore, 1979;
Eilers & Oller, 1980).

The arrangement of the test room is similar to that
used with BOA procedures. The child is placed in an infant
seat or held on the parent's lap at 45 to 90 degrees from the
loudspeaker and reinforcer. The signals are usually presented in a descending pattern, with the initial stimulus
presented at a moderately intense level, e.g. 50 - 60 dB HL.
The stimulus can consist of any auditory signal, including
warbled pure tones, speech, or narrow-band noise. The
response of choice is a head turn towards the sound. This
should be followed immediately by activation of the reinforcer. Commercial reinforcers are available which consist
of battery operated animated toys housed in a plexiglass case.
The examiner controls the toy, activating it after a valid
response to the test signal. If the child fails to respond
after 2 to 3 trials, the intensity level is increased in 10 -
20 dB steps. If there is continuous failure to respond, an
attempt should be made to teach the child to turn toward the
loudspeaker following presentation of the signals. It is
also helpful to couple verbal praise with the visual stimulus
to increase the effectiveness of the reinforcer. When conditioning has been established, the intensity is reduced systematically, until a threshold level is obtained.

With multiply handicapped children, it is best to vary
the test signal and the reinforcer to maintain the child's
interest. We have found that the success of the procedure
depends upon establishing an optimal response-ready state
prior to presentation of each signal. This is most effectively accomplished by having an assistant examiner manipulate
toys or other objects to keep the child occupied while facing
a midline position. It is important to remember that the

activity used to maintain the child's attention should not be more interesting than the reinforcer. During the evaluation, the assistant examiner and parent should be as quiet as possible to increase the interest value of the test signals.

Modifications of the VRA method may be necessary when used with multiply handicapped children. For example, children with poor head control cannot be expected to give a consistent head turn response. However, an eye turn or alerting response may be observed if the child is positioned appropriately. The use of VRA with the visually impaired may be possible if the child has enough vision to perceive movement or flickering lights. We have found that some visually impaired children can be conditioned to give a consistent head turn response to a high intensity, flashing strobe light.

Retarded children may not initially orient toward the source of an auditory stimulus, which necessitates devoting time to teaching them to respond to that stimulus. Greenberg et al., (1978), found a strong age effect for young Down's Syndrome children in relation to eliciting a natural orienting response and for the rate of success for teaching a head turn response. The investigation showed that only 17% of the subjects in the 6 to 12 month category met the initial conditioning criterion (i.e. responding to at least 2 out of 3 stimulus presentations at 50 or 70 dB SPL). Of the 13 infants and young children who failed to meet the conditioning criterion, only 3 could be taught to respond during a single test session. Between the ages of 2 and 3, the percentage of children who localized increased to 75%. It was not until 5 to 6 years of age that all of the subjects exhibited a localization response. Of the children who localized, 75% were judged to yield reliable thresholds. Obviously, VRA can be used successfully with low functioning children, but the examiner must consider the child's developmental level when deciding if the procedure is likely to yield reliable results.

Our experience in using VRA with multiply handicapped children has shown that it can be employed with most children who have a developmental age of at least 6 to 12 months. A schematic of the VRA procedure employed at the Center for Developmental and Learning Disorders is presented in Figure 1. This arrangement is similar to that described by Moore, Wilson

FIGURE 1:   Visual Reinforcement Audiometry (VRA) test
             arrangement.

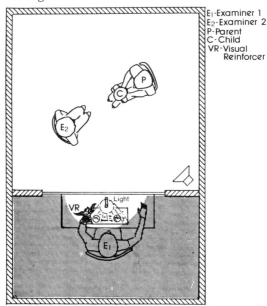

E₁-Examiner 1
E₂-Examiner 2
P-Parent
C-Child
VR-Visual
    Reinforcer

and Thompson (1977) except that the reinforcer is presented
through the observation window of the control room. This
arrangement allows for maximum flexibility when varying the
reinforcer. The visual stimulus may consist of any interesting object or activity. We generally use hand-held puppets
illuminated by an overhead light, which is turned on following a head-turn response. The talk-back microphone can be
used to add voice to the puppet's actions, thus providing
additional reinforcement. The control room lights remain off
between presentations of the stimulus.

Tangible Reinforcement Audiometry

    The use of tangible reinforcers in audiological assess-
ment emerged as a testing method during the 1960s in conjunction with the application of operant conditioning procedures.

The technique developed for use with the retarded, commonly termed Tangible Reinforcement Operant Conditioning Audiometry or TROCA, incorporates well defined stimulus response parameters (Lloyd, Spradlin & Reid, 1968; Bricker & Bricker, 1969; Dahle & Daly, 1974; Fulton, Gorzycki & Hull, 1975). The primary difference between VRA and TROCA is that the former uses visual reinforcement, while the latter relies on the use of a tangible item (e.g. candy, tokens or trinkets) as the reinforcer. Also, whereas most current VRA methods utilize a head-turn response, TROCA procedures usually rely on button or lever pressing and the system tends to be automated. For these reasons, TROCA is most useful in situations where there is a need for a non-ambiguous response and/or highly structured test conditions. Nevertheless, in our experience at least, most handicapped children can be tested more efficiently with a combination of VRA, ABR, and immittance procedures, than with TROCA.

Play Audiometry

Play audiometry is a modification of the standard pure tone technique involving substitution of an interesting play activity for the hand raising response. Since the activity is structured as a game, making the response serves as the reward, but frequent use of praise and encouragement enhances interest and improves the validity and reliability of the results. Of the behavioural procedures utilized with children, play audiometry comes the closest to approximating standard test techniques. The method can be used for measuring pure tone thresholds and/or speech detection, both in sound field and under earphones. The success of play audiometry depends upon establishing a clear understanding of the task and maintaining a high level of interest.

Play audiometry has been shown to be a successful technique for use with the retarded (Schlanger, 1962) and brain damaged (Grey, D'Asaro & Skylar, 1965), but has not been as effective when used with deaf-blind children (Tait, 1977).

Developmentally delayed children can often be conditioned more easily if the initial conditioning is carried out in sound field. Earphones can be introduced once the child has adjusted to the test environment and demonstrates

understanding of the activity. With severely handicapped
children, conditioning can sometimes be facilitated by com-
bining sound with visual and/or vibro-tactile stimuli (St.
James-Roberts, 1975). The added stimulus is then faded out
prior to conducting a threshold search. This technique is
especially useful with visually impaired children and individuals suspect of having profound hearing impairment. In our
experience, play audiometry can be used with most moderately
handicapped children with a developmental age of from 2 to 3
years. However, the presence of physical impairments or
motor co-ordination problems may make it difficult to select
an appropriate response activity. Children with physical
handicaps can frequently be more easily tested using VRA. As
with all techniques, the success of play audiometry depends
upon the skill of the examiner in motivating the child and
structuring the task to accomodate the limitations imposed
by associated handicapping conditions.

Summary of Behavioural Procedures

    The ability to determine when to use a particular
behavioural audiometric procedure is a skill gained from
experience in assessing children with a wide range of handicaps. The experienced clinician soon learns to make this
decision on the basis of information supplied by the parents
and other professionals, and from observation of the child's
behaviour. Considerations which influence choice of procedure include time available for testing, and the purpose of
the assessment. For an initial assessment of auditory sensitivity, VRA is a good choice for children over a wide age
range.

    The results obtained by behavioural audiometry with the
multiply handicapped must be interpreted with caution,
especially when information is based on only one test
session. Williamson, Ross and Woodrow (1978) compared the
results of VRA and play audiometry administered on separate
days to retarded adults and found that, regardless of the
test procedures, lower thresholds were obtained on the
second test. This finding implies that behavioural audiometric procedures are subject to a learning effect when used
with low functioning individuals. This factor should always
be considered when judging the validity of test results
obtained from a single evaluation.

Our experience with BOA, VRA, and play audiometry is
illustrated in Figure 2. This graph represents results based
on 453 audiological evaluations performed on children ranging
from 0 to 36 months of age. The children were seen as part
of a collaborative perinatal infectious disease research
project. Most of the children had congenital CMV, herpes,
rubella, or toxoplasmosis. A small percentage were normal
controls. Approximately 25% had severe multiple handicaps,
and the remainder were at risk for developmental problems.
The majority were seen for sequential evaluations which were
usually conducted at 6 to 12 month intervals. As indicated,
BOA was the procedure most often employed with the 0 to 6
month group, although VRA was used successfully with 28% of
the children, mostly at the 5 and 6 month level. Increase
in the use of VRA rose significantly for the 7 to 12 month
olds and remained the most frequently used procedure until
31 to 36 months, when play audiometry became the technique
of choice.

FIGURE 2:   Percentage of children evaluated by BOA, VRA, and
            play audiometry according to age.

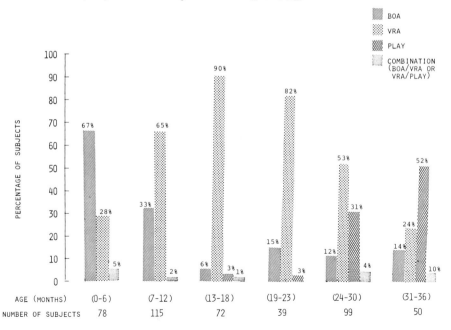

The continued use of BOA with some children beyond 12 months of age was the result of re-evaluations of the more severely handicapped. The finding that BOA was required for some children at all age levels attests to the difficulty of conditioning the multiply handicapped to respond to auditory stimuli. Nevertheless, the fact that VRA and/or play audiometry could be used with the majority past 6 months of age indicates that most handicapped children can be evaluated successfully using conditioned behavioural audiometric procedures.

Table I lists the means, ranges and standard deviations for threshold hearing levels obtained by VRA and BOA for speech detection and pure tones for children in the 0 to 12 month age range. Only children with Type A tympanograms and confirmed normal hearing were included in the analysis. The reduction in mean threshold with advancing age was found to follow a consistent pattern for both BOA and VRA. For each procedure, mean threshold levels were lower for speech detection than for pure tone averages. The finding of a mean SDT of 10 dB and mean pure tone average of 15.6 dB for the 10 to 12 month old children indicates that VRA is an extremely effective prodecure for assessing hearing sensitivity in children who are at risk for developmental disabilities.

TABLE I: Means, ranges and S.D.'s for speech detection and pure tone average (500, 1000, 2000 Hz) dB HL for 1-12 month old children with Type A tympanograms using BOA and VRA

Age (Months)	(1 – 4)		(5 – 9)		(10 – 12)	
	SDT	PTA	SDT	PTA	SDT	PTA
BOA						
Mean	42.1	59.9	28.9	43.5		
Range	15–75	23–95	5–50	27–60		
S.D.	18.5	20.6	13.0	10.0		
VRA						
Mean			18.0	28.8	10.0	15.6
Range			5–35	8–70	0–20	0–25
S.D.			8.5	14.5	5.9	8.2

Number of Subjects   19   43   14

Physiological Procedures

Over the years, hearing scientists have developed many
ingenuous physiological approaches for assessing various
auditory functions. The application of physiological measurement in evaluating the hearing status of the difficult-to-
test child has contributed significantly to our ability to
identify and define auditory problems in severely handicapped
children. Of the available procedures, immittance audiometry
and auditory brainstem response (ABR) audiometry have proven
to be the most applicable for general clinical use.

Immittance Measurements

Our ability to evaluate the hearing of the multiply
handicapped has improved significantly with new procedures
relative to immittance audiometry. The primary problem when
utilizing immittance measurements is that the test requires
the subject to remain relatively still. Crying, yelling,
and kicking may cause difficulty in recording tympanograms
or acoustic reflexes. The child who is active and vocal during tympanometry will yield a very erratic tracing, but by
repeating the procedure with an automatic plotter, the
examiner is usually able to obtain a tympanogram which can be
interpreted. If reflex threshold levels cannot be obtained,
the presence of acoustic reflexes at higher levels can provide
diagnostic information. The creative clinician can, in most
instances, provide some distraction which allows the few
minutes necessary for completion of tympanometry and acoustic
reflex testing. Distraction techniques include filmstrip
cartoons, puppets, bubbles, and animated toys. Restraint,
such as with a papoose board, is usually not successful, but
the restraint provided when a child is held firmly in his
parent's arms often proves helpful. The use of additional
assistance may be essential in obtaining successful measurements. Sometimes it is necessary to have one person to
operate the test instrument, another to provide some distraction, and a third to maintain the probe and earphone on the
child's head. Separating the probe and the earphone from
the head set and using them in a hand-held fashion is helpful.
With some children who seem cognizant of their environment,

it may be helpful to casually demonstrate placement of the
probe tip and earphone on the examiner. It is essential that
the immittance measurements be carried out as quickly as
possible. Selection of a slightly larger probe tip cuff will
usually be more accurate than choosing a slightly smaller one,
and may eliminate the necessity of repeating the procedure.

Immittance reports with retarded children were originally
presented by Lamb and Norris (1969). Fifteen mentally
retarded children and 15 children of normal intelligence were
given acoustic reflex measurements. The subjects had normal
hearing and the acoustic reflex thresholds for each group
were at a similar level, but considerable variability in
thresholds was noted among the mentally retarded subjects. A
normative study by Fulton and Lamb (1972) indicated that
tympanometry can be used successfully with a retarded population and can be used to differentiate type of hearing loss.
Bows (1972) evaluated 23 young retarded children and stated
that immittance measurements are valuable in identifying
cases where there is a conductive component; in differenti-
ating retarded children who require further evaluation; and,
in determining normal hearing in difficult-to-test children.
Bayshore (1976) reported otoscopic and tympanometric results
on 340 developmentally disturbed children and found that only
3% of the population could not be tested. Acoustic reflexes
have also been used successfully to estimate hearing sensitivity in mentally retarded persons (Poole, Sheeley & Hannah,
1982).

One factor to be considered in the evaluation of the
multiply handicapped is the age of the subject. As early
identification of handicaps becomes commonplace, this will
become an even more important factor. Reports by Keith (1973)
of impedance or immittance testing with neonates indicated
that the results of tympanometry did not differ significantly
from the results obtained with older children. In a follow-
up study, Keith (1975) evaluated neonates younger than 36
hours of age and obtained tympanometric results which were
identical with those obtained in his original study. In these
studies, neither acoustic reflexes nor otoscopic evaluations
were obtained. Paradise (1976) studied the correlation
between tympanometric and otoscopic findings in infants and
concluded that tympanometry is a valuable test which has much
to offer in the diagnosis of middle ear effusion. He did not,

however, advocate the procedure with infants less than 7 months of age because of the poor correlation between tympano-metric and otoscopic findings with that age group. This was thought to be related to the highly compliant external auditory canal walls of young infants.

Data from our Center on 363 immittance evaluations with children from 0 to 12 months provides indirect evidence for using caution in interpreting immittance results with children under 7 months of age. Analysis of classification on tympano-grams indicated the presence of a much higher percentage of Type A tympanograms (72.4%) in the 0 to 6 month age level than for the 7 to 12 month age range (44.4%). There was a corresponding increase of Type B tympanograms from 13.5% for the 0 to 6 month olds to 37.1% for the 7 to 12 month olds. The reason for this shift in tympanometric findings is not clear. However, these results may support the findings of Paradise (1976) when he indicated that Type A tympanograms may not accurately reflect middle ear functioning in children under 7 months of age. These findings could also be explained by the evidence provided by Henderson et al., (1982) showing that there is a significant increase in respiratory illness and otitis media for 6 to 12 month old infants, in comparison to 0 to 6 month olds.

A report by Schwartz and Schwartz (1978) of 46 infants ranging in age from 1 to 7 months old, compared otoscopy and impedance results. Considerably better agreement was found between otoscopy and acoustic reflex measurement than with tympanometry and otoscopy. The most diagnostically signifi-cant finding was that the acoustic reflex was absent in all 20 ears with effusion. The authors concluded that their results suggest that while a normal tympanogram may not indicate a mobile tympanic membrane or an effusion-free middle ear system in infants below approximately 6 months of age, a positive acoustic reflex response supports normal middle ear function with this age group.

There is evidence that the acoustic reflex can be elicited in neonates as early as 4 hours (McCandless & Allred, 1978). The reflex was present in approximately 89% of the infants in the study within the first 48 hours after birth when using a 660 Hz probe tone and a 500 Hz stimulus. With a 220 Hz probe tone, only 30% of the neonates had a positive

acoustic reflex, a finding similar to that reported by Keith.
However, the authors reported the 220 Hz probe tone was
superior for tympanometry.

Medication is another factor which one should consider
when evaluating multiply handicapped children by immittance
procedures. There is evidence that nitrous oxide, general
anesthesia, and barbituates have varying and usually negative
influences on immittance test results (Light, Ferrell & Sandberg, 1977; Mitchell & Richards, 1976; Borg, 1976).

An additional area of concern when considering immittance
evaluation of the multiply handicapped child is that of congenital anomalies of the outer and middle ear. The specific
type and/or location of a middle ear anomaly can cause
tympanometric tracings which result in misleading and conflicting results. Large pure tone air-bone gaps and Type B
tympanograms (Jerger, 1975), may be obtained on children with
normal appearing tympanic membranes. Further, the need for
obtaining immittance information was indicated by Libb et al.,
(1980), who found that the presence of Type B tympanograms
was often associated with lowered cognitive function in a
group of Down's Syndrome children.

Hall (1981) reported a study comparing 7 methods of
hearing loss prediction by the acoustic reflex in 869 subjects aged 1 to 20 years. A major limitation in using such
a technique is that middle ear problems occur more frequently
in multiply handicapped children (Downs, 1980) and the substantial (31-67%) proportion of predictive errors in Hall's
study occurred in patients with minor clinically insignificant
tympanometric abnormalities. However, in multiply handicapped
children with normal middle ear function and normal impedance
findings, the methods permit reasonably accurate identification of hearing loss, categorization of degree of loss, or
prediction of hearing loss in dB. In addition to hearing
loss prediction, immittance measurements can provide information relative to perforation of the tympanic membrane,
patency of ventilation tubes, ossicular disarticulations,
loudness recruitment, and non-organic hearing loss. Clinical
experience with the difficult-to-test, including the multiply
handicapped and the very young, indicates that only a very
small percentage cannot be successfully evaluated.

Auditory Brainstem Response
Audiometry

With the exception of immittance, no electrophysiological
procedure has generated more interest amongst audiologists
than auditory brainstem response (ABR) audiometry. In contrast to the problems encountered by the use of cortical
evoked response procedures (Price, 1975), ABR has been found
to be effective when used with difficult-to-test children.
ABR has been shown to be useful in monitoring hearing sensitivity in newborns (Galambos & Despland, 1980; Jacobson
et al., 1980), including premature infants (Schulman-Galambos
& Galambos, 1975; Starr et al., 1977), and the multiply handicapped (Sohmer & Student, 1978). An advantage of ABR is that
it can be administered while the subject is asleep and it is
not affected by sedation (Stockard, Stockard & Sharbrough,
1978). Thus, the procedure is useful for testing children
who cannot be evaluated with the standard behavioural audiological methods described earlier.

Auditory brainstem potentials are recorded through
electrodes placed on the scalp and represent electrical
activity generated by the auditory nerve and various brainstem auditory structures (Davis, 1976). These potentials
are generated by the rapid onset of auditory stimuli and
appear within the first 10 msec. following onset of the
stimulus. Their small voltages necessitate using high gain
amplifiers and signal averagers to enhance the response. In
individuals with normal hearing, the auditory brainstem
response consists of 5 to 7 wavepeaks which, by convention,
are labelled by Roman numerals I-VII (Jewett & Williston,
1971). Waves I, III, and V have been found to be the most
prominent reference points for assessing brainstem auditory
functioning in infants (Starr et al., 1977). Wave V is the
most stable wavepeak and is usually present and easily seen
at near behavioural threshold intensity levels. For this
reason, a clinical judgment of ABR threshold is generally
based on the lowest intensity level at which Wave V can be
elicited.

Since the latency of Wave V has been found to have a
direct inverse relationship to intensity, comparison with
normative latency values can also be used to obtain an
estimate of peripheral hearing sensitivity. However, as

Weber and Fujikawa (1977) point out, estimation of hearing
sensitivity based on latency of response must be made with
caution when latencies do not parallel normative values,
which is often the case in individuals with cochlear impairment. Interwave latencies (e.g. I–V) have been found to be
a sensitive indicator of central auditory brainstem pathway
functioning (Rowe, 1981) and can aid in the diagnosis of
pediatric neurological diseases (Hecox, Cane & Blair, 1981).
Auditory brainstem latencies are influenced by maturation,
and the latency of Wave V has been demonstrated to decrease
with advancing age from birth up to 2 years (Hecox & Galambos,
1974). Thus, clinical application requires establishing age-
related norms for young children. Data collected on young
children at our Center indicates that Wave V latencies tend
to fall into 3 fairly distinct age categories consisting of
0 – 1 month, 2 – 7 months, and 8 – 18 months.

    Broadband click stimuli produce the most clearly defined
response and are most often used to elicit the ABR in
clinical applications. However, clicks are not frequency
specific and the resulting response represents electrical
activity generated primarily from the high frequency basal
region of the basilar membrane (Kileny, 1981). Jerger and
Mauldin (1978) demonstrated that click evoked ABR thresholds
best predict hearing sensitivity in the 1000–4000 Hz region.
The most accurate prediction resulted from multiplying the
ABR threshold by a factor of 0.6.

    Several investigators (Picton et al., 1979; Wood, Seitz
& Jacobson, 1979; Kileny, 1981) have attempted to improve the
frequency specificity of the ABR response by using tone–pips
or filtered clicks to stimulate, and thus examine more
specific regions of the basilar membrane. Although the
higher frequency stimuli (e.g. 2000 and 4000 Hz) appear to
elicit frequency specific responses, the question of whether
low frequency tone pips actually measure hearing for their
equivalent region is less clear (Stapells & Picton, 1981).

    Because of the limitations in interpreting ABR responses,
they should never be used as the sole measure of auditory
functioning. Most clinicians follow a protocol suggested by
Jerger and Hayes (1976) where ABR is one of several measures
used to cross–check results obtained from behavioural,
impedance, and brainstem audiometry.

We have found ABR audiometry to be extremely useful in evaluating infants and other difficult-to-test children. Typically, ABR is employed when impedance and behavioural results are ambiguous, or as a check of estimated sensitivity level prior to recommending amplification in infants or severely handicapped youngsters. When used in this manner, ABR is a vital component of the audiological test battery.

Analysis of ABR audiometry with 49 high risk children who were part of the longitudinal study reported earlier indicates a high percentage of agreement between ABR, behavioural, and immittance results. All of the children had congenital infections and 22 were documented to be multiply handicapped. At the time of ABR testing, the children ranged in age from 1 to 31 months, with a mean age of 8.0 months. ABR using clicks presented at 33.3 per second, was administered as the initial auditory assessment to establish a baseline for hearing sensitivity. The majority of children were tested during sleep following sedation with chloral hydrate. Normal hearing sensitivity by ABR audiometry was defined as at least 2 repeatable tracings with Wave V present at 20 dB HL. Thirty-four (70%) of the children were found to have normal ABR results for both ears. In 9 subjects (18%), ABR indicated a bilateral loss of hearing. Six children (12%) were found to have a unilateral impairment. Follow-up behavioural and immittance test results were available for 38 of the children. The ABR results for 35 agreed with the follow-up findings, for an overall agreement rate of 92%. In other words, ABR accurately predicted normal or abnormal hearing for each ear in 35 of 38 children. Two of the disagreements were subjects with normal ABR thresholds who later exhibited mild to moderate impairments in each ear. One case showed an abnormal ABR in one ear which was found to be normal at a later date. These results are similar to those reported by Jerger, Hayes and Jordon (1980), and further indicate that ABR audiometry can be used effectively in identifying hearing impairment in multiply handicapped infants at an early age. Equally important, ABR results are highly accurate in establishing that an infant has normal hearing. Determining the presence of normal hearing is becoming increasingly important as parents become more cognizant and more concerned about the potential for hearing loss in high risk infants.

There have been few published reports on the use of ABR
with severely handicapped children. Sohmer and Student (1978)
compared ABR results for normal children and children labelled
as having autism, minimal brain dysfunction, and psychomotor
retardation. They found significant differences in some of
the ABR parameters, particularly in Wave latency and the time
interval between Waves, which they interpreted as evidence of
diffuse brain lesions. The most extensive study of ABR with
severely delayed children was reported by Stein, Ozdamor and
Schnable (1981). They conducted ABR audiometry on 82 severely
delayed children suspected of being deaf-blind. Their results
indicated that 43.0% of the children had ABR thresholds
within the normal hearing range. Since all of these children
had previously failed to respond to behavioural testing, the
use of ABR prevented a potential false diagnosis of deafness
in 34 youngsters. It is difficult to overemphasize the significance of the findings of this study.

Clearly, ABR should always be used in helping to make a
determination of peripheral impairment in children who fail
to respond adequately to behavioural tests. We have seen
cases similar to those reported in the above study where ABR
has shown normal hearing when behavioural tests indicate a
severe loss. One can only speculate on whether such children
hear normally in the traditional sense of the term. Other
investigators (Cohen & Rapin, 1978) also report that ABR frequently results in lower thresholds than behavioural audiometry for severely brain damaged children. Thus, one of the
most important roles for the use of ABR audiometry is to
establish the presence of an intact peripheral hearing system
in children who would otherwise be misdiagnosed as hearing
impaired.

Jerger, Hayes and Jordon (1980) point out that when ABR
responses are normal, they contribute valuable information
about peripheral sensitivity. However, when the responses are
abnormal or absent in children with concomitant CNS involvement, the results are ambiguous and must be interpreted with
caution. Worthington and Peters (1980) present evidence
which indicates that one must also be cautious about interpreting the absence of ABRs in individuals who do not demonstrate evidence of neurological dysfunction. Therefore, a
diagnosis of peripheral hearing impairment should never be
based solely upon ABR results.

Figure 3 illustrates the use of ABR in ruling out the presence of a peripheral hearing impairment. This child was referred because of a severe language impairment, behavioural and motor problems. Initial testing by VRA in soundfield produced results which were consistent in indicating a moderate loss. The probability of a loss was supported by the presence of Type A tympanograms with absent reflexes. Although the test results were in agreement with the parents' report of the child's behaviour, the examining audiologist felt that further confirmation was needed. ABR testing was performed under sedated sleep, and the results showed normal responses from 80 to 20 dB HL for each ear (only the responses for the right ear are displayed). Although ABR was useful in ruling out a significant peripheral loss, it did not resolve the question of why stapedial reflexes were absent, or why the child did not respond normally to environmental sounds. ABR waveforms and interwave latencies were within normal limits and subsequent neurological examination failed to reveal any apparent CNS abnormalities. Follow-up audiometric behavioural testing eventually confirmed the presence of normal hearing sensitivity. This case is a good illustration of the limitations of audiological procedures. Limited test results do not always answer all of our questions. In cases such as this, we must rely on long term monitoring and interdisciplinary management.

FIGURE 3:   P.S. (3 yrs.) ABR Wave V latency for click stimuli

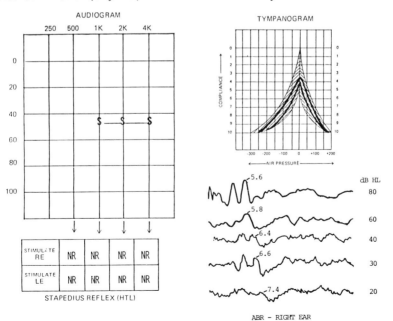

Figure 4 shows the ABR test results on a 5 week old child with a unilateral atresia of the left ear and canal. Immittance measurements resulted in a Type A tympanogram for the right ear. ABR was used to assess the hearing status of the unaffected right ear, and to attempt to determine if there was an associated cochlear impairment. Wave V responses for the left ear reflected the blockage of the outer ear and probable middle ear deformity. Bone conducted clicks were presented to the left mastoid with contralateral earphone masking. The responses shown in Figure 4 indicate hearing by bone conduction down to at least 20 dB HL. Wave V latencies for AC clicks in the right ear were slightly delayed, but Wave V was present down to 30 dB HL. Although the results for bone conducted clicks could not be conclusively determined to originate from the left cochlea, we felt that the child had at least near normal hearing for the right ear, and probable normal cochlear function for the left. Unfortunately, it will be several months before these findings can be confirmed by behavioural audiometry. Nevertheless, the capability of being able to obtain this type of information at 5 weeks of age is immensely important to habilitation, planning and parental counselling.

Figure 4: J.W., age 5 weeks. Goldenhar's Syndrome with atresia of the left outer ear canal.

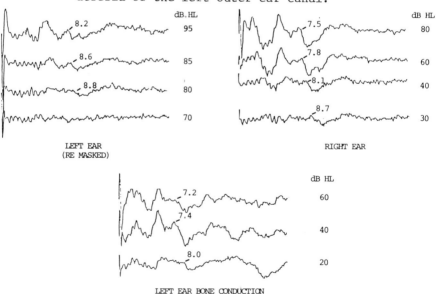

Integration of Information

Although this chapter has presented the various audiological assessment procedures as if they were independent of one another, we would emphasize that all information must be integrated to form a complete picture of a child's hearing ability. Serious errors can be made in attempting to identify or define an auditory disorder on the basis of insufficient information. At the very least, a basic evaluation should assess middle ear function and sensitivity to sounds within the speech frequency range, preferably to pure tones. When a loss is suspected, it must be defined and evaluated in relation to a level of developmental functioning and presence of other impairments. Although this chapter has not addressed evaluation of speech reception skills, some attempt should be made to assess the child's ability to communicate, verbally or manually. Since multiply handicapped children have many needs, other specialists should be consulted to plan for managing follow-up care and for further diagnostic assessment. It is important to remember that evaluation and remediation may need to occur concomitantly, and that they are part of an ongoing process involving the child, family and other agencies. The need to share information and coordinate assessment and remediation strategies with other professionals and other agencies cannot be over-stressed. Too often, parents are left bewildered by contradictory findings and conflicting opinions. These problems can usually be avoided by including parents in the decision making process and taking time to explore available options. Assessment is only one part of a complex process for meeting the needs of the multiply handicapped.

Acknowledgements

The authors wish to acknowledge the contributions made by Anita Ingram and Ruth Bennish for their assistance in preparing this manuscript. Acknowledgement is also extended to Kerk Chan Lim and Sherrill Quinn for their help in data analysis.

Discussion

K. MURPHY

I was intrigued by your comments on the incidence of
apparent middle ear disorders in children over the age of 7
months. Many years ago, I had the good fortune to discuss
that very topic with Mary Sheridan, one of our eminent British
pediatricians. She raised two issues. Is there a possibility
that, up until 6 months of age, ordinary immunities persist.
The other was that when children are over the age of 6 months,
they are often either weaned (that is, they are not using a
bottle any more), or if they are using a bottle, they're using
one with a large hole in the teat. The suckle is different
and the pattern of exercise, therefore, is too. Pressure
around the tympany must also be affected. It was her strong
belief that this was related to change in the incidence of
middle ear disorders in children at that age.

A. DAHLE

Well, I think you've hit on a very important point. In
fact, my co-author, Faye McCollister, made the exact same
statement. She also thought it probably reflected a change
in feeding habits and use of a bottle. She wants to go back
and see if we can get a little better data on that. I'm not
sure how to do it, possibly through some kind of questionnaire,
although it would be much better to follow that in a prospective manner.

M. DOWNS

Do you take into consideration Paradise's study showing
that, of children under 7 months of age, 50% of the ears with
fluid will have normal tympanograms. We did a study showing
an even greater percentage of fluid in ears with normal
tympanograms.

A. DAHLE

Yes. I have included his study in our paper.

P. KILENY

Do you mask the contralateral ear when you do bone conduction ABR? Further, did I understand correctly that you are
waiting for some sort of additional confirmation before you
aid the 5 week old you have shown us?

A. DAHLE

Yes, we mask the contralateral ear. It's interesting though that we have found in our unilateral hearing cases that there is absolutely no crossover without masking. I think it's imperative that you do mask the opposite ear in bone conduction tests.

No, we are not waiting for confirmation. The child was seen in our center because we have the only genetics lab in the state, and the child is from 300 miles away. We have turned over follow-up care to the speech and hearing program in the child's home. I am very hopeful that the child has a hearing aid by now, if one is needed. I would hate to put an aid on a child on the simple basis of the BSER. We got results at 30 dB and maybe the child hears 15 or 10 dB. We recommended follow-up behavioural testing and more evaluation before considering amplification. Obviously, if the 30 dB level held up, there might be a reason to aid.

References

ASHA, Joint Committee on Infant Hearing (Position Statement) ASHA, 1982.

Balkany, T., "Otologic Aspects of Down's Syndrome," Seminars in Speech, Language and Hearing 1:39-48, 1980.

Bayshore, S.R., "The Use of Tympanometry for Screening Developmentally Disabled Children," Audiology and Hearing Education 2:35-40, 1976.

Borg, E., "Dynamic Characteristics of the Intra Muscle Reflex," Acoustic Impedance and Admittance - The Measurement of Middle Ear Effusion (Baltimore: Williams and Wilkins), Feldman, A., and Wilber, L. (Eds.).

Bows, J., "Acoustic Impedance Measurement with Hard of Hearing Mentally Retarded Children," Journal of Mental Deficiency Research 16:196-202, 1972.

Bricker, D.D., and Bricker, W.A., "A Programmed Approach to
Operant Audiology for Low-functioning Children," Journal
of Speech and Hearing Disorders 34:312-320, 1969.

Campbell, C.W., Polomeno, R.C., Elder, J.M., Murray, J., and
Altosar, A., "Importance of an Eye Examination in Identi-
fying the Cause of Congenital Hearing Impairment,"
Journal of Speech and Hearing Disorders 46:258-261, 1981.

Cohen, M.M., and Rapin, I., "Evoked Potential Audiometry in
Neurologically Impaired Children," Evoked Electrical
Activity in the Auditory Nervous System (New York:
Academic Press, Inc.) Newton, F., and Zerlin, S. (Eds.),
1978.

Dahle, A.J., and Daly, D.A., "Tangible Rewards in Assessing
Auditory Discrimination Performance of Mentally Retarded
Children," American Journal of Mental Deficiency 78:625-
630, 1974.

Dahle, A.J., McCollister, F.P., Stagno, S., Reynolds, D.W.,
and Hoffman, H.E., "Progressive Hearing Impairment in
Children with Congenital Cytomegalovirus Infection,"
Journal of Speech and Hearing Disorders, 44:220-229, 1979.

Davis, H., "Principles of Electric Response Audiometry,"
Annals of Otology, Rhinology, and Laryngology (Supplement
28) 85:1-96, 1976.

Davis, H., "The Young Deaf Child: Identification and
Management," Acta Otolaryngologica (Supplement 206), pp.
33-52, 1965.

DiCarlo, L., and Bradley, W., "A Simplified Test for Infants
and Young Children," Laryngoscope 71:628-646, 1961.

Dix, M.R., and Hallpike, C.S., "The Peepshow: A New
Technique for Pure-tone Audiometry in Young Children,"
British Medical Journal 2:719-723, 1947.

Downs, M.P., "Audiometry in Children," International
Audiology 1:268-270, 1947.

Downs, M.P., and Sterritt, G.M., "Identification Audiometry
for Neonates: A Preliminary Report," Journal of Audiology
Research 4:69-80, 1964.

Eilers, R.E., and Oller, D.K., "A Comparative Study of Speech Perception in Young Severely Retarded Children and Normally Developing Infants," Journal of Speech and Hearing Research 23:419-428, 1980.

Eisele, W.A., Berry, R.C., and Shriner, T.H., "Infant Sucking Response Patterns as a Conjugate Function of Changes in Sound Pressure Level of Auditory Stimuli," Journal of Speech and Hearing Research 18:296-307, 1975.

Ewing, I.R., and Ewing, A.W.G., "The Ascertainment of Deafness in Infancy and Early Childhood," Journal of Laryngology and Otology 59:309-333, 1944.

Fulton, R.T., "Standard Pure Tone and Bekesy Audiometric Measures with the Mentally Retarded," American Journal of Mental Deficiency 72:60-73, 1967.

Fulton, R.T., Gorzycki, P.A., and Hull, W.L., "Hearing Assessment with Young Children," Journal of Speech and Hearing Disorders 40:397-404, 1975.

Fulton, R.T., and Graham, J.D., "Conditioned Orientation Reflex Audiometry with the Mentally Retarded," American Journal of Mental Deficiency 70:703-708, 1966.

Fulton, R.T., and Lamb, L.E., "Acoustic Impedance and Tympanometry with the Retarded: A Normative Study," Audiology 11:199-208, 1972.

Fulton, R.T., and Lloyd, L.L., Auditory Assessment of the Difficult-to-Test (Baltimore: Williams & Wilkins), 1975.

Galambos, R., and Despland, P., "The Auditory Brainstem Responses (ABR) Evaluates Risk Factors for Hearing Loss in the Newborn," Pediatric Research 14:159-163, 1980.

Gelatt, J.P., Cherow, E., Holzhoure, E., and Schultz, J., Hearing Impaired Developmentally Disabled Children and Adolescents: An Interdisciplinary Look at a Special Population (Washington, D.C.: American Speech-Language-Hearing Association), 1982.

Gerber, S.E., and Mencher, G.T., Auditory Dysfunction (Houston: College-Hill Press), 1980.

Green, D.D., "The Peep-Show: A Simple, Inexpensive Modification of the Peep Show," Journal of Speech and Hearing Disorders 23:118-120, 1958.

Greenberg, D.B., Wilson, W.R., Moore, J.M., and Thompson, G., "Visual Reinforcement Audiometry (VRA) with Young Down's Syndrome Children," Journal of Speech and Hearing Disorders 43:448-458, 1978.

Grey, H.A., D'Asaro, M.J., and Skylar, M., "Auditory Perceptual Thresholds in Brain Injured Children," Journal of Speech and Hearing Research 8:45-56, 1965.

Hall, J.W., "Hearing Loss Prediction by the Acoustic Reflex in a Young Population: Comparison of Seven Methods," International Journal of Pediatric Otorhinolaryngology 3:225-243, 1981.

Hardy, J.B., Dougherty, A., and Hardy, W.G., "Hearing Responses and Audiologic Screening in Infants," Journal of Pediatrics 55:382-390, 1959.

Hecox, K.E., Cone, B., and Blair, M.E., "Brainstem Auditory Evoked Response in the Diagnosis of Pediatric Neurology Diseases," Neurology 31:832-840, 1981.

Hecox, K., and Galambos, R., "Brainstem Auditory Evoked Responses in Human Infants and Adults," Archives of Otolaryngology 99:30-33, 1974.

Henderson, F.W., Collier, A.M., Sanyal, M.A., Watkins, J.M., Fairclough, D.L., Clyde, W.A., and Denny, F.W., "A Longitudinal Study of Respiratory Viruses and Bacteria in the Etiology of Acute Otitis Media with Effusion," The New England Journal of Medicine 306:1377-1383, 1982.

Jacobson, J.T., Seitz, M.R., Mencher, G.T., and Parrott, V., "Auditory Brainstem Response: A Contribution to Infant Assessment and Management," Early Management of Hearing Loss (New York: Grune & Stratton), G.T. Mencher and S.E. Gerber (Eds.), 1980.

Jerger, J.F., and Hayes, D., "The Cross-Check Principle in Pediatric Audiometry," Archives of Otolaryngology 104:456-461, 1978.

Jerger, J., Hayes, D., and Jordon, C., "Clinical Experience with Auditory Brainstem Response Audiometry in Pediatric Assessment," Ear and Hearing 1:19-25, 1980.

Jerger, J., and Mauldin, L., "Prediction of Sensorineural Hearing Level from the Brainstem Evoked Response," Archives of Otolaryngology 104:456-461, 1978.

Jewett, D.L., and Williston, J.S., "Auditory-Evoked Far Fields Averaged from the Scalp of Humans," Brain 94:681-696, 1971.

Karchmer, M.A., Milone, M.N., and Wolk, S., "Educational Significance of Hearing Loss at Three Levels of Severity," American Annals of the Deaf 124:97-109, 1979.

Keith, R., "Impedance Audiometry with Neonates," Archives of Otolaryngology 97:465-467, 1973.

Keith, R., "Middle Ear Function in Neonates," Archives of Otolaryngology 101:376-379, 1975.

Kent, A., "Audiological Assessment and Implications," Understanding and Evaluating the Deaf-Blind/Severely and Profoundly Handicapped (Springfield, Ill.: Charles C. Thomas), Walsh, S.R. and Holaberg, R., (Eds.) 1981.

Kileny, P., "The Frequency of Tone-pip Evoked Auditory Brain-stem Response," Ear and Hearing 2:270-275, 1981.

Kodeman, F., Powers, T.R., Weller, G.M., and Philip, P.P., "Pure Tone Audiometry with the Mentally Retarded," Exceptional Children 24:303-305, 1958.

Lamb, L., and Norris, T., "Acoustic Impedance Measurement," Audiometry for the Retarded (Baltimore: Williams & Wilkins), Fulton, R., and Lloyd, L., (Eds.), 1969.

Libb, J.W., Myers, G.J., Graham, E., Bell, B., "Correlates of Intelligence and Adaptive Behaviour in Down Syndrome," Paper presented at the 104th Annual Meeting of the American Association on Mental Deficiency, San Francisco, May, 1980.

Liden, G., and Kankkunen, A., "Visual Reinforcement Audiometry," Acta Otolaryngologica 67:281-292, 1969.

Light, M.H., Ferrell, C.J., and Sandberg, R.K., "The Effects of Sedation on the Impedance Test Battery," Archives Otolaryngology 103:235-237, 1977.

Lloyd, L.L., "Use of the Slide Show Audiometric Technique with Mentally Retarded Children," Exceptional Children 32:93-98, 1965.

Lloyd, L.L., and Dahle, A.J., "Detection and Diagnosis of a Hearing Impairment in the Child," A Bicentennial Monograph on Hearing Impairment: Trends in the U.S.A. (Washington, D.C.: A.G. Bell Association), Frisina, R., (Ed.), 1976.

Lloyd, L.L., and Frisina, D.R. (Eds.), The Audiologic Assessment of the Mentally Retarded: Proceedings of a National Conference (Parsons [Kansas] State Hospital and Training Center), 1965.

Lloyd, L.L., Spradlin, J.E., and Reid, M.J., "An Operant Audiometric Procedure for Difficult-to-Test Subjects," Journal of Speech and Hearing Disorders 33:236-245, 1968.

McCandless, G.A., and Allred, P.L., "Tympanometry and Emergence of the Acoustic Reflex in Infants," Impedance Screening for Middle Ear Disease in Children (New York: Grune & Stratton), Harford, E.R., Bess, F.H., Bluestone, L.D., and Klein, J.O. (Eds.), 1978.

Mitchell, O.C., and Richards, G.B., "Effects of Various Anesthetic Agents on Normal and Pathological Middle Ears," ENT Journal 55:36-44, 1976.

Moore, J.M., Wilson, W.R., and Thompson, G., "Visual Reinforcement of Head-turn Responses in Infants Under 12 Months of Age," Journal of Speech and Hearing Disorders 42:328-334, 1977.

Moores, D.E., Educating the Deaf: Psychology, Principles and Practices (Boston: Houghton Mifflin Co.), 1978.

Murphy, K.P., "Development of Hearing in Babies -- A Diagnostic System for Detecting Early Signs of Deafness in Infants," Child and Family 1:16-17, 1962.

Northern, J., and Downs, M., Hearing in Children (Baltimore:
   Williams & Wilkins, Co.), 1978.

Paradise, J.L., Smith, C.G., and Bluestone, C.D., "Tympanometric Detection of Middle Ear Effusion in Infants and
   Young Children," Pediatrics 58:198-209, 1976.

Picton, T.W., Quellette, B.A., Hamel, G., and Smith, A.D.,
   "Brainstem Evoked Potentials to Tone Pips in Matched
   Noise," Journal of Otolaryngology 8:289-314, 1979.

Poole, P.B., Sheeley, E.C., and Hannah, J.E., "Predicting
   Hearing Sensitivity and Audiometric Slope for Mentally
   Retarded Persons," Ear and Hearing 3:77-82, 1982.

Price, L.L., "Evoked Response Audiometry," Auditory Assessment of the Difficult-to-Test (Baltimore: Williams &
   Wilkins), Fulton, R.T., and Lloyd, L.L. (Eds.), 1975.

Rowe, M.J., "The Brainstem Auditory Evoked Response in
   Neurological Disease: A Review," Ear and Hearing 2:41-51,
   1981.

Schlanger, B.B., "Effects of Listening Training on Auditory
   Thresholds of Mentally Retarded Children," ASHA 4:273-275,
   1962.

Schulman-Galambos, C., and Galambos, R., "Brainstem Auditory
   Evoked Responses in Premature Infants," Journal of Speech
   and Hearing Research 18:456-465, 1975.

Schwartz, D.M., and Schwartz, R.H., "A Comparison of Tympano-
   metry and Acoustic Reflex Measurements for Detecting
   Middle Ear Effusion in Infants Below Seven Months of Age,"
   Impedance Screening for Middle Ear Disease in Children
   (New York: Grune & Stratton), Harford, E.R., Bess, F.H.,
   Bluestone, C.D., and Klein, J.O. (Eds.), 1978.

Sheeley, E.C., "Audiological Assessment," In Proceedings of
   the Special Study Institute, Assessment and Education of
   Deaf-Blind Children (Sacramento, California, State Department of Education), 1978.

Sohmer, H., and Student, M., "Auditory Nerve and Brainstem
   Evoked Responses in Normal, Autistic, Minimal Brain
   Dysfunction and Psychomotor Retarded Children," Electroencephalography and Clinical Neurophysiology 44:389-388,
   1978.

Stapells, D.R., and Picton, T.W., "Technical Aspects of
   Brainstem Evoked Potential Audiometry Using Tones," Ear
   and Hearing 2:20-29, 1981.

Starr, A., Amlie, R.N., Martin, W.H., and Sanders, S.,
   "Development of Auditory Function in Newborn Infants
   Revealed by Auditory Brainstem Potentials," Pediatrics
   60:831-839, 1977.

St. James-Roberts, I., "Cross-modal Facilitation of Response
   in Behavioural Audiometry with Children," Journal of
   American Audiology Society 1:119-125, 1975.

Stein, L.K., Ozdamor, O., and Schnable, M., "Auditory Brainstem Response (ABR) with Suspected Deaf-Blind Children,"
   Ear and Hearing 2:30-40, 1981.

Stockard, J.J., Stockard, J.E., and Sharbrough, F.W., "Non-
   pathological Factors Influencing Brainstem Auditory Evoked
   Potentials," American Journal of EEG Technology 18:177-209,
   1978.

Suzuki, T., and Ogiba, Y., "Conditioned Orientation Reflex
   Audiometry," Archives of Otolaryngology 74:192-198, 1961.

Tait, C.A., "Hearing and the Deaf-Blind Child," State of the
   Art: Perspectives on Serving Deaf-Blind Children
   (Sacramento: California State Department of Education),
   Lowell, E.L., and Rouin, C.C. (Eds.), 1977.

Thompson, G., and Weber, B.A., "Responses of Infants and
   Young Children to Behavioural Observation Audiometry
   (BOA)," Journal of Speech and Hearing Disorders 39:140-147,
   1974.

Thompson, G., Wilson, W., and Moore, J., "Application of
   Visual Reinforcement Audiometry (VRA) to Low-Functioning
   Children," Journal of Speech and Hearing Disorders 44:80-
   90, 1979.

Watrous, B.S., McConnell, F., Sitton, A.B., and Fleet, W., "Auditory Responses of Infants," Journal of Speech and Hearing Disorders 40:357-367, 1975.

Weber, B.A., "Comparison of Two Approaches to Behavioural Observation Audiometry," Journal of Speech and Hearing Disorders 13:823-825, 1970.

Weber, B.A., and Fujikawa, S.M., "Brainstem Evoked Response (BER) Audiometry at Various Stimulus Presentation Rates," Journal of the American Audiology Society 3:59-62, 1977.

Williamson, D.G., Ross, R., and Woodrow, S., "A Comparison of Two Response-Reinforcement Methods in Pure-tone Testing of the Retarded," Journal of the American Audiology Society 4:36-38, 1978.

Wood, M.H., Seitz, M.R., and Jacobson, J.T., "Brainstem Electrified Responses from Selected Tone Pip Stimuli," Journal of the American Audiology Society 5:156-162, 1979.

Worthington, D.W., and Peters, J.F., "Quantifiable Hearing and no ABR: Paradox or Error?" Ear and Hearing 1:281-285, 1980.

MOBILE AUDIOMETRY FOR THE
MULTIPLY HANDICAPPED HOSPITALIZED CHILD
FROM BIRTH TO SIX YEARS

Martha Rubin
Gene Kunreuther
Neil Lombardi
Lexington Hearing and Speech Center, Queens, New York

Testing the handicapped for hearing loss is not easily accomplished, even under the most optimal conditions. Developmental delay and sensory-motor deficits usually alter a child's behaviour, consequently, more often than not, hearing impairment remains an invisible handicap, undocumented and undiagnosed. Accordingly, the multiply handicapped infant and young child present confusing and misleading behaviours causing inexperienced caretakers to further miss a diagnosis of hearing impairment. For example, Bergstrom (1976) observed that, on the average, the deaf child is first suspected at age 10 months, detected at 21 months, and receives training and amplification at 27 months. Furthermore, hearing impairment in some multiply handicapped infants is undetected because little or no identification audiometry occurs after discharge from the acute care hospital following birth. An unpublished analysis (Rubin, 1981), of the Infant Program at the Lexington School for the Deaf showed that this time frame was particularly applicable to the multiply handicapped deaf infant in that institution. On the average, such children were admitted to the Lexington program at 27 months, as compared with the deaf infant of deaf parents who was admitted at 4 months, or the deaf infant of hearing parents who was admitted at 18 months.

Recently, a series of articles appeared in which multiply handicapped infants were examined for hearing loss prior to their discharge from a neonatal intensive care unit (NICU). Since graduates of an NICU are known to be at increased risk for neurological, motor and sensory disorders, Despland and Galambos (1980) tested 91 ICU infants with Auditory Brainstem Response Audiometry (ABR). They identified 11 with hearing disorders, 3 with neurological problems, and 3 with both disorders, and found a 15% incidence of hearing loss. In a

207

later study, Galambos, Hicks and Wilson (1982) found a 16%
incidence of hearing loss among 890 babies in an NICU when
tested with ABR. They concluded that at least 2% had severe
hearing losses for which amplification would be necessary,
and that 10% would later have reduced hearing sensitivity.
This is a very high yield, which a longitudinal study has not
yet validated. It is note-worthy that Simmons reported
different results from screening over 1500 NICU babies with
the Crib-O-Gram. At Stanford Medical Center in California,
they found that 31 of the 1,554 babies screened (2%) had moderate to profound hearing loss (Simmons, 1980). The discrepancy between studies may be attributed to the greater sensitivity of the ABR test over the Crib-O-Gram, and to a 10 dB
difference in pass-fail criteria. Simmons' data approximate
accepted incidence rates. The most common risk factor in the
Simmons (1980) study was intra-uterine and neonatal anoxia
which occurred in 73% of the NICU infants. Robertson (1978)
in a Canadian study utilizing the five point 1972 High Risk
Register, found a 3% overall incidence of deafness, results
which were validated through ongoing audiological evaluation.
Thus, three techniques have been used for NICU screening:
ABR; Crib-O-Gram; and the High Risk Register.

Although the NICU yields a 2%-4% incidence of severe
hearing impairment in the nursery, there has been no program
approaching universal testing of these infants in the United
States. The 1982 Position Statement developed by the U.S.
Joint Committee on Infant Hearing (Appendix I) addresses
testing this population only indirectly by describing seven
categories which place infants at risk for hearing loss.
Typically, graduates of an NICU are lost to hearing testing
once they leave the hospital and return home. Only 8 States
in the United States offer free follow-up testing to families.
Audiological evaluation is difficult to arrange in the U.S.
because it is time consuming, can devour a family's expendable
income, and seems unimportant compared to the neonates'
struggles for existence. Some children need ongoing skilled
nursing care which families cannot manage at home and, thus,
are subsequently admitted to a residential facility where
rehabilitation is fostered, but where hearing testing is not
part of the program. A small hospital cannot afford the
equipment or expense of an audiological suite, much less the
certified staff needed for ongoing professional services. A
mobile audiological unit may answer this unmet need.

Mobile audiometry has been utilized to great advantage in both identification audiometry in the schools and baseline audiometrics in industry. In most instances, the vehicle used to provide these services only carries the specialized audiological equipment required to serve a specific need. A few vehicles, however, are equipped with a broad array of diagnostic audiometric equipment so that they can function as complete hearing centers-on-wheels.

An opportunity arose to assess the benefits of mobile audiometry to the small residential hospital when a collaborative program was established between the Lexington Hearing and Speech Center and St. Mary's Hospital for Children. The Lexington Hearing and Speech Center has operated a versatile, multi-purpose mobile audiological unit for 4 years, enabling certified staff to test over 30,000 people, including groups of institutionalized, developmentally disabled children and adults. The St. Mary's Hospital children were referred for testing on Lexington's mobile unit (testmobile). Among these children was a large number of youngsters whose medical charts showed them to be NICU graduates. The purpose of this paper is to examine the use of mobile audiometry in a hospitalized group of children aged birth to 6 years.

Description of the Agencies

St. Mary's Hospital for Children, owned and operated by the Sisters of St. Mary, accepts severely handicapped children for convalescence and rehabilitation, based on their potential. It is the only multi-disciplinary, extended care facility in New York City which provides rehabilitative medicine, birth defects and genetic counselling, and care for intractable asthma. Eighty-five beds are divided into 4 wards. Included are 16 children age birth to 2 years, and 40 children age 2 to 6 years on 2 of the wards. There is an Early Education Department with an Infant Stimulation Program directed by certified Early Education Specialists. The Lexington Hearing and Speech Center has sent a team of 3 audiologists and its well equipped diagnostic vehicle to St. Mary's on a monthly basis. The program has been in effect since December, 1979, and has rendered 42 months of service.

The testmobile contains an IAC 1204 sound chamber, a Grason-Stadler 1702 clinical audiometer with speakers and earphones, a Madsen Z070 impedance bridge, an X-Y plotter,

and an otological chair (Figure 1).   Referral for audiological
evaluation is made by staff physician, nurse, or therapist, to
a speech/language pathologist who is the liaison between the
agencies.   Usually, 8 children are seen for evaluation per
day.   All children in the birth to 2 year category are
evaluated within 1 month of admission.

Selection of Subjects

There were 48 children (birth to 6 years) selected as
subjects, of which 19 were females and 29 males.   Sixty percent (29 children) were less than 24 months old at the time
of their initial hearing test.   Subjects (Ss) were seen for
audiological tests and retests by the same certified audiological team during a 3 1/2 year time frame.

FIGURE 1:   Lexington Mobile Hearing and Speech Center.

211

Birth History

St. Mary's Hospital for Children medical charts were
meticulously reviewed by the authors. The charts showed that
at least 32 children had been in an NICU and that among these,
25 were at risk for hearing loss according to the High Risk
Register. The NICU babies were characterized as neonates who
had severe asphyxia and anatomical malformations of the head
and neck. In addition, 7 non-ICU children were identified as
high risk for hearing loss according to birth history, bringing the total to 32 out of 48 who were at risk. Table I
lists the 7 categories of high risk and shows the numbers of
Ss who had one or more risk conditions.

The medical charts did not show family history of hearing loss because, in many cases, parents were not available
for interview or, when present, the question was not asked.
The most prevalent condition in birth history was severe
asphyxia (35 cases) and included infants with Apgar scores
of 0-3 and/or those who failed to institute spontaneous
respiration by 10 minutes and those with hypotonia persist-
ing to 2 hours of age. The second largest number of children
(25) had anatomical malformations involving head and neck.
Among these, 4 had severe asphyxia or respiratory distress as
well. In the entire group of 48, there were only 5 children

TABLE I: Classification of subject's(s) birth history accord-
          ing to 7 categories of the High Risk Register
          (JCIH, 1982).

Condition	No. of Ss.
Family history of hearing loss	0
Birthweight less than 1500 grams	9
Hyperbilirubinemia	3
Anatomic malformation of head and neck, dysmorphic appearance, syndromal	24
Morphologic abnormalities of pinna	1
Bacterial meningitis	1
Severe asphyxia	20
Failure to institute spontaneous respiration	11
Hypotonia	2
Apgar scores of 0-3	2

without traumatic birth history, who were not at risk according to High Risk Register, but who were admitted with chronic
asthma. The remaining 2 were admitted post-trauma.

Length of Hospitalization

Although the average length of hospitalized stay was 6
months to 1 year, 7 Ss were hospitalized for 3 to 4 years and
10 for almost 3 years. One died during this program.

Frequently, St. Mary's children were taken to acute care
hospitals for treatment; some were admitted for emergency
surgery or reconstructive surgery and were then readmitted
for skilled nursing care. A majority was admitted for
residential care directly from an acute care hospital. For
example, one youngster had 4 acute care hospital admissions
during his 18 months at St. Mary's and he had had 25 admissions prior to entering St. Mary's. His case was not atypical.

Description of Handicaps

Many of the children had severe motor dysfunctions as
well as ongoing respiratory distress, problems which were
expected in view of their stormy birth histories. At various
times, 10 Ss had tracheotomy tubes. The 5 children with
chronic intractable asthma constituted the only stable group.

Specific disorders known to result in hearing handicap
are included in the list of handicaps shown in Table II.
Genetic syndromes (Down's and Pierre-Robin) placed 3 subjects
at risk for hearing loss (Konigsmark & Gorlin, 1976; Northern
& Downs, 1978). Three with renal disease were suspect for
hearing loss (Fraser, Sproule & Haiai, 1980), along with 4
with cleft palate (Gould, 1979), and 4 with cerebral palsy.

Table II also shows 6 with Spina Bifida and 6 with
myelomeningocele, both of which are complex congenital
anomalies. Spina Bifida is often complicated by hydrocephalus, a condition which appeared in our medical charts without
specification of the degree of damage. Spina Bifida children
are known to have language disorders and delay (Culatta &
Culatta, 1978), as are children with myelomeningocele (Van
Nort, 1977).

TABLE II: Description of handicaps among population according to number.

Classification	No. of Cases
Cardio-Pulminary	
Bronchial Asthma	7
Broncho-Pulmonary Dysplasia	4
Congenital Heart Disease	1
Fetal Alcohol Syndrome	2
Hyaline Membrane Disease	1
Hydrocephalus	6
Patent Ductus Arterosis	2
Respiratory Distress Syndrome	13
Congenital	
Phocomelia	1
Cranial-Facial	
Cleft Palate	5
Syndromes	
Boller-Gerold	1
Cornelia de Lange	1
Down's	2
Pierre-Robin	1
Weyer's	1
Infectious	
Bacterial Meningitis	1
Neoplastic	
Bilateral Retinoblastoma	1
Neurologic	
Cerebral Palsy	4
Spina Bifida (Polygenic)	6
Myelomeningocele	6
Seizures	9
Renal Disease	3

Only 1 child had a previous hearing test. Cyanotic at
birth, this girl had a cleft palate, club foot, retarded
motor function, and other birth defects. Pierre-Robin
Syndrome was ruled out. She had had a single audiological
test at 11 months of age, while in an acute care hospital
awaiting surgery.

Procedures

Audiological Evaluation

Each child was scheduled for test and retest within 2
months in the sound room on the testmobile. The pure tone
audiometric techniques utilized were behavioural observation
audiometry (BOA), visual reinforcement audiometry (VRA), or
serial play audiometry. Speech audiometry measured the
threshold of detection, a threshold of intelligibility for
at least 10 spondaic words or pictures, and discrimination
tests. Soundfield and ear phone testing were used, as predicated by the child's skills and abilities.

As testing developmentally delayed children is not easy
and the test paradigm should be consistent, we were careful
to control our procedures. In BOA, for example, the initial
stimulus was always presented at a suprathreshold level in
order to elicit a response and to ascertain that the stimulus
was a heard event. A descending approach was used until 3
responses indicated threshold. The team of 3 audiologists
needed to agree completely upon responses for threshold
measurement. Test-retest reliability was judged good if
results were within +10 dB. If results were considered
accurate, a 6 month re-check was scheduled. If results were
equivocal, the child was scheduled for retest 1 month later.

Impedance audiometry was attempted on all children.
Testing included tympanometry and elicitation of stapedius
muscle reflexes contralaterally. Unfortunately, ABR was not
available for use on the testmobile.

Medical History

Prior to testing, a medical summary was furnished to the testmobile staff, which became part of the audiological chart. This was usually the Hospital Admission Summary or a recent Comprehensive Care Case Summary. Further history was provided by the professional nurse who accompanied the child and who observed the entire test procedure. This also offered a form of individual inservice training for house staff.

Medical Referral

Referral was made for otological examination when impedance audiometry was abnormal during 3 tests or after a 3 month interval between tests. All tympanograms were categorized as Type A, B, or C, according to Jerger (1976). Type A represents a well defined compliance, maximum around an air pressure differential of 0 mm H_2O. Type B tympanograms have a flat or gradually falling shape, and Type C reflect negative air pressure greater than -100 mm H_2O.

Classification of Hearing Loss

Children were categorized into 6 groups on the basis of the average audiometric findings at 500, 1000, and 2000 Hz, either in the better ear through ear phones, or in the soundfield. The following classification was used for hearing levels:

0-25 dB	Hearing within normal limits
26-40 dB	Mild hearing loss
41-55 dB	Moderate
56-70 dB	Moderate-Severe
71-89 dB	Severe
90+ dB	Profound

Results of Audiological Testing

Incidence of Hearing Loss

There were 219 evaluations provided in this program. More than half of the 48 children were seen 2 or 3 times. Some children were seen as many as 14 times when impedance results did not confirm or disagreed with audiometric findings. For example, in some cases impedance audiometry indicated a middle ear disorder not discernible audiometrically because the air conduction audiogram was normal or because of the presence of a sensorineural loss. Results showed that 2 children had a severe hearing loss, 1 had a moderate-severe loss, 5 had moderate losses, 17 had mild losses, and 33 had normal hearing. On the basis of these findings, it is estimated that 4% had severe losses and 16% had handicapping sensorineural losses.

Test Techniques

In this study, 29 children were under 24 months at the time of the first test. Since this group was primarily characterized by sensory, motor, and cognitive deficits as well as failure-to-thrive, many (except for 5 with chronic asthma) were estimated to be seriously developmentally delayed. Psychological reports support this observation. Therefore, BOA was used to evaluate 38 children; but, during this program, 8 of the 38 had hearing sensitivity confirmed by serial play audiometry. VRA was used with only 3. This was not surprising, considering the developmental age of the children, their lack of eye contact, and the effect of new admissions. Serial play audiometry was used initially with 7 children.

Impedance Findings

Considering the excellent skilled nursing care and daily medical examinations which the children received, there was an alarmingly high incidence of abnormal tympanometry. There were 22 children who had Type B or Type C tympanograms. Of these, 16 never displayed a Type A. Rubin (1978) found a 61% incidence of abnormal tympanometry in a group of young deaf children, but this percentage dropped to 12% in the same group after 3 years of age.

Some children continued to display abnormal tympanometry. For example, 1 child, following multiple unsuccessful medical treatments, had confirmed middle ear pathology for 9 months

and eventually had to have myringotomies and ventilation
tubes inserted. On the basis of these clinical findings,
7 children were referred to the Lexington Hearing and Speech
Center for otological examination.

It was thought that children with tracheotomy tubes
might show abnormal tympanometric findings, but inspection
of the data showed this to be not true.

Normal Hearing Group

Audiological findings indicated that 33 children (69%)
had hearing within normal limits. Table III indicates that
reflexes were in agreement with audiometric results and
present in 15Ss, absent in 16, and could not be established
in 4. This result is not surprising, given the overall
incidence of 45% of abnormal tympanometry in this hospitalized
group. The reliability and validity of audiological evaluations were judged to be good because of test-retest
consistency.

Behavioural observation audiometry was the test technique
of choice with 20 children. VRA succeeded with 3, while 5
more responded initially with BOA, and then, as they matured

TABLE III: Analysis of normal hearing results according to
            number of subjects (N), test technique (test),
            and impedance finding.

					Reflexes		
N	Test	Norm Tymp	Abn Tymp	Pres	Abs	Could Not Test	Ss 6 mo
10	BOA	x		x			
2	BOA	x				x	
6	BOA		x		x		
5	BOA/SP		x		x		
2	BOA	x			x		x
1	VRA	x					
2	VRA		x		x		
4	SP	x					
1	SP		x		x		
33		19	14	15	16	2	2

developmentally, were able to perform serial play. All children were eventually tested audiometrically, although many were not testable during their initial evaluations.

Five admitted for chronic asthma were thought to be representative of the general population, rather than the developmentally disabled. None had been in an NICU and all had hearing within normal limits.

Children With Hearing Loss

It is not surprising that 14 of the 15 children with suspected hearing loss had stormy birth histories requiring neonatal intensive care, while the remaining child had been in an ICU following post-natal trauma. Eleven of the 14 children had respiratory distress at birth and were cyanotic, and 3 had a severe seizure disorder. These children resemble Simmons' (1980) patterns of deafness. In addition, of the 5 children known to have cleft palates, 4 had a hearing loss.

Genetic defects contributed to this group. All the children with Down's Syndrome, Pierre-Robin Syndrome, Cornelia de Lange Syndrome, and with bilateral retinoblastoma with deletion of the long arm of chromosome 13 had a confirmed loss. Table IV lists the various test techniques used and shows that 53% had abnormal impedance findings. Reflexes were

TABLE IV: Analysis of subjects' (Ss) hearing levels according to hearing level, number of subjects (N), test technique (Test) and impedance findings (N=15).

N	Hrng Level	Test	Norm Tymp	Abn Tymp	Reflexes Pres	Abs	Could Not Test
3	mild	BOA	x		x		
3	mild	BOA		x		x	
1	mild	VRA	x		x		
4	moderate	BOA		x		x	
1	moderate	BOA					x
1	mod-severe	BOA		x		x	
1	severe	SP	x			x	
1	severe	BOA	x			x	
N=15			6	8	4	10	1

present in only 4 cases. Absent reflexes were the result of
sensorineural hearing loss. Two children with unilateral
sensorineural hearing loss were not included in this group.

Audiological Management

     Boothroyd (1982) listed the objectives of audiological
management of the hearing impaired child as follows:

     1. to ensure that the child has appropriate hearing
         aids;
     2. to keep the aids in perfect working order;
     3. to establish full time use of the aids;
     4. to conserve hearing;
     5. to create an optimal acoustic environment;
     6. to provide diagnostic information.

     Many of these objectives require a parent, parent-
surrogate, or a teacher in an educational setting to translate
them into action. In the current program, the parents were
not available on a daily basis. According to the social
worker's chart notes, many did not visit at all. Our atypical
children were usually in need of the services offered by a
variety of specialists, including an audiologist, nurse,
physician, teacher, physical and occupational therapist, and
speech/language pathologist. Yet it was essential that the
number of these supplementary caregivers be limited in order
to foster a familiar and trusting relationship (Connor et al.,
1978). Rather than using numerous, well-meaning professional
workers, each performing designated traditional roles, a
transdisciplinary approach was employed in which the speech/
language pathologist was the primary programmer. Dealing with
passivity and auditory deprivation of the hearing impaired
children was the responsibility of the speech/language pathologist, while the skilled nurse became the nurturing parent
capable of fostering strong attachments and basic trust. Thus,
the audiologist recommended amplification, but it was the
speech/language pathologist who subsequently trained the house
staff and then created an optimal acoustic environment on the
ward by carrying out the audiologist's recommendations (e.g.
sound toys which the hearing impaired child could perceive
were introduced into the crib). The audiologist provided
diagnostic information which the speech/language pathologist
presented at case conferences, and it was the latter who
attempted to establish full time use of amplification which,
for ill children, was a difficult task.

The usual contribution of the audiologist in planning rehabilitation was limited in this process, as can be seen in the
following illustrative case study.

Case Study

L.D. is a 5 year old male admitted to St. Mary's
Hospital at age 16 months with a diagnosis of
cyanotic congenital heart disease, transposition
of the great vessels, brain damage secondary to
cardiac arrest, tracheostomy, gastrostomy, and
developmental retardation with seizure diathesis.

L.D., who was cyanotic at birth and in an NICU,
underwent 2 unsuccessful surgical procedures
before discharge. At 11 months, following cardiac
arrest, he was re-admitted to an acute care hospital.
Constant seizures were shown in electroencephalography. L.D. was then admitted to St. Mary's
Hopsital, where he has been for a period of 5 years.
He is closely monitored for respiratory and cardiac
distress. Medications include Dilantin, Digoxin,
Lasix and Valium.

L.D. was seen initially in the Lexington test-mobile
at 22 months. He was among the first group evaluated
audiologically. On that occasion, the results of
soundfield BOA audiometry indicated a severe bilateral
sensorineural hearing loss. Tympanometry was normal
(Type A), with reflexes elicited only in the left
ear at 500 Hz (115 dB HL), and 1000 Hz (120 dB HL).
Retested 1 month later, eye blink, eye widening,
and eye shifts were found in response to warbled
pure tones and to speech presented in the soundfield. Speech detection was 60 dB HL. Amplification was not recommended because of poor prognosis.

During 1979, L.D. was seen on 3 occasions. BOA
indicated a severe sensorineural hearing loss
bilaterally. Tympanometry resulted in Type A
tympanograms, and reflexes could not be established
because there was an insufficient sensation level
to elicit them. A sound stimulation program was

initiated and continued through 1980. During
that year, L.D. sustained repeated attacks of
otitis media, there being 4 episodes in 3 months.

In January, 1981, L.D.'s progress was reviewed
in a Comprehensive Care Conference. It was
noted that this 3 year old child showed periodic
self-induced vomiting which decreased when the
boy was occupied. Intensive stimulation was
recommended for all areas, especially audition.
Earmolds were fabricated in February and a hearing
aid evaluation was performed on the test-mobile
comparing performance with 2 post-auricular prostheses. Utilizing BOA, it was found that L.D.
responded at 30 dB HL to warbled tones and at 20 dB
HL to speech in the soundfield. He received a
post-auricular hearing aid in February, 1981.
Staff noted that he was more alert and responsive
to his environment, but that he used the aid only
while attending Early Education and Infant Stimulation sessions during the day. Hearing aid evaluation has continued, in part, to determine if there
is an aided difference between ears.

L.D. occasionally played with small toys and
remained totally dependent on staff for daily
living activities at a reported social age of
41 months. He began to imitate labial sounds
and responded appropriately by pointing to body
parts when named. Staff recommended that he use
his aid as much as possible. A plastic shield was
made by the occupational therapist to help keep
the aid on while he was in his crib (Figure 2).

In 1982, L.D. made several successful home visits
and arrangements were made to transfer him to
live with his grandmother. His personal wheelchair was delivered. Conference notes showed
that fine motor co-ordination improved (e.g. he
placed rings on a cone or took bean bags in and
out of buckets), he used amplification during
waking hours, and healthwise, he was judged
basically stable with profound retardation.

FIGURE 2:   Patient using a post-auricular hearing aid with a
            plastic shield to keep the prosthesis in place
            during crib rest.

L.D. was followed audiologically for 3.6 years,
during which time there were 10 diagnostic
evaluations and 8 rehabilitation sessions.
Because this child was gravely ill during this
period, 2 years elapsed before personal amplification was provided. Auditory brainstem response
audiometry will be scheduled at the Lexington
Hearing and Speech Center.

                        Discussion

    The children in this study all needed skilled nursing
care, residential placement, and a variety of other services
to meet their needs. Their failure-to-thrive was evident
during the initial audiological evaluations, by their lack

of affect, poor eye contact, and, in some instances, posture
like a rag doll. With the exception of the group of children
with chronic asthma and 2 children with post-natal trauma,
32 were graduates of an NICU with a predictable high risk of
hearing impairment. The 2% to 4% incidence of severe hearing
loss is remarkably similar to those rates reported by Despland
and Galambos (1980), Galambos, Wilson and Hicks (1982),
Simmons (1980), and Robertson (1978). Furthermore, the 16%
incidence of handicapping hearing loss is nearly identical to
the data presented by Galambos et al., (1982). Yet the reader
should recall that, regardless of the proclivity of these
children for hearing loss, only one child had a single test
of auditory sensitivity prior to our evaluations. The use of
mobile audiometry facilitated diagnosis of hearing impairment
and subsequent habilitation. In this setting, mobile audiometry was a valuable mechanism which focused the need for
audiological services. Of course, there are both advantages
and disadvantages to a program such as the one described.

Advantages of Mobile Audiometry

    Early Diagnosis of Hearing Loss

    Insofar as mandatory hearing screening exists in only a
few states in the United States, early identification of
hearing loss exists more in the literature than in reality.
Although NICU graduates are at risk for hearing loss and a
High Risk Register does work, children are being diagnosed
past the second year of life. Multiply handicapped children
are known to be at risk by virtue of their birth history.
They can be evaluated early with mobile audiometry while
they are hospitalized, or while they reside in a developmental
center. Children who require skilled nursing care can have a
more meaningful rehabilitation course if sensory deficits such
as hearing loss are identified early.

    Ease of Ongoing Audiological
    Evaluation

    The developmentally disabled child requires expert
management in order to develop motorically, cognitively, and
socially into an independent, happy human being. It is
evident that great burdens are placed on the family to manage

several appointments per week and several serious operations
during their child's habilitation. In this study, parents
were mostly absent during the hospitalization. At the time
of discharge, most children went to a foster home or a center.

The mobile unit gets to the heart of the matter of
transportation by providing an on-site service in a systematic
way. Although a few children were lost to follow-up, most
had a diagnostic work-up completed before they left the
hospital. The time frame was appropriate to the task.

Cost-Effectiveness

Fitting a multi-purpose unit with audiological equipment
is not inexpensive. Cost, however, can be depreciated over
an 8 year period while the van serves a wide variety of
social agencies, schools, and industry. It is less costly
than establishing an audiology suite in a small hospital!
A hospital like St. Mary's (85 beds) is too small to support
its own service. For it, use of a mobile unit is very cost-
effective.

Disadvantages of Mobile Audiometry

Inadequate Interface With
Hospital Staff

Time constraints prevented the audiological staff from
active participation in case conferences and observations of
children in early education activities. A transdisciplinary
approach was necessary when the program was undertaken, but
in the end there was a lack of audiological input into
rehabilitation plans. This disadvantage was more of a
scheduling problem than a philosophical one.

Lack of Extensive Diagnostic
Tests on the Mobile Unit

The hearing status of developmentally disabled young
children is difficult to assess. In this study, for example,
some children were tested 8 or 9 times before agreement was
obtained between tests. In 2 cases, excessive crying prevented tympanometry, while in another, we wondered whether

an intracranial hemorrhage had affected the facial nerve and obliterated reflexes. ABR would have been welcomed for a population with so many neurological deficits, not only in terms of helping to validate a diagnosis, but in yielding important information about the auditory system. For example, in a study of deaf-blind children, Stein and his colleagues (1981) showed a significant number of infants and children who appeared deaf but were not when tested with ABR. There is no question but that ABR should be scheduled for use with all multiply handicapped children to assist in the confirmation of hearing loss.

Conclusion

1. Mobile audiometry offers a unique opportunity to identify the multiply handicapped hearing impaired hospitalized child.

2. All multiply handicapped infants should be evaluated for hearing loss by any reliable testing method because of the high yield of hearing impairment within that group.

3. Children who have graduated from a neonatal intensive care unit are at risk for hearing loss, inasmuch as that population yields an incidence of 2% to 4% severe hearing loss and approximately 16% handicapping hearing loss.

4. A high number of children with cleft palate have a handicapping hearing loss.

References

Bergstrom, L., "Congenital Deafness," Hearing Disorders (Boston: Little, Brown & Co.), Northern, J.L. (Ed.), 1976.

Boothroyd, A., Hearing Impairments in Young Children (Englewood Cliffs, N.J.: Prentice-Hall), 1982.

Connor, F.P., Williamson, G.G., and Siepp, J.M., Program Guide for Infants and Toddlers with Neuromotor and Other Developmental Disabilities (New York: Columbia University Press), 1978.

Culatta, B., and Culatta, R., "Spina Bifida Children's Non-Communicative Language: Examples and Identification Guidelines," Allied Health and Behavioural Sciences 1:22-29, 1978.

Despland, P.A., and Galambos, R., "The Auditory Brainstem Response (ABR) is a Useful Diagnostic Tool in the Intensive Care Nursery," Pediatric Research 14:154-158, 1980.

Fraser, F.C., and Haiai, F., "Frequency of the Brachio-oto-renal (BOR) Syndrome in Children with Profound Hearing Loss," American Journal of Medical Genetics 7:341-349, 1980.

Friedrich, B.W., "Clinical Evaluation of Hearing in Developmentally Disabled Children," Audiology Journal of Continuing Education - Tapes (New York: Grune & Stratton, Inc.), Vol. 5, No. 8, 1980.

Galambos, R., "Use of ABR in Infant Testing," Early Diagnosis of Hearing Loss (New York: Grune & Stratton, Inc.), Gerber, S.E. and Mencher, G.T. (Eds.), 1978.

Galambos, R., Hicks, G., and Wilson, J.J., "Hearing Loss in Graduates of a Tertiary Intensive Care Nursery," Ear and Hearing 3:87-90, 1982.

Gould, H.J., "Aspects of Hearing in Craniofacial Malformation," Audiology Journal of Continuing Education - Tapes (New York: Grune & Stratton, Inc.), Vol. 4, No. 5, 1978.

Jerger, S., Jerger, J., Mouldin, L., and Segal, P., "Studies in Impedance Audiometry: Children Less Than 6 Years Old," Selected Readings in Impedance Audiometry (Dobbs Ferry, New York: American Electromedics Corp.), Northern, J.L. (Ed.), 1976.

Joint Committee on Infant Hearing (Position Statement), Pediatrics, September, 1982.

Konigsmark, B.W., and Gorlin, R.J., Genetic and Metabolic Deafness (Philadelphia: Saunders Co.), 1976.

Northern, J.L., and Downs, M.P., Hearing in Children (Baltimore: Williams & Wilkins), 1978.

Robertson, C., "Pediatric Assessment of the Infant," Early Diagnosis of Hearing Loss (New York: Grune & Stratton), Gerber, S.E., and Mencher, G.T. (Eds.), 1978.

Rubin, M., "Serous Otitis Media in Severe-Profound Hearing Impaired Children, Age 0-6," Volta Review 80:81-85, 1978.

Rubin, M., Unpublished Analysis of Lexington School's Infant Center Population, Annual Report of Lexington School (1980-1981), New York.

Simmons, F.B., "Patterns of Deafness in Newborns," Laryngoscope 90:448-453, 1980.

Stein, L.K., Ozdamar, O., and Schnable, M., "Auditory Brainstem Responses (ABR) with Suspected Deaf-Blind Children," Ear and Hearing 2:30-41, 1981.

Van Nort, J.B., "Myelomeningocele: Educational Importance," Division of the Physically Handicapped, Homebound and Hospitalized Journal (Council for Exceptional Children) 3:7-9, 1977.

Appendix I
Joint Committee on Infant Hearing
Position Statement

Early detection of hearing impairment in the affected
infant is important for medical treatment and subsequent
educational intervention to assure development of communication skills.

In 1973, the Joint Committee on Infant Hearing Screening
recommended identifying infants at risk for hearing impairment
by means of five criteria and suggested follow-up audiological
evaluation of these infants until accurate assessments of
hearing could be made. Since the incidence of moderate to
profound hearing loss in the at-risk infant group is 2.5%+5%,
audiologic testing of this group is warranted. Acoustic testing of all newborn infants has a high incidence of false
positive and false negative results and is not universally
recommended.

Recent research suggests the need for expansion and
clarification of the 1973 criteria. This 1982 statement
expands the risk criteria and makes recommendations for the
evaluation and treatment of the hearing-impaired infant.

1. Identification

A. Risk Criteria

The factors that identify those infants who are AT
RISK for having hearing impairment include the following:

1. A family history of childhood hearing impairment;

2. Congenital perinatal infection (e.g. cytomegalo-
    virus, rubella, herpes, toxoplasmosis, syphilis);

3. Anatomic malformations involving the head or neck
    (e.g. dysmorphic-appearance including syndromal and
    non-syndromal abnormalities, overt or submucous
    cleft palate, morphologic abnormalities of the
    pinna);

4. Birthweight less than 1500 grams.

5. Hyperbilirubinemia at level exceeding indications
    for exchange transfusion;

6. Bacterial meningitis, especially H. influenza;

7. Severe asphyxia which may include infants with
    Apgar scores of 0-3 who fail to institute
    spontaneous respiration by 10 minutes and those
    with hypotonia persisting to two hours of age.

B. Screening Procedures

The hearing of infants who manifest any item on the
list of risk criteria should be screened, preferably under
supervision of an audiologist, optimally by 3 months of age,
but not later than 6 months of age. The initial screening
should include the observation of behavioural or electrophysiological response to sound.* If consistent electrophysiological or behavioural responses are detected at
appropriate sound levels, then the screening process will be
considered complete except in those cases where there is a
probability of a progressive hearing loss; e.g., family
history of delayed onset, degenerative disease, or intra-
uterine infections. If results of an initial screening of an
infant manifesting any risk criteria are equivocal, then the
infant should be referred for diagnostic testing.

II. Diagnosis for Infants Failing Screening

A. Diagnostic evaluation of an infant under 6 months of
age includes:

1. General physical examination and history including:

    a) examination of the head and neck;

    b) otoscopy and otomicroscopy;

    c) identification of relevant physical abnorm-
        alities;

    d) laboratory tests such as urinalysis and
        diagnostic tests for perinatal infections.

2. Comprehensive audiological evaluation:

    a) behavioural history;

---

* This Committee has no recommendations at this time
regarding any specific device.

b)   behavioural observation audiometry;

c)   testing of auditory evoked potentials, if
indicated.

B.   After the age of 6 months, the following are also
recommended:

1.   Communication skills evaluation;

2.   Acoustic immitance measurements (Impedance
measurements);

3.   Selected tests of development.

III.   Management of the Hearing Impaired Infant

Habilitation of the hearing-impaired infant may begin
while the diagnostic evaluation is in process. The Committee
recommends, however, that whenever possible, the diagnostic
process should be completed and habilitation begun by the age
of 6 months. Services to the hearing impaired infant under 6
months of age include:

A.   Medical management:

1.   Re-evaluation;

2.   Treatment;

3.   Genetic evaluation and counseling when indicated.

B.   Audiologic management:

1.   Ongoing audiological assessment;

2.   Selection of hearing aid(s);

3.   Family counseling.

C.   Psychoeducational management:

1.   Formulation of an individualized educational
plan;

2.   Information about the implications of hearing
impairment.

After the age of 6 months, the hearing impaired infant
becomes easier to manage in a habilitation plan but s/he will
require the services listed above.
(Joint Committee on Infant Hearing ASHA 24:1017-1018, 1982.)

SELECTIVE IMPAIRMENT OF LATE VERTEX
AND MIDDLE LATENCY AUDITORY EVOKED RESPONSES

Paul Kileny
David A. Berry
Glenrose Hospital, Edmonton, Alberta

The discovery in the late 1960s of methods to record the brainstem auditory evoked response gave a significant boost to the electrophysiological assessment of peripheral auditory function in the very young or the severely handicapped. Today, auditory brainstem responses (ABR) are effectively utilized:

1)   to determine hearing sensitivity in neonates and infants (Schulman-Galambos & Galambos, 1975; Mokotoff et al., 1977; Galambos & Despland, 1980);

2)   for the detection of brainstem lesions (Starr & Hamilton, 1976);

3)   as measures of peripheral auditory pathway maturation (Salamy & McKean, 1976);

4)   to monitor the outcome of perinatal asphyxia (Kileny et al., 1980);

5)   as indicators of hearing aid efficacy (Kileny, 1982).

Although the identities of the neural generators of several ABR components (beyond Wave II) are unclear, the current notion is that the ABR originates from the peripheral portions of the auditory pathway, including the auditory nerve and the brainstem (Moller et al., 1981; Starr & Achor, 1980).

With the introduction of brainstem responses into clinical practice, the interest in middle latency (MLR) and late vertex auditory evoked (LVAER) responses and their clinical utilization declined. The relative ease with which

brainstem responses may be acquired contributed significantly
to this trend. However, the ABR provides a rather restricted
view of auditory function, one which excludes the central
portion of the auditory pathway. With some interesting
exceptions, basically the ABR provides an indication or an
approximation of peripheral hearing sensitivity (Worthington
& Peters, 1981).

The exact generators of the MLR and the LVAER are also
not known, but the temporal characteristics and some clinical
data suggest that they are generated central to the ABR and
probably reflect auditory neuro-electrical activity in the
thalamus, primary and secondary auditory cortex and temporal-
parietal cortex (Picton et al., 1974). Unlike the ABR, the
LVAER is affected by stages of sleep (Kevanishvili & Von
Specht, 1979; Skinner & Antinoro, 1969), and certain drugs
which may alter its configuration and/or peak latencies
(Pradhan & Galambos, 1962). The MLR is quite resistant to
drugs and is not appreciably altered by the state of the
subject (Mendel et al., 1975; Kileny et al., 1982).

Several recent studies have emphasized the clinical
utility of these later components of the auditory evoked
response. For instance, it has been documented that following
unilateral temporal-parietal lesions, the amplitude of the N1
component of the LVAER was markedly depressed (Knight et al.,
1980). With bilateral temporal lobe lesions, MLRs were either
intact (Parving et al., 1980), or disrupted (Ozdamar et al.,
1982). In another case study (Michel et al., 1980), bilateral
lesions involving the supratemporal planes resulted in an
absence of LVAERs. Based on a study of neurologically
impaired multiply handicapped children (some with hypsa-
rhythmic EEGs), Cohen and Rapin (1978) regarded the early and
late auditory evoked potentials as "complementary methods".
In some of the cases described by those authors, there were
major discrepancies between the early brainstem responses
which reflected normal peripheral auditory thresholds, and
late cortical evoked responses which were absent or were only
elicited at high, suprathreshold levels, suggesting profound
hearing loss.

Inasmuch as the brainstem components of the auditory
evoked response reflect neuroelectrical activation of the
peripheral portion of the auditory pathway, the ABR alone
may provide misleading results when dealing with cases with

possible central lesions. Does one send a multiply handicapped infant with no behavioural responses to auditory
stimuli but normal ABR thresholds, home with a diagnosis of
normal auditory function? While, at the moment, there seems
to be little we offer the patient with central auditory dysfunction, a different course of action would be indicated for
them as compared to those with normal auditory function or a
peripheral hearing impairment.

This study is a demonstration of the benefits and the
significance of auditory evoked responses beyond the ABR
(e.g. MLR & LVAER) when testing infants and children with
suspected diffuse or localized brain lesions. The ABR alone
may not provide sufficient diagnostic information. The
presence of MLRs and LVAERs, in addition to normal ABR thresholds, would provide strong evidence of normal peripheral and
central auditory function.

Material and Methods

Subjects

This report involves 15 patients aged 6 weeks to 15
years, referred to the Audiology Department at the Glenrose
Hospital. Twelve of the 15 were between 8 to 20 months old
at initial testing. In each case, there was evidence of
neurological involvement in the form of hypotonia, spasticity,
and/or convulsive disorder. The apparent time of insult
varied from prenatal and perinatal (i.e. IUGR, perinatal
asphyxia) to post-natal (i.e. accidental suffocation, drown-
ing). Hypoxia or anoxia was a precipitating or primary
factor in 13 of the 15 patients. Focal CNS lesions were
demonstrated in 2 of the 15. Formal or informal behavioural
testing either elicited no responses to auditory stimuli, or
suggested elevated thresholds. With two exceptions (Cases 1
and 4) where slight or mild peripheral hearing losses were
suggested, the ABR indicated normal bilateral peripheral hearing sensitivity with Waves I through V present in all cases.
Both EEG and CT scan results were available on 14 patients.
CT scan results could not be obtained in one case. Table I
summarizes the CT scan and EEG results for the group. Every
patient had abnormal CT scan and/or EEG results. In 8 of our
patients, only the EEG or the CT scan results were abnormal

(4 each). CT Scan diagnoses included: sub-arachnoid hemorrhage, generalized atrophy, and dilated ventricles. In several cases, a combination of 2 or all 3 of the above could be found. EEG results included generalized supression with or without spikes, generalized epileptiform activity, and a single case with hypsarhythmia.

TABLE I: Summary of CT Scan and EEG results.

	Positive	Negative
CT Scan	10	4
EEG	11	4

Procedures

The assessment of behavioural responses to auditory stimulation was based on informal observations, startle responses, Behavioural Observation Audiometry, and/or Visual Reinforcement Audiometry (Wilson, 1978). With the 2 oldest patients (3.5 and 15 years old), play and conventional audiometry were utilized.

Auditory brainstem responses (ABR), middle-latency responses (MLR), and late vertex auditory evoked responses (LVAER) were recorded from all patients with a vertex to ear-lobe (or mastoid) electrode configuration. The contralateral earlobe or mastoid served as the ground. Neuroelectrical activity was pre-amplified, filtered (150-3000 Hz for ABR; 30-100 Hz for MLR; 1-30 Hz for LVAER) and averaged by a Nicolet CA-1000 averager or a Nicolet MED-80 mini computer. For ABR, 2048 sweeps of 20.48 msec. duration were summed, compared to 1024 sweeps of 60-102.4 msec. duration for the MLR and 50-100 sweeps of 512 msec. duration for the LVAER.

Auditory brainstem responses were elicited by unfiltered clicks alternated in polarity and presented at a rate of 17.1/sec. In every case, responses were elicited by 60 dB and 20 dB HL clicks. Brainstem responses to 20 dB clicks were accepted as evidence of normal peripheral hearing sensitivity. The MLRs were elicited by 60-70 dB HL unfiltered

clicks presented at a rate of 6.7/sec. No attempt was made to
establish an MLR threshold, merely to verify their presence
for suprathreshold stimuli. In those cases where ABR thresholds were above 20 dB HL, the MLRs were elicited at 40-50 dB
above ABR thresholds. LVAERs were elicited by 1000 Hz tone-
bursts gated with rise-fall times of 5 msec. and a plateau of
10 msec. presented at 60 dB HL or 40-50 dB above ABR threshold
at a variable rate ranging from 1/sec. to 1.9/sec.

Figure 1 illustrates MLRs from 2 healthy infants and an
adult. Wave V of the ABR and Pa of the MLR are the most
prominent components, along with No of the MLR (15 msec.).
Pb may be detected in the first (adult) and the second recordings. The adult and the infant MLRs exhibited similar
latency characteristics (Mendelsohn & Salamy, 1981). Figure 2
is an illustration of replicated LVAERs recorded from a
healthy 4 week old. A small N_1 (109 msec.) and a larger P_2
voltage exceeded 1.5 microvolts.

FIGURE 1:   Middle-latency auditory evoked response (MLR). In
this and all following figures, an upward deflec-
tion of the trace represents vertex positivity.
Peak latencies are designated in msec.

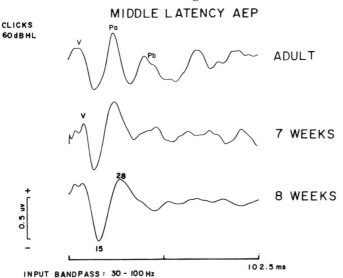

MIDDLE LATENCY AEP

FIGURE 2:   Late vertex auditory evoked responses (LVAER)
            recorded during quiet sleep from a normal 4 week
            old male. Peak latencies are designated in msec.
            N_1 (109 msec.), P_2 (245 msec.), N_2 (389 msec.).

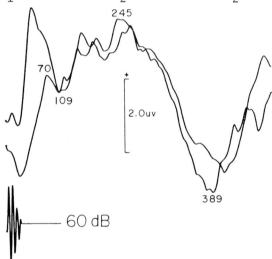

        Figure 3 summarizes the evoked response audiometry
battery currently utilized in our facility. It includes
brainstem, middle-latency, and late vertex auditory evoked
responses recorded from a 4 week old male infant during
natural sleep. Both the 60 dB and the 20 dB brainstem
responses are well defined with prominent Waves I, II, III,
and V (VI and VII may also be detected in the 60 dB ABRs).
The MLR is characterized by Wave V, Po and Pa (Pb is also
detectable in this record). The late vertex response features
a well defined N_1 (100 msec.) and P_2 (210 msec.) complex that
exceeds 2.0 microvolts.

        Table II is a summary of the initial auditory evoked
response results from our 15 patients. ABR was present in all
subjects. Wave V, and in most cases Waves I, III, and V, were
clearly detectable in all. ABR abnormalities consisted of
prolonged interpeak latencies in 6 cases. MLRs were recorded
in only 11 of our patients. The MLR was absent in 2 cases and
was abnormal (prolonged peak latencies) in 3 cases. LVAER
abnormalities consisted mainly of peak reversals (4 cases).
The LVAER was absent in 11 cases.

FIGURE 3:   The auditory evoked response battery in a normal 4
            week old male infant. ABR - auditory brainstem
            responses; MLR - middle-latency responses; LVAER -
            late vertex responses (N_1-100 msec., P_2-210 msec.).

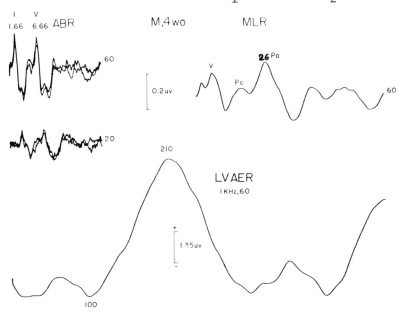

Thirteen of the patients are being followed with behavioural audiometry. In 9, the evoked potential studies were
repeated once or twice. Improvements in behavioural responses
were noted in 5 of the 9. In all 5, behavioural improvement
(i.e. some response to auditory stimuli where previously there
was none; closer coincidence between ABR and behavioural

TABLE II: Summary of Auditory Evoked Potential studies.

	Absent	Impaired	Negative
ABR	–	6	9
MLR	2	3	6
LVAER	11	4	–

---

thresholds) coincided with improvements in MLR or LVAER (i.e.
replicable responses where previously there were none, or a
normalization of evoked potential configuration). Of the 6
patients not re-evaluated by evoked potential, 2 have expired.
Both were severely asphyxiated at birth, and had subsequent
seizures and frequent apneas. In both cases, the LVAERs were
absent.

Autopsy reports are available in 1 of the 2 cases, a male
who expired at 2 months-11 days of age. The examination of
the brain revealed the following: hypoxemic, laminar and
multifocal neuronal depletion with replacement astrocytosis in
cerebral cortex, rarefaction and diminution of convolutional
white matter with astroglial hyperplasia, mild ex-vacuo hydrocephalus and hypoxemic neuronal depletion of cerebellar cortex.

Following are 5 typical living cases representative of
this entire group of patients. They reflect the complexities
of response and diagnosis seen in the multiply handicapped
child.

    Case 1.

    A female born to a 26 year old primigravida mother
    at 38 weeks gestation, the child was delivered by
    Caesarean section due to intrauterine growth retarda-
    tion. Apgars measured at 1 and 5 minutes were 5 and
    8, respectively. The amniotic fluid was meconium
    stained. Birthweight was 1860 gms. The baby had
    an abnormal appearance, especially her facies. She
    fed poorly initially and showed no evidence of eye
    contact or startle. At 7 months of age, following
    a 1 month history of seizures, hypsarhythmia was
    revealed upon EEG examination. She was subsequently
    medicated with Phenobarb and Rivotril. She appeared
    to be very hypotonic and small for her age. Subse-
    quent surgery revealed an absent left kidney and
    she remains on medications for high renin hyper-
    tension. At 20 months of age, she presented with
    optic atrophy, spastic quadriplegia and convulsive
    disorder. The results of a CT Scan were negative.

    The patient was referred to audiology at 8 months
    of age, at which time behavioural testing revealed
    no apparent response to sound. Figure 4 illustrates
    the ABRs and the LVAERs obtained at that time.

FIGURE 4:   Case 1 - Auditory brainstem responses (ABR) and
            late vertex responses (AEP).

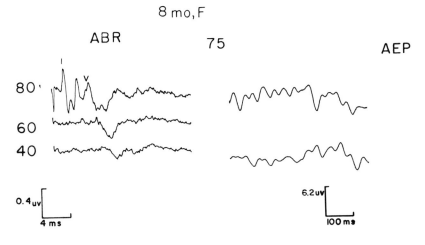

8 mo, F

Waves I through VI of the ABR were detectable
following stimulation with 80 dB clicks.   No
responses could be elicited by clicks below
40 dB HL.   The late components of the auditory
evoked (AEP) response were clearly absent.   At
18 months of age, a 55-60 dB soundfield speech
awareness threshold was obtained.   Subsequently,
she was fitted with hearing aids which provided
her with a speech awareness threshold of 35-40 dB.
Since then, there have been some fluctuations in
this patient's unaided hearing thresholds, as the
problem was compounded by bilateral serous otitis
media.   The evoked response studies were repeated
again at 27 months of age, at which time ABR
thresholds to unfiltered clicks were 50 dB HL
bilaterally.   Her MLRs were characterized by
prolonged Pa peaks (latency 37.2 msec.) and some
replicable but atypical activity was obtained
within the latency range of the LVAER.   At present,
the patient is in an institution for the severely
retarded, as she presents with severe intellectual
and language delay.

Case 2.

This male patient developed normally until the
age of 6 months. At that time, he was suffocated
accidentally in a plastic wrap. Subsequently, he
developed numerous seizures and exhibited marked
hypotonia. After discharge from the hospital, he
developed marked spasticity and according to the
parents and his physician, exhibited no responses
to visual and auditory stimuli. An EEG performed
3 days after admission to the hospital was normal.
The initial CT Scan results were normal, however,
subsequent CT Scans revealed bilateral temporal
lobe cerebral infarcts.

The patient was referred to audiology at 11 months
of age, approximately 5 months following his
accident. Figure 5 illustrates the auditory
brainstem responses to 60 dB and 20 dB HL clicks
following right ear stimulation. Identical
responses were obtained following a left ear
stimulation. These responses suggest a peripheral
hearing sensitivity of at least a 20 dB HL.

FIGURE 5:   Case 2 - Auditory Brainstem Responses.

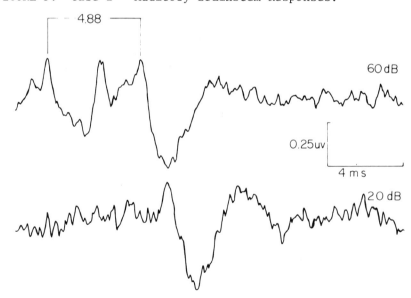

Waves I, III and V are well defined with the I-V
peak latency slightly prolonged (4.88 msec.).

Figure 6 illustrates our attempt to obtain middle-
latency auditory evoked responses from this patient.
The top trace is a control MLR obtained from a
normal subject. The second and third traces were
recorded from Case 2. No replicable activity could
be detected following Wave V of the auditory brainstem response. The bottom trace is a "no stimulus"
control run.

Behavioural observation audiometry performed soon
after the evoked response studies indicated soundfield thresholds in the 75 to 85 dB HL range.
Visual evoked responses elicited by light flashes
were absent bilaterally. Speech-language assessment revealed a severe expressive and receptive

FIGURE 6:   Case 2 - The second and the third trace are
            attempts at obtaining MLRs from this patient at
            11 months of age. The top trace is an MLR from
            a normal control. The bottom trace is a "no
            stimulus" control. Notice the absence of Wave V
            of the ABR.

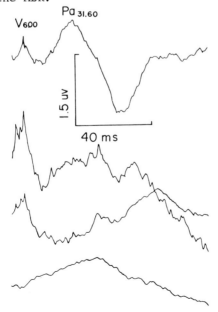

language delay; the patient was functioning at approximately a 4 month level. He was assessed again at 19 months, at which time he was still functioning at the 4 month level. His vocalizations were randomly produced, but he seemed to respond by cessation of activity to his name, and to noise makers.

Auditory evoked response studies repeated at 33 months of age are illustrated in Figure 7. The MLRs are characterized by a poorly resolved Pa peak which is partially replicated. The LVAERs obtained following right ear stimulation (AD; CZA2) were not significantly different from the "no stimulus" control run (C). Those obtained following left ear stimulation (AS; CZA1) did differ from the control run and exhibited some low amplitude replicable activity (less than 0.6 microvolts), characterized by a positive polarity peak at approximately 100 msec. post-stimulus latency. Behavioural observation audiometry performed on the same date (33 months) indicated awareness of speech and warble tones in the 65-70 dB HL range. The patient continues to have seizures and presents with spastic quadriparesis. He is on medication for seizure control.

FIGURE 7:   Case 2 - MLRs and LVAERs obtained from this patient at 33 months of age.

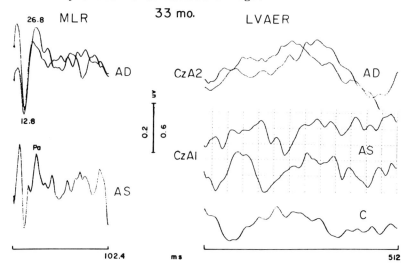

Case 3.

Admitted at 10 1/2 months of age, this female with
convulsions and severe dehydration secondary to
gastroenteritis, was started, and then maintained
on Phenobarb and Dilantin. Behaving at the 2 month
developmental level at the time of admission, she
exhibited increased deep tendon reflexes. Prior to
this admission, she had been developing normally.
A CT Scan was negative, the EEG appeared initially
within normal limits, however, several days later
it became epileptiform. The patient had very poor
head control and exhibited some hypotonia. She
responded to bright light, but did not fixate or
follow, and exhibited roving, disassociated eye
movements. She did not appear to respond to any
auditory stimuli.

Evoked potential studies were performed for the
first time at 11 months of age, 2 weeks following
admission. Figure 8 illustrates the results of
ABRs, LVAERs, and Visual Evoked Responses (VEP)
elicited by light flashes. The ABRs were well
defined and were detectable down to 20 dB HL,
suggesting normal peripheral hearing sensitivity.
The responses shown in this figure are from the
patient's left ear. Identical responses were
obtained from the right ear. The LVAER was
essentially absent. Visual evoked responses
were well defined and replicable. The patient
was seen again at 16 months of age when brainstem, late components, and middle components
were attempted. A partially replicated Pa peak
was detected. As can be seen in Figure 9, there
was definitely replicable activity in the late
vertex component time domain. There was also a
marked difference between late vertex responses
obtained during sleep and those obtained while
the patient was awake. This difference consisted
of a polarity inversion at around 20 msec. post-
stimulus latency. The LVAER obtained during sleep
is quite similar to those shown in Figures 2 and 3,
with a reasonably replicated $N_{100}-P_{200}$ complex.
Behavioural responses the same day consisted of
a startle at 80 to 85 dB HL.

FIGURE 8: Case 3 - Brainstem responses (ABR), late vertex
responses (AEP) and visual evoked responses (VEP)
obtained soon after admission at 11 months of age.

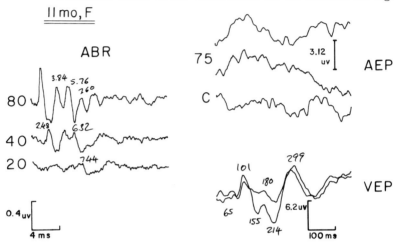

FIGURE 9: Case 3 - Middle-latency (MLR) and late vertex (AEP)
auditory evoked responses at 16 months of age.
C = "no stimulus" control.

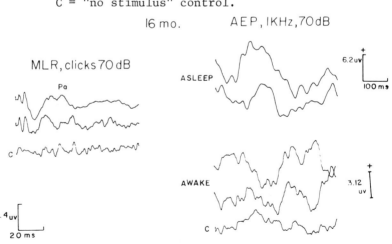

Evoked potential studies were repeated again at
27 months of age. Well defined and replicable
MLRs were obtained, as well as symmetrical late
vertex auditory evoked responses consisting of
an N_{105}-P_{239} complex. Behavioural thresholds
were still difficult to determine, but the
patient was responding much more consistently to
various auditory stimuli. This is an example of
a significant improvement of electrophysiological
indicators of auditory function, with a partial
improvement of behavioural responses.

FIGURE 10:   Case 3 - Middle-latency (MLR) and late vertex
              (AEP) auditory evoked responses obtained at
              27 months of age. C = "no stimulus" control.

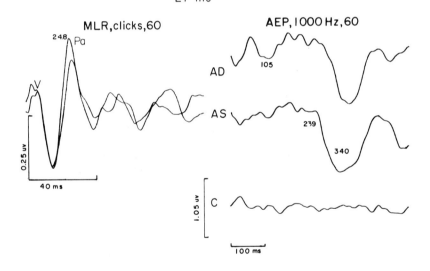

Case 4.

Born to a hypoparathyroid and diabetic mother on insulin during pregnancy, this female with multiple congenital anomalies including a hypoplastic mandible and cleft palate, was diagnosed as having a caudal regression syndrome. In addition, she had numerous asphyxial episodes. Although a CT Scan performed at 6 weeks of age revealed slightly enlarged ventricles, an EEG done at 3 months was considered normal.

The child was referred to audiology at 11 months of age, at which time, with the exception of a possible orientation response to white noise presented at 85 dB, there were no consistent responses to sound. Tympanograms suggested some middle ear involvement. Auditory evoked potential studies performed at the time revealed the following:

1) brainstem responses within normal limits with 30 dB HL unfiltered click thresholds bilaterally;

2) MLRs within normal limits;

3) the LVAERs had an unusual configuration charac-terized by replicable positive polarity peaks at a post-stimulus latency of 80 msec.

This patient was seen again at 17 months of age. She was still unable to suck or swallow, and was fed through a naso-gastric tube. The foster mother reported some vocalization, very inconsistent response to sound, and no attempt whatsoever at imitation. The patient startled to voice at 65 dB HL and responded inconsistently to warble tones at 30 dB HL presented in the soundfield. Tympanograms were within normal limits bilaterally. MLRs were again found to be within normal limits, and the LVAERs were again characterized by a replicable positive polarity peak with a latency of 101 msec.

FIGURE 11:   Late vertex auditory evoked responses elicited
by binaural stimulation from Case 4 at 8 months
of age.   These responses are characterized by a
positive polarity peak at 80 msec post-stimulus
latency.

8m.o.f.

LV AE R , I 0 0 0 Hz, 6 0 dB, bin.

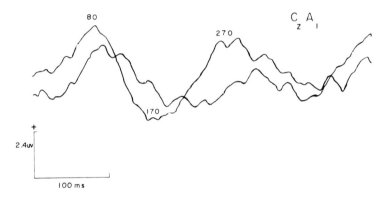

Case 5.

This little boy was a forceps delivery at 30 weeks
gestation, due to a persistent occiput posterior
presentation, at which time fetal distress was
reported.   He weighed 3180 gms, and was noted to
be lethargic, and subsequently developed seizures.
Apgars were 4 at 1 minute, and 7 at 5 minutes.   He
underwent an exchange transfusion and was noted to
have clotting abnormalities, possibly due to
asphyxia.   A CT Scan done immediately after birth
demonstrated a subarachnoid hemorrhage posteriorly
in the interhemispheric fissure.   The results of an
EEG done at 4 months of age were normal.   At 5
months of age, a repeated CT Scan revealed dilated
ventricles.

Behavioural and ABR testing between 11 months and
2 years indicated a mild bilateral hearing loss
and normal middle ear function.   The boy was fitted

with a mild gain hearing aid and was monitored
frequently until, at 3 years of age, behavioural
audiometry indicated normal unaided thresholds.
This was also confirmed by ABR.

At 3 1/2 years of age, the child presented with
an expressive language and articulation delay,
an apparent central processing dysfunction, and
perceptual deficits. MLRs and LVAERs were
recorded at that time, with the patient relaxed
but awake, sitting in his mother's lap. Figure
12 illustrates the MLRs obtained from this patient,
characterized by an absent or delayed Pa peak
(40.4 msec). Figure 13 illustrates the LVAERs.
Their configuration was atypical, exhibiting a
consistent positive polarity at 80-130 msec
post-stimulus latency.

FIGURE 12:   Case 5 - MLRs obtained at 3 1/2 years of age.
             These responses are characterized by a delayed
             Pa peak.

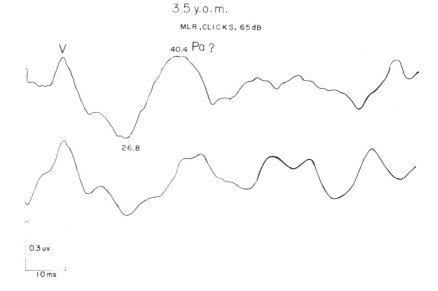

3.5 y.o.m.

MLR, CLICKS, 65 dB

FIGURE 13:   Case 5 - Late vertex auditory evoked responses
              characterized by positive polarity peaks at 80-130
              msec. post stimulus latency obtained at 3 1/2
              years of age.

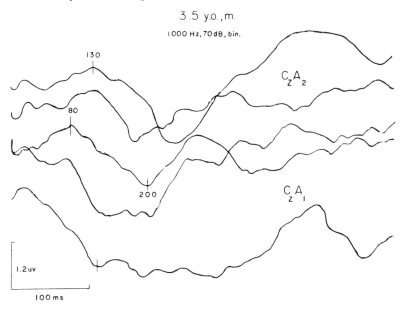

3.5 y.o.,m

1000 Hz, 70 dB, bin.

Discussion

The major issues raised by this report of 15 patients
with multiple problems relate to the interpretation and the
functional significance of the evoked potential data.   First,
as also shown by Worthington and Peters (1981), an absence of
recognizable ABR does not necessarily mean an absence of
measurable functional hearing.   Conversely, as demonstrated by
the results of this study, the presence of an ABR does not
necessarily coincide with functional hearing.   The ABR is, at
best, an indicator of peripheral hearing sensitivity which, in
the absence of neurological involvement, coincides, in most
cases, with functional hearing abilities.   This study clearly
suggests that, for neurologically involved patients, it is
risky to equate functional hearing abilities with ABR results,
as such a practice may be misleading.   In those cases, as
recommended by Cohen and Rapin (1978), a careful investigation
with a complete evoked response battery is warranted.   Then,
the ABR serves to rule out a peripheral hearing loss, while

the LVAER and the MLR assess the integrity of those higher
order auditory centers necessary for awareness of auditory
stimuli.

In the cases presented here, an absence or an unusual
configuration of LVAER elicited by suprathreshold stimuli (a
clear polarity reversal) was associated with one of the
following conditions:
- no response to auditory stimuli;
- significantly elevated behavioural auditory thresholds
  relative to ABR thresholds;
- in older children, severe delays in language development.

In general, improvements in LVAER correlated well with
behavioural responses to auditory stimuli.

The late vertex auditory evoked response occurs within a
post-stimulus latency range of 50-500 msec., and is considered
to be generated by the frontal association and/or the primary
auditory cortex (Picton et al., 1974). In waking adults, it
consists of a vertex-negative peak with a latency of 80-110
msec. (N_1) followed by a positive peak at 160-180 msec. (P_2).
In sleep, P_2 is delayed to approximately 200 msec., a prominent N_2 appears at approximately 300 msec., and N_1 is markedly
diminished or disappears (Davis, 1976; Kevanishvili & Von
Specht, 1979). The latencies of the waking LVAER components
have been reported to be greater and more variable in infants
and children of preschool age, and to assume a more typical
configuration during sedative-induced sleep. Under those conditions, they are characterized by a prominent positive
polarity peak at a post-stimulus latency of approximately 300.
msec. (Skinner & Atinoro, 1969). Figures 2 and 3 display
infant LVAERs recorded during sleep in our evoked potential
laboratory. Both exhibit small N_1 components (100 and 109
msec.,respectively), and more prominent P_2 components (210 and
245 msec.,respectively). The N_1-P_2 voltage exceeded 1.5
microvolts in both cases. These responses are in general
agreement with published norms for this age group (Barnet
et al., 1975). The late vertex auditory evoked response
undergoes maturational changes consisting of latency reduc-
tions and modifications of amplitude ratios of the N_1, P_2, and
N_2 components. By 4 months of age, a complete maturation of
the responses is reached (Davis & Onishi, 1969).

In our patients, the LVAER was either absent or exhibited
an unusual configuration on the initial examination (performed
in most cases soon after neurological problems became evident,
or soon after the insult). Twelve of the 15 patients were on

barbiturate (i.e. Phenobarb) and/or anticonvulsant medication (i.e. Dilantin or Rivotril) when tested. Barbiturates may induce increased or attenuated peak amplitudes, changes in peak latencies, and with deep anesthesia, disappearance of some or all components (Kiang et al., 1961; Pradhan & Galambos, 1963; Teas & Kiang, 1964; Borbely & Hall, 1970).

Polarity reversal at the same recording site as seen in our patients has not been reported to occur as a result of barbiturate anesthesia. A reversal of polarity of the late vertex auditory evoked response reportedly occurs when the active electrode is moved below the Sylvian fissure (Vaughan & Ritter, 1970). The explanation for this phenomenon is that above and below the Sylvian fissure, the electrode sees opposite poles of the dipole consisting of the primary auditory cortical projection in the superior surface of the temporal lobe. If one accepts this explanation, the polarity inversion in some of our patients could be due to topographical or morphological changes in the generator of the LVAER, and hence, our vertex electrode may see the opposite pole of a dipole, instead of the standard expected one. Another explanation for this response pattern is that it may be the result of an immature generator; similar LVAERs were recorded from premature infants (Barnet et al., 1975). It may be concluded that the abnormal LVAERs (or their absence) in the cases presented in this study must have been a consequence or the sign of central nervous system pathology.

Knight et al., (1980) found that the amplitude of the N_1 component of the LVAER was reduced consistently with well defined and well documented temporo-parietal lesions. Such accurate lesion localization did not occur in our patients. One fairly homogenous sub-group consisted of 4 patients in whom a generalized cortical atrophy was diagnosed on CT Scan. In all, the LVAER was absent, and the MLR was within normal limits.

It is interesting to note that both an abnormal CT Scan demonstrating a well defined anatomical lesion, and an abnormal EEG were not present in all of our cases. At least one of these examinations, however, did yield positive results for each case.

The MLRs occur within a post-stimulus latency range of 10-100 msec. and are presumed to originate central to the generators of the ABR. Some possible generators are the thalamus, primary-auditory cortex, or secondary auditory projections (Picton et al., 1974; Davis, 1976). There have been

conflicting reports in the literature concerning the effects
of temporal lobe lesions on the MLR. Parving et al., (1980)
described a patient with auditory agnosia and documented
bilateral temporal lobe lesions, who exhibited normal MLRs
(Pa latency = 30 msec.). On the other hand, Ozdamar et al.,
(1982) described a patient who has also presented with
bilateral temporal lobe lesions. He demonstrated inconsistent
awareness to sound, impaired pure tone sensitivity, and
abnormal MLRs (Pa was missing bilaterally). Based on their
respective results, the two groups of investigators arrived at
opposite conclusions regarding the role of the primary
auditory cortex in the generation of the MLR.

     Two of our patients had documented bilateral temporal
lobe lesions: Case 2 reported above; and a 7 month old male
infant with convulsive disorder, irritability, and spastic
quadraplegia secondary to severe birth asphyxia. A CT Scan
performed at 6 weeks of age revealed cystic changes in the
temporal regions and dilated lateral and third ventricles.
Both patients exhibited normal ABRs elicited by 60 and 20 dB
clicks, and recognizable MLRs (Case 2 had no MLRs initially).
Thus, our findings are in agreement with those of Parving
et al., (1980). Those investigators raised the question but
ruled out the possibility that the MLR may be of myogenic
origins and is, therefore, unaffected by temporal lobe
lesions. Our experience with the MLR recorded in the operating room following the administration of muscle relaxants also
rules out major myogenic contribution to the MLR when elicited
by moderate intensity stimuli (Kileny et al., 1982). We must
conclude that the primary auditory projections located in the
temporal lobe may not be the sole or specific generators of
the MLR.

                            Conclusions

     Several conclusions may be drawn from this study. First,
the battery approach to auditory evoked potentials for children with proven or suspected brain lesions provides more
meaningful information about auditory function than ABR alone.
It is important to note that no attempt was made in our work
to establish thresholds for the MLR and LVAER. Attempts were
made to elicit responses at levels which were well above ABR
threshold. Parving et al., (1980) found that the threshold of
the late vertex response is a poor predictor of central

hearing dysfunction. Although we made no systematic attempt to determine whether LVAERs could be elicited by higher intensity stimuli (in cases where they were absent with standard stimuli), in the few cases where this was attempted, the LVAER is utilized as a strictly suprathreshold device, its status will correlate well with the types of central auditory dysfunctions found in our patient group.

As the use of the MLR was somewhat restricted with our group, it is more difficult to make a similar statement concerning its usage. While it is well known that MLRs may be elicited at levels very close to behavioural thresholds (Musiek & Guerkink, 1981), we recommend that in the context used in this study (the multiply handicapped child), it should also be elicited by suprathreshold stimuli.

The MLR and the LVAER did not provide specific site of lesion information. These later auditory evoked potentials are better suited to determine function rather than provide specific site of lesion information. In the future, the auditory evoked response battery may be used in order to monitor progress in these types of patients. More information could be derived if measurements were performed with multiple electrode arrays, especially in those cases presenting with inverted polarity responses. As the imaging techniques become more and more sophisticated, there may be better correspondence between specific sites of lesions and the results of evoked potential studies.

Acknowledgements

We wish to acknowledge the ongoing support of the Glenrose Hospital and to thank the staff audiologists for their contributions with the patient population described here. Many thanks to Drs. Kurt Hecox and Thomas Campbell for their helpful suggestions and comments during the various stages of the preparation of this study.

References

Achor, L.J., and Starr, A., "Auditory Brainstem Responses in
    the Cat: I. Intracranial and Extracranial Recordings,"
    Electroencephalography and Clinical Neurophysiology
    48:154-173, 1980.

Barnet, A.B., Ohlrich, E.S., Weiss, I.P., and Shanks, B.,
    "Auditory Evoked Potentials During Sleep in Normal Children
    from Ten Days to Three Years of Age," Electroencephalo-
    graphy and Clinical Neurophysiology 39:29-41, 1975.

Borbely, A.A., and Hall, R.D., "Effects of Pentobarbitone
    and Chlorpromazine on Acoustically Evoked Potentials in
    the Rat," Neuropharmacology 9:575-586, 1970.

Cohen, M.M., and Rapin, I., "Evoked Potential Audiometry in
    Neurologically Impaired Children," Evoked Electrical
    Activity in the Auditory Nervous System (New York:
    Academic Press), Naunton, R., and Zerlin, S. (Eds.), 1978.

Davis, H., "Principles of Electric Response Audiometry,"
    Annals of Otology, Rhinology, and Laryngology Volume 85,
    Supplement #85, 1976.

Davis, H., and Onishi, S., "Maturation of Auditory Evoked
    Potentials," International Audiology 8:24-33, 1969.

Galambos, R., and Despland, P.A., "The Auditory Brainstem
    Response (ABR) Evaluates Risk Factors for Hearing Loss in
    the Newborn," Pediatric Research 14:159-163, 1980.

Kevanishvili, Z.Sh., and Von Specht, H., "Human Slow Auditory
    Evoked Potentials During Natural and Drug-Induced Sleep,"
    Electroencephalography and Clinical Neurophysiology
    47:280-288, 1979.

Kiang, N.Y.S., Neame, J.H., and Clark, L.F., "Evoked Cortical
    Activity from Auditory Cortex in Anesthetized and
    Unanesthetized Cats," Science 13:1927-1928, 1961.

Kileny, P., "Auditory Brainstem Responses as Indicators of
    Hearing Aid Performance," Annals of Otology, Rhinology,
    and Laryngology 91:61-64, 1982.

Kileny, P., Connelly, C., and Robertson, C., "Auditory Brainstem Responses in Perinatal Asphyxia," International Journal of Pediatric Otorhinolaryngology 2:147-159, 1980.

Kileny, P., Dobson, D., and Gelfand, E.T., "Middle Latency Auditory Evoked Responses During Open-Heart Surgery with Hypothermia," In Preparation, 1983.

Knight, R.T., Hillyard, S.A., Woods, D.L., and Neville, H.J., "The Effects of Frontal and Temporal-Parietal Lesions on the Auditory Evoked Potential in Man," Electroencephalography and Clinical Neurophysiology 50:112-124, 1980.

Mendel, M.I., Hosick, E.C., Windman, T.R., Davis, H., Hirsch, S.K., and Dinges, D.F., "Audiometric Comparison of the Middle and Late Components Awake and Asleep," Electroencephalography and Clinical Neurophysiology 38:27-33, 1975.

Mendelson, T., and Salamy, A., "Maturational Effects on the Middle Components of the Averaged Electroencephalic Response," Journal of Speech and Hearing Research 46:140-144, 1981.

Michel, F., Peronnet, F., and Schott, B., "A Case of Cortical Deafness: Clinical and Electro-physiological Data," Brain and Language 10:367-377, 1980.

Mokotoff, B., Schulman-Galambos, C., and Galambos, R., "Brainstem Auditory Evoked Responses in Children," Archives of Otolaryngology 103:38-43, 1977.

Moller, A.R., Janetta, P., Bennet, M., and Moller, M.B., "Intracranially Recorded Responses from the Human Auditory Nerve: New Insights into the Origin of Brain Stem Evoked Potentials (BSEP)," Electroencephalography and Clinical Neurophysiology 52:18-27, 1981.

Musiek, F.E., and Guerkink, N.A., "Auditory Brainstem and Middle Latency Evoked Response Sensitivity Near Threshold," Annals of Otology, Rhinology, and Laryngology 90:236-240, 1981.

Ozdamar, O., Kraus, N., and Curry, F., "Auditory Brain Stem and Middle Latency Responses in a Patient with Cortical Deafness," Electroencephalography and Clinical Neurophysiology 53:224-230, 1982.

Parving, A., Salomon, G., Elberling, C., Larsen, B., and
    Lassen, N.A., "Middle Components of the Auditory Evoked
    Response in Bilateral Temporal Lobe Lesions," Scandinavian
    Audiology 9:161-167, 1980.

Picton, T.W., Hillyard, S.A., Krausz, H.I., and Galambos, R.,
    "Human Auditory Evoked Potentials: I. Evaluation of
    Components," Electroencephalography and Clinical Neuro-
    physiology 36:179-190, 1974.

Pradhan, S.N., and Galambos, R., "Some Effects of Anesthetics
    on the Evoked Responses in the Auditory Cortex of Cats,"
    Journal of Pharmacology and Experimental Therapeutics
    139:97-106, 1963.

Salamy, A., and McKean, C.M., "Postnatal Development of
    Human Brainstem Potentials During the First Year of Life,"
    Electroencephalography and Clinical Neurophysiology
    40:418-426, 1976.

Schulman-Galambos, C., and Galambos, R., "Brainstem Auditory
    Evoked Responses in Premature Infants," Journal of Speech
    and Hearing Research 12:394-401, 1969.

Skinner, P., and Antinoro, F., "Auditory Evoked Responses In
    Normal Hearing Adults and Children Before and During
    Sedation," Journal of Speech and Hearing Research
    12:394-401, 1969.

Starr, A., and Hamilton, A.E., "Correlation Between Confirmed
    Sites of Neurological Lesions and Abnormalities of Far-
    Field Auditory Brainstem Responses," Electroencephalography
    and Clinical Neurophysiology 41:595-608, 1976.

Vaughan, H.G., and Ritter, W., "The Sources of Auditory
    Evoked Responses Recorded from the Human Scalp," Electro-
    encephalography and Clinical Neurophysiology 28:306-367,
    1970.

Wilson, W.R., "Behavioural Assessment of Auditory Function
    in Infants," Communicative and Cognitive Abilities - Early
    Behavioural Assessment (Baltimore: University Park Press),
    Minifie, F.D., and Lloyd, L.L. (Eds.), 1978.

Worthington, D.W., and Peters, J.F., "Quantifiable Hearing
    and no ABR: Paradox or Error?" Ear and Hearing 1:281-285,
    1980.

HEARING IMPAIRMENT IN DOWN'S SYNDROME CHILDREN

Wesley R. Wilson
Richard C. Folsom
Judith E. Widen
University of Washington, Seattle, Washington

One might ask: "Why the special interest in the Down's Syndrome population?" First, Down's Syndrome is one of the most common forms of mental retardation, Coleman (1978) reporting an incidence figure of 1:696 births. Second, since a diagnosis based on physical characteristics can be made at birth, identification of this population occurs early and habilitative planning may begin immediately. Third, there is evidence that Down's Syndrome infants between 6 and 10 months of age show a decline in cognitive and motor development (as measured by the Bayley Scales of Infant Development - BSID) which is unequalled at other future time periods (Carr, 1970; Dicks-Mireaux, 1972). Fourth, there is data (VanderVeer & Schweid, 1974; Barnard, 1975) suggesting that Down's Syndrome infants in a parent-focused intervention program show the most favourable developmental progress when enrolled prior to 30 months of age. Hayden and Haring (1977) also point to the importance of an early educational program for this population.

The communication handicap of Down's Syndrome children is well documented; however, the causative factors underlying that problem are not well understood. It is known that this population demonstrates a substantially higher incidence of hearing impairment than normals, and that this loss is usually present in early infancy. In addition, recent work in our laboratory suggests that Down's Syndrome children may also process auditory information differently than normal children. This chapter focuses on those areas of our longitudinal study of Down's Syndrome infants, children and young adults. The procedures used include the Auditory Brainstem Response (ABR) in addition to the behavioural approaches of Behavioural Observation Audiometry (BOA) and Visual Reinforcement Audiometry (VRA). This combined behavioural and electrophysiological approach has allowed an attempt to answer questions regarding hearing sensitivity, maturation of the central nervous system, onset of sound localization, and speech-sound discrimination abilities.

Etiology of Down's Syndrome

Down's Syndrome is due to a genetic imbalance caused by
the presence of an extra set of 21 chromosomes. In over 90%
of the cases (Smith & Wilson, 1973) the imbalance is a fault
in chromosome distribution which has occurred in the development of the egg or the sperm, or in the first division of the
fertilized egg. Some of Down's Syndrome cases occur because
of translocation of a third number 21 chromosome. In those
cases, the extra number 21 chromosome has broken and is
attached to the broken end of another chromosome. The genetic
imbalance represented by either Full 21 trisomy or Translocation 21 trisomy produces a recognizable pattern of altered
development originally described by Langdon Down in 1866 --
thus the name, Down's Syndrome.

Effect on Hearing, Speech and
Language

        Incidence of Hearing Problems

        As a population, Down's Syndrome individuals present a
variety of abnormalities besides mental retardation, with
hearing loss as one of the most frequent (Coleman, 1978).
Although the incidence figures for hearing loss vary considerably depending on procedural variables and criteria used to
specify loss, it is agreed that the occurrence of hearing loss
is much more frequent in the Down's Syndrome population than
in the population at large (Glovsky, 1966; Fulton & Lloyd,
1968; Brooks, Wooley & Kanjilal, 1972; Balkany et al., 1979;
Keiser et al., 1981). Studies utilizing appropriate test
techniques report that the majority of these losses are mild
to moderate in severity, varying 20 to 40 dB above normal
threshold (Greenberg et al., 1978; Thompson, Wilson & Moore,
1979; Balkany et al., 1979). Additionally, the majority of
impairments appear to be conductive in nature. Balkany and
his co-workers (1979) found that among the 78% of ears
identified with losses greater than 15 dB HL, 83% were of a
conductive nature. Many of these losses were the result of
otitis media. The studies of Brooks et al., (1972), Schwartz
and Schwartz (1978), and Balkany et al., (1979) demonstrate
that the incidence of middle ear disease reported in an
unselected sample of asymptomatic children with Down's
Syndrome is approximately 60%. In addition, Balkany et al.,
(1979) report a large number of cases with conductive losses
not associated with otitis media.

Speech and Language Problems

Anecdotal reports suggest that Down's Syndrome children show greater delays in speech and language development than in other performance parameters, and greater delays in speech and language than other groups of mentally retarded children (Lyle, 1960, 1961; Evans, 1977; Blager, 1980). The contributions of hearing loss to this delay are unknown. Although early hearing loss is known to have a significant effect on speech and language development of normal infants, it has received little consideration in most studies on the speech and language development of Down's Syndrome children. One notable exception is the work of Downs and her colleagues in Colorado, who have compared the language abilities of Down's Syndrome children who have had several years of hearing aid usage, to a similar group who have not been aided (Downs, 1980; see chapter by Downs in this volume for details). However, in view of the multiplicity of otologic abnormalities which have been reported for Down's Syndrome, it is unlikely that loss of hearing sensitivity is the only auditory problem contributing to speech and language delay. Distortion in the transmission and processing of speech signals as they pass through abnormal structures from the outer ear to the auditory cortex is certainly an additional contributing factor.

Abnormalities in Auditory
Structures

Nearly every part of the auditory system of Down's individuals has been reported to be anatomically abnormal. The longitudinal dimension of the pinna is significantly shorter than normal in a majority of cases (Aase, Wilson & Smith, 1973; Balkany et al., 1979). The pinna is typically low set (Aase et al., 1973; Balkany, 1980). The diameter of the ear canal averages 1/2 to 2/3 the size of age-matched normal children (Balkany, 1980). It is often narrow to the point of being stenotic (Schwartz & Schwartz, 1978). Even the cerumen is different; it tends to be drier and flakier (Balkany, 1980).

Aside from the increased incidence of upper respiratory infections leading to otitis media, abnormalities in the middle ear may contribute to the prevalence of middle ear effusion. Some authors speculate that the generalized hypotonia seen in Down's Syndrome may extend to the tensor veli

palatini, thus affecting the opening of the Eustachian tube
(Schwartz & Schwartz, 1978). The epithelium of the middle
ear may be roughened due to Vitamin A deficiency, increasing
the chance of effusion (Coleman, Schwartz & Schwartz, 1979).
Other reported middle ear abnormalities include erosion of
the ossicles due to chronic otitis media, as well as congenital malformations and stapes fixation (Igarashi et al., 1977;
Balkany, 1980).

In regard to the inner ear, Igarashi et al., (1977) and
Harada and Sando (1981) studied temporal bones from Down's
Syndrome children and found that the length of the cochlear
spirals was shorter than that of normal controls in a large
percentage of cases. In addition, Balkany (1980) speculated
about the possible existence of inner ear conductive losses
in several children whose sensitivity failed to improve
following surgical treatment. Inner ear conductive losses
may reflect physical changes in the basilar membrane and/or
tectorial membrane (Davis, 1978).

Although there are no reports of specific abnormalities
of the VIIIth nerve, anatomical differences in brainstem
neural structures which could affect the transmission of
signals to the brain have been noted. Crome, Cowie and
Slater (1966), and Crome and Stern (1972) reported that the
cerebella and brainstems of Down's Syndrome subjects were
2/3 of normal weight. This disproportionate reduction in the
size of those areas compared to total brain weight was likened
to the proportion seen in infants, and viewed as possible
evidence of lack of development of those structures. In
addition, Palo and Savolainen (1973), and Banik et al.,
(1975) reported evidence of abnormal or incomplete myelination, also reflecting possible abnormal neuronal growth and
synaptogenesis.

Other Possible Changes in
Auditory Behaviour

These anatomic data are extended by behavioural evidence
of auditory deficits other than loss of sensitivity. The
frequent inability of Down's Syndrome infants to localize to
a sound source, to learn a simple task dependent upon an
auditory cue, or to perform simple speech-sound discrimination tasks at the same developmental age as normals, may point
to differences in ability to process auditory information
(Greenberg et al., 1978; Thompson et al., 1979).

Bilovsky and Share (1965), Rohr and Burr (1978), Rynders, Behlen and Horrobin (1979), and McDade and Adler (1980) have shown that Down's Syndrome children have lower verbal-auditory abilities than do other etiological classes of mentally retarded children. They also reported that the verbal-auditory abilities of Down's Syndrome children are poorer than the corresponding processes in visual-motor channels. A study of Zekulin et al., (1974) suggested that Down's Syndrome subjects were more susceptible to auditory distraction than were non-Down's mentally retarded or normal subjects. They found that Down's individuals were unable to habituate to auditory distraction.

Differences in Evoked
Potentials

In their efforts to find electrophysiological factors which might correlate with mental retardation, Barnet and her co-workers (1967, 1971) studied the auditory-evoked cortical potentials of Down's infants. Barnet and Lodge (1967) found that the amplitude of responses to clicks was significantly larger in Down's infants, and Barnet, Ohlrich and Shanks (1971) reported there was also no progressive decrement in the amplitude of the Auditory Evoked Response (AER) with repetitive stimuli, as would be the case with normals. Responses of Down's infants resembled those of neonates who had not yet developed the response decrement which characterizes older normal infants and adults. Barnet and colleagues postulated that the difference between Down's Syndrome and normal infants might reflect underlying differences in brain mechanisms governing sensory input. For example, they suggested high amplitude evoked potentials may indicate the presence of abnormally diffuse and hyper-synchronous neural responses. The persistence of high amplitudes during repetitive stimulation may indicate a defect of the inhibitory mechanisms which normally result in response habituation (Barnet & Lodge, 1967; Barnet et al., 1971).

The abnormally large auditory-evoked cortical potentials exhibited by the Down's infants in Barnet's studies have since been reported in Down's Syndrome adults by Straumanis, Shagass and Overton (1973a) and Yellin, Lodwig and Jerison (1980). The increased amplitudes of the auditory-evoked potentials obtained from Down's subjects have also been

reported for other sensory modalities. Bigum, Dustman and
Beck (1970), and Higashi et al., (1972) reported greater
amplitude visual-evoked potentials in Down's children than in
normal children. Likewise, the Down's adults in studies by
Gliddon, Busk and Galbraith (1975), and Yellin, Lodwig and
Jerison (1979) showed larger visual-evoked potentials than
normal. Somatsosensory-evoked potentials have also shown
increased amplitudes in Down's children and adults (Bigum
et al., 1970; Straumanis, Shagass & Overton, 1973b).

It is unlikely that the auditory-evoked potential differences seen in the Down's population are isolated to the
cortex. In fact, the reports of underdevelopment of the
brainstem and lack of myelination of its neural structures
suggest that differences at subcortical levels are also likely.
The recent emergence of the ABR as a tool for the study of
auditory function allows for further exploration of the
auditory abnormalities in Down's Syndrome at these subcortical
levels.

Squires et al., (1980) from the Mental Retardation
Research Center at UCLA, published one of the first comparative studies of the auditory brainstem response in Down's
individuals. The responses of 16 Down's adults were compared
with a group of retarded adults of unknown etiology and a
group of non-retarded control subjects. As a group, the
Down's subjects showed shorter central conduction times (Wave
V minus Wave I latency, or I-V interval) than the normal
group. The unknown etiology subjects tended to show longer
I-V interwave intervals than normal. Absolute Wave V
latencies for the Down's subjects tended to be short despite
the fact that the investigators did not control for hearing
loss. Generally, peak amplitudes were reduced for the Down's
group.

The effects of 3 click intensities (40, 55, and 70 dB
nHL)[1] on Wave V latencies showed that latency-intensity
functions did not differ across the 3 groups studied by Squires
et al., (1980). However, changes in Wave V latency as a

---

[1] We have adopted the term dB nHL to indicate the intensity
of the signal in electrophysiologic audiometry relative to
the mean threshold of a jury of normally hearing young
adults.

function of 3 click repetition rates (20, 50, 100 clicks per second) did show differences. Wave V latencies in the Down's group were more resistant to fast click rates than were those of the normal or unknown etiology group. That is, the Down's subjects showed less latency change as stimulus repetition rates increased than did the other groups. Squires and her associates concluded that their data indicate abnormal functioning of the auditory brainstem pathway in the Down's group as a whole, and imply that both peripheral and central processing disorders accompany and possibly contribute to retardation.

Current Studies at the University of Washington Child Development and Mental Retardation Center

Over the past 6 years, a series of studies at the University of Washington Child Development and Mental Retardation Center have explored the auditory function of Down's Syndrome individuals. The studies have attempted to chart the development of auditory abilities using both electrophysiological and behavioural assessment procedures. Specifically, the Auditory Brainstem Response (ABR) has been used, along with Behavioural Observation Audiometry (BOA) and Visual Reinforcement Audiometry (VRA). These offer a combined approach which allows accurate assessment of hearing at an earlier age than previously possible, thereby providing better understanding of the age of onset and types of hearing loss in Down's children. Specific methodologies include the recording of ABRs at various stimulus intensities and presentation rates in Down's and normal children, as well as assessing hearing function using BOA and VRA. Our effort is designed to answer questions regarding hearing sensitivity, maturation of the central nervous system, onset of sound localization, and development of speech-sound discrimination abilities.

Subjects

Down's Syndrome

A total of 190 Down's subjects ranging in age (CA) from birth to 21 years have been seen. Infants have been selected from an educational training program at the University of

Washington and older subjects from surrounding school districts and training programs. Diagnosis of Down's Syndrome is based on chromosomal tests, as reported in medical records. Almost all of the Down's subjects were Trisomy 21 (non-mosaic) type; the exceptions are noted in the specific studies. A parental questionnaire was used in subject selection to exclude any children who:

1. were in poor general physical health;

2. evidenced additional handicaps;

3. had uncorrected gross visual defect;

4. were under the influence of medication which noticeably altered the normal level of functioning at the time of testing.

Normal Controls

Infants and children matched by either chronological (CA) or developmental age (DA) to the Down's Syndrome sample, have been selected based on mail solicitation in the greater Seattle area. Introductory letters explaining the nature and scope of the project were sent to parents of newborns. Parental response cards indicating a desire to participate were computer filed, and parents re-contacted as their children reached the appropriate age. A parental questionnaire was used again in selection. For older children, telephone solicitation and contact with schools was used to obtain subjects. All subjects, both Down's and controls, were paid for participation in the studies. Participation was voluntary. The process described is ongoing, and further subjects will be added by the same method as our work continues.

Behavioural Procedures

Behavioural assessment of auditory thresholds in infants is based on observation of overt responses to controlled auditory signals. The two general approaches which have been employed clinically may be differentiated by whether or not reinforcement is applied. Until completion of recent work in our lab, procedures involving some form of instrumental conditioning were restricted in use to infants over 12 months of age.

Behavioural Observation
Audiometry

For infants under 12 months of age and/or young, retarded
children, audiologists usually resort to BOA in which no conditioning is employed. A number of investigators have pointed
to shortcomings in this procedure. For example, Weber (1969,
1970) and Ling, Ling and Doehring (1970) have shown it may be
difficult to control observer bias; Moore, Thompson and Thompson (1975) demonstrated the infant may habituate quickly to
the signal, making it difficult to determine whether absence
of response is due to habituation or hearing loss; and Thompson and Weber (1974) found that the threshold obtained will
vary widely across a group of presumed normal hearing infants.

In an attempt to overcome some of the apparent shortcomings of BOA, we added a number of procedural controls. First,
we focused on the issues of potential observer bias. We
utilized 2 observers who were "blind" to the signal condition
and who were required to vote independently following each
presentation of either a signal or a control. More specifically, the observers were under earphones and heard a masking
signal each time a judgment period occurred. This signal cued
them that they were to observe the infant's behaviour over a
short time interval and then were to vote: a) Yes (+) there
was a response; b) Questionable Response (?); or c) No (-)
there was no response during the judgment period. During 25%
of the judgment periods, no signal was presented to the infant
although the observers were blind to this fact. These control
intervals were used to determine accuracy or false alarm rate.
During the remaining 75% of the judgment periods, signals of
varying intensities were presented. The observers were not
aware of the signal intensity.

Two signals, counter-balanced across subjects, were used
in the BOA procedure to avoid order effects. One consisted of
a broad-band noise presented with an average 2-second duration.
Acoustic analysis of this complex signal indicated that the
major concentration of energy was between 1000 and 8000 Hz,
with slightly decreasing energy in the lower frequencies out
to 125 Hz and falling off sharply above 8000 Hz. The second
signal was a high-pass (2000 Hz and above) filtered version of
the original broad-band signal. A strict presentation protocol
was employed. Successive changes in signal intensity were
determined by the observers' votes on the preceding presentation with negative or questionable responses resulting in 10 dB
increases. Signal intensity was raised until observer votes of

either [+,+] or [+,?] were obtained. This point was recorded
as the minimum response level for that stimulus condition.
The second signal was then presented in the same ascending
fashion. Each signal condition was repeated.

Visual Reinforcement Audiometry

Our VRA procedure, as applied to threshold assessment,
has the infant seated on the parent's lap. The test room
examiner is seated on the side of the subject opposite the
loudspeaker and keeps the infant actively but quietly occupied
in a midline position by manipulation of interesting toys.
When this examiner signals that the subject is in a response-
ready state, the control room examiner presents the initial
auditory stimulus at 50 dB SPL. Each subject is required to
meet a conditioning criterion by responding to 2 out of 3
stimulus presentations at a single intensity level. If the
infant or young child does not satisfy the criterion at 50 dB
SPL, the intensity is increased to 70 dB SPL, and the conditioning is again attempted, including a pairing of the stimulus and the visual reinforcer. The signals employed were the
same as described for the BOA procedure.

Once the infant meets criterion, a threshold search is
initiated with threshold defined as the lowest intensity level
at which at least 3 out of 6 responses occur. The intensity
is decreased 20 dB following each positive response, and
increased 10 dB after each failure to respond. To measure
false-positive responses, control trials are randomly included
at a 30% rate throughout the procedure, with a minimum of 3
controls per test. Control trials are initiated when the
infant is in a response-ready state and consist of a timed
No-Signal interval identical in duration to the Signal-
Response intervals. The threshold obtained from the subject
is arbitrarily considered unreliable if the rate of false-
positive responses exceeds 20%.

The visual reinforcer consists of a 3-dimensional stuffed
toy animal, capable of movement when an electric circuit is
activated. The reinforcer is enclosed in a smoked plexiglass
container located near the loudspeaker, and is controlled by
an AND-gate circuit comprised of an automatic timer and 2 vot-
ing switches. Initiation of a signal activates the timer; if

both judges vote affirmatively that a response has occurred
during the following 4 seconds, the visual reinforcer is
automatically activated for approximately 2 seconds (Wilson
et al., 1976). A positive response is defined as a complete
head turn toward the loudspeaker. Eye movement only is considered "No Response "

For assessment of speech-sound discrimination, infants
are presented with one member of a contrastive stimulus pair
at the rate of 1 syllable per second at 50 dB SPL. While the
infant is entertained at midline, the speech stimulus is
changed during a 4 second interval. The infant is reinforced
for a head-turn in response to the change by the activation of
an animated toy. Initially, the figure stimulus is presented
at a higher intensity than the ground stimulus. Once the
infant has demonstrated responses to the intensity and/or
speech signal difference, the intensities are equated. Each
infant is then presented with 3 experimental and 3 control
trials. The infant must respond appropriately 5 out of 6
times to reach significance (see Wilson, 1978, and Moore &
Wilson, 1978, for additional details on test procedures and
studies of normal infants).

Electrophysiological Procedures

Electrophysiological procedures are defined as those
which include electrophysiological monitoring of either
autonomic nervous system reflex activity to sound or direct
recording of the bioelectrical correlates of the original
acoustic signal at various stations along the auditory
nervous system. Response averaging may be included. Electric
response audiometric procedures involve the recording of
neuroelectrical potentials which represent the brain's
responses to sounds. These various recorded responses are
classified by latency or site of origin, and can be divided
into 4 primary categories: electrocochleography (1 to 5
msec.), auditory brainstem responses (Wave V latency 6 - 8
msec.), primary cortical response (12-50 msec.), and the late
cortical response (50-300 msec.). Of these responses, the
ABR offers the greatest ease of recording and stability of
response under a variety of subject states, in addition to
providing a low-level (VIIIth Nerve and lower brainstem)
measure of hearing sensitivity.

Auditory Brainstem Response
Audiometry

The amplified DC logic output of an electronic timer
(Grason-Stadler 1216A), set to a duration of .1 msec. was
delivered to an earphone to generate an acoustic rarefaction
click.   Intensity and rate have varied depending on the study.
Intensity is expressed in dB re: the mean threshold of 10
normally hearing young adults and is designated dB nHL.

Electroencephalic activity was recorded by gold plated
EEG electrodes attached to midline of the forehead (active)
and ipsilateral mastoid (reference).   The contralateral mastoid served as the site for the ground electrode.   The impedance of the electrodes was maintained at under 5000 ohms.   The
response was amplified (x 500000) and passed in a frequency
band between 100 and 3000 Hz (Grass P-511J).   This bioelectric
activity was then fed to a signal averager (Fabri-tek 1010)
set to scan a 10 msec. epoch.   The final averaged response
was the result of 1024 stimulus presentations.   All tracings
were written out on an X-Y recorder (Hewlett-Packard 7035B).
In the more recent studies, the response was digitized and
transferred to a general purpose minicomputer (Digital Equipment Corporation MINC-11) for digital storage and later
latency and amplitude analysis.

Stimulus intensity conditions were presented in a quasi-
randomized order.   To aid in the confirmation of the Waves to
be scored, each condition was replicated at least once and
super-imposed in different colours when plotted.   When time
and consistent subject state allowed, each replicated condition was repeated.

Tracings were scored by measuring the distance in centi-
meters (cm) from the stimulus onset to the peak of Wave I or
V.   Calibration of the X-Y recorder to display the 10 msec.
epoch over a 20 cm span allowed the time in msec. to be calculated from this measurement.   Following the test session,
each tracing was scored by 2 judges, working independently,
who were blind both to the subject category (i.e. control or
Down's Syndrome), as well as to stimulus condition.   Each
replication was scored separately, then averaged within each
stimulus condition.

Impedance Audiometry

Tympanometric measurements, including calculation of ear canal volume, were obtained for both ears using an American Electromedics (Model 81) electroacoustic impedance bridge. The compliance meter of the bridge and the X-Y recorder were calibrated prior to each test. Periodic checks assured accuracy of the manometer.

Results

Behavioural Studies

In the behavioural assessments of hearing sensitivity, BOA was used with younger infants as well as older infants who had not, as yet, learned the VRA task. This procedure, which does not use reinforcement, yielded high inter-judge agreement. The rate of scored responses during the control trials was very low, indicating the "blind" observer techniques we employed were appropriate. However, the use of BOA techniques with Down's infants resulted in the same wide range of variability as seen with normally developing infants, thus reducing its effectiveness as a measure of hearing sensitivity. In both the Down's and normal groups, the range of responses was on the order of 50 - 60 dB which renders any definition of "normal" sensitivity impossible. This finding is in agreement with previous work with older normal infants in our lab (Thompson & Weber, 1974).

Greenberg et al., (1978) investigated the effectiveness of VRA with 46 Down's Syndrome children between the ages of 6 months and 6 years. Twenty-five of the subjects were also administered the Bayley Scales of Infant Development (BSID) by a trained psychometrician during a separate session which fell within 2 weeks of the audiometric testing.

VRA sound field threshold procedures, as previously described, were used. Each subject was required to respond to 2 out of 3 presentations at either a 50 or 70 dB SPL conditioning level. If the subject failed to satisfy initial conditioning criterion, an attempt was made to teach the turning response. If consistent responses occurred within a maximum of 10 teaching trials, the original test procedure was again attempted.

The results showed inter-judge reliability was excellent. The examiners disagreed on only 1% of the responses elicited from nearly 600 stimulus presentations. If the disagreement occurred during a stimulus trial, it was considered no response, and if during a control trial, it was considered a false response.

Table I details the number of subjects who successfully completed each phase of the study, including a breakdown by chronological age. Twenty-eight (68%) of the Down's subjects met the response criterion at 1 of the 2 initial conditioning levels. A large percentage (71%) who eventually achieved threshold, conditioned to the 50 dB SPL signal, and did not require the 70 dB SPL signal. No systematic relationship existed between the initial conditioning level and the threshold obtained.

Of the 13 infants and young children who failed to meet the initial conditioning criterion, only 3 could be taught to respond during the single visit used in this study. The time required to accomplish the training task ranged from 4 to 7 minutes.

TABLE 1:   Number of Down syndrome subjects meeting initial conditioning or training criterion and threshold criterion as a function of chronological age (from Greenberg, Wilson, Moore and Thompson, 1978).

Chronological Age (in months)	N	Number of Subjects Who Met Initial Conditioning Criterion	Number of Subjects Not Meeting Initial Conditioning Criterion Who Were Taught to Respond	Number of Subjects Yielding Thresholds Unreliable	/Reliable
6-12	6	1	0	0	1
13-24	7	3	2	0	5
25-36	7	5	1	0	5
37-48	7	6	0	1	5
49-60	4	3	0	0	3
61-72	10	10	0	4	6
Totals	41	28	3	5	25

A strong age effect did occur relative to the initial
conditioning as shown in Figure 1. Although 68% of the total
population met criterion (2 out of 3 correct responses), the
range was from 17% for the youngest group (6 - 12 months of
age), to 100% for the oldest group (5 - 6 years of age).

Threshold criterion was met by 30 of the 31 subjects who
initially conditioned or who could be taught to respond. One
child who initially conditioned, stopped responding before
threshold criterion could be reached. The thresholds for 5
subjects were considered to be unreliable because of a rate of
false-positive responses in excess of 20%, leaving 25 subjects
who yielded reliable thresholds. As is apparent in Table I,
only 1 of 6 Down's Syndrome infants under 13 months of age
(chronologically) was able to complete the threshold task.
Above that age, an approximately equal proportion of successful tests compared to number attempted was obtained for each
age category. Interestingly, the majority of the unreliable
thresholds, as defined by a high rate of false-positives,
occurred in subjects in the oldest age category - 5 years of
age.

FIGURE 1:   Percentage of Down syndrome subjects meeting initial
            conditioning criterion as a function of chronological
            age (from Greenberg, Wilson, Moore and Thompson, 1978).

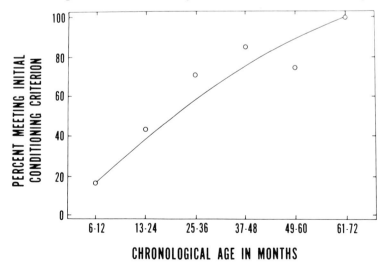

Table II provides the thresholds obtained by the Down's children, as well as the number of trials and amount of time required to complete threshold testing. Of the 25 subjects yielding reliable thresholds, the values ranged from 30 to 60 dB SPL with a mean of 38.4 dB and median and mode of 30 dB. These values may be compared to those obtained with the same procedure and signal on 75 normal 6 to 18 month old subjects by Wilson, Moore and Thompson (1976)* who found thresholds ranging from 10 to 40 dB with a mean of 22.5 dB and a median and mode of 20 dB. As is evident, the median and mode threshold values obtained in the present investigation are elevated by 10 dB over the values for the normal infants.

The final question in this study concerned the effectiveness of the VRA procedure with Down's children as related to age. Figure 2 plots the number of successful (+) and unsuccessful (-) audiometric tests as a function of chronological age, BSID mental age equivalent, and BSID psychomotor age equivalent. As would be expected, the proportion of successful tests increases as age increases, regardless of which age scale is considered. However, if one is interested in predicting potential success with the procedure for a clinical population similar to the one studied, the BSID mental age equivalent score provides the most distinct (bimodal) distribution between successful and unsuccessful tests with the dividing point being a BSID mental age equivalent to at least 10 months.

TABLE 2:   Auditory thresholds obtained including the number of trials and time required to complete testing of Down syndrome subjects (from Greenberg, Wilson, Moore and Thompson, 1978).

Audiometric Threshold (dB SPL)	Number of Subjects	Trials Range	Trials Mean	Time (Min) Range	Time (Min) Mean
30	13	7-24	13	7-20	10
40	5	9-22	14	5-15	11
50	5	12-21	16	6-13	10
60	2	22-23	22.5	—	—
Unreliable	5	11-19	15	—	—
Not obtained	1	6	—	—	—

*References to dB in the Wilson, et al, 1976; Greenberg, et al, 1978; Wilson, Moore and Thompson, 1976; and Thompson, et al, 1979 studies are in SPL.

FIGURE 2: Number of successful and unsuccessful VRA threshold
tests as a function of BSID mental age equivalent,
chronological age, and BSID psychomotor age equivalent (from Greenberg, Wilson, Moore and Thompson,
1978).

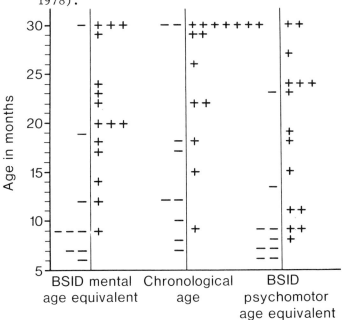

The results of the Greenberg et al., (1978) study provided a partial picture of the localization abilities of
Down's Syndrome infants. Previous studies using the same
methodology (Moore et al., 1975; Wilson et al., 1976; Moore,
Wilson & Thompson, 1977) have demonstrated that normal infants
5 months of age and over will initially localize to a sound
source and then continue with a very high rate of response
under conditions of visual reinforcement. In the present
study, when chronological age is considered, only a small
percentage of Down's infants 6 to 12 months of age and
slightly less than 50% of those 13 to 24 months of age showed
initial localizations to the sound. Between ages 2 and 3,
they localized at a rate of approximately 75%, and it was not
until 5 to 6 years of age that all subjects localized. Certainly, the fact that localization is substantially delayed
is not surprising, since a developmental delay is symptomatic
of this population. It is interesting to note, however, that
whereas young normal infants shift from no response to this

procedure at 4 months of age, to high response at 5 months of
age, nothing approaching such a tight grouping occurred in
the Down's group. Again, this simply attests to the wide
individual variation present in this clinical population.

Because it was expected that chronological age would be
a very poor predictor of success with the VRA procedures, the
BSID scales were used to provide an estimate of developmental
level. It was hypothesized that if the Down's group was considered on the basis of individual developmental age, as contrasted to chronological age, results would be similar to
those found with normally developing infants. However,
whereas Wilson et al., (1976) found normal infants 6 months
of age and older accomplished the VRA threshold procedure
with a high rate of success, the present study found Down's
subjects did not achieve a high success rate until 10 to 12
months BSID mental age equivalent.

This particular finding has 2 important implications.
First, it would suggest that the clinician involved in testing young Down's children might best predict potential success
with the VRA procedure based on developmental age with the
fence being 10 to 12 months. Second, it raises a theoretical
question concerning why Down's children normalized on developmental age, continued to show an age gap as compared to normal infants. Whether or not this difference reflects an
inappropriate scaling of the abilities of the Down's Syndrome
infants based on the BSID, or reflects an inability to deal
as effectively with auditory cues in a modality-specific
manner, cannot be determined from this study.

In their study of the use of auditory cues, Moskowitz
and Lohmann (1970) reported that attention, as measured by
the orienting reflex threshold, was substantially poorer in
a Down's group compared to a normal group. A question of
interest would be to match Down's and normally developing
infants by developmental level and compare abilities in both
tactile and visual modalities on tasks similar to those of
the present study. Such a procedure should provide information as to whether or not the findings in this study are
modality specific, suggesting a greater difficulty in processing auditory information in this population, or whether,
in fact, they reflect a greater cross-modality developmental
delay than predicted by BSID scales.

In an extension of the Moskowitz and Lohmann study, Thompson et al., (1979) investigated the application of VRA to a population of 21 low functioning, mentally retarded infants and children as part of an ongoing clinical program. All children successfully completing the VRA threshold procedure were then tested using visually reinforced infant speech discrimination (VRISD) to test its clinical applicability. The tape recorded contrastive pairs used in the study represented a discrimination found easy for normally developing 6 month old infants [sa] vs. [va], and a discrimination found to be difficult for both 6 and 12 month olds [fa] vs. [θa] (Eilers, Wilson & Moore, 1977).

The children ranged in age from 10 months to 6 years-6 months. Their developmental ages based on psychological tests or teachers' estimates, ranged from 1 month to 4 years-9 months. Fourteen of the children were diagnosed as having Down's Syndrome, while 7 evidenced undifferentiated mental retardation. The VRA paradigm was the same as used in past threshold studies.

In Procedure 1, each child was presented with 15 complex noise signals at 70 dB SPL with no reinforcement (baseline trials). Following teaching trials, each child received a second set of 15 stimulus presentations in which appropriate head-turn responses were visually reinforced. If a child failed to show and/or could not be taught a head-turn response in the teaching trials, the procedure was considered a failure. Of the 6 children who failed, 2 were functioning at the 1 month level and had not developed a head-turn response; 2 were functioning at the 5 to 9 month level and were capable of performing a head-turn response, but could not be conditioned during teaching trials. Two children were functioning in the 3 to 4 year range but also failed to condition to the task during teaching trials. These latter gave evidence of hearing the auditory signals. For example, one repeatedly said "What's that?" when the signal was presented, but failed to provide a head-turn response. Those children were tested satisfactorily by a combination of play and speech audiometry. No child failed the VRA procedure because of excessive false-positive responses.

Results for Procedure 1 are shown in Figure 3. The data reflect the total number of localization responses to each stimulus presentation for 15 children under reinforcement and no reinforcement conditions. Two distinct patterns are apparent. First, the number of responses in the no reinforcement (baseline) condition decreased as a function of stimulus

FIGURE 3:   Total number of children showing auditory-localizati
            responses to 15 stimulus presentations under conditi
            of no reinforcement and visual reinforcement (from
            Thompson, Wilson and Moore, 1979).

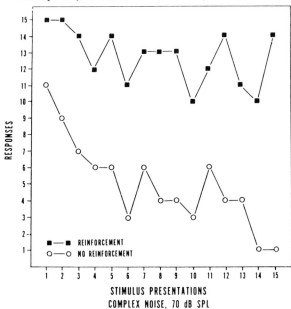

trials. The initial stimulus presentation produced responses
from 11 children (of 15), while the 14th and 15th presentations produced a response from only 1 child. Second, the
number of children responding in the reinforcement condition
remained reasonably high for all 15 stimulus presentations,
none of which produced fewer than 10 responses. The reinforcement condition resulted in significantly more responses
(t=7.09; df=14; p ≤ 0.01) than the baseline condition. The
difference between conditions tended to be greater as the
number of stimulus presentations increased.

    In Procedure 2, the complex noise stimulus was used to
establish hearing thresholds for 15 children who were capable of responding to VRA. Thresholds were obtained at 30 dB
for 10 children, 40 dB for 2 children, and 50 dB for 3
children.

Results of hearing assessment and tympanometry were used to determine which children required medical follow-up. Referral was made if tympanometry produced abnormal results, or if threshold levels exceeded 30 dB. A normal tympanogram was defined as an observable compliance peak occurring at pressures within ± 100 mm equivalent water pressure. Decision for referral of children whose thresholds exceeded 30 dB was based on:

1. a study by Wilson et al., (1976) which found that 90% of normal infants show complex noise thresholds of 30 dB or lower;

2. the Greenberg et al., (1978) study in which the modal complex noise threshold for Down's children was 30 dB.

Of the 10 children who responded to 30 dB, 4 showed normal or marginally normal tympanograms and required no medical disposition. Of the remaining 6, one had drainage tubes in place at the time of testing, was under medical care and required no further disposition. Five showed abnormal tympanograms in one or both ears and were referred for medical examination resulting in treatment ranging from wax removal to insertion of drainage tubes. Of the 5 showing reduced hearing thresholds (40 or 50 dB), all demonstrated abnormal tympanograms and all were referred for medical evaluation. One was diagnosed as having no problem, one was referred to an ear specialist for further evaluation, and 3 had middle ear pathology requiring either medication or surgical procedures.

Of the entire sample of 21 children, including those who were testable by VRA and those who were not, 11 (52%) were referred for medical evaluation. Nine (43%) either received medical treatment for ear pathology or were referred to an ear specialist for further evaluation.

Procedure 3 explored, on a pilot basis, the feasibility of applying the VRISD procedure to low functioning children. Of the 15 who successfully completed the VRA threshold pro- cedure and were candidates for the discrimination task, 5 were excluded due to hearing loss. Additionally, 1 child was unable to remain for the extra time required for the task.

Of the remaining 9 children, 4 successfully discriminated [va] vs. [sa] only, and a fifth discriminated both [va] vs. [sa] and [fa] vs. [θa]. Of the remaining 4 who did not give evidence of discrimination, 3 completed the [va] vs. [sa] task if one token was more intense than the other, as in training, but could not discriminate between the pair when the intensity cue was removed. The remaining child could not complete the task, even with the intensity cue added.

Table III details the VRA and VRISD results as a function of developmental age. VRA was an effective test procedure for 15 of the 21 (71%) children seen in this study. As is evident, success rate is highly dependent on developmental age. If all infants developmentally under 9 months are excluded, the procedure was effective on 88% of the children. VRISD was an effective procedure for 5 out of 9 (56%) children tested.

TABLE 3:   Effectiveness of VRA and VRISD as a function of developmental age (from Thompson, Wilson and Moore, 1979).

Developmental Age in Months	VRA Results [1]	VRISD Results [2]
1	—	Not Tested
1	—	Not Tested
7	—	Not Tested
7	—	Not Tested
9	+	Not Tested: Hearing Loss
12	+	+
16	+	Not Tested: Hearing Loss
17	+	Not Tested: Hearing Loss
19	+	Not Tested [3]
21	+	+
23	+	+ +
24	+	Not Tested: Hearing Loss
26	+	Not Tested: Hearing Loss
30	+	+
30	+	—
30	+	+
30	+	—
34	+	—
37	—	Not Tested
50	—	Not Tested
57	+	—

[1] + in VRA column means successful test.
[2] + in VRISD column means discrimination of (va) versus (sa).
+ + means discrimination of (va) versus (sa) and (fa) versus (θa).
— means unsuccessful test.
[3] Insufficient time for VRISD at time of test.

Thresholds using VRA were obtained on several children who were functioning well under 2 years of age, and on 1 Down's Syndrome child who was functioning at the 9 month level. These findings support the Greenberg et al., (1978) contention that VRA is appropriate for use on Down's children, providing their functional age is approximately 10 to 12 months. The difference between normal infants who typically respond to VRA at 5 to 6 months (Wilson et al., 1976), and Down's infants normalized on developmental age, suggests the value of further study to determine if the finding is modality or paradigm specific. Are Down's children delayed in auditory skills relative to other aspects of their development? Is there something about the VRA procedure itself which does not tap competence in the auditory area to the same degree as tests in other modalities (motor, social, etc.)? An answer that the finding is modality specific would have educational implications, as well as theoretical ones.

Results from the Thompson et al., (1979) study suggest that VRA is an effective and practical procedure for assessment of low functioning children in an ongoing clinical program. There was good agreement between VRA and tympanometry, as evidenced by the finding that all 5 children showing depressed hearing thresholds also had abnormal tympanograms. The high percentage (52%) of children referred for medical evaluation is consistent with previous reports discussed earlier in this chapter on the incidence of middle ear involvement in Down's children. Of interest is the fact that of the 11 children referred, 9 required medical management for outer or middle ear problems. This finding re-affirms the need for careful monitoring of the hearing and middle ear status of Down's children, and also indicates that the combination of VRA and tympanometry was an accurate predictor of those requiring medical attention.

The results of VRISD procedure on the easy contrast – [va] vs. [sa] – showed that only 56% of those subjects who completed the VRA threshold task gave evidence of successful discrimination. This can be compared to the 100% success rate for normal 6 and 12 month old infants in earlier work (Eilers et al., 1977). The discrimination task was included in this study primarily to determine its applicability to a clinical population. The choice of stimuli pairs was based on previous studies with normals – not on clinical

or educational import. Even given these limitations, the
results are interesting in terms of suggesting that the task
or the process of discrimination may be more difficult for
mentally retarded children than for normal infants at comparable developmental ages. The fact that some of the children
in the current study could correctly discriminate the contrast
when an intensity cue was added, but could not discriminate
without this additional cue, may suggest that the failure to
discriminate is not totally task related.

More recent work from this laboratory provides additional
information on the question of age of effectiveness of the
VRA threshold procedure. Wilson (1980) has shown that most
of the normally developing control infants could perform the
task at 6 months; most of the Down's infants could not, a
finding consistent with previous research (Greenberg et al.,
1978; Thompson et al., 1979). At 12 months, however, we have
found that 80% of the Down's subjects were assessable by VRA,
suggesting that our earlier VRA studies with Down's subjects
may have underestimated their abilities, and that VRA may be
an effective assessment tool at an age younger than previously believed possible.

This apparent difference is tempered somewhat by differences in subject selection and testing procedure. Down's
infants in the Wilson (1980) study were assessed longitudin-
ally, which allowed younger infants previous exposure and
familiarity with the reinforcement procedure, in addition to
regular training trials (albeit unsuccessful), prior to
establishing the VRA task as part of their response repertoire. Additionally, all Down's subjects in this study had
been enrolled in a parent-focused infant stimulation program,
in most cases, some time between birth and 6 months of age.
This may have also resulted in favourable developmental
progress.

Results: Electrophysiological
          Studies

Folsom, Widen and Wilson (1982) examined the post-natal
maturation of ABR latencies in Down's and normally developing
infants. It is known that the latency for Wave V decreases
with increased central nervous system maturation, up to 18
months. Since Down's individuals are reported to differ in
terms of cochlear and neural structures, there was reason to
believe that their time frame for maturation of the ABR may be
different as well.

Figure 4 illustrates responses recorded from one Down's and one normal subject at 12 months. These tracings were selected as they reflect typical waveforms and latencies for their respective groups. Latency differences for Wave I and V can be observed, with the Down's child showing shorter latencies.

ABR results across age at 60 dB nHL were examined for statistical significance using a two-factor Analysis of Variance design. Subjects selected for analysis were those deemed to be free from hearing loss at the time of testing. For the study, hearing loss subjects were defined as having:

1. no response at 20 dB nHL;
2. Wave I values at 60 dB nHL, which were absent or prolonged beyond two standard deviations.

In the subset presumed to have normal hearing, there were Wave V differences between groups (p $\leq$ .01) and across age (p $\leq$ .01). There was no interaction between groups and age, suggesting that mean differences were similar across age. No differences were observed between groups for Wave I or Wave I to V values at any age, although there was a trend at 12 months toward shorter I to V intervals in the Down's group.

FIGURE 4:   ABR results from a selected subject in each group. Latency values for these subjects approximate the respective group means. Vertical dotted lines represent positions of wave I, III, and V in the control group [click intensity = 60 dB nHL; rate = 13.3/sec; 1024 sweeps] (from Folsom, Widen and Wilson, 1983).

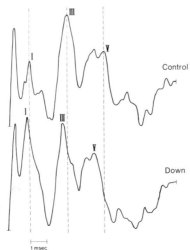

Figure 5 reflects the mean ABR Wave I and Wave V latencies
for the Down's and normal control subjects across the 3 age
groups. The graph illustrates that the magnitude of difference between the 2 groups for Wave V only is greatest at 12
months of age.

Figure 6 (a, b, c) reflects the Wave V latency differences between groups as a function of intensity (dB)nHL for
each age. The latency-intensity functions tend to overlay
for ages 3 and 6 months. At 12 months, however, a clear
divergence is seen for 40 and 60 dB nHL with the Down's group
showing shorter latencies than the control infants.

The intensity results were treated statistically for
each age. For the analysis, only those infants with datum
points at all intensity levels were included. This resulted
in slightly different group mean values for the latency-
intensity functions, particularly at 6 months of age. No
differences between groups were observed for 3 or 6 months;
however, there were differences at 12 months between groups
(p $\leq$ .05) and, as expected, across intensity (p $\leq$ .01). In
addition, there was a significant interaction between groups

FIGURE 5: Mean ABR wave I and V latency values for Down
          syndrome and control infants at ages three, six
          and 12 months. Vertical bars represent +/- twice
          the standard error of the mean [click intensity =
          60 dB nHL; rate = 13.3/ sec] (from Folsom, Widen
          and Wilson, 1983).

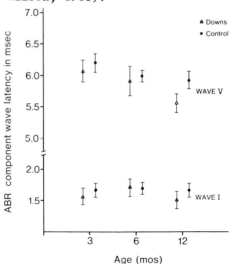

FIGURE 6 A, B, C: Mean ABR wave V latency values for Down
                    syndrome and control infants as a function
                    of intensity in dB nHL. Vertical bars rep-
                    resent +/- twice the standard error of the
                    mean [click rate = 13.3 /sec] (from Folsom,
                    Widen and Wilson, 1983).

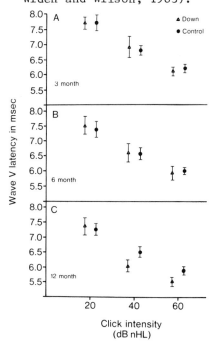

and intensity (p ≤ .01). At this age, that interaction
implies that the difference between Down's and control
infants was not uniform across intensity. Simple main effect
comparisons at each intensity for the 12 month group show no
difference between groups at 20 dB nHL. There were, however,
significant differences seen at 40 dB (p ≤ .01) and at 60 dB
(p ≤ .01), resulting in steeper latency-intensity functions
for the Down's group.

     The results of this study demonstrate that the ABR of the
Down's infant is similar in waveform morphology to the normal
infant. However, clear differences exist between groups when
comparisons of Wave V latencies are made across age. Additionally, the Down's group shows a steeper latency-intensity slope.
The finding of shorter latencies in the Down's group was
unexpected, particularly when reported neural and auditory
abnormalities are taken into consideration.

Clearly, our understanding of neural development in Down's
Syndrome and/or the underlying cochlear and neural mechanisms
which generate the ABR in Down's Syndrome is incomplete.

Squires et al., (1980) have also reported shorter ABR
latencies in Down's adults when compared to normals and other
retarded individuals. Our findings are consistent with their
latency differences, particularly for our 12 month group,
where we show the greatest mean difference between groups.

Implications can be drawn from the present study regarding the alteration of Wave V latency values as a function of
chronological age in Down's Syndrome. While significant
group differences in the absence of a group-by-age interaction
implies similar differences across age, Figure 5 illustrates
that it is only at 12 months of age that any substantial
difference occurs between mean values. This suggests that
Wave V change across age in Down's infants proceeds on a
different time course than in normal infants. That is, the
Wave V latency "matures" more rapidly. In fact, at some
point between 6 and 12 months, the Down's infants' Wave V
values reach those of normal young adults (5.6 msec. at 60
dB nHL; 13.3/sec.). Consequently, the latency norms developed
from normal infants may not adequately serve as norms for
Down's children after 6 months of age. Hearing levels in
Down's infants which were determined using the expected
latency curves for normal infants beyond 6 months of age may
underestimate a possible hearing loss and result in false-
negative findings. Beyond this age, there is approximately
a 10 dB difference between the means of each group, with up
to a 30 dB difference between the extremes of $\pm$ 2 standard
deviations for both the controls and Down's group.

The differences reported here between groups appear to
be intensity dependent and were seen only at the higher
intensity levels of 40 and 60 dB HL. This finding suggests
that cochlear function in Down's infants may differ from
normals by 12 months, as evidenced by latency-intensity
functions significantly steeper in the Down's group.

In the most recent and extensive study in our center,
Widen (1982) tested the hypothesis that Down's individuals
show more rapid changes in their ABR to increasing intensity
than normals. Her subjects ranged in age from 15 to 21 years.
In addition, she used a matched group of normals. She found

all subjects were able to respond in a reliable manner to the
behavioural testing included in the pre-experimental protocol.
Click thresholds were obtained at the same level as the best
of the 5 pure tone thresholds (within +5 and -10 dB) for both
groups, suggesting that behavioural test results are as
reliable for the Down's subjects as for controls. The controls responded at lower levels to both pure tone and click
stimuli than did the Down's subjects. The discrepancy between
groups was greatest at 8000 Hz and there was greater variability within the Down's group.

By criterion, all subjects showed normal tympanograms
with compliance peaks between +50 and -100 mm. equivalent
water pressure. Measurements of ear canal volume taken during
tympanometry revealed significantly smaller ear canals for the
Down's subjects (mean = .7 cc) than for the control subjects
(mean = 1.3 cc), (p $\leq$ .001).

The latency-intensity functions for both the experimental
and control groups were developed from their mean ABR Wave V
latencies for 20, 40, and 60 dB nHL and are graphically por-
trayed in Figure 7. As expected, there is a systematic
decrease in Wave V latency as signal intensity is increased
from 20 to 60 dB for both groups. Examination of these
functions shows that at 20 dB, Wave V latencies for Down's
subjects are longer than the controls. By 60 dB, however, the
mean latency of the Down's group is shorter than the controls.
Thus, the slope of the function is steeper for the Down's
subjects than for the control group.

Significant differences were seen between groups and
across intensity (p $\leq$ .05). In addition, a significant interaction was found between groups and intensity conditions. The
mean Wave V latency for the Down's group was significantly
longer at 20 dB (p $\leq$ .01) and significantly shorter at 60 dB
(p $\leq$ .05) than the control group. No significant difference
was found between groups for the 40 dB condition.

To facilitate comparison of data from individual subjects,
latency changes as a function of intensity were quantified for
each subject by computing the shift in latency between two
intensity conditions. Latency shifts from 20 to 40 dB, from
40 to 60 dB, and from 20 to 60 dB were calculated for each
subject. In a sense, these values are the numerical representation of the individual latency-intensity curves. On the

FIGURE 7:   Mean ABR wave V latencies for Down syndrome and
            control groups as a function of intensity.   Stan-
            dard deviations are represented by vertical bars
            [click rate = 33.3/sec] (from Widen, 1982).

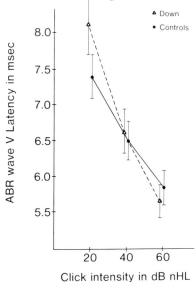

average, a 40 dB increase in click intensity resulted in a
1.54 msec. change in ABR Wave V latency for the normal control
subjects.   By comparison, a 40 dB increase in signal strength
resulted in a 2.44 msec. change in the Wave V latency for
Down's subjects.   The rate of change was proportional for the
2 groups.   That is, both groups showed a greater latency shift
between 20 and 40 dB (60% of the total shift) than between 40
and 60 dB.

     Although amplitude of the ABR is considered to be a less
stable measure than latency, the expected increase in Wave V
amplitude with increasing intensity was evident for both control and experimental groups, as can be seen in Figure 8.   The
amplitude of the ABR is significantly reduced in Down's subjects compared to the control group, and these differences
remain essentially constant across intensity.   Unlike the
latency-intensity function, the slope of the amplitude-
intensity function did not differ between the 2 groups.

FIGURE 8: Mean ABR wave V amplitudes for Down syndrome and
control groups as a function of intensity. Standard deviations are represented by vertical bars
[click rate = 33.3/sec] (from Widen, 1982).

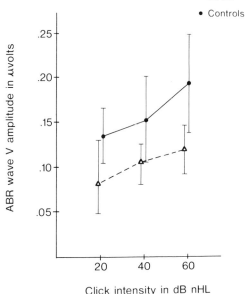

Click intensity in dB nHL

ABR threshold for each subject was calculated in dB nHL
and in dB relative to each subject's own behavioural threshold
for the click stimulus (SL or Sensation Level). The effect of
any differences in hearing level between groups should be
minimized when using a Sensation Level reference. ABR thresholds were at significantly higher intensity levels for the
Down's subjects than for the controls. This was the case
using both decibel referents.

Just as there was good agreement between pure tone and
click thresholds, there was also good correspondence between
ABR and behavioural click thresholds. This is of particular
interest to audiologists who have wondered if retarded subjects
possessed the cognitive or attending capabilities to respond
to signals at threshold levels during behavioural testing.
Theoretically, if the subject is unable to attend to threshold
level stimuli, an electrophysiological procedure which requires
no active participation on the part of the subject is expected
to yield a lower threshold. With the Down's subjects in our

study, however, ABR threshold was actually elevated compared
to behavioural click thresholds. On the average, ABR thresholds occurred at 5 to 15 dB above click thresholds for the
control subjects (mean: 8 dB SL), and at 5 to 20 dB SL (mean:
13 dB SL) for Down's subjects.

Discussion

The results of Widen's (1982) investigation support the
hypothesis that Down's individuals show abnormally rapid
changes in their ABRs as a function of changes in stimulus
intensity. Strong support is provided by the finding of
significantly steeper latency-intensity functions for the
Down's group than for the controls.

An abnormally steep latency-intensity function is usually
associated with a sensorineural hearing loss with loudness
recruitment. None of our Down's subjects was thought to have
a hearing loss. Although hearing sensitivity was not quite as
good as that of the age-matched peers in the controls, generally their hearing levels did fall "within normal limits". It
is likely that an audiologist reviewing the results of behavioural tests would conclude that hearing sensitivity is adequate for communication, and would not make additional recommendations. Nonetheless, only 2 of the 15 "normal hearing"
Down's subjects showed ABR latency-intensity functions comparable to those of the normal controls. The 2 were the only 2
with 8000 Hz hearing threshold levels of 10 dB or better.

The possibility of cochlear abnormality in many Down's
individuals seems likely. Thirteen of the 15 subjects in this
study showed a loss of hearing at 8000 Hz. Their abnormally
steep latency-intensity curves suggest an abnormal response to
increases in intensity similar to those seen in cases of
cochlear hearing loss with loudness recruitment.

Anatomical studies of the temporal bones of Down's children offer additional support for cochlear involvement. Two
studies report shorter cochleas in Down's Syndrome (Igarashi
et al., 1977; Harada & Sando, 1981). Although the effect of a
shorter cochlea on hearing sensitivity is not known, a high

frequency loss would not be inconsistent with that finding. Strong support for cochlear pathology in Down's Syndrome also comes from Harada and Sando (1981), who found that 7 of 12 Down's temporal bones showed apical endolymphatic hydrops. Information about hearing in those ears was not available. However, a typical symptom of endolymphatic hydrops is loudness recruitment. Furthermore, more often than not, patients with hydrops or Meniere's show abnormally steep ABR latency-intensity functions.

The possibility that an alteration of intensity might produce shorter Wave V latencies has been considered. That is, it is possible that the auditory system might respond as if the stimulus was more intense in those cases with a recruiting, sensorineural hearing loss. The findings of this study suggest that was the case for many of the Down's subjects. Most cochlear hearing losses reach, but do not exceed, normal latency values once threshold is sufficiently surpassed. Wave V latencies for the Down's subjects tended to exceed the normal range, resulting in absolute values shorter than normal. This difference between Down's subjects and reported cases of cochlear hearing loss suggests that steeper latency-intensity functions alone may not account for all the differences seen between Down's and control latencies at intense levels of stimulation.

Squires et al., (1980) investigated another hypothesis, the possibility of smaller head size among the Down's Syndrome subjects accounting for the shorter latencies. They found no correlation between head size and Wave V latencies within the Down's group, although as a group, Down's head measurements were smaller.

Attempts to explain differences between male and female Wave V latencies have focused on the size of auditory nerve structures, despite the absence of correlations between skull size and latencies. It seems reasonable that size may, indeed, influence latency. The results of the present study are consistent with reported sex differences. Male control subjects yielded significantly longer ABR Wave V latencies than females. Likewise, Down's males showed longer latencies than Down's females. Down's Syndrome individuals, known to have a smaller pinna, ear canals, cochlea, and brainstem, have a shorter latency than the controls.

It seems likely that the short latencies result from a complex set of factors, including size and steeper latency-intensity functions. These factors may interact with other factors (e.g. conductive hearing loss or brainstem abnormality) within individuals to produce a confusing audiological picture. If the ABR is to be used as part of the hearing assessment of Down's Syndrome people, the audiologist should take particular care to record responses at a number of stimulus levels and to base interpretation upon response threshold, as well as latency. If the ABR is to be used with Down's Syndrome to assess neural integrity of the brainstem, the likelihood of high-frequency hearing loss and the probability of short latencies at supra-threshold levels of stimulation must be recognized.

Summary

Based on longitudinal study of Down's infants, children and young adults, our work to date allows the following conclusions:

1. The hearing sensitivity of Down's infants and young children can be tested reliably with ABR and VRA procedures; however, in the case of VRA, the Down's infant must be older than a normally developing infant to complete the test successfully. The BOA procedure does not provide reliable results with this population, as has also been found with some normally developing infants.

2. Both the ABR thresholds and the VRA thresholds were elevated for the Down's group, and there was good agreement between the electrophysiological and behavioural test results.

3. Head turning behaviour, and perhaps localization ability, develop more slowly in Down's individuals than normals.

4. Results from a limited sample of Down's children demonstrated that, of those able to accomplish the VRA hearing threshold test, most did not demonstrate the ability to discriminate speech sounds when tested with the same procedure. This finding is in contrast to that of normally developing infants.

5. The ABR in Down's individuals is smaller in Waveform
    morphology to normal controls. However, clear differ-
    ences exist between groups when comparisons of Wave V
    latencies are made across age. Consequently, the
    latency norms developed from normal infants may not
    serve adequately as norms for Down's children after 6
    months of age. Hearing loss in Down's infants which
    is determined using the expected latency curves for
    normal infants may underestimate the possible hearing
    loss.

6. The latency-intensity function of Wave V of the ABR
    for Down's subjects is steeper than for normal control
    subjects. Mean Wave V amplitude for the Down's sub-
    jects was reduced when compared to normal controls.
    Abnormally steep latency-intensity functions are usu-
    ally associated with abnormal cochlear function,
    raising the possibility of cochlear abnormality in
    many Down's individuals.

Acknowledgements

The research reported in this chapter was supported by
research grants from The Deafness Research Foundation and from
the National Foundation-March of Dimes. During a portion of
the project, Dr. Widen was supported, in part, by the Gatzert
Fellowship, University of Washington. The authors wish to
thank Douglas B. Greenberg, John M. Moore, and Gary Thompson
for their substantial contributions to the research, and also
Linda Hesketh for her assistance in data collection and in
preparation of this manuscript, and Dolorita Reandeau for her
assistance in data collection. A particular thanks is extended
to Phyllis Doyle, Valentine Dmitriev, and Patricia Oelwein, and
the Program for Children with Down's Syndrome and other
Developmental Delays, Child Development and Mental Retardation
Center, University of Washington, and to the special children
and families who contributed so greatly to these studies.

References

Aase, J.M., Wilson, A.C., and Smith, D.W., "Small Ears in Down's Syndrome: A Helpful Diagnostic Aid," Journal of Pediatrics 82:845-847, 1973.

Balkany, T., "Otologic Aspects of Down's Syndrome," Seminars in Speech, Language and Hearing 1:39-48, 1980.

Balkany, T., Downs, M.P., Jafek, B.W., and Krajicek, M.J., "Hearing Loss in Down's Syndrome," Clinical Pediatrics 18:116-118, 1979.

Banik, N.L., Davison, A.N., Palo, J., and Savolainen, H., "Biochemical Studies of Myelin Isolated from the Brains of Patients with Down's Syndrome," Brain 98:213-218, 1975.

Barnard, K.E., "Infant Stimulation," Down's Syndrome (Mongolism): Research, Prevention and Management (New York: Brunner/Mazel), Koch, R., and de la Cruz, F.F. (Eds.), 1975.

Barnet, A.B., and Lodge, A., "Click-evoked Responses in Normal and Developmentally Retarded Infants," Nature 214:252-255, 1967.

Barnet, A.B., Ohlrich, E.S., and Shanks, B.L., "EEG Evoked Responses to Repetitive Auditory Stimulation in Normal and Down's Syndrome Infants," Developmental Medicine and Child Neurology 13:321-329, 1971.

Bigum, H.B., Dustman, R.E., and Beck, E.C., "Visual and Somatosensory Evoked Responses from Mongoloid and Normal Children," Electroencephalography and Clinical Neurophysiology 28:576-585, 1970.

Bilovsky, D., and Schare, J., "The ITPA and Down's Syndrome: An Exploratory Study," American Journal of Mental Deficiency 70:78-82, 1965.

Blager, F.B., "Speech and Language Development of Down's Syndrome Children," Seminars in Speech, Language and Hearing 1:63-73, 1980.

Brooks, D.N., Wooley, H., and Kanjilal, G.C., "Hearing Loss
    and Middle Ear Disorders in Patients with Down's Syndrome
    (Mongolism)," Journal of Mental Deficiency Research
    16:21-29, 1972.

Carr, J., "Mental and Motor Development in Young Mongol
    Children," Journal of Mental Deficiency Research 14:205-220,
    1970.

Coleman, M., "Down's Syndrome," Pediatric Annals 7:36-63,
    1978.

Coleman, M., Schwartz, R.H., and Schwartz, D.M., "Otologic
    Manifestations in Down's Syndrome," Down's Syndrome Papers
    and Abstracts for Professionals 2:1, 1979.

Crome, L., and Stern, J., Pathology of Mental Retardation
    (Baltimore: Williams and Wilkins), 1972.

Crome, L., Cowie, W., and Slater, E., "A Statistical Note on
    Cerebellar and Brainstem Weight in Mongolism," Journal of
    Mental Deficiency Research 10:69-72, 1966.

Davis, H., "Abnormal Hearing and Deafness," Hearing and
    Deafness (New York: Holt, Rinehart & Winston), Davis, H.,
    & Silverman, S.R. (Eds.), 1978.

Dicks-Mireaux, M.J., "Mental Development of Infants with
    Down's Syndrome," American Journal of Mental Deficiency
    77:26-32, 1972.

Down, J.L., "Observations on Ethnic Classifications,"
    London Hospital Reports 3:259-262, 1866.

Eilers, R.E., Wilson, W.R., and Moore, J.M., "Developmental
    Changes in Speech Discrimination in Infants," Journal of
    Speech and Hearing Research 20:766-780, 1977.

Evans, D., "The Development of Language Abilities in Mongols:
    A Correlational Study," Journal of Mental Deficiency
    Research 21:103-117, 1977.

Folsom, R.C., Widen, J.E., and Wilson, W.R., "Auditory
    Brainstem Responses in Down's Syndrome Infants," Arch.
    Otolaryngol. 109:607-610, 1983

Fulton, R.T., and Lloyd, L.L., "Hearing Impairment in a
Population of Children with Down's Syndrome," American
Journal of Mental Deficiency 73:298-302, 1968.

Gliddon, J.B., Busk, J., and Galbraith, J.C., "Visual Evoked
Responses as a Function of Light Intensity in Down's
Syndrome and Nonretarded Subjects," Psychophysiology
12:416-422, 1975.

Glovsky, L., "Audiological Assessment of a Mongoloid Population," Training School Bulletin 63:27-36, 1966.

Greenberg, D.B., Wilson, W.R., Moore, J.M., and Thompson, G.,
"Visual Reinforcement Audiometry (VRA) with Young Down's
Syndrome Children," Journal of Speech and Hearing Disorders
43:448-458, 1978.

Harada, T., and Sando, I., "Temporal Bone Histopathologic
Findings in Down's Syndrome," Archives of Otolaryngology
107:96-103, 1981.

Hayden, A.H., and Haring, N.G., "The Acceleration and Maintenance of Developmental Gains in Down's Syndrome School-
age Children," Research to Practice in Mental Retardation:
Care and Intervention - Volume 1 (Baltimore: University
Park Press), Mittler, P. (Ed.), 1977.

Higashi, Y., Yasui, M., Monotani, Y., Kawasaki, H., Asai, T.,
and Shingyoji, I., "Visually Evoked Potential of Retarded
Children," Clinical Electroencephalography 14:541-549, 1972.

Igarashi, M., Takahashi, M., Alford, B.R., and Johnson, P.E.,
"Inner Ear Morphology in Down's Syndrome," Acta Otolaryngologica 83:175-181, 1971.

Ling, D., Ling, A.H., and Doehring, D.G., "Stimulus Response
and Observer Variables in the Auditory Screening of Newborn
Infants," Journal of Speech and Hearing Research 13:9-18,
1970.

Lyle, J.G., "The Effect of an Institution Environment Upon
the Verbal Development of Imbecile Children; II: Speech
and Language," Journal of Mental Deficiency Research
4:1-13, 1960.

Lyle, J.G., "Comparison of the Language of Normal and Imbecile Children," Journal of Mental Deficiency Research 5:40-51, 1961.

McDade, H.L., and Adler, S., "Down's Syndrome and Short-term Memory Impairment: A Storage or Retrieval Deficit?" American Journal of Mental Deficiency 84:561-567, 1980.

Moore, J.M., Thompson, G., and Thompson, M., "Auditory Localization of Infants as a Function of Reinforcement Conditions," Journal of Speech and Hearing Disorders 40:29-34, 1975.

Moore, J.M., Wilson, W.R., and Thompson, G., "Visual Reinforcement of Head-Turn Responses in Infants Under 12 Months of Age," Journal of Speech and Hearing Disorders 42:328-334, 1977.

Moore, J.M., and Wilson, W.R., "Visual Reinforcement Audiometry (VRA) With Infants," Early Diagnosis of Hearing Loss (New York: Grune & Stratton, Inc.), Gerber, S.E. & Mencher, G.T. (Eds.), 1978.

Moskowitz, H., and Lohmann, W., "Auditory Threshold for Evoking an Orienting Reflex in Mongoloid Patients," Perceptual Motor Skills 31:879-882, 1970.

Palo, J., and Savolainen, H., "The Proteins of Human Myelin in Inborn Errors of Metabolism and in Chromosomal Anomalies," Acta Neuropathologica 24:56-61, 1973.

Rohr, A., and Burr, D.B., "Etiological Differences in Patterns of Psycholinguistic Development of Children of IQ 30-60," American Journal of Mental Deficiency 82:549-553, 1978.

Rynders, J., Behlen, K., and Horrobin, J., "Performance Characteristics of Preschool Down's Syndrome Children Receiving Augmented or Repetitive Verbal Instruction," American Journal of Mental Deficiency 84:67-73, 1979.

Schwartz, D.M., and Schwartz, R.H., "Acoustic Impedance and Otoscopic Findings in Young Children with Down's Syndrome," Archives of Otolaryngology 104:652-656, 1978.

Smith, D.W., and Wilson, A.A., The Child With Down's Syndrome (Mongolism) (Philadelphia: W.B. Saunders Co.), 1973.

Squires, N., Aine, C., Buchwald, J., Norman, R., and Galbraith, G., "Auditory Brain Stem Response Abnormalities in Severely and Profoundly Retarded Adults," Electro-encephalography and Clinical Neurophysiology 50:172-185, 1980.

Straumanis, J.J., Shagass, C., and Overton, D.A., "Auditory Evoked Responses in Young Adults with Down's Syndrome and Idiopathic Mental Retardation," Biological Psychiatry 6:75-79, 1973a.

Straumanis, J.J., Shagass, C., and Overton, D.A., "Auditory Evoked Responses in Down's Syndrome," Archives of General Psychiatry 29:544-546, 1973b.

Thompson, G., and Weber, B.A., "Responses of Infants and Young Children to Behaviour Observation Audiometry (BOA)," Journal of Speech and Hearing Disorders 39:140-147, 1974.

Thompson, G., Wilson, W.R., and Moore, J.M., "Application of Visual Reinforcement Audiometry (VRA) to Low-functioning Children," Journal of Speech and Hearing Disorders 44:80-90, 1979.

VanderVeer, B., and Schweid, E., "Infant Assessment: Stability of Mental Functioning in Young Retarded Children," American Journal of Mental Deficiency 79:1-4, 1974.

Weber, B.A., "Validation of Observer Judgments in Behavioural Observation Audiometry," Journal of Speech and Hearing Disorders 34:350-355, 1969.

Widen, J.E., The Effects of Intensity on the Auditory Brain-stem Response in Down's Syndrome Unpublished Doctoral Dissertation: University of Washington, 1982.

Wilson, W.R., "Behavioural Assessment of Auditory Function in Infants," Communicative and Cognitive Abilities-Early Behavioural Assessment (Baltimore: University Park Press), Minifie, F.D., & Lloyd, L.L. (Eds.), 1978.

Wilson, W.R., Lee, K.H., Owen, G., and Moore, J.M.,
    Instrumentation for Operant Infant Auditory Assessment
    (Seattle: Child Development and Mental Retardation Center),
    1976.

Wilson, W.R., Moore, J.M., and Thompson, G., "Sound-field
    Auditory Thresholds of Infants Utilizing Visual Reinforce-
    ment Audiometry (VRA)," paper presented at the 1976
    American Speech and Hearing Association Convention,
    Houston, Texas.

Yellin, A.M., Lodwig, A.K., and Jerison, H.J., "Effects of
    Rate of Repetitive Stimulus Presentation on the Visual
    Evoked Brain Potentials of Young Adults with Down's
    Syndrome," Biological Psychiatry 14:913-924, 1979.

Yellin, A.M., Lodwig, A.K., and Jerison, H.J., "Auditory
    Evoked Brain Potentials as a Function of Interstimulus
    Interval in Adults with Down's Syndrome," Audiology
    19:255-262, 1980.

Zekulin, X.Y., Gibson, D., Mosely, J.L., and Brown, R.I.,
    "Auditory-Motor Channeling in Down's Syndrome Subjects,"
    American Journal of Mental Deficiency 78:571-577, 1974.

IS THERE HEARING HELP FOR DOWN'S SYNDROME?

Marion P. Downs

University of Colorado, Health Sciences Center, Denver, Colorado

Whenever a population of mentally retarded children is screened for hearing, an inordinate number of them are found with significant losses. One of the reasons may be that a large percentage of these children have Down's Syndrome, a group in which hearing loss occurs almost as part of the symptomatology. The identification, diagnosis and management of these hearing losses have been the subject of a long-term study at the University of Colorado Health Sciences Center. The results of the study are not only significant for Down's Syndrome individuals, but seem to indicate that indepth studies of other clinical pathologies with multiple handicaps could reveal ear abnormalities specific to those entities.

Identification

Reports of the prevalence of conductive hearing loss in Down's individuals range from 2.6% to 60%, while that of sensorineural losses ranges from 16% to 52.6% (see Table I). One reason for this variability may be that clinicians, fearing that testing this population is a difficult procedure, may not have pursued testing with sufficient vigor. Since 1971, when adequate infant stimulation programs were developed for Down's children, their improved psychomotor and language development have made testing far more feasible. It should be remembered that Down's children who have been in an intensive infant stimulation program are performing 95% of the tasks expected of normal children (Coleman, 1980). Therefore, this group is now available for all the standard testing techniques clinicians use with children of comparable mental age.

TABLE I: Comparison of previous studies: Prevalence of
          hearing loss in Down's population

Study	Criterion	Abn. (%)	Cond. (%)	S/N (%)	Mixed (%)
Glovsky 1966	20 dB	73	2.6	52.6	18.4
Brooks 1972	"Tympanometry & Audiometry"	77	60	36	
Fulton/Lloyd 1973	25 dB	40	54.8	22.6	22.6
Schwartz/ Schwartz 1978	Tympanometry & Pneumatic-Otoscopy	67			
Denver Study	15 dB	78	54	16	8

From Downs, M.P., "The Hearing of Down's Individuals",
    Seminars in Speech, Hearing, Lang., Vol. 1:25-38, 1980.
    With permission of Brian C. Decker, Inc., Division Thieme-
    Stratton, Inc.

Subjects

The 107 subjects in our initial survey were selected by
a cluster, non-random sampling procedure (Krajicek, 1980).
They ranged from 2 months to 60 years and were selected from
community-based programs within 120 miles of Denver.

Tests

The tests utilized on this population are shown in
Table II (Downs, 1980). The kinds of tests each performed
were dictated by the functional age of the individual. For

TABLE II: Tests performed on Denver population.

	Tests	Number Able To Be Tested
Group 1:	Sound Field SRT's, Air and Bone SRT's, Pure Tone Air and Bone Discrimination Test	34
Group 2:	All of the above except Discrimination	46
Group 3:	Air and Bone SRT's	11
Group 4:	Sound Field and Bone SRT's	8
Group 5:	Sound Field SRT's	5
Group 6:	Awareness and Localization	3

From Downs, M.P., "The Hearing of Down's Individuals, Seminars in Speech, Hearing, Language, 1:25-38, 1980. With permission of Brian C. Decker, Inc., Division Thieme-Stratton, Inc.

Group 2, the discrimination tests could not be given because the examiner could not understand the child's speech patterns using standard PB-K discrimination lists. It is possible that picture discrimination or sentence discrimination tests might have produced results from most of this Group. Groups 3, 4, 5 and 6 contained the younger members of the study.

Speech reception thresholds were obtained by toy identification, a simple and highly motivating procedure. Audiometry was done with play conditioning techniques using a piggy bank with pennies to put in it. Reinforcement consisted only of smiles, words or enthusiastic hand clapping, which were quite sufficient to keep the children cooperating as long as necessary.

Results

Our criterion level of 15 dB pure tone average as handicapping (Roeser & Downs, 1981; Lewis, 1976) yielded a higher
prevalence of hearing loss than any other study in the literature (conductive - 54%; sensorineural - 16%; mixed - 8%).
Seventy-eight percent of our population showed hearing losses
in one or both ears at levels greater than 15 dB. Sixty-five
percent had binaural hearing losses of greater than 15dB. A
composite audiogram of the means of the conductive losses is
shown in Figure 1. The composite sensorineural losses are
shown in Figure 2, the mixed losses in Figure 3.

FIGURE 1:   Conductive losses: a) Composite audiogram of
          means; b) Range of air conduction thresholds;
          c) Range of bone conduction threshold.

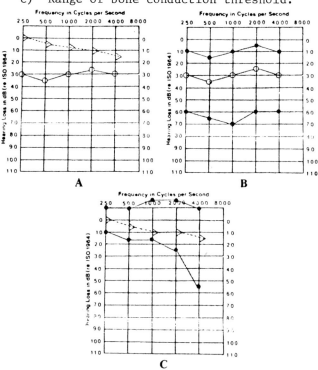

Figures 1, 2 and 3 are reprinted from Downs, M.P., "The Hear-
ing of Down's Individuals," Seminars in Speech, Hearing,
Language 1:25-38, 1980. With permission of Brian C. Decker,
Inc., Division of Thieme-Stratton, Inc.

FIGURE 2:   Sensorineural losses: Composite audiogram of
            means and range.

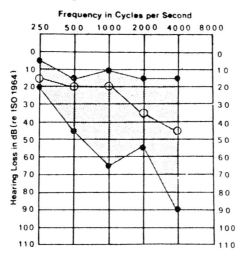

FIGURE 3:   Mixed losses: a) Composite audiogram of means;
            b) Range of air conduction; c) Range of bone
            conduction.

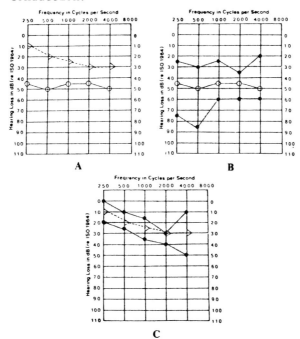

For our purposes, we assume that both monaural and
binaural losses are handicapping; indeed, there is now hard
evidence that monaural hearing losses produce lower academic
skills in school children than was previously thought (Bess,
1982). Therefore, we will take 78% as the prevalence figure
for handicapping hearing losses in Down's children. Although
duration of hearing loss and its effects are not considered
at this point in the discussion, the high overall incidence
should serve as a guide to those dealing with this population.

Diagnosis

Something is going on in the ears of the Down's population that is not evident to even the practiced eye of the
otolaryngologist. Sixty percent of our cases of conductive
loss could be explained by middle ear effusion or chronic
otitis media, but 40% could not be explained on that basis.
On microscopic pneumatic otoscopy and impedance tympanometry,
the 40% had normal physical findings yet significant hearing
loss, or they had losses too severe to be explained by negative pressure ($>$ 20 dB) or by middle ear effusion ($>$ 35 dB).
In addition, 20% of the conductive losses had normal tympanograms. A medical-surgical and temporal bone investigation
was thus indicated in order to complete the diagnoses of the
conductive hearing losses which had been found.

Surgical Findings

Four ears with unexplained conductive hearing losses
were brought to surgery. A number of abnormal middle ear
conditions were found, including:

1. Anterior fixation of the stapes footplate;

2. Mildly abnormal ossicular chain;

3. Malformed stapes;

4. Widely dehiscent facial nerves.

Stapedectomies were performed on the 4 ears, but none of these procedures produced significantly improved hearing levels, a negative result also encountered by Goodhill (1978), Shea (1977), and House (1977). House termed this lack of improvement to be due to "inner ear conductive hearing loss". It was not clear, however, what it was that caused such an "inner ear loss".

In addition to the surgery on our study cases, 12 operative procedures on patients with Down's Syndrome and chronic otitis media were reviewed by Balkany (1980). The following findings were reported:

1. Malformed or eroded malleus: 4 of 12 cases
   (Remodeling by infection);

2. Malformed or eroded incus: 8 of 12 cases
   (Remodeling by infection);

3. Stapes malformation: 7 of 12 cases
   (Most likely congenital);

4. Facial nerve canal widely dehiscent: 3 of 12 cases
   (Congenital).

The patients in this latter series all had cholesteatomas, but they represented residents in a state institution, a setting where there may be a higher than normal prevalence of chronic otitis media. In our 107 Down's people living at home, only 1 had a cholesteatoma. The difference may reflect the difficulty of maintaining otological health care in an institutionalized population, a situation exacerbated by the presence of congenital problems leading to middle ear disease.

Temporal Bone Findings

Five temporal bones received from 3 Down's children were examined in the laboratory of the University of Colorado Health Sciences Center. Ages of the subjects ranged from 3 days to 14 months. The results are remarkably similar to the surgical findings:

1. Malleus involved in acute and chronic inflammation:
   2 of 5 ears;

2. Incus involved in severe lymphocytic inflammation:
   2 of 5;

3.   Deformed stapes: 4 of 15;

4.   Widely dehiscent facial nerve canal: 3 of 5.

Perhaps the most significant temporal bone study was reported in 1981 by Harado and Sando, who examined the middle and inner ears of 12 temporal bones of Down's patients 3 to 15 years.   The following abnormalities were found.

Middle Ear Abnormalities   Inner Ear Abnormalities

Hypoplasia of epitympanum   Reduced number of cochlear
Narrow round window niche   turns
Remnant of mesenchymal tissue   Apical endolymphatic hydrops
   in round window niche in   Cyst in stria vascularis
   rest of middle ear   Hemorrhage in perilymphatic
Middle ear inflammation   spaces
Ossicular abnormalities   Wide communication of
Remnant of stapedial artery   saccular and utricular
Wide angle of facial genu   spaces
Large bony dehiscence of   Abnormal semicircular canals
   facial canal   Abnormal vestibular aqueduct
Cartilage remnant of otic
   capsule
High jugular bulb

The most common abnormality observed was a remnant of mesenchymal tissue in the round window niche.   The authors postulated that such tissue might cause a conductive loss if one of the following factors was also present:

1.   Complete obstruction of the round window niche by the tissue (present in 3 cases);

2.   Presence of such tissue in the epitympanum and tissue surrounding the ossicles (present in 2 cases);

3.   Tissue accompanied by other abnormalities, such as narrow round window niche with a small opening to the middle ear cavity (present in 1 case).

Here we have the first evidence of a reason for the "inner ear conductive loss" which has baffled surgeons and audiologists. The condition appears to be a congenital abnormality which may be specific to Down's Syndrome. However, the possibility arises that whenever chromosomal defects are present, one should look for some accompanying inner or middle ear abnormalities. We know this is true in First and Second Arch Syndromes, but other conditions should also be studied.

Management Study

Can the functioning of Down's children be enhanced by the use of amplification at an early age? This question naturally follows from the information gleaned in the studies described above. We set out to answer it in a controlled study with a young population of Down's children. The initial effort encountered problems which reduced the value of the results, so a second study was initiated. Both studies will be described, because each provides useful information.

Study I

Population

Nineteen Down's subjects ranging in age from 4 to 35 months were selected. A random sample of 8 children in the group were given hearing aids. Eleven were unaided. The aid chosen was the Qualitone DAO, which, at the time, had the most favourable SSPL, gain, and frequency response (SSPL $<$ 90 dB, gain $<$ 30 dB, flat frequency curve) for their mild hearing losses. One hearing aid was given, but ear molds were made for each ear so that the aid could be alternated every week.

Tests

Initially, and at 4 month intervals for 20 months, the children were given the following evaluative tests:

            Language: REEL (Receptive Expressive
                       Emergent Language Scale)
                       0-4 years;
            I.Q. - Development: Bailey Scale
                       (0-36 months)
                       Stanford Binet (24 months-)

    Results

        No significant differences have been observed between
    the aided and the unaided groups in this study. However, so
    many problems were encountered wearing aids that none of the
    group met our criteria for successful hearing aid usage,
    namely, 8 hours a day. Four of the 8 aided children wore
    the devices only an insignificant length of time per day, if
    at all. The other 4 did not meet our criteria, although the
    mothers made some effort to put the aids on the children
    once a day.

        The reasons for the mothers' inability to apply the aids
    were numerous, and provided a learning experience for all of
    us. What we had failed to recognize was the inordinate
    amount of pressure put on parents of Down's children.
    Intense infant stimulation programs, concern over heart con-
    ditions, treatment for upper respiratory problems, and other
    physical conditions, are putting burdens on these parents
    beyond their coping abilities. The problems associated with
    the wearing of a hearing aid seemed insurmountable to them.
    Not recognizing this over-burdening, we failed to provide
    the support required. Factors which contributed to the
    failures in hearing aid usage included:

        1. Trouble with ear mold fittings;

        2. Difficulty of maintenance of aids on ears;

        3. Insufficient counselling;

        4. Inadequate support systems;

        5. Improper therapy;

        6. Low parental tolerance level.

Armed with a fresh understanding of the problems, we undertook to repeat the study. The goal of determining whether the functioning of these children could be improved by amplification was too important to be side-tracked.

Study II

Population

Twelve Down's children, age 6 to 27 months, were selected from the patient rolls of the University of Colorado Health Sciences Center. Eight of the 12 were given hearing aids (Qualitone DAO).

Tests

The same evaluations were made as listed above, but it was felt that test administrations could be applied once a year for 3 years.

Procedure

With our new insights, we attempted to improve our procedures with the hearing aids in the following manner:

1. The hearing aid dealer who fitted the ear molds was, by now, an expert in applying molds to these tiny ears. Parents were counselled as to the problems they might encounter, and were told we would all help with them.

2. The need for some adhesive application to hold the aids in place was faced from the very start. Either surgical tape or a special gum was used to keep the aid on the child's head.

3. Everyone concerned with the study made a special effort to give more counselling. The project director called the parents every week to see if any problems were encountered, and to check on the number of hours the aids were worn.

4. Close contact was kept with the stimulation programs
    to assure that all support systems were adequate.
    The close touch that was kept with the parents
    assured them of the support of the personnel.

5. Special hearing aid therapy was given to this group,
    rather than relying on the stimulation programs, as
    had been done in the previous study. Audiologists
    and Speech Pathologists familiar with hearing aid
    orientation and auditory training were involved with
    the group.

6. Our personnel undertook a sharp change in attitude,
    from pressure-producing to support-giving. We
    understood the degree of stress that all of the
    stimulation programs and physical problems put on
    the parents, and we attempted to foresee when a
    tolerance level was exceeded. We then pulled back
    from our demands, and tried to give help rather than
    pressure.

The tremendous success of the infant stimulation programs
for Down's children has made it mandatory for parents to
participate in them. They can cause great feelings of guilt
and pressure in the parents. The addition of a hearing aid
program is just another burden for parents, unless handled
extremely cautiously.

Results

In an informal evaluation of the preliminary results of
our work by Dr. Florence Blager, the Speech/Language Pathologist involved in the study, the following tentative conclusions have been made:

1. In the first part of the study (Study I), hearing
    aid use was sporadic and, thus, application of hear-
    ing aids did not seem to override any basic develop-
    mental delay.

2. All 8 of the children in the second part of the
    study (Study II) appear to be wearing their aids the
    required amount of time per day. Complete follow-up

tests have not been given, but preliminary research data is available and, in addition, anecdotal reports have been quite satisfactory. Where hearing aids have been worn more consistently, 2 data points indicate that expressive language scores are rising in the aided children and falling in the unaided children. Further, parents indicate that they are encouraged by their child's progress and only affirmative feelings have been expressed. Thus, we feel that regardless of the outcome of the actual testing, there have already been positive results.

If the trend toward improved expressive language persists in the aided group, we will observe whether it modifies, in any way, the amount of drop which occurs in retarded children when cognitive skills should normally be developing. If so, that may mean that early hearing aid amplification may be a treatment of choice for Down's Syndrome individuals. The same consideration may also apply to other groups of children with specific handicaps. This, of course, would also require further study.

Discussion

G. MENCHER
The malformations and conductive loss you described intrigue me. I know that the etiology is completely different, but this problem is similar to one we see in Rubella children – that is, a congenital conductive hearing loss which may, in part, be due to stapes malformation, appears to be cochlear in origin. I wonder if you would like to comment on that?

M. DOWNS
In regard to the Rubella children, we do have, as you know, one temporal bone from a Rubella child which shows a congenital fixation of the stapes, which may account for any conductive hearing loss. I understand that quite a few children in Australia have been operated on for that condition. They did not get any improvement in hearing as a result. It may well be that additional study is necessary.

A. BOOTHROYD

From what we know of cochlear mechanics, I would have expected that obliteration of the round window would have affected bone conduction and air conduction thresholds equally. My understanding is that obliteration of the round window would diminish bone conduction thresholds because there is, for some unknown reason, then no capacity for the cochlear partition to move.

M. DOWNS

I agree with you. That thought occurred to me too. But evidently, in this case, the bone conduction method of testing obviates that. I don't know why. I think it should be looked into. Any suggestions on that? You have asked a good question, and one that I've thought of too, but to which I do not have an answer.

PARTICIPANT

Since you're an expert on ear mold fittings now, would you be willing to give us some information on what you do with your young children?

M. DOWNS

One of our hearing aid dealers who has done all of the fittings has just become so expert in doing this, that we aren't having the troubles that we've had before. These are unusually small ear canals, as you know, and the shape of the ear is such that it is difficult to keep the ear mold in. It's a matter of developing expertise in fitting them, and a willingness to go back (and you are going to have to go back) and make other ear molds. Every 3 months we have to make new ones. That is true of any child at that age who is given a hearing aid. It's always a problem, but I think expertise is the name of the game.

PARTICIPANT

Are you aware of the particular material he uses?

M. DOWNS

No, we use a soft material mostly.

PARTICIPANT
    I'd like to know more about the 5 factors influencing
your program, particularly the counselling and parental
tolerance levels. Can you give us a point-by-point analysis
of where that fell apart and what you've done to change it?

M. DOWNS
    Well, it fell apart in the first study because we didn't
do it. We assumed that the language stimulation programmer
whom we had contacted and who knew what we were doing, would
be able to handle these things. They had therapists in the
group, but they didn't have really good hearing therapists
who understood hearing aid usage. We realized that we had to
have good expertise working with the children. Everybody in
the study now understands that parents must be listened to;
they must be counselled at all steps and constantly. The
weekly phone calls are really the essence of it. I think
that is very important. Call them up. Ostensibly, we call
them to get a count as to how many hours the child has worn
the hearing aid, but in that call we also let them tell us
what their problems are. Then, if they have any problems,
we have a nurse, Dr. Krychek, who goes out to the home. If
there are any problems, she really trouble-shoots at all
stages of the game. That part must be done.

References

Balkany, T.J., "Otologic Aspects of Down's Syndrome,"
    Seminars in Speech, Language & Hearing 1:39-48, 1980.

Bess, F.H., Personal Correspondence (Study to be published in
    Ear and Hearing, 1983).

Downs, M.P., "The Hearing of Down's Individuals," Seminars in
    Speech, Language & Hearing 1:25-38, 1980.

Goodhill, V., Personal Correspondence, 1978.

Harada, T., and Sando, I., "Temporal Bone Histopathologic
    Findings in Down's Syndrome," Archives of Otolaryngology
    107:96-103, 1981.

House, H., Personal Correspondence, 1977.

Krajicek, M., "The Down's Syndrome Population," Seminars in Speech, Language & Hearing 1:9-24, 1980.

Lewis, N., "Otitis Media and Linguistic Incompetence," Archives of Otolaryngology 102:387-390, 1976.

Roeser, R., and Downs, M.P. (Eds.), Auditory Disorders In School Children (New York: Thieme-Stratton, Inc.), 1981.

Shea, J., Personal Correspondence, 1977.

LANGUAGE DISORDERS IN
NEONATALLY ASPHYXIATED CONGENITALLY DEAF CHILDREN

Sanford E. Gerber
Carol A. Prutting
Elizabeth Wile
University of California, Santa Barbara, California

Asphyxia (hypoxia, anoxia), when it occurs in the neonatal period, is the most common cause of cerebral palsy,
accounting for 75% - 80% (Jilek, Travnickova & Trojan, 1970).
In North America, it is also the second most frequently
occurring etiology of congenital deafness (Robertson, 1978;
Mencher, 1981). It is the most frequent cause of brain
damage in the neonatal period, and occurs in 13.8 of 1000
live births (Anderson, 1952). Furthermore, "The perinatal
period is a time when the CNS is exposed to an unusually high
danger of hypoxic damage" (Jilek, Travnickova & Trojan,
1970). It has been observed that both the auditory brainstem responses (Kileny, Connelly & Robertson, 1980) and the
middle evoked potentials (Mendelson & Salamy, 1981) of
asphyxiated babies differ from normal infants. Finally, the
data reported here suggest that neonatal asphyxia may also
be commonly associated with language disorders in both the
hearing and severe-to-profound hearing impaired populations.

Communicative disorders - speech, language, and/or
hearing - have causes which are frequently not immediately
obvious. As indicated by Knobloch and Pasamanick (1959),
there is an assumed "...continuum of reproductive causality"
the consequences of which vary in degree. The kinds of
subtle functional behavioural alterations we observe in
children with mild/moderate speech and language delay or
difficulty are assumed to have etiological roots very early
in life. Why do we make such an assumption? Because, in
the absence of any identifiable post-natal disease or
injury, but in the presence of phonological or syntactical
dysfunction, one must look for an earlier and more generalized etiology.

Consider the child of 5 or 6 years of age whose speech
and language abilities are mildly retarded and who is of
normal intelligence, has no history of disease or trauma,
and whose parents have good speech and language and are also
of normal intelligence. What could have produced a difficulty? In the case of more obvious organic disturbances,
particularly profound hearing loss, we look to the perinatal
period for high risk factors such as family history, prenatal
disease, or neonatal asphyxia. We know that the high risk
register for hearing loss (e.g. Gerber & Mencher, 1978) was
primarily designed to find the deaf infant. But it is
apparent that high risk children who are not deaf have learning or language difficulties when seen later in life (Mencher
et al., 1978). If we can identify in detail how these
children differ from other children, then perhaps we can
identify them early enough in life so that intervention
becomes more efficacious.

It is economically impossible and pragmatically of
little value to perform detailed neurological examinations
of all newborns. In fact, it has been shown that neither
hypoxia nor hyperbilirubinemia correlate highly with neurological abnormality (Heimer, Cutler & Freedman, 1964).
Children who have actual or potential neurosensory handicaps
are probably not found randomly in the total population, but
are found in groups which are characterized by unfavorable
genetic inheritance or adverse environmental influences
operating during the fetal, perinatal, or neonatal periods.

In order to determine the role neonatal asphyxia may
play in the etiology of neurosensory handicaps, Gerber (1980)
conducted a retrospective study (one of the methods suggested
by Graham et al., 1962) of the birth histories of 190 children who had speech or language disorders for which there was
no evident disease or trauma etiology. All subjects in the
study were at least 5 years old at the time of the initial
speech and language evaluation. Children were excluded if
their birth histories included any medical diagnosis which
could have disturbed speech and language development, such
as prenatal rubella, overt central nervous system abnormality, neonatal meningitis, or hydrocephalus. Hence, severely
disordered children such as those with cerebral palsy or
profound hearing loss were excluded.

Birth records of children who fit these criteria were read at the hospital where the child was born. Only those children who suffered neonatal asphyxia which required some kind of external control to facilitate optimum respiration (such as endotrachial intubation) were considered to be the neonatally asphyxiated group. The type of delivery was also recorded, as non-vertex deliveries are known to promote asphyxiant illnesses.

Of the 190 speech and language disordered children, Gerber reported 19 (10%) experienced respiratory distress requiring assisted ventilation. While 19 children is not a large number, the proportion found was striking. Gerber observed that 10% of the children who had speech and/or language difficulties, but, in the main, did not have hearing impairments, and who did not have any other evident cause for their speech and language dysfunction, had a history of neonatal asphyxia.

Gerber's 10% reflects an incidence of neonatal asphyxia in a group of speech/language dysfunctional children which is about 6 times that reported by Robertson (1978) for the asphyxiated population in general, and should be considered, he believes, a significant finding.

On the basis of the Gerber retrospective study, it seems evident that neonatal asphyxia is related to speech and language dysfunction. It also has been well documented by others (Robertson, 1978; Mencher, 1981) that asphyxia during the neonatal period is a frequent cause of hearing impairment. These two findings forced us to question the various relationships among neonatal asphyxia, language dysfunction, and severe-to-profound hearing impairment. It was for that purpose that the study to be discussed in this chapter was designed. Briefly, 10 severe-to-profoundly hearing impaired subjects were given a battery of language tests to determine the effects of neonatal asphyxia on language.

Subjects

Subjects were 10 severe-to-profoundly hearing impaired children between the ages of 6 and 10 years, selected on the

basis of parental reports and school records. All 10 children
were attending school in Total Communication classrooms. All
subjects had been exposed to Signing Exact English (SEE II)
for at least 1 year. Nine subjects were reported to be within
the normal range on nonverbal intelligence tests (WISC-P and/
or Leiter). No scores were available for 1 subject, but she
was reported by her teacher to be functioning at a level
similar to the other children.

Five children were reported to have required some form
of assisted ventilation following birth, and were intubated
for at least 48 hours. Neonatal asphyxia had specifically
been designated as the cause of the hearing impairment in 1
of the subjects. Rubella was reportedly the cause of 1
subject's hearing loss, with 3 reported to be due to unknown
causes.

The remaining 5 subjects were used as controls. These
children had not required breathing assistance at birth. All
were full term and normal weight. Two were listed as being
hearing impaired as the result of hereditary influences, 2
were listed as unknown etiology, and 1 had meningitis at 2
months.

Procedures

Four subtests from the *Clinical Evaluation of Language
Functions* (CELF), (Semel & Wiig, 1980) were chosen to assess
specific areas of language. They were chosen on the basis
of difficulty, applicability, and time required for administration. Conferences with the speech/language pathologist
and psychologist involved with the children aided in the
selection of the appropriate materials. Those subtests
administered (with examples) were:

Subtest Area of Assessment

Receptive   Example of Item

1. Word and sentence structure   "The boy is being
                                      followed by the dog"

3. Linguistic concepts   "Point to the line that is
                                      not yellow"

5. Processing oral directions   "Point to the last circle"

Expressive

8. Producing Names on Confrontation (Timed test)
    (1) colour   "Red"
    (2) shape   "Circle"
    (3) colour and shape   "Red circle"

The children were taken from the classroom, and the subtests, administered in one sitting, were presented in Signing
Exact English by a fluent signer. Responses were noted by
the examiner and a reliability observer. Subtests were
untimed, except for Number 8 (Producing Names on Confrontation). On any one procedure, and as recommended, testing was
discontinued after erroneous responses on 5 consecutive items.
Children were required to pass the trial items for each subtest before beginning assessment.

Because the children were unable to follow multiple
directions with multiple components, and after trial administration, consultation with teachers, and the speech/language
pathologist, subtest 5 (Processing Oral Directions) was
administered in adapted form. Hence, individual items were
separated. For example, "Point to the white triangle and the
black square" became "Point to the white triangle" and "Point
to the black square". All other subtests were administered
as designed.

Testing was done in a 5' by 7' room with the child seated
across from the examiner. The reliability observer was sitting
to the left of the examiner while the pictorial stimuli were
positioned to the right of the examiner, facing the child.
Children were given a positive reinforcer (stamp) after each
response and after it was determined that this would provide
increased motivation.

Results

The experimental group had mean scores lower than those
of the control group on all receptive subtests (Figure 1).

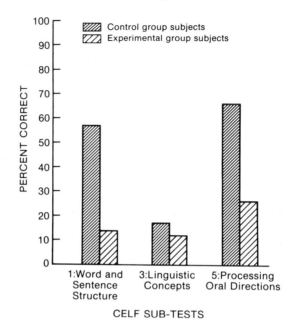

CELF SUB-TESTS

Figure 1. Mean Scores on CELF Sub-tests

Subtest 1, Word and Sentence Structure, produced mean scores of 57% for the control group and 14% for the experimental group (on 52 items). All 5 controls scored higher than the 5 experimental subjects. Although the N was not large, and complete statistical analysis was not possible, the difference between groups was so large it was believed to be significant.

As mentioned, scores on Subtest 3, Linguistic Concepts, did not appear to differentiate between the two groups. Percentages obtained were 17% for the control group and 12% for the asphyxia group (44 items). The lack of an apparent clinically significant difference was thought to be a reflection of the overall language difficulties of hearing impaired children, and not a true indication that "no difference" exists.

Subtest 5, Processing Oral Directions, produced mean scores of 66% for the control group and 26% for the asphyxia group (90 items). With only one exception, the control

group children scored above all of the experimental subjects.
Although not confirmed by formal statistical procedures, this
difference was thought to be significant. It was of interest
to the examiners that, prior to the adaptation of this Subtest, no important differences were identified.

The 3 timed tests, Producing Names on Confrontation,
also produced marked differences (Figure 2). Although the
CELF manual calls for scoring only the results of the third
condition (colour and shape), we scored all 3 tests, and
differences were exhibited in all 3 conditions (colour,
shape, colour and shape). Mean times for the first condition
(colour only) were 35 seconds for the control group and 54
seconds for the asphyxiated group. With only one exception,
the control group children took less time than the experimental group. The one exception may have been age related.
The oldest participant in the study was a member of the
experimental group, and it was his score which was the
exception to all the others in the group.

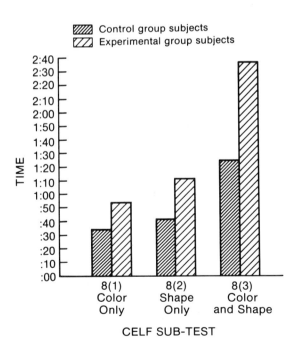

Figure 2.   Mean Times on CELF Sub-test 8

Results of the final Condition (colour and shape)
resulted in a mean score for the control group of 1 minute-
25 seconds, with a mean of 2 minutes-36 seconds for the
experimental group. With only one exception, the control
group children took less time than the experimental. The
one exception was, again, the oldest subject in the study,
a member of the experimental group.

Relative time differences were also determined for both
groups (Figure 3). The differences between single aspect
Conditions and Condition 3, which required production of 2
aspects, were found to be greater for the asphyxia group.
The time difference between Condition 1 and Condition 3 was
52 seconds for the control group, and 1 minute-41 seconds
for the asphyxiated group. The relative time differences
for Conditions 2 and 3 were 47 seconds for the control group
and 1 minute-24 seconds for the experimental group. These
time differences are thought to be clinically significant
and indicative of the processing difficulties encountered by
the children in the experimental group.

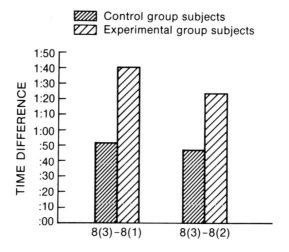

Figure 3. Time Differences on CELF Sub-test 8

Our results revealed differences between the two groups on all but 1 subtest. Although the children did not rank the same on all subtests, a consistent pattern of better scores for the control group was exhibited (Table I). We submit that this finding is clinically significant and in a larger study would be statistically significant.

TABLE I: Raw scores.

		IQ*	1	3	5	8(1)	8(2)	8(3)
Control Subjects	1	107	22	20	69	:46	:41	1:53
	2	102	32	0	47	:40	:44	1:25
	3	98	35	8	70	:20	:25	1:00
	4	91	26	4	60	:36	:53	1:27
	5	--	33	5	62	:33	:38	1:27
Experimental Subjects	6	93	20	12	4	1:05	1:33	2:10
	7	118	0	2	33	:55	1:00	2:30
	8	118	11	6	9	:51	1:00	3:00
	9	94	2	2	21	1:09	1:42	3:51
	10	98	4	4	58	:32	:41	1:27

*IQ scores are either WISC Performance or Leiter scores adjusted to be equal to the WISC-P.

Discussion

Gerber (1980) concluded that neonatal asphyxia should be recognized as "A valid high risk criterion for the development of communicative disorders" including, but not limited to, peripheral auditory dysfunction. One might suppose that the incidence of neonatal asphyxia, if it were significant, would cause severe neuromotor and/or neurosensory problems which would be evident shortly after birth. In the Graham et al., (1962) study, the authors considered only convulsions and neuromotor disorders to be "positive" neurological findings. Such things as "speech disturbance" and "facial asymmetry" were called "essentially normal". This is, of course, not true. It has been observed that hypoxia may cause damage to the immature cerebral cortex of the newborn infant, but this damage may remain latent since, at that time, the cerebral cortex is not yet fully operational. Furthermore, in patients where there is hypoxic damage to higher brain centers, "...a developmental conflict occurs that hampers the organism seriously...". (Jilek, Travnickova & Trojan, 1970).

Animal studies have shown that the apparent reversibility of hypoxia in lower neural centers is greater than in higher centers such as the cortex. In humans, 7.4% of survivals develop signs of cerebral lesion a year later (Krynski et al., 1973). The pathology associated with asphyxia, while it occurs primarily in the lower auditory centers, will also occur in more central portions of the auditory pathway, essentially sparing the cochlear elements. There are apt to be regions of severe atrophy in the auditory cortex of an anoxic patient, marked necrosis, and also replacement of cortical nerve cells by glia and macrophages (Dublin, 1978).

Gerber (1980) concluded, "...we believe that speech pathologists and audiologists should seriously consider neonatal asphyxia as a high risk condition for speech and language disorders. We should expect some school aged children to develop speech and language problems which could have been due to neonatal asphyxia." The results of the study reported here indicate that the same conclusion can be reached with the severe-to-profound hearing impaired population. In short, speech/language pathologists, audiologists, educators, etc. should look beyond the child's hearing impairment to other possible complicating factors, such as asphyxia during the neonatal period.

Gerber found 10% of his speech/language disordered children had a history of neonatal asphyxia. Our study found that, on a battery of language tests and without exception, those children with a history of neonatal asphyxia performed below their hearing impaired peers who did not have such a history.

Although this study was not carried out on a large number of children, the results should be considered carefully. Preliminary findings indicate that neonatal asphyxia does affect the language abilities of severe-to-profound hearing impaired children. As we reach that level of management where more emphasis is placed on etiology as a factor in treatment, consideration of asphyxia during the early neonatal period should result in a program better suited to the individual child.

Just as neonatal asphyxia is considered a high risk factor for hearing loss, it should also be considered a high risk factor for speech/language disorders for both the hearing and hearing impaired populations. As such factors receive due consideration, differential assessment and remediation can be undertaken to the good of the child and the communicatively handicapped population as a whole.

Acknowledgements

The authors wish to thank Ms. Miriam Gottlieb for her assistance in data collection and analysis. Her support for the project was invaluable. We would also like to thank the faculty and staff of the Oster School, without whose participation a study could not have been done. Special thanks to Mr. Bud Mardock and the children of Oster School.

Discussion

I. RAPIN

I would like to report some interesting data pertaining, not to the deaf, but to the language impaired. I had the privilege of hearing a paper given by Lowe, Lawson and Ingvar about cerebral blood flow patterns in children with language disorders, and children with the common receptive/expressive language difficulty representing the bulk of hearing impaired. They were able to show that there was decreased cerebral blood flow. But interestingly, not in the cerebral cortex as one might have expected, but in the periventricular white matter which is an area of the nervous system which we know to be involved in a rather common pathology seen in neonatal

asphyxia called periventricular lucomalacia. It's interesting
to think that we, perhaps, have been thinking of cortex,
cortex, cortex, all the time, and it may be that we also have
to consider white matter involvement and pathologies too. Of
course, some authors, particularly Geshwind and others who are
concerned with adult aphasia, have been telling us that there
are forms of aphasia which are not necessarily due to the
destruction of a vocal area of the cortex, but rather to
impaired communication between the cortical and/or cortical-
subcortical areas concerned with language processing.

S. GERBER
    We have found a number of these things. For example, all
of us, I suspect, have had experience with a child who has an
abnormal or missing auditory brainstem response, yet who
behaves like a hearing child. That is the case of the test
wagging the audiologist. We often see that as these children
get older, the ABR becomes normal. I don't know the answer
to this question, but I have a hunch that it's the same group.

I. RAPIN
    Indeed, absent brainstem auditory evoked response in
patients who are not deaf has been described, not only in
early infancy, but in some adult patients - particularly in
some patients with multiple sclerosis. The explanation which
has been proposed for this observation is that not all fibres
are conducting at the same velocity because of the abnormality
of some fibres and not of others. As a result, one has
desyncronization of the volly and, therefore, one cannot
record well syncronized stimuli at the various relays of the
central auditory pathway. I think that that's really quite a
different situation than from what I've described because
what I'm talking about in the language disordered children has
to do with the white matter of the cerebral hemispheres,
which is quite far away from the brainstem.

T. CAMPBELL
    You stated there is a difference between the control
group and other children - your experimental group - on the
language measures. How did you test that?

S. GERBER
    With the CELF Test.

T. CAMPBELL
How do you test the differences between groups? You said there was a significant difference between the groups.

S. GERBER
I did not mean statistical significance, and I meant to make that clear. We felt that the N - the number - was too small. Had we employed a statistic, we would have been the victim of statistics. The children did have similar audiograms. They were all profoundly impaired. They were all in special classes for the hearing impaired. They all had normal intelligence in the WISC ($\pm$ 1/2 standard deviation).

T. CAMPBELL
Do you have any other measures, like some structural measures (e.g. MLU) or comprehension measures?

S. GERBER
Not at this time. There are some things we want to do as we expand the study. Psychologists in schools for the deaf like to use the WISC Performance Scale, which is fine. I would like to see them use the WISC Verbal too. What I really want to do is a double blind study where we take test results, sort them out, and then go back to an analysis such as "Here's a group where the verbal and the performance is the same"; or "Here's a group where verbal is better than performance", and so on. Then we would go back to the birth records and see how all the results correspond.

T. CAMPBELL
But at this time, you really don't know if the two groups are significantly different?

S. GERBER
Statistically different? No, we do not.

P. KILENY
I think we must reiterate again and again, and continue to caution people not to rely too heavily on brainstem responses. We have patients who are similar to the patients described here; patients who have much better thresholds as

measured by middle components than by brainstem auditory
evoked responses. In some cases, you cannot really get any
coherent brainstem responses, but you do see very nice
middles ... including the Galambos 40 Hz.

References

Anderson, F.W., "Symposium on Cerebral Palsy: Part I.
    Obstetrical Factors in Cerebral Palsy," Journal of
    Pediatrics 40:340-375, 1952.

Dublin, W.B., "The Auditory Pathology of Anoxia," Otolaryn-
    gology 86:27-39, 1978.

Gerber, S.E., "Communicative Disorders and Asphyxia Neo-
    natorum," Paper Presented to the XVth International
    Congress of Audiology, Krakow, Poland, September, 1980.

Gerber, S.E., and Mencher, G.T. (Eds.), Early Diagnosis of
    Hearing Loss (New York: Grune & Stratton), 1978.

Graham, F.K., Ernhart, C.B., Thurston, D.B., and Craft, M.,
    "Development Three Years After Perinatal Anoxia and Other
    Potentially Damaging Newborn Experiences," Psychological
    Monographs 76:522, 1962.

Heimer, C.B., Cutler, R., and Freedman, A.M., "Neurological
    Sequelae of Premature Birth," American Journal of Diseases
    of Children 108:122-123, 1964.

Jilek, L., Travnickova, E., and Trojan, S., "Characteristic
    Metabolic and Functional Responses to Oxygen Deficiency in
    the Central Nervous System," Physiology of the Perinatal
    Period (Vol. 2) (New York: Appleton-Century-Crofts),
    Stave, U. (Ed.), 1970.

Kileny, P., Connelly, C., and Robertson, C., "Auditory
    Brainstem Responses in Perinatal Asphyxia," Paper Presented
    to the 1980 Annual Meeting of the Canadian Speech and
    Hearing Association, Winnipeg, Manitoba.

Knobloch, H., and Pasamanick, B., "Syndrome of Minimal Cerebral Damage in Infancy," Journal of the American Medical Association 170:1384-1387, 1959.

Krynski, S., Diament, A.J., Levisky, D.L., and Dominques, W.M., "Perinatal Anoxia and Mental Retardation," Acta Paedopsychiatrica 39:347-355, 1973.

Mencher, G.T., "Prologue: The Way We Were," Early Management of Hearing Loss (New York: Grune & Stratton), Mencher, G.T., and Gerber, S.E. (Eds.), 1981.

Mencher, G.T., Baldursson, G., Tell, L., and Levi, C., "Mass Behavioural Screening and Follow-up," Paper Presented at the National Research Council-National Academy of Sciences, Assembly of Behavioural and Social Sciences, Meeting of The Committee on Hearing, Bioacoustics, and Biomechanics, Omaha, Nebraska, 1978.

Mendelson, T., and Salamy, A., "Maturational Effects on the Middle Components of the Averaged Electroencephalic Response," Journal of Speech and Hearing Research 24:140-144, 1981.

Robertson, C., "Pediatric Assessment of the Infant as Risk for Deafness," in Gerber, S.E., and Mencher, G.T. (Eds.), Early Diagnosis of Hearing Loss (New York: Grune & Stratton), 1978.

Semel, E.M., and Wiig, E.H., Clinical Evaluation of Language Functions (Columbus: C.E. Merrill Publishing Co.), 1980.

DEVELOPING PREPARATORY SKILLS
FOR USING AUGMENTATIVE COMMUNICATION AIDS

Elaine M. Heaton
Barbara L. Strohbach
Glenrose Hospital, Edmonton, Alberta

There is an increased survival rate among extremely low
birthweight infants and severely asphyxiated children who
present with multiple handicaps. As outlined by Robertson
(1982) and in this volume, improved ability to select children who should be followed by the Neonatal Clinic has resulted
in increased referral for evaluation and possible intervention. The multiple problems encountered include various combinations of hearing disorders, neurological deficits, mental
retardation and/or visual impairment.

For those children without a potential to develop functional oral speech, decisions must be made regarding the types
of intervention strategies which seem most appropriate. Many
reports are available regarding the use of total communication, signing, finger spelling and other such methods with
hearing impaired or mentally retarded children (Fristoe &
Lloyd, 1978; Goodman & Kroc, 1981; Silverman, 1980; Wilbur,
1979). Information is also available regarding approaches
which have been used with deaf/blind children, the child's
primary disability strongly influencing the strategy chosen.

The purpose of this paper is to address possible avenues
of intervention with the multiply handicapped hearing
impaired child unable to develop adequate manual dexterity
for use with signing or other forms of manual communication.
Many of the strategies described will have application to the
broad spectrum of multiply handicapped children, even those
without hearing loss.

Effective intervention strategies for multiply handicapped children require ready access to a multidisciplinary
team. Experience has shown that the core members of this team
should be a physiatrist, a speech pathologist, a biomedical
technologist, and an occupational therapist. The use of a

core team presupposes that the child has previously been
evaluated by a pediatrician, otolaryngologist and an audiologist. In many cases, depending upon the age of the child
and the specific deficit areas suspected, evaluation also may
be performed by physical therapists, ophthalmologists, psychologists, educators, social workers, and other specialists.

Evaluation of the multiply handicapped child is extremely
complex and time consuming, particularly when the child shows
no evidence of interaction with the environment. Under such
circumstances, questions concerning etiology are paramount
(e.g. retardation vs. physical handicap vs. deafness). However, the advent of evoked response audiometry has made it
possible to make more accurate predictions concerning the
child's response to sound and amplification (Kileny, 1981,
1982; Kileny & Berry, 1982; Connelly & Oviatt, 1979). Further,
some of the strategies described later can enable the core
team to make predictions about whether the child understands
or can be taught the concept of causality. As such, these
strategies also have the potential to predict whether a child
can learn to interact with the environment. Without such
strategies and associated resources, many professionals may
discount any possibility of teaching functional skills to the
non-interactive child.

With the multiply handicapped population, evaluation and
intervention are a continuously interwoven process. All
intervention plans should be geared towards maximum functional
use of cognitive, communicative and locomotive skills. Whenever the prognosis for the acquisition of functional ability
in any one of these areas is poor, the applicability of a
technological device or "technical aid" which might assist the
child to interact more effectively in the environment should
be considered. As the child's abilities develop, intervention
plans should be reviewed to ensure that they remain appropriate to the skills and needs of the child. This also
ensures that intervention plans take maximum advantage of
current advances in technology.

Advantages and Limitations of
Augmentative Communication Systems

Most of the strategies and equipment described here rely
on the visual modality, making them especially applicable for
the educational development of the hearing impaired population.

It would be necessary to more specifically evaluate their applicability to the child with a severe visual impairment. The cognitive limitations of each child would also restrict the degree of sophistication to which a system may be developed. However, physical handicap need no longer be a limiting factor in the development of an augmentative communication system.[1] Indeed, for children with a good prognosis for learning to read and spell, a highly sophisticated system can easily become a reality. In order to derive maximum potential from an augmentative communication system, the technological skill must be available, on-site, to develop a customized access device. Readers are advised to check patent laws governing equipment to prevent violations resulting from modifications of commercially manufactured units. This paper will not discuss some of the more "traditional" telecommunication aids used by the hearing impaired (e.g. TTY).

There is, throughout this paper, a strong emphasis on the use of strategies and equipment to improve the child's interaction abilities. However, their use should be seen as a means to an end, the "end" being development and enhancement of communication experiences. The nonspeaking child is continuously faced with breakdowns in the knowledge-context interaction process, and is deprived of opportunities to clarify or redefine unique word-referent pairings and mismatches (Carlson, 1981). Recent advances in available technology to facilitate communication should not be allowed to become the primary focus, as it cannot eradicate the problem but only reduce the limitations.

When developing intervention strategies for a child with sensory, cognitive, communicative and/or locomotive deficits, integration of information from a complete evaluation is of paramount importance. Use of this information as a data base, and close consultation with an involvement of the family, is the next essential step. An indepth awareness of the child's repertoire of responses forms the basis of the plan. The

---

[1]"Given the state of the art regarding the development and use of communication techniques, there is no nonspeaking person too physically handicapped to be able to utilize some augmentative communication system." Position Statement on Nonspeech Communication (ASHA, 1981).

degree to which it is possible to model, and by successive approximations, shape those responses into a broader repertoire, becomes the clinical challenge.

Development of Choice Strategies and an Awareness of Causality

It is necessary to work with the family to develop a framework within which the child can begin to make choices and thereby have more impact on the immediate environment. By means of demonstration, modelling, successive approximation, and shaping of response (Ault, 1977), the child learns to modify events rather than being a passive recipient. No attempt will be made to describe in detail the mechanics for developing choice strategies, but an outline of a successful hierarchy is summarized in Table I.

To teach awareness of causality (referred to as "means-end" and "operational causality" in the Piagetian literature), it is necessary to select a stimulus which will catch attention and maintain interest. A stimulus which combines movement and sound seems to be the most effective, with battery operated toys encompassing the most essential components. Examples of procedures for assessing various developmental levels of means-ends and causality have been published by Miller et al., (1980).

Morris (1981) described in detail the rationale and strategies which may be used for developing means-ends, object permanence and reciprocity in communication within meaningful contexts. She emphasized the benefits to be obtained through insightful interaction with the child at mealtimes, and alerted readers to an awareness of their own nonspoken messages conveyed by their body language. Close interaction activities such as those seen at mealtimes, have considerable dynamic potential for building the prerequisite skills necessary to use an augmentative communication system.

TABLE I: Hierarchy for developing choice strategies*

Analyse responses:

- is there any consistent response to "not want", food, place, handling (by whom?)
- if no consistent response apparent, what behaviours might be shaped?

Can child indicate preference?

- between 2 very dissimilar objects?
- between 2 similar objects?
- between a real object and nothing?
- between 2 objects using finger cues? (i.e. objects not present)
- between 2 activities using finger cues?

Expand choice selection to 3 objects, then 4 objects.

Can child associate a picture with an object? If not, develop picture recognition by:

- pointing out and labelling pictures in books
- matching picture to object
- matching object to picture using 2 pictures
- matching object to picture expanding number of pictures to 3, then 4
- matching pictures to photographs
- asking child to correctly indicate picture from auditory label without object or photograph present.

Can child successfully indicate:

- between 2 pictured objects?
- between 3, then 4, then 5, then 6?

* Adapted from Mahood, J.A. and Jenner, M. "Let's Be Realistic". A paper presented at the Canadian Speech and Hearing Association Convention, Edmonton, May 6, 1981.

Accessing Adapted Toys

     Many severely physically disabled children are unable to
turn on or off a battery operated toy. Many severely retarded
children are unable to combine adequate manual dexterity with
the necessary understanding of the concept of turning on or
off such a toy. Having mother control the device may result
in momentary attention from the child, but it does not foster
an ability to determine when, or for how long, it is used. As
with the majority of events in such a child's environment,
manipulation of a toy by an outsider reinforces the role as a
passive responder, as long as the child is developmentally
beyond Sensorimotor Stages IV and V. However, with minimal
adaptations and with minimal physical demands being placed
upon the child, it is possible to create a situation in which
the individual is able to control the activity, becoming an
active participant in the environment. As reported by Shane
(1981), there is little data available to support the claims
that playing with adapted toys is extremely beneficial to
severely handicapped children. However, clinical observation
suggests that these methods ensure a more stimulating and
challenging learning environment.

     While some adapted toys are available commercially, ser-
vices exist to adapt others (Giles, 1982). The cost of such
services can be reduced significantly by adapting battery
operated toys at home. The equipment needed is inexpensive
and the technique does not require a high level of expertise.
As shown in Figure 1, the 3 elements of the system are the
toy, a wafer, and a remote switch. Instructions for building

FIGURE 1:   Adapting a battery operated toy: the wafer (arrow)
            is inserted between the battery and negative
            terminal.

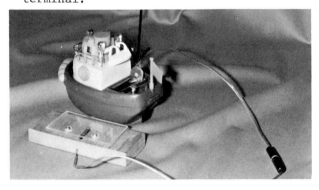

a wafer and switch or for making a remote access to the
battery compartment have been described by Wethered (1982).
Using this simple adaptation, the child is able to make the
toy move by depressing the switch and, of course, make the
sound and activity stop by simply releasing the switch. Once
the child has learned how to control the activity of the
device, independent play may be possible for the very first
time. Such a simple process has the potential to cause
dynamic changes in a child's (and family's) behaviour and can
lead to knowledge of causality which, in turn, can result in
an ability to modify one's environment.

Selection of Access Devices

     The type of access device (or switch) selected depends
upon the physical skills of the child, the most frequently
used being the touch switch (Figure 2). Many different access
devices are available commercially, but these are obviously
more expensive than those home-made. It is relatively simple
to build a custom switch, once the basic principles of the
system are understood (Wethered, 1982). The selection of the
switch is governed by the child's functional level. For
example, in the earlier developmental stages, it may be appropriate to expect the infant merely to reach out and touch or
grasp. However, with additional training and practice, the
child may be able to progress to a directional selection
switch such as a joy stick.

FIGURE 2:   Several types of control switches. From left to
            right: joy stick switch; slot selection switch;
            optical head pointer; manual pointer; touch switch.

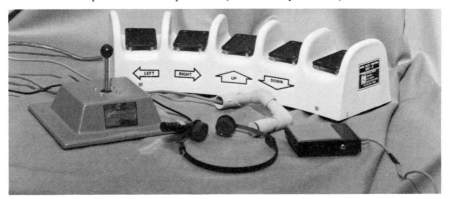

The switch need not be operated by a fist or finger, but may be manipulated by any part of the body over which there is effective control (e.g. elbow, foot, knee, head). The physical location of the access device will also vary according to the child's effective range and accuracy of motion. Consequently, access device selection, activation and placement may require long-term experimentation.

Timers

As the next step in developing preparatory skills for using augmentative communication systems, it may be desirable to teach the child to maintain or repeat a specific activity. With the mechanical system described under the "Accessing Adapted Toys" section, the toy will continue to operate as long as contact with the switch is maintained. For many reasons (e.g. wishing to teach the child to repeat the action, or wishing to maintain the toy's activity for a child who can only make fleeting contact with the access device), it may be desirable to have the toy operative for a specified time period and then stop until contact is made again. This can be achieved by inserting a timer into the system, as illustrated in Figure 3. Timers are available commercially (or can be produced cheaply at home). Some have counters attached so that it is possible to record how frequently the child caused the toy to operate within a specific time period.

FIGURE 3:   Time controlled operation of toy. A timer is inserted into the system so that the toy will operate for a specified length of time when contact is made with the switch.

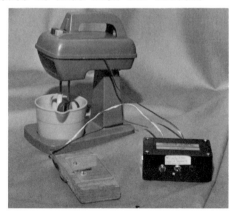

Positioning

There is little value in attempting to develop choice
strategies for an awareness of causality with the severely
physically handicapped child if the child is positioned
incorrectly. Improper positioning may increase manifestations of the physical disability and decrease functional
attention span. For many children, separate seating arrangements are necessary for wheelchair use, table work, eating,
and play. Custom-made seats are often required. As the
child grows, positioning equipment will need frequent modification. Whenever an augmentative communication system is
required, the physical requirements of equipment must be
considered in designing the seat (e.g. a child who uses a
HandiVoice may require special adaptations to the lap tray,
as shown in Figure 4).

While the majority of children with hearing loss are
exceptionally alert visually and use vision to obtain maximum
information from environmental cues, some with additional
problems cannot maintain an upright head position. This may
be the result of a lack of muscular control, or a lack of
awareness. Use of a head position trainer (available commercially, or custom made), can be effective when teaching awareness of upright head posture (Wethered, 1982). The device

FIGURE 4: An adaptation to a lap tray to accommodate the
           HandiVoice 120.

can be attached to a battery operated toy, tape recorder, or
television set. Provided the child is able to hear music, a
tape recorder is the most effective reinforcer (i.e. cause/
effect is most easily understood in that the music stops when
the head position drops, and the music starts when the head is
returned to the upright position). Teaching the child to
maintain an upright head posture greatly enhances development,
increasing awareness and facilitating the ability to benefit
from situational cues and eye/face contact with other people.

Aids to Communication

Once a child has learned causality and is able to move
on to higher cognitive level tasks, use of an access device
as an interface to the toy may be eliminated. However, for
those children with the additional complication of a physical
handicap, the use of a switch control system may be an
integral part of the long-range intervention plan. Ideally,
the same control switch is used to activate the augmentative
communication system, power wheelchair, and various environmental controls and technical aids.

Once an understanding of causality and the need to
interact with people has been established, consideration can
be given to developing more advanced communication skills.
As stated earlier, this paper will not discuss those hearing
impaired children who have the physical ability to use total
communication and signs, but rather will address the range of
systems available where normal limb function is not possible.
In determining which augmentative system is appropriate, the
child's language level, cognitive abilities and motoric
limitations are always in the forefront of any decision
(Coleman et al., 1980; Shane & Bashir, 1980; MacDonald, 1976).
The system selected will require modification as the child
develops. In some situations, an augmentative system may be
an interim step towards oral speech.

A brief description of the capabilities of some of the
commercially available equipment is outlined at the end of
this chapter. Such equipment ranges in cost from less than
$200.00 to over $10,000.00. A regularly updated catalogue of
equipment is available through the *Non-Vocal Communication
Resource Book* (Vanderheiden, 1978).

Content Format

The content (i.e. vocabulary, linguistic complexity, etc.) and format utilized by each device should be based upon the needs and the cognitive and linguistic abilities of the child (MacDonald, 1976). Simple pictures or photographs can be used to enable the child to make choices between 2 or more items or activities. Symbol systems such as PIC, Blissymbolics, or Rebus are available for the next level of sophistication. Letter, word or phrase format is generally utilized at the highest level of sophistication (see Table II).

Selection of appropriate vocabulary for the system has considerable influence upon how well the system is accepted and used. Many times the vocabulary appears to represent those ideas which adults need or want the child to communicate. However, such a vocabulary may not meet the developmental and personality needs of the child. Carlson (1981) recommends training the family, teachers, and those around the child to become sensitive to evolving vocabulary needs to that the content of the communication system more closely resembles the speaking child's self-selected lexicon.

TABLE II: A hierarchy of some frequently used display formats.

AUGMENTED COMMUNICATION SYSTEMS : DISPLAYS

PICTORAL	PHOTOGRAPHS PICTURES LINE DRAWINGS
SYMBOLIC	PIC: BLACK AND WHITE OUTLINE DRAWINGS WHICH INCLUDE PICTOGRAMS AND IDEOGRAMS. BLISSYMBOLIC: A SEMATICALLY BASED, GRAPHIC NONALPHABET COMMUNICATION SYSTEM CONTAINING PICTOGRAPHIC, IDEOGRAPHIC AND ARBITRARILY ASSIGNED COMPONENTS. REBUS: PICTORAL SYMBOLS WHICH ARE SOUND BASED, INTERSPERSED WITH TRADITIONAL ORTHOGRAPHY - A PRE-READING AID.
TRADITIONAL ORTHOGRAPHY	LETTER PHRASE LETTER, WORD, PHRASE, SENTENCE COMBINATIONS

Equipment Format

     The range of equipment available is expanding continu-
ously. The format selected may be the traditional communications board or some variation on that theme (e.g. ring binder,
slate, "Bliss apron", "Communication bracelet"). It may be an
eye-pointing chart such as a plexiglass Etran, or it may be
more sophisticated electronic hardware incorporating the use
of microprocessors. Some examples of communication aids are
shown in Figure 5.

     Messages may be indicated using either a *direct selec-
tion mode* or a *scanning mode*. *Direct selection* means that the
specific item is indicated by a "pointing response" (by any
part of the body), thereby requiring adequate motoric control
over a specified body part with a specified degree of accuracy
to actually make the response. In the *scanning mode*, the
message elements are presented one at a time and the child
indicates, in any possible manner, when the correct selection
is displayed (e.g. Zygo 100, the HandiVoice 120 in the scroll
mode, as shown in Figure 6).

     The way in which the child actually informs the equip-
ment of his selection varies widely, depending upon physical
limitations. It may be as simple as using a finger, fist or
toe. However, in many cases, a head pointer is required.
This may be either mechanical in nature or a light beam indicator attached to the head. The response repertoire may be

FIGURE 5: A selection of examples of augmentative communica-
           tion aids. From left to right: Blissymbol board;
           picture board; eye pointing board.

FIGURE 6:   A selection of augmentative communication aids
            which can be used in a scanning mode. From left
            to right: Zygo 100; Handivoice 120; Express 1.

limited only to eye pointing for the most physically involved
individuals. Some experimental work is also being done using
myoelectric switches to activate equipment.

     The layout of the selected vocabulary on the communica-
tion system can have significant impact on the efficiency with
which the system is used. Waters (1982) suggests that the
most frequently used items should be located in close prom-
imity to the "functional centre" of the layout. He defines
that centre as that area from which the user can most readily
move to all other parts of the board. Waters states that it
is maximum physical control <u>working with</u> the power of microelectronics which results in the most efficient output in
communication. Optimal independence requires <u>both</u>.

     The output format may be immediate, hard copy, or stored
in a memory unit and then produced when the listener is available. Immediate output includes the listener who communicates
with the child by watching which item is selected. Immediate
output can also be synthesized or recorded speech (e.g. the
Form-A-Phrase) or an LED. Hard copy output can include a
strip printer (as in the Canon Communicator), or a page
printer (as in the hard copy attachment for the microcomputer),
or the standard output of a typewriter (see Figure 7). Several electronic communication aids permit the user to build the
message and store it in memory until the listener arrives,
thereby reducing listener dependency. Aids which feature memory storage include the Zygo 100 and the Handivoice 110 and 120.

FIGURE 7:   A selection of augmentative communication aids
            which have a printing output.   From left to right:
            Canon Communicator; Sharp's Memowriter.

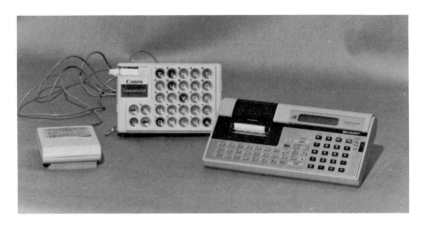

Adaptations to Equipment

    Many nonspeech patients are unable to use commercially
available equipment without special adaptations, some of which
can be made relatively simply and inexpensively (e.g. grid for
HandiVoice 110 as shown in Figure 8).   Other adaptations
require the services of a rehabilitation enginner, and none
must violate patent laws.   Finally, because the factory-
designed vocabulary and content of some commercial aids is
inappropriate to the needs and skills of some users, many
units can be re-programmed to the needs of the individual,
thereby considerably enhancing applicability.

Recent Advances in Computers

    The rapid development of computer technology has created
an entirely new range of aids for the handicapped (Perry,
1980).   It is now possible to access all functions of a microcomputer through a single switch scanning control.   If the
child is able to access the system through a directed scanning
control (as contrasted with row and column scanning), the
speed of operation may become as fast as that possible using
the traditional keyboard control.

Both commercial learning programs and those custom
designed for each child enable handicapped individuals to
learn at their own rate, in a 1-to-1 situation. The potential
for improved and accelerated learning is far reaching, and at
a cost considerably cheaper than the traditional high teacher-
student ratio found in most centers for the disabled. The use
of visual display on the terminal, combined with the computer's
continual interaction with its user, reduces misunderstanding
and makes this a dynamic teaching approach for the hearing
impaired. The potential for eliminating those situations in
which the hearing impaired child fails to hear the complete
instructions, or misunderstands the content of the message,
represents a significant advance to us all.

The microcomputer can also assist the older child to
complete exercises which would require extra note taking or
homework. The relatively inexpensive addition of a hard copy
printing unit may enable the child to complete typewritten
assignments with almost as much ease as his non-handicapped
peers.

Not only has the advent of video games made independent
use of leisure time a reality for the severely physically
handicapped/hearing impaired child, the microcomputer also
has the ability to control environmental aids such as tape
recorders and household appliances. This added degree of
independence is invaluable in developing attitudes of self-
worth in severely handicapped people.

FIGURE 8:   Custom-made grid for the HandiVoice 110.

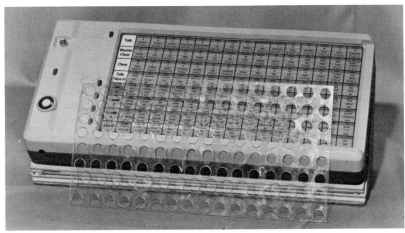

Using a microcomputer as an augmentative communication
system increases the child's potential for greater linguistic
competence. Programs have been developed for individual
children which greatly increase the speed of their communication by predicting words and phrases which the child uses
frequently. Programs can be developed to continually expand
the complexity of utterances, along the lines of language
intervention recommended by Bloom and Lahey (1978).

Some vocabulary studies are currently in progress utilizing the transcript of conversations of hearing impaired
persons who use several types of deaf telecommunication
systems such as the electrowriter, the TTY, and a computer
messaging system. There are several purposes to this study,
one of which is to develop clinical guidelines for the
selection of word sets to accelerate communication. These
"speed word" sets will be a combination of letters, letter
groupings, syllables and words (Vanderheiden, 1982).

Summary

Utilizing elements of the foregoing information, the
reader should be able to predict the types of intervention
strategies and equipment which would be applicable for each
individual child. A hierarchy which might be considered
during the selection process is outlined in Table III.

The newcomer in this area is referred to standard texts
(e.g. Schiefelbusch, 1980; Silverman, 1980) for detailed
information on evaluation parameters. It should be remembered
that evaluation, experimental intervention and training are
long-term activities and that the strategies utilized must be
modified continuously to meet the changing needs and developing
skills of each individual.

It is no longer acceptable for the professional to discount, on first contact, the potential of a severely physically handicapped hearing impaired, mentally retarded infant.
Ongoing technical advances and increased professional awareness dictate that we take time to investigate the possibility
of liberating and developing previously masked potential in
multiply handicapped hearing impaired children.

TABLE III: Selection of an augmentative communication
system: examples of prerequisite skills needed
to use some of the systems currently available.

AUGMENTED COMMUNICATION SYSTEMS:
HIERARCHY OF SELECTION

IF PATIENT CAN RECOGNIZE AND POINT TO PICTURES
- USE PICTURE BOARD
- ZYGO 100/16

IF PATIENT CAN RECOGNIZE AND SELECT BLISSYMBOLS
- USE BLISSYMBOL BOARD
- BLISSYMBOL SCANNER
- BLISSYMBOL MICROCOMPUTER SYSTEM

IF PATIENT CAN UNDERSTAND AND FORM SIGNS
- USE SIGN LANGUAGE
- ASL
- SIGNED ENGLISH
- AMERIND

IF PATIENT CAN RECOGNIZE AND SELECT WORDS
- USE WORD BOARD
- HANDIVOICE 110
- FORM-A-PHRASE LAP TRAY
- EXPRESS 111

IF PATIENT CAN SPELL WORDS
- USE SPELLING / WORD BOARD
- HANDIVOICE 110/120
- FORM-A-PHRASE
- MEMOWRITER
- CANON COMMUNICATOR
- EXPRESS 111

A Selection of Commercially Available Communication Aids

Etran   - use with eye pointing only
                             - can be modified to use as a picture
                               board, word-phrase board or
                               spelling board.

Zygo 100/16   - a scanning device to be used when
                               patient has essentially no pointing
                               skills
                             - can be modified to use as a picture
                               board, word-phrase board or
                               spelling board.

Si Di Ki/Communication   - use with fairly accurate pointing
Board   (degree of resolution will depend
                               upon fineness of pointing combined
                               with range of movement)
                             - can be modified to use as a picture
                               board, word-phrase board or
                               spelling board.

Scanners   - use when patient has extremely
                               limited pointing skills (with
                               finger, fist, head pointer, toe,
                               etc.)
                             - various scanners are commerically
                               available; e.g. Blissymbol scanner,
                               Zygo 16, Zygo 100, HandiVoice 120.

Canon Communicator   - compact typewriter with strip
                               printout. Machine comes with 2
                               types of key guard.

Sharp's Memowriter   - compact calculator/typewriter with
                               strip printout. Requires very fine
                               pointing skills, unless the
                               expanded keyboard is purchased.

HandiVoice 110   - microcomputer-based word board with
                               synthesized speech output. 440
                               word/phrase/phoneme memory. Adult
                               male voice only.

Form-A-Phrase   — microcomputer-based unit with
                               recorded speech output. 128/word/
                               phrase memory. Can be programmed
                               for patient-specific vocabulary.
                               Can be used as a word board with
                               the lap tray attachment. Can be
                               used in a manner similar to the
                               HandiVoice 120 (i.e. memorization
                               of 3-digit codes) with the other
                               3 attachments. Selection of
                               specific attachments depends upon
                               pointing accuracy.

Express III   — a microprocessor-based unit with a
                               40 character line printer and LCD.
                               A speech output and remote display
                               are optional. The unit may be used
                               via direct selection, scanning or
                               directed scan. Can be programmed
                               easily for patient-specific
                               vocabulary.

Acknowledgements

The authors wish to thank those persons who have
assisted in the development of this paper, particularly
Thomas F. Campbell, Ph.D., and Michael Webster, Ph.D., for
their thoughtful critique; Paul Kileny, Ph.D., and Thomas F.
Campbell, Ph.D., for their invaluable assistance in photo-
graphing the equipment; and Ken Warman for bringing the
reality of computer-assisted systems to Glenrose Hospital.

References

Ault, R.L., Children's Cognitive Development (New York:
    Oxford University Press), 1977.

Bloom, L., and Lahey, M., Language Development and Language
    Disorders (New York: John Wiley & Sons), 1978.

Carlson, F., "A Format for Selecting Vocabulary for the Non-
    Speaking Child," Language, Speech and Hearing Services in
    the Schools 12:240-245, 1981.

Coleman, C.L., Cook, A.M., and Myers, L.S., "Assessing Non-
    Oral Clients for Assistive Communication Devices," Journal
    of Speech and Hearing Disorders 45:515-526, 1980.

Connelly, C., and Oviatt, D., "Physiologic Measures in
    Pediatric Audiology," Human Communication 4:299-305, 1979.

Fristoe, M., and Lloyd, L., "A Survey of the Use of Non-
    Speech Systems with the Severely Communication Impaired,"
    Mental Retardation 16:104-107, 1978.

Giles, S., "The Early Education Program of United Cerebral
    Palsy of New York City," Communication Outlook 3:8, 1982,

Goodman, L., and Kroc, R., "A Classroom Sign Communication
    Program for the Severely Handicapped," Language, Speech
    and Hearing Services in the Schools 12:233-239, 1981.

Kileny, P., "Auditory Brainstem Responses as Indicators of
    Hearing Aid Performance," Annals of Otology, Rhinology,
    and Laryngology 91:61-64, 1982.

Kileny, P., "The Frequency Specificity of Tone-Pip Evoked
    Auditory Brain Stem Responses," Ear and Hearing 2:270-275,
    1981.

Kileny, P., and Berry, D., "Selective Impairment of Late
    Vertex or Middle Latency Auditory Evoked Responses in
    Multiply Handicapped Children," This Volume.

Lloyd, L.L. (Ed.), Communication Assessment and Intervention
    Strategies (Baltimore: University Park Press), 1976.

MacDonald, E., "Identification of Children at Risk," Non-
    Vocal Communication Techniques and Aids for the Severely
    Physically Handicapped (Baltimore: University Park Press),
    Vanderheiden, G.C., & Grilley, P. (Eds.), 1976.

MacDonald, E., "Design and Application of Communication
    Boards," Non-Vocal Communication Techniques and Aids for
    the Severely Physically Handicapped (Baltimore: University
    Park Press), Vanderheiden, G.C., & Grilley, P. (Eds.),
    1976.

Miller, J., Chapman, R.S., Branston, M.B., and Reichle, J., "Language Comprehension in Sensorimotor Stages V and VI," Journal of Speech and Hearing Research 23:284-311, 1980.

Morris, S.E., "Communication/Interaction Development at Mealtimes for the Multiply Handicapped Child: Implications for the Use of Augmentative Communication Systems," Language, Speech and Hearing Services in the Schools 12:216-232, 1981.

Perry, R.L., "Help for the Handicapped," Owning Your Home Computer (Chicago: Playboy Paperbacks), 1980.

Robertson, C., Shea, R., Whyte, L., "Prospective Identification of Infants with Hearing Loss and Multiple Handicaps," This Volume.

Schiefelbusch, R.L. (Ed.), Nonspeech Language and Communication (Baltimore: University Park Press), 1980.

Shane, H.C., "The Value of Toys," Communication Outlook Vol. 3:8, 1981.

Shane, H.C., and Bashir, A., "Election Criteria for the Adoption of an Augmentative Communication System," Journal of Speech and Hearing Disorders 45:408-414, 1980.

Silverman, F.H., Communication for the Speechless (Englewood Cliffs, New Jersey: Prentice Hall), 1980.

Vanderheiden, G.C. (Ed.), Non-Vocal Communication Resource Book (Baltimore: University Park Press), 1978.

Vanderheiden, G.C., "Vocabulary Studies," Communication Outlook 2:12, 1982.

Waters, P.D., "Maximization of Minimum Control Function and Increasing Efficiency," Communication Outlook 3:11, 1982.

Wethered, C.E., "Teacher-Made Response-Contingent Materials," Strategies for Helping Severely and Multiply Handicapped Citizens (Baltimore: University Park Press) Anderson, R., Greer, J., & Odel, S. (Eds.), 1982.

Wilbur, R.B., American Sign Language and Sign Systems (Baltimore: University Park Press), 1979.

SELECTION OF OPTIMAL MODALITIES AS AVENUES OF LEARNING IN DEAF, BLIND, MULTIPLY DISABLED CHILDREN

Kevin Murphy
David J. Byrne
Royal Berkshire Hospital, Reading, England

Research information concerning any aspect of behavioural change in severely subnormal children seems to begin from the implicit notion that such children present a quantifiable series of assets and deficits. Such research seems designed to enhance the assets and to overcome the deficits. Laudable though this may be, it does not seem to coincide with our experiences in a series of studies of the behaviour of the children at the Mary Sheridan Unit of Borocourt Hospital near Reading.

Three projects comprise the body of this report. Before reviewing those, however, it might be useful to consider the reality of the condition often faced by the therapist-educator. All the studies which follow are based on certain fundamental criteria. These are that the child must be capable of maintaining sufficient attention focus to begin to identify:

1. that he exists;

2. that others exist;

3. that he has needs;

4. that these needs can be met;

5. that some of these needs will be met by him;

6. that some (if not most) of these needs will be met by others.

Two brief accounts of children in our care will illustrate these points.

Sabina presented for diagnosis rolled in a fetal
ball, only able to express frustration by shriek-
ing or drumming her heels on the wall. She could
not absorb solid food, was grossly undernourished,
lacked physical strength and the fundamental energy
from which any creative behaviours could be fuelled.
Preliminary investigation showed, however, that she
was aware of the existence of others and had some
primitive identification skills through the use of
touch and odor. The diagnostic problem was to
devise a system by which the child could acquire
enough energy and motivation to expand existing
rudimentary conceptual skills. However, before
any skills could be taught, Sabina had to be trained
to absorb (and indeed to eliminate) sufficient food
to fuel the flow of energy without which training
was impossible.

Stevie was functioning at a far higher level of
development than Sabina, but was described as
autistic because he seemed incapable of idenfity-
ing the existence of others and/or relating to
them. He fed well and had no difficulty in metabo-
lizing his food as a source of strength and energy,
which, unfortunately, was totally unstructured,
often taking the form of self-stimulation. He was
not able to recognize that he had needs which could
be met in any consistent and/or predictable fashion
by persons other than himself. The problem was to
find ways in which he identified the presence of
others, their demands on him, the meaning of such
demands, and obtain the motivation to relate in a
positive manner to such demands by complying with
their meaning.

We were faced with two intriguing problems. In the first
case, how were we to create an internal consistency for Sabina
in which she could maintain attention focus long enough to
identify simple, logical structures, cause, effect, reinforcement contingencies, pleasure and displeasure. Ultimately, she
needed to know that others wished her to behave in certain
ways, and the ways in which others wished her to behave. In
Stevie's case, we were faced with controlling unstructured
energy, channelling it in a constructive, consistent and
purposeful behaviour. The problem was to convince him of a
notion of predictability, that others exist, and that his
needs are real and can be identified, signalled and met.

The initial stages of therapy with Sabina centered on the processing of food for energy. In fact, the initial malnutrition problem was overcome surprisingly easy, energy flowed quite quickly, but then the problems really began to emerge. In Stevie's case, we were already accustomed to patterns of unpredictable behaviour. But when Sabina, a child heretofore almost totally passive, developed sufficient energy to produce behaviours, those tended to follow patterns which, at first, were totally unpredictable and required careful study and evaluation.

We have reached a point at where we can assert, therefore, that without controlled, consistent energy, even deviant behaviour is impossible. We cannot yet say that energy will be utilized to further the cause of learning. All too soon it became clear that both Sabina and Stevie could become locked in self-stimulatory behaviour which precluded attention focused to other inputs.

When we consider the complexities of behaviour exhibited by multiply disabled children, it is all too easy to forget that, prior to the presentation of evidence of progress, evidence of controlled behaviour is essential. In the next section of this chapter, we illustrate the extent to which self-distracting mannerisms can dominate the spontaneous behavioural repertoire of the child, often thwarting the learning of new skills. Further, we outline procedures which researchers and clinicians have, to varying degrees, found successful in bringing such mannerisms under control. A hugh amount of unmeasured and unmeasurable precedent progress is required to ameliorate non-productive "chaotic" behaviours and to substitute the patterns required by the experimenter. Each child who comes to therapy has certain repertoires of behaviour from which, for statistical purposes, baselines can be formulated. We would stress, however, that these baselines are often no more than quantifications of consistent measurable patterns of compliance (or, of course, non-compliance). The real problem is to identify and describe those patterns of behaviour which the experimenter knows to be underlying features, though their description and quantification do not yield easily to statistical treatment.

To summarize, the writers wish to stress that there are at least 2 precedent requirements to control behaviour:

1. The presence of sufficient energy to fuel any behaviour;

2. The amelioration of self-distracting behaviours.

The results presented in this report are only those which can
be measured and analyzed; as an infrastructure, there is a
considerable amount of behaviour which, at least in the case
of this paper, has not been analyzed. The primary case to
be made here is that children can be trained, that they can
learn to learn, that when learning occurs, residual sensory
function, in some cases, appears to be heightened, and that
programs of training can be devised to meet such ends.

Developmental Issues, Sensory Learning
and the Multiply Handicapped Child

        Many deaf, blind, retarded children are never able to
use the auditory modality meaningfully. Often, even with
highly structured conditioning, no gain is made in creating
that auditory situation in which children attend, decode and
learn. Normally, the orienting auditory reflex grows consistently and reliably as a result of reinforcement provided by
the auditory stimuli which act as attention-centering mechanisms. However, if the auditory modality is deficient, significance is reduced and reinforcement becomes less frequent.
Indeed, Mark and Hardy (1958) claim that "cerebral damage or
faulty development interferes primarily with the establishment
of the meaning of sound". Similarly, we feel that provision
of auditory stimulation inconsistently reinforced by a mal-
functioning central auditory system leads to unstructured
learning processes. The influence of audition is reduced to
a minimum as the individual learns to disregard auditory
stimuli. In time, the relevance of auditory stimulation to
everyday behaviour can diminish to a point where response is
virtually non-existent. Although there is now considerable
use of visually communicated language by the hearing impaired,
for the purpose of this discussion, priority is placed upon
audition in the development of speech and language. This is
partly because that is the natural manner in which language
is developed and partly because the multiply disabled child
may have more effective residual hearing than residual visual
function.

        The problem is even more difficult when recognizing and
evaluating a hearing loss in a severely or profoundly retarded
child. Unless a loss is moderately severe, an auditory impairment frequently goes undetected among the associated multiple

handicaps of the mentally retarded. Other disorders, such as emotional disturbance and associated conditions of brain damage prevalent among retarded individuals, may also confuse and obfuscate diagnosis. Murphy and Byrne (1980) expanded on this concept when they said,

> "The commonest result of such mixed symptomatology has been a tendency on the part of pediatricians and developmental psychologists to confuse acuity or 'sensitivity', to use the North American expression, with function. The child may be given behavioural tests of vision or hearing resulting in depressed performance and, hence, false assumptions about acuity. Such pessimistic scoring with all the attendant consequences of faulty labelling cannot but modify prognostic statements and discourage all but the most independent parent from engaging in the early therapy so vital to progress. At the other extreme there can also be a danger of over-optimistic counselling based on thresholds derived from tests of end organ and brainstem function. It is essential to stress, therefore, that in the case of multiply disabled children who are also severely to profoundly mentally retarded, modification of function must be the basis of therapy, while modification of acuity provides the caveats upon which prescription of prostheses is based and towards which therapy may be ultimately directed."

Reliable auditory thresholds are necessary prerequisites for a satisfactory training program, based on functional use of residual hearing. Paradoxically, in light of present educational approaches to retarded children, it is of only minimal use for any further development of the auditory modality. Knowledge of auditory thresholds will not result in a response to superthreshold stimuli if the child cannot decode information embedded in the stimuli he is hearing. One often finds mentally retarded children with apparently normal visual and/or auditory acuity not functionally using those modalities. When there are decoding difficulties, superthreshold stimuli are pertinent only when they are interpreted as novel. Conventional auditory training or hearing rehabilitation (Guberina, 1972) has had only limited success with even the moderately retarded (Rittmanic, 1959). In our experience,

similar techniques applied to the severely or profoundly
retarded child have proven futile. Years of non-attendance
to the auditory channel cannot be remedied by provision of an
appropriately adjusted hearing aid or other source of
amplification.

Sensory Stimulation

     It is difficult to ascertain whether inattention thwarts
learning or whether it results from the boring and unrewarding
character of the learning process, if that process is not
relevant to the behavioural repertoire of the individual. It
is obvious that when there is failure to develop an association between stimulus, response and reward, test responding
will be inadequate and reward occurrence would appear random
and unstructured.

     Neurophysiological research has illustrated how animals
respond to sensory stimuli as pleasurable or unpleasurable.
Children who attend to, code, and thus learn from sensory
stimuli, also find such stimuli either pleasurable or unpleasurable. Studies of cranial self-stimulation (Brady, 1958;
Olds, 1958; Olds & Milner, 1954; Olds & Olds, 1963) have shown
that animals will continually stimulate electrodes surgically
implanted in specific regions of the brain. These regions,
namely parts of the hypothalamus and thalamus, the pre-optic
and septal areas, and the amygdaloid nucleus (Olds, 1958),
constitute an area known as the limbic system. It has frequently been observed that access to electrodes implanted at
the above locations results in persistent self-stimulation.
Furthermore, such activity overrides more common behaviours
such as eating, drinking, sex, etc., activities which normally
preoccupy the animal's time and are necessary for maintaining
life. Accordingly, it seems logical to assume that, as the
animal chooses to preoccupy itself with cranial self-
stimulatory activity having little obvious survival value,
some sort of reward experience must be derived. Indeed,
Campbell (1973) has gone so far as to term the areas of the
limbic system which elicit continuous self-stimulatory behaviour as the 'pleasure areas'.

     The deliverance of pleasure is not the only function of
the limbic system. It also contains nerve fibres and neurons
subserving a variety of activities (i.e. heartbeat, breathing,
etc.). Furthermore, by placing other stimulating electrodes,
animals can be made to eat, drink, fly into a rage, etc.,
(Campbell, 1973).

The close proximity of the 'pleasure areas' and the controllers of other behaviour which play a vital part in an animal's daily routine have led Campbell to conclude that an association exists between the two. To be more exact, he suggests that behavioural reactions initiated in specific regions of the limbic system are controlled by neural messages from the 'pleasure areas'. Thus, ultimately, fundamental behaviours are governed by the 'pleasure areas', and their performance is motivated by the acquisition of the reward of pleasure.

Pfaffman (1960) has suggested that the senses are the channels of communication between the external environment and the nervous system. The senses can be divided into 3 groups of receptors: "distance", "near", and "internal". The distance sensors are the visual, auditory and olfactory. The near sensors involve touch, taste, temperature, pressure and vibration. The internal sensors incorporate the neuromuscular information derived from posture and movement, activity of internal organs, and possibly hormonal influences. Therefore, one can define the near and internal sense modalities as those which receive their impulses by direct stimulation, while distance senses require a transmission medium through which appropriate energy impulses pass to reach them.

Vision and hearing allow us to create a picture of the world in which we live. Visual information helps us to understand the function of the space around us and how persons, objects and events relate to that space. Hearing, like vision, has, at first, an alerting and scanning function. However, at a much more sophisticated level, it allows us to categorize our world, organize thoughts through language, and communicate at the symbolic vocal level.

The detection of events and the detection of pleasure within those events is mediated by the senses. If, as Campbell suggests, pleasure is derived through activation of the limbic system, one would expect to find a link between the senses and the areas of the limbic system which generate pleasure. Indeed, there does seem to be increasing evidence of the existence of a sensory viscerosomatic influx into the limbic system which relates to the "hedonic and reinforcing features" of self-stimulation (Nagoun, 1958). Kish (1966), used the term "sensory" reinforcer to refer specifically to the response contingent presentation of a sensory stimulus of moderate intensity to change a subsequent behaviour.

Several other studies have also demonstrated that pleasurable reward obtained through sensory stimulation increases
rate of performance. Barnes and Kish (1961) successfully
utilized auditory reinforcement in an operant conditioning
experiment with mice. Harlow (1960) cited the potential application of touch as a potent reinforcer, while others considered the reinforcing effects of light onset (Kish, 1955),
olfaction (Kish, 1966), and gestation (Pfaffman, 1960).

Investigations of sensory reinforcement with humans have
been confined, in the main, to studies of the vibrotactile
sensory modality, and there are comparatively few of these.
Schaefer (1960) was the first to demonstrate that vibration is
a reinforcing stimulus when he "shaped" both a button pressing
and a pill taking response in a 17 month old. Meyerson, Kerr
and Michael (1967) showed that vibratory stimulation can
maintain lever-pressing behaviour from a profoundly retarded
4 year old. The reinforcing effectiveness of vibration was,
however, found to decrease in subsequent sessions.

Bailey and Meyerson (1969) reinforced a lever pressing
response by a profoundly retarded child by contingent application of vibrotactile stimulation. Rehagen and Thelen (1972)
and Myrvang reported by Barton (1975) have also demonstrated
the effectiveness of vibration as a reinforcer with retarded
children.

It appears from this discussion that sensory stimulation
is an effective means of gaining access to the 'pleasure
areas' of the brain. That is not to say that it is the only
means of obtaining reward. However, its simplicity and
effectiveness does suggest that it might be a fundamental,
perhaps primitive, means of acquiring pleasure.

There is a pressing need for reinforcers which, especially in applied clinical settings, can be easily administered,
result in a high rate of response acquisition, and are resistant to satiation. Sensory stimulation may be such a
reinforcer.

If such reinforcement is to be incorporated into clinical
treatment, a problem arises deciding which form of sensory
stimulation provides the most effective reinforcement.

A Hierarchy Within the Senses

Sherrington (1906) suggested the possibility of a phylo-
genetic hierarchy of sensory usage, an idea which is in
accordance with the general assumption that the so-called
lower senses or near senses (gustatory, cutaneous, kinesthetic
and somatic) develop first and the higher or distance senses
(visual, auditory) develop later in the evolution of species.

Schachtel (1956) suggesting a similar idea, described an
infant's progressive shift in its central mode of perception
from an autocentric mode (primarily utilizing the near receptors) to an allocentric mode (primarily involving the distance receptors). The autocentric mode is seen to be involved
primarily with sensory quality and feelings of pleasure or
displeasure. The allocentric mode is thought to come later
in development, as interests in the objects' qualities and
exploration become important. This shift is consistent with
Piaget's (1952) conceptualization of the developmental
sequences of the sensory-motor period, during which change
from reflex behaviour to increased goal directedness occurs.

Such ideas are supported by comparatively few studies.
Nevertheless, it is evident that, with maturity, development
from touch to vision occurs. Renshaw et al., (1930) found
younger children to be more accurate in tactile kinesthetic
localization than they were in visual localization, while the
pattern was reversed in older children. Zaporozhets (1961)
reported that exploration of novel situations by young children changed from tactile to visual modalities with age, while
Tarakanov and Zinchenke (1960) reported better recall after
tactile than after visual exploration in young children.

Murphy (1978) applied the idea of a hierarchy in sensory
receptor usage in clinical and audiological testing. He
argued that auditory response is minimal when testing hungry,
cold, or otherwise distressed neonates or infants, because
olfactory and tactile dominance may prevent response to visual
or auditory inputs unless the latter are so intense as to
cause startle or greater discomfort. In the same paper,
attention was drawn to comments made by Hardy and Bordley
(1973) concerning young infants with normal hearing but
affected by rubella, who failed to respond to audiological
screening tests. The authors concluded that "...all children
with known trauma or abnormality of function should be carefully examined to identify the extent to which they have
matured in the sensory hierarchy".

The above statement has far reaching implications for the
diagnosis, treatment and training of mentally handicapped
children. At present, there is a great deal of attention paid
to the static evaluation of a person's intellectual status.
Perhaps that type of approach, when applied to the retarded,
should be refocused to a more dynamic, qualitative analysis of
the capacity to process sensory inputs. Taylor (1964) reinforced that point in a discussion of the 2 distance senses,
vision and hearing, when he described the development of
response to auditory stimuli as follows:

> In the early months, a baby usually can cope with
> one source of stimulation at a time. Development-
> ally, vision is usually in advance of hearing, so
> that in the early months, response to visual
> stimulation usually means the ignoring of auditory
> inputs. At about 7 months, the baby is less bound
> to the visual system and can, if left free from
> visual stimuli, respond to auditory stimuli. In
> the maturation of the nervous system, the brain
> learns to cope with competing stimuli so that
> there is an integration of the various modalities.

Predictions concerning function are usually confidently
based on patterns of response. However, in the case of the
multiply disabled child, it is essential to separate notions
of potential function from those of present response. By now,
it should also be obvious that patterns of response may be
modified by the intrusion of extraordinary stimuli which may
be present in the test situation. Just as normal young
infants, if visually or kinesthetically distracted, will not
respond to sounds below the threshold of startle, so too,
untrained multiply disabled children cannot be expected to
respond to sound if distracted by stereotypic behaviour or
tactile or neuromotor sensations. Therefore, present notions
of response measurement may well need to be revised.

If we apply the concept of a sensory hierarchy to the
education of multiply disabled children, it follows that the
physical environment is critical to the optimal functioning of
sensory, intersensory and sensory motor development. In the
case of the normal child, there is almost universal understanding that particular skills must be taught utilizing the sensory
input system(s) which best facilitate the learning of each
skill at each developmental stage. For the mentally handicapped child, however, such a universal law requires radical

rethinking. Intersensory development is often severely out of
phase with chronological age. Thus, teaching such children
should not be carried out using more traditionally accepted
modes of sensory interaction, but rather through the use of
a "sensory exchange" related to the extent to which a child
has progressed on the sensory hierarchy.

"Autocentric" or "Allocentric"

Schopler (1966), Stayton (1971) and Ohwaki and Stayton
(1976) have considered the problem of hierarchies in sensory
receptor usage among the mentally handicapped. Both Schopler
and Stayton failed to demonstrate mental age differences in
tactile and visual preference. Ohwaki and Stayton, who criti-
cized the two earlier studies because they did not distinguish
between Schachtel's (1959) hierarchical modes of perception,
argued that the key theoretical issue should not be a comparison of developmental trends in modality preference, but rather
a comparison of autocentric and allocentric perception. Their
experiment demonstrated a developmental shift from a preference for vibrotactile stimulation to one of visual stimulation.
However, their use of Schachtel's formulation to achieve this
is not clear. They have equated near-sense usage with the
autocentric mode and visual sense usage with the allocentric
mode. Such a distinction is unrealistic because there can be
both autocentric and allocentric perception within the same
modality (Piaget & Inhelder, 1956).

In the field of the multiply disabled, Danella (1973) has
shown that there can be a great deal of exploration by the
near senses. Alternatively, the distance senses can be used
in the autocentric mode (i.e. in the case of such self-
stimulation behaviours as light play).

While the idea of shift from autocentric to allocentric
perception seems valid, especially with normal children, these
concepts must be treated with caution when applied to the
severely retarded child whose behaviour often appears bizarre,
chaotic, self-stimulatory and undirected. The majority of
children on the Mary Sheridan Unit spend in excess of 70% of
their free time engaged in self-stimulatory, stereotyped
behaviours. With this in mind, the writers disagree with
Ohwaki's and Stayton's (1976) statement that a comparison of
developmental trends in modality preference is not a key
issue. Moreover, the need for investigation of a sensory
hierarchy among mentally retarded children is seen as essential to planning a therapeutic regime.

Modality Preference

Byrne and Stevens (1980) have investigated the sensory
modalities of a sample of 16 severely and profoundly mentally
handicapped children with sensory deficits. It was demonstrated that, among the children who were not blind, there
was a significant positive correlation between a shift from
the tactile to the visual modality and an increase in Behavioural Quotient as reflected on the Fairview Self Help Scale
(1969). Because each subject had to perform the same operant
to elicit the various stimuli offered once exploratory behaviour had ceased and the task became automatic, the balance of
autocentric-allocentric behaviour inherent in the task was
kept constant. The above correlation suggests that, with
increasing ability and independence or maturity, there is an
increasing dominance of the distance receptors. If this
result is evidence for a sensory hierarchy, then it emphasizes
the need to refocus our attention to the possibility that the
sensory inputs utilized in teaching, training and treatment
with the retarded should be related to a position on the sensory hierarchy. To date, research into the training of the
mentally handicapped using sensory stimuli in an operant conditioning paradigm (Kish, 1966) has not taken this factor into
account (e.g. Bailey & Meyerson, 1969; Schaeffer, 1960;
Johnson, Fürth & Davey, 1978; Jones, 1979). Many studies have
investigated vibration as a sensory reinforcer because of its
astonishing efficacy. However, Byrne and Stevens (1980) have
shown that since not all children prefer the same sensory
stimuli, the choice of a reinforcer should be child specific.
Moreover, since the use of sensory modality is related to
Behavioural Quotient, persistence in use of the same stimulus
may limit the opportunity to learn through sensory inputs best
related to developing behavioural age. In other words, the
clinical application of sensory stimuli chosen by the clinician
rather than by the child may prevent optimal learning.

Byrne and Stevens (1980) have shown:

1. There may be a shift to usage of visual from the
    tactile modality with increasing Behavioural Quotient;

2. That while some children prefer only vibrotactile
    stimulation and others only visual stimulation, there
    are those who are equally responsive to both.

This suggests that rather than there being a complete shift from near sense dominance to distance sense dominance, a gradual transition occurs in which near and distance senses are accorded equal importance. Further, while dominance may be transferred to the distance senses, the near senses would appear to maintain the supportive information. Murphy and Byrne also reported that while children with visual impairments preferred visual stimuli, children with auditory impairments did not show any preference for either filtered white noise or vocal praise. This suggests that the auditory modality develops later than the visual, a contention supported by Taylor (1964), Murphy (1978), and Johnson, Furth and Davey 1978). If further research supports this, it would certainly bring into question the efficacy of vocal praise with the mentally handicapped, except as a basis for staff encouragement or for the furtherance of rapport.

The following points are important with respect to the emergence of sensory function in the deaf, multiply disabled child:

1. Sensory response in infants tends to follow a hierarchical pattern;

2. The sense of touch is more easily controlled and replicated than the sense of smell and seems less vulnerable to satiation than taste;

3. Vision seems to block audition;

4. Audition as a basis for reinforcement strategies seems to be confined to children who are at a higher level of function;

5. From the foregoing, it has become clear that the most likely areas of reinforcement with the Mary Sheridan Unit children who are severely to profoundly educationally subnormal, are tactile and visual;

6. Children who respond consistently to visual stimuli may be regarded as functioning at a higher level than those who respond to tactile;

7. Shift from tactile to visual reinforcement may be accepted as a sign of functional progress;

8. If one is able to identify the child's preferred modality, that particular stimulus should be used in an operant conditioning paradigm (where operant conditioning refers to increasing the probability of a response in a particular stimulus environment by following the response with reinforcement). In this way, skills such as self-help, communication and motor skills, still fundamental to survival, may be taught to individuals who have failed to acquire such abilities through the use of more 'traditional' reinforcers in conventional educational settings.

Identifying the Preferred Modality

Identification of types of stimuli likely to be most effective is not without difficulty. Rincover (1978) utilized sensory extinction to identify individual stimuli which might serve as potent reinforcers for teaching autistic children. He based his findings on a study of the individual sensory components of the self-stimulatory behaviours frequently indulged in by a population of 3 autistic children. Self-stimulation, characterized by a large amount of stereotyped repetitive behaviour such as rocking, hand flapping and head rolling, is a characteristic of most children with severely limited behavioural repertoires. Observers report that children seem to "use" the behaviour to stimulate themselves, providing sensory input from the movements of their own bodies. Rincover, by elimination of the stimulating components of various stereotypic movements (e.g. a blindfold to eliminate a visual component; a vibrator to eliminate a proprioceptive component) found that during such a sensory masking, there was a marked reduction in self-stimulatory behaviour, a finding which supports the hypothesis that self-stimulatory behaviour is maintained by sensory reinforcement (Kish, 1955).

If recognition and elimination of the rewarding components of self-stimulatory behaviour lead to a gradual extinction of stereotypies, then the fact that an individual selects a particular form of self-stimulation presumably indicates that the sensory stimulation is the most rewarding for that particular individual. The sensory components of the stereotyped movement may be the most effective type of sensory reinforcement and the sense involved is the obvious choice for use in operant conditioning. There will be further discussion of the point in the section dealing with children's responses to sensory stimuli.

Development of skills should result in a spontaneous shift in responsivity from one sensory modality to another. However, the alternative possibility is that a child may per- severate in the most pleasurable modality, one in which motor patterns, even though involving fine and gross motor skills, are related to the individual rather than to the environment. The child may seem to be "stuck" at that point. Self- stimulation precludes attention to other higher order sensory inputs and the skills relevant to their deployment. However, it is environmentally directed skills which would allow for progression along a sensory hierarchy. In fact, the shaping of environmentally directed skills can be influential in the amelioration of self-stimulatory behaviour.

As we have mentioned above, perseveration on one sensory modality limits the possibility of learning taking place through other senses. For example, a child with tactile dominance may fail to organize the visual inputs which contain spatial information about the environment, or fail to organize the auditory inputs necessary for the transmission of informa- tion in speech. In such a case, strategies would be necessary to encourage the use of distance sense information. Thus, in the case where there may be no spontaneous shift from one sensory modality to another, the use of secondary reinforce- ment strategies to allow for generalization from one modality to another may be necessary. Through bisensory presentation of stimuli, intersensory links can be developed between the dominant modality and the modality to which generalization or cross-modal conditioning should take place. Cross-modal con- ditioning refers to the fact that with acquaintance of a stimulus feature through one sensory modality, less practice will be required for its recognition or correct use in a different modality.

It is important to stress that cross-modal transfer is not dependent upon verbal mediation, as confirmed by Hermelin and O'Connor (1968), when they demonstrated vision to touch facilitation in subnormal and autistic subjects. Similarly, St. James-Roberts (1972) cleverly demonstrated the possibility of visual to auditory transfer in a small sample of communica- tion disordered children. In doing so, he established

reliable responses across a range of frequencies where all
previous attempts of audiometric assessment had failed. By
experimental technique, the author had made auditory signals
pertinent to subjects for whom, formerly, the functional significance of auditory stimuli was negligible and in whom the
orientation reflex was minimal. Our own experience certainly
agrees with these results. Patients in our care who have not
hitherto responded to sound, have done so after training in a
cross-modal system using auditory and tactile inputs, after
consistent responses had been developed to tactile inputs
alone.

Sensory and Intersensory Function as
a Basis for Communication

For all children wearing hearing aids, tactile information is derived from the effort of voicing (cranial, thoracic
or laryngeal proprioceptive functions) and from the sound of
the voice as it resonates the earmold. Every hearing aid
wearer, therefore, receives bimodal (i.e. auditory and tactile)
stimuli from his own voicing. Unless held by the person speaking, tactile inputs are otherwise restricted. That is, the
other proprioceptive cues are absent, thus, an infant has to
learn to identify the presence of voices other than his own by
the absence of proprioceptive inputs on the one hand, and by
pitch differentiation on the other. The multiply disabled
child may be neither intellectually nor experientially capable
of making such judgments. Hence, additional information of a
tactile nature has to be supplied; namely, presentation of
stimuli to the cochlea and to the cranium simultaneously, and
amplification of proprioceptive inputs.

One of the early components of auditory stimulation of
the hearing impaired is the maintenance of voicing, so that,
eventually, it may be used purposively and so that the child
can learn to discriminate between his own voice and that of
others. Identification of voice difference is added to other
visual, gustatory and tactile components so that notions of
demanding need satisfaction and environmental manipulation
emerge. The cognitive skills required for such behaviour may
be of very low order in the multiply disabled child. At the

early stages of therapy, we have adopted the principle that
discrimination between self-initiated stimuli and environmentally initiated stimuli will take time. Every step must be
taken to assist these discriminations in order that needs
will, in fact, be signalled in such a way that meeting those
needs will reinforce signalling. This will, in turn, form
the basis for a primitive communication modality.

In our earlier sections, we have stressed the need for
developed cognitive manipulation of sensory inputs. Working
with older children, we have seen that the tactile components
described below can be "faded" in order to encourage the more
normal processes of auditory monitoring. However, we have
also discovered that, though specific signals can be generalized from the tactile to the auditory, in many cases the
development of new generalizations must also begin at the
tactile level. Therapeutically, we retain tactile inputs as
an integral part of sensory learning so that incidental auditory generalization may be concurrently derived from the
tactile modality.

The parents of multiply disabled children await any
contact with the child which indicates a realization of their
presence and role. The encouragement of such communication is
of inestimable value to the child and is essential to parental
bonding and continued stimulation. Much of our effort with
older children is also directed toward the recreation of bonding and the facilitation of pleasure and pride in communication, especially where such structures have lapsed. We cannot
adequately stress the need to evoke satisfaction from simple
communication and the capacity to signal and identify needs.

Similar comments apply to notions of exploration and
curiosity. The what and why of objects outside ourselves
can only be derived from the capacity to identify that objects
exist outside ourselves. Hence, exploration of the environment is an essential aspect of sensory and sensory-motor
learning. Just as we say that to teach language to the deaf
child is dependent upon a purpose and function for that language, so the multiply disabled child requires purpose before
cognitive functioning can be encouraged.

How, then, is the child to be presented with stimuli
tied to objects, activities or events in such a way that they
encourage examination and the coding of linguistic structures

for further identification? In our early work with older
children, we used massive vibro-tactile inputs to encourage
conforming behaviour as a basis for primitive learning. In
the last year, we have found that objects can be given a
tactile identity not simply related to weight, heat or texture.
For example, a hand-held vibrator can be applied to a number
of objects in order to attract exploration. When exploration
occurs, the vibro-tactile components are removed and the
identification process continues either in usage or in further
investigation. For instance, a child may be encouraged to
grasp an object by vibro-tactile stimulation, but having
grasped it, will be allowed to investigate it by the handling,
mouthing and smelling processes typical of a given stage of
development. In another example, the approach of others may
be related to need satisfaction if vibro-tactile stimulations
are added to olefactory inputs, preliminary to feeding or social
contact. We have described our equipment in an earlier paper
(Murphy & Byrne, 1980, pp. 410-414). The reader is referred
to that earlier reading for more information. In that earlier
contribution, we referred to the "3 P's of communication",
which are Pleasure, Pride, and Purpose. We have seen enough
pleasure and pride generated by mother and child in the use
of communication to recognize that there is a danger in seeing
communication merely as a focus of pleasurable interchange.
We do not encourage communication solely as a source of
emotional satisfaction. The social, emotional, intellectual,
and administrative virtues derived from communication are
obvious to us. The child, however, is not in our fortunate
position. It is essential, therefore, to proceed from the
child's restricted view of communication for pleasure related
to the indication/satisfaction of needs to the more complex
view of sophisticated communication.

Research

    In this section, we describe the population, equipment
design, experimental procedures and results achieved in a
series of experiments relating patterns of responses to a
variety of sensory stimuli and independent assessment of self
help skills through the Fairview Self Help Scale (Ross, 1969).

The research may be summarized into 3 categories:

1. Previous research led to the superficial conclusion
    that vibro-tactile reinforcement strategies are appli-
    cable to all patients. Our research investigating
    the validity of that conclusion considered selection
    of the most effective sensory reinforcer for each
    child in the research population. There was a signi-
    ficant correlation between the relevant sensory modal-
    ity and position on the Fairview Self Help Scale.

2. Having discovered the most effective sensory rein-
    forcement paradigm, we investigated the possibility
    of developing self help skills in laboratory and
    then in domestic circumstances. In the course of
    this work, we noted that awareness of and pride in
    success are highly effective reinforcers. These take
    time to develop and should be a major aspect of
    training strategy.

3. Skill development becomes most effective when related
    to a capacity to make choices. Communication of
    these choices, though difficult, can be achieved.
    Results from this part of the project underlined the
    temporal, intellectual and emotional prerequisites
    of communication.

Experiment 1: Multiply Handicapped
Children's Responses to Vibro-
Tactile and other Sensory Stimuli

Specific Aims

Because confirmation of a sensory hierarchy could be of
value diagnostically, and because it was hoped to link the
acquisition of self help skills with the consistent selection
of a particular sensory usage, the present study examined the
following questions:

1. Would children respond more consistently to alterna-
    tive sensory stimuli than they do to vibration?

2. Would a capacity to do well in situations involving
    distance receptors (hearing and vision) rather than
    near receptors (touch) correlate with higher scores
    on an index of skill development?

3. Would a relationship between type of sensory input
    utilized, its position on a sensory hierarchy, and
    the child's score on an index of skill development:

    a) prove diagnostically significant?

    b) provide a basis for therapy?

Subjects

The subjects, all residents at the Mary Sheridan Unit,
Borocourt Hospital, a ward for sensorily handicapped children
with behavioural problems, were ambulatory and exhibited
behaviour consistent with severe mental retardation. There
were 12 males and 4 females with a mean age of 10 years, 11
months, and a range of 5 to 15 years. Two subjects were
blind, the balance visually impaired. There were 4 normal
hearing, 7 hearing impaired, and 5 deaf children in the
group. One subject exhibited hemiplegia.

Procedure

In addition to formal experimental procedures, all Ss
were evaluated by the Fairview Self Help Scale. The Fairview
Self Help Scale scores behavioural items ranging from simple
self help skills to such early educational development as
reading. Scores were presented in the form of a Behavioural
Quotient (B.Q.) resulting from a summation of evidence provided by a teacher, nurse and psychologist from our staff.

All experiments were conducted under laboratory conditions in an 11' x 8' room, with relatively constant illumination from a fluorescent tube.

Subject (S.) accompanied by Examiner (E.) sat at a table
facing a 1-way observation screen, on the other side of which
recording took place. A clock and electric counter were used
for tallying the number of responses. A lever was mounted on
the table by which the S could elicit a stimulus from a multi-
mode output system.

The following test/situational paradigms were employed:

1. White noise (65 dB) from 2 speakers placed in the
    corners of the room behind the S;

2. Vibration through a hand unit mounted centrally on the underside of the table. Frequency was fixed at 50 Hz. Auditory intensity was 56 dB;

3. Light from a wall-mounted filament lamp of 500 watts, 3' from the S. at eye level;

4. An "auditory social" condition where E. would say "good boy" or "good girl" whenever S. pressed the lever. E. did not touch S.;

5. A condition in which manipulation of the lever was not rewarded by any other sensory stimulus.

In each trial of 5 minutes duration, S. would press a lever to elicit a 3 second stimulus (with exception of condition 5). To renew the stimulus, it would be necessary for S. to press the lever again. If S. did not press within 13 seconds, E. would prompt with a tap on the elbow, followed immediately, if no response occurred, by E. moving S.'s hand to the lever. If necessary, E. would complete the sequence by pressing S.'s hand to the lever.

Each S. was given 50 trials in random order, consisting of 10 trials for each of the 5 conditions. Four trials were given daily at regular intervals, such that there were at least 45 minutes between sessions.

Results

Each child's score on a given condition was counted at the end of a 5 minute trial, and then the procedure was repeated for each of the next 5 conditions. Results analyzed by a 2-way analysis of variance showed:

a) that individuals had significantly different scores for the different conditions. The scores from each of the switch pressing conditions were examined for significance against the score from the condition in which no stimulus could be elicited. Of the 16 subjects, 4 scored markedly higher in the vibro-tactile condition, 2 markedly higher in the visual condition, and 7 scored equally for the vibro-tactile and visual stimulation. This result clearly

illustrates that the arbitrary use of vibration as a
sensory stimulus is not justified, and that careful
selection of sensory modality is essential.

b) There was a significant subjects effect on the analysis of variance, which meant that the absolute level
of the 5 conditions varied significantly from individual to individual.

c) There was also a significant interaction effect.
That is, differences between the scores of one condition and the scores of another varied between individuals (i.e. visual and vibration). In view of these
findings, it was felt that a more searching analysis
should be made of correlations between each individual's B.Q. and the differences between the means of
the scores of any pair of the 5 conditions.

We were particularly interested in whether an increased
tendency to score higher on those conditions involving vision
and hearing would be related to a higher B.Q. A partial answer to that question was found by considering the children who
were not blind. For that group, there was a statistically
significant correlation between B.Q. and the difference between
scores on the visual and vibratory conditions. Further, when
the ratio of those scores was compared with B.Q., an even
greater significance emerged.

The fact that the majority of children did not score
significantly higher under the 2 auditory conditions than
under any of the other 3, indicates that auditory stimuli are,
in general, less successful with such a population, or else
the pattern of auditory stimulation used in the current experiment was at fault.

Discussion

The major change in behaviour in the experimental group
was the diminution of stereotypies and an associated development of compliance with the research strategies. For the
majority of the children, such a change was unexpected. This
has led to a reappraisal of the philosophy of care for such
children, and an attempt to predict the extent to which
research methods may be used therapeutically. Two main
features were discerned in the results. First, the vibro-
tactile and visual modalities were the most effective source

of stimulation. This phenomenon (with only 3 exceptions)
related to the whole group, irrespective of sensory function –
be it auditory, visual, audio-visual or simply tactile.
Secondly, the auditory modality was the least effective source
of stimulation for the group.

From these results, we concluded that:

a)   if a child diagnosed as clinically blind, scored well
     in all conditions, the accuracy of that diagnosis
     must be suspect;

b)   where children score high under the vibro-tactile
     condition but low under the others, there are good
     grounds for suspecting:

     i)   impaired visual function;

     ii) good prognosis for the acquisition of self help
          skills, even if the children later prove to be
          blind and deaf.

We also theorized that children with minimal conceptual
function lack the capacity to organize sensory stimuli. As
cognitive skills emerge, there is:

1.   a resultant increment in capacity to organize inputs;

2.   a consequent emergence of sensory function (which
     appears to mirror the normal development of a
     sensory hierarchy).

Given useful sensory residua, these developments will, in
turn, lead to improvements in the development of self help
skills. The particular attraction of this hypothesis is its
potential value as the basis for a therapeutic program.

With only 5 exceptions, all S.s found the vibro-tactile
condition to be an effective source of stimulation. Three of
the 5 did not consistently respond to any sensory input, and
they scored lower on the Fairview Self Help Scale. Children
with high B.Q.s tended to score higher under all 5 conditions
than did children with low B.Q.s. These latter children
tended to score high only under the vibro-tactile condition.

Within the test procedures outlined above, the validity
of scores achieved need not be affected by the current state
of sensory function. In those cases where clinical findings
indicate lack of sensory function, it would be feasible to
identify potential areas of skill development by means of a
restricted test battery. The blind child, for instance, would
not be put through a visual condition series, nor the deaf
child through an auditory series. Hence, by using a modified
series of trials in which only those conditions relevant to
that sensory or sensory-motor function are utilized, valid
results can be expected. By following such a strategy, the
therapist learns to focus on observed function and to be prepared to examine statements about acuity or sensitivity with
a measure of caution.

When training personnel, we have found it necessary to
encourage differentiation between clinically diagnosed acuity
and subjectively observed function. Due to "labelling"
effects, therapists tend to expect that diagnosed levels of
acuity will result in commensurate levels of usage of that
acuity (i.e. of function). As a result, they tend to have
unrealistic goals for some children, and lower levels of
expectation for others. Unless proper guidance and training
is given, a clinician can easily be discouraged by failure
to reach expected targets or bewildered by the unexpected
emergence of sensory function. We have found that, where
staff become accustomed to using B.Q. scores as an index of
prognosis for skill maturation, the notion of a hierarchy in
the development of sensory function has provided an additional
basis for prognostic statements.

"Caveat" Experiments

Certain experimental features required secondary investigations which we described as "caveat" studies.

Caveat I: Because vibrator units produce noise, it was
possible that the aural rather than the vibro-tactile stimulus
was the reinforcer. A trial was made in which:

a)   the lever used in previous experiments produced no
     sensory reward;

b)   an auditory and vibration stimulus was produced;

c)   by means of tape recordings of the vibrator noise,
     auditory stimuli alone were produced.

Condition b) was the only factor which significantly reinforced lever pressing. We were able to conclude that the auditory condition alone was not the reinforcer.

Caveat II: Visual, auditory, vibro-tactile and gustatory reinforcers were compared for efficacy in a simple lever pressing task. The vibro-tactile reinforcer was found to be significantly more effective.

Caveat III: Though these results were relevant to severely subnormal children, they might be less relevant to a similar population with the additional complication of severe autism. A small population (6) of such children repeated the trials described above. The vibro-tactile stimuli were found to be the only significant task reinforcers.

Experiment 2: The Efficacy of
Using Sensory Reinforcers to
Shape Motor, Self Help and
Communication Skills

In Experiment 1, the distinction between sensory "acuity" or sensitivity and sensory "function" motivated us to search for those stimuli children could experience and use as a basis of cognition. Such functional use of a sense organ increases a child's ability to use sensory information and allows the production of planned change in the immediate environment. Therefore, a task was devised which, when completed, produced an immediate and detectable change in the sensory stimuli presented to a child. The task also required very simple neuromotor skills and allowed for accurate measurement and recording by an experimenter.

As described earlier, a lever which a child could press in order to elicit various sensory stimuli from a multi-modal output system was mounted on a table. Results showed that the majority of children who took part in the study could perform a simple structured task when either vibration or a strong light was made contingent upon its completion. In order to investigate whether the results obtained in the first experiment were applicable to the acquisition of other tasks and skills, we attempted to teach skills using the sensory stimulis to which the children were most responsive. The procedure for isolating that stimulus was described in Experiment 1. A strategy was developed by which performance or partial performance resulted in immediate sensory stimulation. Such a teaching strategy could be interpreted as operant conditioning: the performance of a skill being the operant, and the sensory stimulus being the (sensory) reinforcer (Kish, 1955).

Specific Aims

The specific questions investigated were:

1. Could the children learn various motor, self help and communication skills without the use of sensory reinforcers?

2. What is the effect on the acquisition of skills when sensory reinforcers are introduced?

3. How does the rate of learning vary when sensory reinforcers have been introduced compared to when no such reinforcers are used?

Subjects and Procedures

Eleven severely/profoundly retarded children displaying varying levels of sensory handicap were chosen as subjects. All except one subject were ambulant. The experimental environment was the same as Experiment 1.

For the majority of skills taught, S. accompanied by E. sat at a table facing a 1-way observation screen. Recording took place from the other side of the screen. A foot switch was available to E. so that a sensory reinforcer could be administered while allowing E.'s hands to be free.

Three experimental conditions were utilized in the teaching of skills:

1. Completion of the required task was not reinforced by a sensory stimulus;

2. When required, vibration was presented through a hand vibrator mounted centrally on the underside of the table;

3. Light was presented from a wall mounted filament
    lamp 3' from the subject, at eye level.

The Fairview Self Help Scale was used as the index of
skill development. The B.Q. was determined as in Experiment 1.

Design

The same experimental design was adopted for teaching all
skills. A baseline was established in which there was no
reinforcement. Ten sessions of 2 minutes each were spread
equally over 5 days. Baseline sessions were followed by teaching divided into units (or cells) to make subsequent analysis
easier. Each cell comprised 24 sessions, each 2 minutes, of
1 of 2 types designated as A or B, presented in random order.

During the B. sessions, the most effective sensory
stimulus for each child (established using the same procedure
as in Experiment 1) was introduced as a reinforcer, whereas
during the A. sessions it was not. Not more than 8 sessions
were administered each day.

Such a procedure broadly resembles an intermittent
reinforcement paradigm and was chosen because such paradigms
have been shown to be important for long-term success and
generalization.

The total number of cells completed in this investigation
was 71. Sixty-two of these involved communication, 4 self
help, 2 fine motor, and 3 gross motor activity.

Each child's score on 1 condition was counted at the end
of a 2-minute session and the procedure was repeated for each
of the conditions during the baseline and cell sessions. The
data thus derived was subjected to linear regression analysis.

The baseline measures were not included in the analysis,
as no child produced any consistent pattern of spontaneous
operants during these sessions. Their incidence was minimal
and occurred randomly over sessions, the children often sitting passively or being absorbed in self-stimulatory behaviour.
This situation was particularly true for the sessions involving the teaching of communications signs, which formed 86% of
the data of the investigation. For instance, for the majority
of the communication signs, no spontaneous operants were produced. Such baselines probably do not portray a true picture.
The limitations with regard to such baselines have been outlined earlier.

Results and Discussion

For 62% of the A. conditions, learning occurred. It is
likely that the B. conditions influenced the A.s as they were
presented in the randomized sequence. Learning occurred in
the B. conditions for 81.1% of the skills taught.

From such results, it would seem as if Condition B. is
initiating learning and, in turn, causes learning to occur in
Condition A., thus explaining the marked differences between
A.s and the baseline measures, even though in both, no sensory
reinforcer was utilized. That preliminary conclusion is
supported by the fact that for 35.1% of the skills taught,
there were statistically significant differences ($\geq.05$),
thus indicating that in those instances, children were learning the skills significantly faster in Condition B. than in
Condition A. The vibro-tactile stimulus was used in 70% of
the cases in which skills were learned significantly faster
under Condition B.

For 94.6% of the skills taught, there were also differences which indicated that the children's level of responding
was statistically significantly higher in Condition B. than in
Condition A. The higher level of responding when sensory
reinforcers are used for teaching has obvious implications for
the children's self occupation activities. Generally, when
left to their own devices, they tend to involve themselves in
repetitive manneristic behaviour. By structuring the sensory
environment so that most extraneous distracting (sensory)
stimuli are eliminated, it is possible to teach and maintain
skills which are constructive and resemble play by normal
children. A normal child's play is usually adaptive, however,
undergoing continuous change, the child generating an apparently infinite range of play activities. In contrast, the
purposive play of our population is usually pre-taught and is
then repeated again and again by the child, with little
change over time. Detailed future research is essential in
this area, not only to establish the sequence of skills to be
utilized in self occupation, but also to develop sensory
training equipment which is functional, easy to operate, and
capable of maintaining the child's level of response. Such
research will obviously be closely linked to investigations
involving the reduction of stereotypes.

The two skills not statistically significant at the 5% level utilized the vibro-tactile stimulus as the reinforcer in the B. condition. These were also the only 2 skills in which there was no difference between the A. and B. conditions. For all the skills which utilized light as a reinforcer in the B. condition, the level of responding was significantly higher when light was, in fact, used as the reinforcer.

Finally, through time sampling of behaviours at the appropriate times of day (e.g. observing children at meal times to ascertain whether they use the "food" sign, or at dressing times for the "coat" sign), a memory check was carried out 12 months after the investigation to establish whether the children had retained the skills taught. Thirty-five of the 37 skills were retained by the population.

Conclusions

All subjects displayed a capacity to learn a variety of motor, self help and communication skills (the investigation concentrated mainly on communication signs). It was discovered, however, that sensory reinforcement was necessary for the children to acquire such skills. The sensory reinforcer used for teaching was isolated using a procedure similar to Experiment 1. Vibro-tactile inputs were not used as a panacea. Eight of the children required the contingent use of vibro-tactile inputs in the B. condition of the cell structure, while 3 required visual inputs.

Recognition and Identification
Using Communication Signs

The learning of symbolic codes releases the child from complete dependence on his immediate environment. Such independence, besides allowing recollection of the past and prediction of future events, also allows the initiation of change. In the previous section, we concentrated on the child's ability to acquire visual and tactile codes. The basis of such codes is the demand-response arc.

The Demand-Response Arc

Therapy carried out in the fine motor and self help areas
encourages the child to explore objects for their function.
Eventually, clinicians hope to develop socially meaningful
patterns of behaviour which utilize objects in the same
manner. In other words, we are attempting to develop a meaningful demand-response arc (e.g. a demand is made of the
child to which he responds with a meaningful pattern of
behaviour). The physical and verbal prompts utilized when
developing trainable motor skills are the initial stages of
this process. That is the beginning of the receptive function of communication and of language. On the other hand,
the demand symbol* is the initial example of the child making
a demand on the adult. The demand signal in this type of
child has 3 components:

1. the child has to identify a need in himself and to
    see someone outside himself as a potential source of
    satisfaction;

2. the child must identify the specific item in the
    environment that will satisfy his need;

3. by means of a consistent pattern of training (or
    reinforcement), the notion of a relationship between
    an expressive pattern of behaviour on his part and
    the satisfaction of the need will be developed.

Once more, we see needs leading to expression, which in turn,
leads to satisfaction. This interlinking of skills in trans-
mitting and of knowing what to transmit is fundamental to all
communication learning. Therefore, such demand-response arcs
form the basis of the communicative process.

---

*   "The spoken word, at first a sign because it reaches the
    child embedded in a situation, becomes a signal as he
    hears it in the absence of the situation; becomes a symbol
    as he himself utters it with some direction of his atten-
    tion towards the situation; becomes linguistic as it is
    bound into a system of relationships, syntactic and seman-
    tic". (Lewis, 1968). Such a definition also applies to
    visual and tactile codes. As visual codes are commonly
    referred to as signs, the demand symbol has been referred
    to in this account as a communication sign."

In Section II, we investigated whether the child could learn the necessary specific motor pattern associated with an item in his environment. However, the experimental environment was very restricted. Twelve months after the completion of the investigation, the results of time sampling procedures indicated that the children could still appropriately use all the signs that they had previously learned. The production of signs was situation specific, however, in that they would only sign "food" when sitting at the meal table, or "coat" when they were preparing for an outing, etc.

On the basis of this result, a new experiment was designed to determine if a child's signs are temperospatially locked, or if children can recognize a number of objects presented in a randomized sequence and identify each object by producing the correct sign. In the writers' past experience, given such a situation, many children will persevere on the motor pattern of the sign of the first object they have been asked to identify. The major question under consideration in this new investigation was: "Could children recognize a number of objects presented in a randomized sequence and subsequently identify each object by producing the correct sign?"

Subjects and Procedures

Four children (3M, 1F) all with visual and auditory handicaps and displaying behaviour consistent with severe mental retardation, were the subjects. Experimental conditions re: the room, light, and other factors were similar to those of previous experiments. The Fairview Self Help Scale was again used as an index of skill development, with the B.Q. determined as in previous studies.

The identification of objects by producing the appropriate sign was part of the therapeutic program. There were always 24 trials within a therapeutic session. Therefore, for 2 objects, 12 trials for each object were randomized to form the therapeutic session. Similarly, for 3 objects, 8 trials, and for 4 objects, 6 trials were administered.

The child was presented with 3 options of response:

1. the motor pattern for the correct sign was produced;

2. an incorrect motor pattern was produced;

3. the child did not respond.

For the purpose of this investigation, correct and incorrect
responses were recorded. Incorrect responses included both
the production of the incorrect motor pattern and not responding. If the child did not respond in 10 seconds, the next
trial was presented.

Results and Discussion

The results showed that the number of correct discriminations not due to chance was very infrequent. When they
did occur, they were rarely immediately followed by another
such session. A possible cause of this may have been that
the experimenter who carried out the research was not the
same person who taught the children the original signs. This
may have produced a failure to generalize. If the results
were not due to this (and only future research can resolve
that issue), the present situation looks ominously bleak.
Future research should, therefore, not only examine whether
failure to generalize is the main causative factor in failure to discriminate, but also whether original teaching
designs can be organized so as to promote consistent sign
discrimination at later stages. It should be noted, however,
that the fact that there were significant runs of correct
discrimination responses suggests that the potential to be
able to learn to discriminate is present, even if it is
inconsistent.

Summary, Conclusions and Suggestions
for Future Research

Throughout this chapter, one central theme has led to a
series of relatively minor experiments designed to examine
the validity of hypotheses developed. The results of these
were applied to the investigation of the consequences of
their application. In turn, the results of these were used
to develop a logical structure within which an approach to
improved learning could be developed for a multiply disabled
population which is also mentally retarded.

Central Theme

The central theme examined the validity of the traditional approach to mental subnormality which assumes that the
major problem in such children is a severe defect of intelligence. Previous experience had raised the interesting
speculation that the problem is not merely, or only, a function of cognition, but also of the capacity to use the senses
as a prerequisite to such cognition. Sensory function was
thought to be vulnerable to various distracting phenomena,
and it has become increasingly clear that reduction of stimulus content or quality is essential if the capacity to focus
sensory attention is to develop. It also became increasingly
clear as time went on that self-distraction is a major barrier
to the acquisition of sensory information basic to cognition.

Hierarchy of Sensory Response

At first, self-distraction was identified predominantly
as stereotype. However, as increased use was made of the
theory of a hierarchy of sensory response, it became clear
that inadvertent use of the inappropriate sensory modality
might not only be unproductive with regard to learning, but
might also prevent it. Following this discovery, experiments
were constructed which related optimal sensory stimuli to a
level in a hierarchy of skill development. As a result, a
correlation between low order skills and low order sensory
response functions was identified. This discovery not only
gave credence to the original tentative hypothesis, but
allowed the development of a logic which would explain the
apparent recovery of sensory or motor function in the children
under investigation. It became clear that the capacity to
focus attention on sensory input led to experimental usage of
such senses as reinforcers in teaching situations. Moreover,
growth in success by the children increased the likelihood of
further success. This, in turn, increased attention, led to
considerable self-regard on their part, and produced what
might well be described as "an explosion" of learning skills.
Helping children to learn, therefore, was seen as:

1. learning to focus sensory attention;

2. identification of the optimal sensory mode for
    reinforcement;

3. use of reinforcement to help learning to learn;

4. as learning skills developed, to reduce the strength of the reinforcing stimulus;

5. to see the sensory function in its own right and to develop cross-modal transfer, as a result of which, improved function in a previously defective sense would be possible; and,

6. to use these improved sensory skills as a basis for further learning, in particular, for the development of locomotor and self help skills, and as a basis for communication.

Mental Subnormality as a
Condition Amenable to Therapy

We found ourselves questioning the validity of the notion that mental subnormality is, as it were, a static condition based on a fundamental lack of cognitive capacity or potential. As soon as we showed that children could be trained to respond, we were faced with the task of identifying:

1. which sense to stimulate;

2. how much stimulation to apply;

3. how to apply it (i.e. by what forms of equipment and under what circumstances);

4. for what purposes we could apply it; and,

5. how to extend such usage to the investigation of that increased development in cognitive ability which appears to follow increased sensory awareness.

In the early stages of our experiments, we examined the notion of a sensory hierarchy. Having done so, we then compared the efficacy of vibro-tactile sensation to that of visual and auditory stimuli for the Mary Sheridan Unit population. Soon we were able to select relevant sensory reinforcers and to re-examine the validity of the original pessimistic diagnosis of each child's sensory state. As increased

sensory skills developed, children were shown to have a
higher potential for learning. Major improvements in gross
and fine motor skill emerged. Self-regard and amenability
were seen to be capable of improvement and, at the same time,
the serious consequences of self-distraction by stereotypic
behaviour were revealed.

There were certain emphases early in the research which
would have been examined in a different manner if the writers
had known then what has been learned in the course of the
study. Because the children were relatively unstimulated and
untrained when the work began, there was a tendency to assume
that certain patterns of stimulation had a specific quality
rendering them more effective than any (or all) others.
Hence, the equipment first developed was based on vibro-
tactile stimulation. The enthusiasm this equipment provoked
nationally and internationally could well have led to a
failure to progress further in the development of other
sensory stimuli. It soon became clear, however, that there
is no "one best way" for all children. Indeed, it is
unlikely there is even a "one best way" for any given child.
As each child grows in skills, so there is a gradual shift in
the efficacy of reinforcement from the tactile to the visual
modality. Future research will investigate the extent to
which the auditory sense can be used more effectively as a
reinforcer.

There is no doubt that vibro-tactile stimulation provided a key which, as it were, "unlocked" the capacity of
our population to respond. Once response had been initiated,
the development of skills, the efficacy of other sensory
inputs, and the use of systematic communication patterns all
became feasible. Considering the present state of development of our population, it is unlikely that vibration would
have the same dramatic effect as it did when we began with
them. Other patterns of reinforcement will be needed and
research will be directed to this end.

Another potential area of research is stereotypic
behaviour. There is a tendency in the mental subnormality
field to ignore such behaviour unless it is extremely
bizarre or leads to self-mutilation. Such behaviours
obviously do need control and eradication. The particularly
self-distracting aspects of stereotypes with their associated

reduction of attention focus and subsequent interference with growth in learning skills demand urgent attention.

Learning to Learn

Fundamentally, our research has established that mentally subnormal children can learn to learn. Gross motor skills lead to, or are accompanied by development of fine motor skills. How far, however, can we go in the "higher order" or distance senses? Will we be able to develop fine auditory skills which can lead to discrimination of sound and then, eventually, some speech comprehension? There is no doubt that in the case of one child in our population, this has begun to emerge. Future research should concentrate on such goals and the optimal processes for achieving them.

Parallel Research

Skills learned can be forgotten. For children with considerable learning capacity, a few lapses of memory can be irrelevant. For a population such as the one investigated in this study, loss of skill can be a source of considerable discouragement and trauma to staff, and of great significance to the child.

Generalization of skill from one task to another, or from one environment to another, requires protracted training and support of children and staff alike. There is a dearth of research in this area. We would, therefore, add it to our voluminous catalogue of information urgently required for the development of learning skills in multiply disabled children.

Discussion

P. ALEXANDER

Dr. Murphy, I have the distinct sense that you approach children in your care from the perspective of a child with a complex series of problems, one of which happens to involve the auditory modality. As I view programs elsewhere, I sometimes get the impression that the professionals involved view the child as having a problem with deafness, and some other things. This implies that, perhaps because of our professional training, we see the child first through our own involvement. I wonder two things; first, which sense do you get most from viewing programs both in Europe and North America? Also, to what extent does viewing the problem of the child from a rather narrow perspective negatively influence the care that we provide?

K. MURPHY

First of all, it's very difficult to know what anyone means these days by "hearing", when dealing with the severely mentally retarded population. All I can say is that one has to think in terms of growth of function. To me, it doesn't matter an awful lot where success arises, so long as success arises quickly and consistency is developed. Once consistency develops, communication can develop; and if we're lucky, from communication we may then get round to an improved evaluation of auditory function.

References

Bailey, J., and Meyerson, L., "Vibration as a Reinforcer with the Profoundly Retarded Child," Journal of Applied Behavioural Analysis 2:135-137, 1969.

Barnes, G.W., and Kish, G.B., "Reinforcing Effects of Manipulation in Mice," Journal of Comparative Physiological Psychology 54:713-715, 1961.

Brady, J.V., "Temporal and Emotional Factors Related to Electrical Self Stimulation of the Limbic System," Reticular Formation of the Brain (Boston: Brown & Co.), Jasper, H.H. (Ed.), 1958.

Byrne, D.J., and Stevens, C.P., "Mentally Handicapped Children's Response to Vibrotactile and Other Stimuli as Evidence for the Existence of a Sensory Hierarchy," Apex Journal of the British Institute of Mental Handicaps 8:96-98, 1980.

Danella, E.A., "A Study of Tactile Preference in Multiply Handicapped Children," American Journal of Occupational Therapy 27:457-463, 1973.

Foale, M., and Patterson, J.W., "Hearing of Mental Defectives," American Journal of Mental Deficiency 59:264-258, 1954.

Hardy, W.G., and Bordley, J.W., "Problems in the Diagnosis and Management of the Multiply Handicapped," Archives of Otolaryngology 98:269-274, 1973.

Harlow, H.F., "Primary Affectional Patterns in Primates," American Journal of Orthopsychiatry 30:676-684, 1960.

Hermelin, B., and O'Connor, N., "Like and Cross Modality Responses in Normal and Subnormal Children," Quarterly Journal of Experimental Psychology 12:48-53, 1960.

Johnson, D., Furth, H., and Davey, G., "Vibration and Praise as Reinforcers for Mentally Handicapped People," Mental Retardation 16:339-342, 1978.

Jones, C., "Uses of Mechanical Vibration with the Severely Mentally Handicapped, Part I," Apex Journal of the British Institute of Mental Handicap 7:81-82, 1979.

Jones, C., "Uses of Mechanical Vibration with the Severely Mentally Handicapped, Part II," Apex Journal of the British Institute of Mental Handicap 7:112-114, 1980.

Kish, G.B., "Learning When the Onset of Illumination is Used as a Reinforcing Stimulus," Journal of Comparative and Physiological Psychology 48:261-264, 1955.

Lewis, M.M., Language and Personality in Deaf Children (Slough: National Foundation for Educational Research in England and Wales), 1968.

Mark, H., and Hardy, W., "Orienting Reflex Disturbances in Central Auditory or Language Handicapped Children," Journal of Speech and Hearing Disorders 23:237-242, 1958.

Meyerson, L., Kerr, N., and Michael, J., "Behaviour Modification in Rehabilitation," Experimental Analysis (New York: Appleton-Century Crofts), Bijou, S., & Baer, D. (Eds.), 1967.

Murphy, K.P., Investigation of the Incidence of Hearing Loss in the Mentally Retarded, Confidential Report for the R.N.I.D., 1977.

Murphy, K.P., Early Development of Auditory Function, Paper Presented to the National Convention of the American Speech and Hearing Association, San Francisco, 1978.

Murphy, K.P., and Byrne, D.J., "The Blind-Deaf Multiply Disabled Infant," Early Management of Hearing Loss (New York: Grune & Stratton, Inc.), Mencher, G.T. & Gerber, S.E. (Eds.), 1980.

National Development Group, Helping Mentally Handicapped People in Hospital, Department of Health and Social Security, 1978.

Ohwaki, S., and Stayton, S.E., "Preference by the Retarded for Vibratory and Stimulation as a Function of Mental Age and Psychotic Reaction," Journal of Abnormal Psychology 85:516-522, 1976.

Olds, J., "Self Stimulation and Differentiated Award Systems," Reticular Formation of the Brain (Boston: Little & Co.), Jasper, H.H. (Ed.), 1958.

Olds, J., and Milner, P., "Positive Reinforcement Produced by Electrical Stimulation of Septal and other Regions of Rat Brain," Journal of Comparative and Physiological Psychology 47:419-427, 1954.

Olds, M.E., and Olds, J., "Approach Avoidance Analysis at Rat Diencephalon," Journal of Comparative Neurology 120:259-295, 1963.

Pfaffman, C., "The Pleasures of Sensation," Psychological Review 67:253-268, 1960.

Piaget, J., The Origins of Intelligence in Children (New York: International University Press), 1952.

Piaget, J., and Inhelder, B., The Child's Conception of Space (London: Routledge & Paul), Langdon, F.J. & Lunzer, J.L. (Translators), 1956.

Rehagen, N.J., and Thelen, M.H., "Vibration as Positive Reinforcement for Retarded Children," Journal of Abnormal Psychology 80:162-167, 1972.

Renshaw, S., "The Errors of Cutaneous Localization and the Effect of Practice on the Localizing Movement in Children and Adults," Journal of Genetic Psychology 28:223-238, 1930.

Rincover, A., "Sensory Extinction: Procedure for Elimination of Self-Stimulatory Behaviour in Developmentally Disabled Children," Journal of Abnormal Child Psychology 6:299-310, 1978.

Rittmanic, P.A., "Hearing Rehabilitation for the Institutionalized Mentally Retarded," American Journal of Mental Deficiency 63:778-783, 1959.

Ross, R.T., Fair View Self Help Scale (California: Fair View State Hospital), 1969.

Schachtel, E.G., "The Development of Focal Attention and the Emergence of Reality," Psychiatry 17:309-324, 1954.

Schachtel, E.G., Metamorphosis: On the Development of Affect, Perception, Attention, and Memory (New York: Basic Books), 1959.

Schaefer, H., "Vibrations as a Reinforcer for Infant Children," Journal of Experimental Analysis of Behaviour 3:160, 1960.

Schopler, E., "Visual Versus Tactile Receptor Preference in Normal and Schizophrenic Children," Journal of Abnormal Psychology 71:108-114, 1966.

Sherrington, C.S., The Integrative Action of the Nervous System (London: Cambridge University Press), 1906.

St. James-Roberts, I., The Development of Multi-modality Assessment Procedures for use in the Audiological Testing of Children Ph.D. Thesis, University of Newcastle, 1972.

Stayton, S.E., "Multi-Modality Responding as a Function of Mental Age and Retardation," Journal of Perceptual and Motor Skills 33:1122, 1971.

Tarakanov, V.V., and Zinchenke, B.P., "Comparative Analysis of Touch and Vision: Communication VI, Voluntary and Involuntary Learning of Form in Pre-School Age (in Russian)," Daklady Akademiia. Pedagogicheskikh. Nauk. R.S.F.S.R. Volume 5, 1960.

Taylor, I., Neurological Mechanisms of Hearing and Speech in Children (Manchester: University Press), 1964.

Zaporozhets, A.V., "The Origin and Development of the Conscious Control of Movements in Man," Recent Soviet Psychology (New York: Liveright), O'Connor, N. (Ed.), 1961.

THE CALIFORNIA SCHOOL FOR THE DEAF: SPECIAL UNIT PROGRAM

Eugene LaCosse
California School for the Deaf, Fremont, California

The Special Unit program at the California School for the Deaf in Fremont serves fifty-six deaf, multihandicapped children ranging in age from elementary to high school. The Unit, as well as the other three educational departments in this large state residential program, do not provide week-end care. The other three departments (elementary, junior high, and senior high schools) serve normal deaf children, deaf learning disabled, deaf low functioning, and the deaf ortho-pedically handicapped able to function within the regular classroom. Students who attend the program generally origin-ate from the San Francisco Bay area and Northern California. There is another state residential school for the deaf in Riverside, which serves children from Southern California and maintains a program similar to Special Unit.

The name of our program is the Deaf Multihandicapped Unit. Total communication is its philosophy, and that of the entire school.

The Special Unit student is the deaf child who has additional handicapping conditions which significantly inter-fere with his/her ability to benefit from regular classroom instruction. Accordingly, there are many elements which dis-tinguish the Special Unit from the regular deaf program. To begin with, the Special Unit provides a small student-teacher ratio (4-1, 5-1) and is non-text book oriented. Instruction emphasizes functional skills for living. Behav-iour modification strategies are utilized extensively within the program. Individual and/or group sign language therapy is available for students who demonstrate more severe language deficiencies.

Program Description

Staff

   Staff of the Special Unit consists of a principal,
psychologist, consulting psychiatrist, vocational teacher,
communication skills teacher, 13 classroom teachers, a
teaching assistant, and a secretary.

   The Principal is responsible for the overall supervision
of the Unit and is the co-ordinator of all administrative and
instructional activities. He reports to the Director of
Instruction.

   The Psychologist plays a significant role in the area of
assessment. She is responsible for administering and interpreting a variety of intelligence, diagnostic and achievement
tests. She also assists in the development of behaviour
management strategies for the staff.

   A psychiatrist is available on a consultation basis
once a week. He also participates in the assessment process
and makes recommendations concerning the appropriateness of
placement for children with significant emotional problems.

   The vocational teacher devotes a good portion of the
day to the Special Unit, exposing students to a variety of
vocational tasks and work environments. He also helps them
discover and explore their areas of interest. After completion of the program, capable students participate in the
regular vocational exploratory and/or training program.
Ultimately, students may choose to participate in a work
experience program providing on-the-job training, on or off
campus.

   The communication skills teacher works in the Unit on a
full-time basis. She evaluates students' expressive and
receptive signing skills and provides individual and group
signing instruction. Speech therapy, aural habilitation and
audiological services are not provided by this person, but
are available through the Communication Skills Department.

Currently, there are 4 elementary, 3 junior high, and 6 high school level teachers. They are all credentialed as Teachers of the Deaf and receive continuous inservice training re: the deaf, multihandicapped. The basic subjects they teach are functional language, reading, mathematics, social studies (community awareness) and applied practical science. Instruction is generally non-text book oriented, and requires many teacher-designed materials. The materials are frequently made by the teaching assistant. The role of the teaching assistant is not the same as that of a teacher's aide. Rather, that person is responsible for the maintenance, supervision and distribution of teacher-designed materials.

Wherever possible, Special Unit students are integrated into the regular school physical education program, while others are in an adaptive/remedial physical education course. That program emphasizes the development of body awareness, teamwork, appropriate social behaviour and a positive self-image. A perceptual-motor program is provided by the classroom teachers, especially at the elementary and junior high levels.

Many Special Unit students integrate with the regular deaf children during meal times, recess, school-wide assemblies, and some after school activities. Some Unit children are capable of being mainstreamed into regular physical education classes, vocational classes, and regular residential settings. The program encourages the mainstreaming of qualified children whenever possible.

Objectives

The major objectives of the Unit are the development of self-awareness, survival skills and appropriate social behaviour. Ultimately, our goal is for the child to be able to function independently or semi-independently and be qualified for employment, vocational training or placement in a sheltered workshop. The Unit curriculum ("The Curriculum for the Development of Self-Awareness, Survival and Independent Living Skills") developed by the Unit staff, concentrates on 12 functional goals:

1.   Communicates with others;

2.   Able to take care of self;

3. Recognizes life threatening situations;

4. Displays appropriate behaviour in public;

5. Accepts and follows directions;

6. Has basic idea of money;

7. Uses leisure time effectively;

8. Uses transportation to best of ability;

9. Understands basic sexuality;

10. Writes and uses personal data;

11. Shops and prepares food for self;

12. Knows time concepts.

Behaviour modification strategies are used to increase
educational progress, appropriate attending behaviour and
appropriate social interaction. Clear expectations and
immediate consequences are vital for the Unit's children.
The importance of positive reinforcement cannot be overemphasized. In some cases, the psychologist is needed to
develop individualized behavioural programs. To date, it
appears that the use of money is one of the most effective
reinforcers.

Weekly composition books are exchanged among Unit
teachers, Unit residential counsellors and the child's
parents/guardians. This is one vehicle for open communication and insures that all concerned parties are fully aware
of important events of the week. For instance, if a child
has a bad week in school, the teacher will make a note of
this in the book and when the parents/guardians read it, they
may talk to the child accordingly. Consequently, the child
will see that the school and parents do work together as a
team. The team approach in working with the whole child is
an important aspect of the entire program. Open and frequent
communication is emphasized among staff and parents/guardians.

Criteria for Admittance

Having established criteria for admittance is crucial. Focus is placed on the appropriate types of deaf, multi-handicapped students who can best be served. Deafness must be the primary handicap. However, with multihandicapped children it may be difficult to determine which handicap interferes the most with learning.

Basically, the criteria for the Unit are as follows:

1. The child is functioning on at least an educable, mentally retarded level, or has the intellectual capacity to eventually do so.

2. The child's hearing loss requires a specialized program for deaf children.

3. Additional handicapping conditions do not prevent the child from benefiting in an educational setting, in contrast to a treatment setting or a developmental center. Deaf-blind children are not served. They receive services from the Deaf-Blind Unit at the California School for the Blind in Fremont.

4. The child is able to at least:

   a) function in small group situations more than 50% of the time and does not require 1-to-1 supervision;

   b) conceptualize presence of life-threatening situations;

   c) demonstrate internal control so as not to be abusive to self or others;

   d) respond to others and initiate contact voluntarily for more than basic needs;

   e) learn simple mobility patterns, (e.g. able to find his/her way to and from school and residence cottage, vocational shop, sym, etc.);

   f) demonstrate some self-help skills.

5. Priority admission is given to elementary age children.

The criteria are often difficult to apply to elementary age applicants. Special consideration needs to be given when the cause of a child's behaviour is ambiguous. For example, in younger children, behaviour can be the result of normal immaturity or a true handicap. It is easier to make this distinction in older children.

Assessment

The California School for the Deaf receives many applicants for the Special Unit program. In the case of a deaf child currently enrolled in another school department on the campus, a referral to the Unit for further assessment can be made. At the applicant's preliminary evaluation by the psychologist and/or the psychoeducational specialist, all records are reviewed. As a result of the preliminary evaluation, a determination will be made as to the appropriateness of further assessment or referral. Assessment will not continue when a child is functioning on a trainable mentally retarded level or exhibits severe acting-out aggressive behaviour.

After preliminary evaluation, and when there is an appropriate space in the Unit, as well as the residence cottage, the child will enter the Unit strictly on an assessment basis. The assessment period lasts 4 weeks and, in special circumstances, may be extended an additional 4 weeks. During that time, the child will participate as much as possible in all school and cottage activities.

Team

The Unit assessment team consists of the Principal, Psychologist, Teacher(s), cottage counsellor(s), communication skills teacher and other staff when appropriate. Areas assessed are cognitive functioning, adaptive behaviour, gross and fine motor skills, social and emotional behaviour and adjustment, communication skills, self-help/independent living skills, pre-vocational skills, and others. A psychiatric consultant is available during the assessment period. In-house meetings take place to discuss the child and the appropriateness for placement or the need for further referral(s). For example, if hearing loss or severe autism is questioned, a referral for further evaluation may be recommended.

Placement

At the end of the assessment period, a meeting is called
with the child's parents, a local school or agency representative, the Unit assessment team, and any other involved individuals. Determination of the appropriateness of the Unit for
the child is based on the evaluations and recommendations made
by the team. If the child's placement in the Unit is not
appropriate, the school may provide recommendations for programming or alternative placement. The assessment process is
difficult because of the nature of the handicaps. The program
design of the Unit is not appropriate for children requiring
extensive psychiatric treatment and/or excessive custodial
care.

There is a growing deaf multihandicapped population. It
is important to note that not only high school applicants are
increasing in number due to the Rubella epidemic in the 1960s,
but that the incidence of elementary age applicants is also
increasing. As noted in the *Hearing Aid Journal* (Klein &
Vernon, 1982), epidemic growth in the spread of sexually
transmitted diseases (herpes) will significantly increase the
number of congenitally deaf, multihandicapped children born in
the next decade.

Assessment Tools

As the Unit enters its seventh year, it has become
increasingly apparent that instructional and assessment
materials need to be continually re-evaluated. They need to
be upgraded and reviewed with an ultimate goal of enhancing
their validity and significance. For instance, in the field
of deaf education, the Stanford Achievement Test for the
Hearing Impaired (SATHI) developed by the Office of Demographic Studies at Gallaudet College in Washington, D.C., is
given to deaf students. The advantages of the SATHI are in
the statistics. The scaled scores can be used to indicate
changes and performance levels of individual deaf students.
These scores can be used when comparing one child to a nation-
wide population of deaf children. In this respect, the grade
equivalent scores are not used or looked at singularly. This
adaptation serves as a model for assessment of the deaf,

multihandicapped. However, it is evident that tests need to be developed which have been standardized on deaf, multi-handicapped children and attention needs to be focused on the improvement of existing assessment tools for this population.

Some standardized tests are used, such as the Leiter, American Association on Mental Deficiency Adaptive Behaviour Scale, and Bender-Gestalt tests. There is one problem, however, which continues to exist. Very often, children in our Unit appear to understand directions, when they really do not. Their initial responses, therefore, can be very mis-leading. In the case where borderline results are obtained, the decision for placement rests heavily on the team's sub-jective judgment. We find that the most accurate picture of the child's functioning level is provided by the teacher, who interacts with that child on a daily basis.

The need for assessment tools for the deaf, multi-handicapped child should be addressed in depth. Standardiza-tion of teacher-made tests is one area which should be explored. Currently, the Unit is considering the formaliza-tion of pre- and post-diagnostic tests. These tools will be designed so that they can be used in conjunction with the existing curriculum.

There is need for continual research and development in the field of deaf, multihandicapped. Psychology, sociology, family counselling, medicine, and related disciplines should address the problems of assessment and treatment. These pro-fessionals provide an objective framework within which the teachers' subjective evaluations can be most effective.

Transition

Working and dealing with the deaf, multihandicapped is very challenging and difficult. Endless concern for the successful and effective transition by the deaf, multihandi-capped child from the school environment into society often haunts the professionals in the field. Klein and Vernon (1982) mentioned that there are no provisions for post-secondary programs or further training programs for the rising deaf, multihandicapped population. Economic restraints create tremendous obstacles for the young adults in this group after leaving school. This concern also applies to many financial

problems dealing with handicapped children in general.
Federal law 94-142 (Education for all Handicapped Children),
as written, does not provide for these people after leaving
school.   There is an ongoing need for vocational rehabilitation, sheltered workshops, half-way houses, and other innova-
tive programs to help in the transition from school to society.
Concerned professions have, thus far, been shortsighted and
negligent in recognizing and addressing that problem.

Professional Interaction

Improvement of services to deaf, multihandicapped people
should be realized through regular professional interaction
to address problem areas.   Inservice training should not be
accepted as the only traditional vehicle to facilitate further
improvement.   Various sectors of the professions in the field
of exceptional/handicapped education, as well as rehabilitation, should interact at conventions, workshops and seminars.
The inclusion of deaf, multihandicapped professionals into
helping organizations or associations should not be ignored.

Monthly or bimonthly meetings and activities with various
professionals, including those working with the deaf, multihandicapped, should occur.   This should include educational
and psychological staff from state hospitals, treatment centers
and developmental centers.   Psychological and psychiatric
associations should also be included.   The emphasis should be
on intensive professional awareness and development.   Problems,
issues, concerns and experimental approaches should be
addressed as they apply to the best interests of the deaf,
multihandicapped.

Conclusion

In the late 1960s, we were told about the birth of a
large Rubella deaf population.   In the 1970s, we were told to
prepare for working with and teaching them.   Now, in the early
1980s, we are dealing with this population.   In the late 1980s,

as they leave school, minimal programming will have been
developed for them. We are reaching a point where there
needs to be critical questioning of our direction. In
addition, our task will become even more difficult due to
the predicted herpes-induced deaf, multihandicapped population coming in the next decade (Klein & Vernon, 1982).
Obviously, there is a valid need for immediate professional
action and interaction.

The challenging and frustrating field of the deaf,
multihandicapped will continue. It is going to evolve,
based on what we have been and are doing, as well as what
we should be doing next.

Discussion

I. RAPIN
How many teachers in the entire school are deaf? I
think that is tremendously important and needed, to have
professionals who are deaf working with the deaf. I agree
with you that a period of diagnostic observation is very
important. As a Neurologist, I am often asked to state the
potential and what the future is for a given child. I think
the most reliable method is to observe what the child can do.
You mentioned that it takes 4 weeks and sometimes 8 weeks. I
wonder whether that is really enough?

E. LaCOSSE
We have about 75 - 80 classroom teachers, not including
support service positions. How many teachers are deaf? I'm
not sure about the percentage, but I would say 35%, probably
a little bit more. In answer to your second question, really
4 weeks is not adequate. We are under Federal Public Law
No. 94-142. The law clearly says that you cannot continue,
you have to stop the child after 30 days of assessment. We
need to comply with the law. But, your point is well taken.
The important thing is to re-evaluate the child again. Some
abnormal children are so cute, they seem to be o.k., but when
the child gets bigger and starts to fight back, you realize
there's something wrong. You need to re-evaluate. Is something wrong neurologically, or is there something wrong
psychologically? We really need to look at each individual
child's problems every year.

References

Curriculum for the Development of Self-Awareness, Survival,
and Independent Living Skills, California School for the
Deaf, Fremont.

Klein, N., and Vernon, M., "Hearing Impaired in the 1980s,"
Hearing Aid Journal 35:17-19, 1982.

Special Unit Admission Policy, California School for the
Deaf, Fremont.

WORKING WITH PARENTS TOWARD ACCEPTANCE AND BEYOND

Sara C. McClain
Glenrose Hospital, Edmonton, Alberta

"Working with parents" includes counselling for emotional support, education (including clinic/home visits, and parent groups), and training in skills to use with the child. Matkin (1980) suggested that it is important for the parent to be present and involved in the audiological assessment. When a hearing loss is assessed and a preschool program for hearing impaired is monitoring the child and family during the first year of life, that is often the first non-medical habilitative service accessed.

Because the infant is wearing a hearing aid, the audiologist and the teacher of the hearing impaired or speech pathologist will continue to monitor the baby's use of the aid, level of response to sound, reactions to the care giver, and visual attending. At this stage, the work with the parent is ongoing, diagnostic treatment. The goal is to keep the aid on and working. It is not advisable at this stage to overwhelm parents by the presentation of great amounts of information (Stream & Stream, 1978; Moses, 1981). Cober-Ostby (1979), while providing guidelines for counsellors in an Arizona program for severely handicapped hearing impaired, developmentally disabled, made the point that, because of the usually long process of diagnosis, parents of these children move slowly through the stages of emotional response. At least a partial working through of the stages of the grieving process will likely be repeated at each new crises of the infant's development.

Parent-Child Programs

The parents should be asked to carry a notebook about and for their child. The teacher will use it to write things she wants the mother to observe regarding the infant's behaviour. The parents enter the child's responses, as well

as questions which arise between scheduled treatment periods.
These questions are answered as they occur. Parents are apt
to be very occupied and pre-occupied with all the usual and
special kinds of care which the infant requires.

Various combinations of home demonstration, clinic visits
and home visits, as well as group meetings, can address
aspects of parent training and counselling in a co-operative
framework. The atmosphere of the sessions should foster the
attitude that the parent is the prime care giver, the expert;
now, how can we accomplish the goals together. The crucial
element is a shared trust and shared observation, which
enables the parent to honestly evaluate what is seen in the
child's behaviour. One way of achieving this is in a small
group where 2 or 3 parents can alternately observe and interact with their own child, the other children, and with each
other.[1]

McInnes and Treffrey (1982), in their recent book on
deaf/blind children, have written not only for teachers and
interveners, but for families as well. They made the point
that a multiply sensorially impaired child requires programming 24 hours a day and, thus, the role of the parents must be
active.

To develop responsiveness in the child and to begin to
bring him into contact with his environment requires the co-
operative efforts of parents and teachers alike. Each small
gain is an achievement for all.

"...it is through the active, rather than the reactive
behaviour of the infant that cognition develops (Kaufman,
1979)." This interactive approach, a piagetian one, is the
focus of many programs today. The parent-infant interaction
program as described by Bromwich (1981), has much to recommend
it in the kinds of support that can be offered to parents.
It can be modified for use with multiply handicapped, hearing
impairec children. The parent centered approach as advocated
most eloquently by Luterman (1979), is another very effective
program for those who choose it. While, admittedly, not
universally applicable, it is a powerful way to help parents
toward useful advocacy for their children.

----

1   Preschool formats are discussed in Stromer & Miller (1982),
    and Simmons-Martin & Calvert (1979), and Simmons-Martin
    (1978).

Another approach to programming for deaf/blind is parent education based on an adult education model (Kershman, 1980). Although the competencies outlined by Kershman are important to parents, on looking back over years of experience, it seems as though the model lacks a developmental approach and places overwhelming demands on parents. The danger of parent "burnout" from attempting to accomplish too much too soon is a real danger.

Parents' groups are a strong element of support for those who are able to participate in them. They choose topics for monthly evening discussions and arrange social occasions. In addition, they contact and interact with other parent groups for information and action of mutual interest, and present information on needs to government.

Multiply handicapped infants will be involved with many hospital services. Parents grow slowly into a realization of the child's limitations. With additional diagnostic information, they may have to adjust their expectations again. They may need respite and ask for techniques for handling behaviour. There are surprising gains as some infants respond to the hearing aid or to physiotherapy programs. Because these changes are usually gradual, however, the teacher can provide information slowly, so that when decisions are necessary, they can be made by the parent with confidence and full comprehension of all the implications.

In a society where more and more mothers must work outside the home, nurturing is shared with a day care worker or babysitter. These individuals must be part of the counselling plan, along with the parents and the teacher. With many multiply handicapped, the social worker, speech pathologist, occupational therapist, and physiotherapist will be included in the planning and training. The role of the social worker may be very important in providing information to the parents with reference to appropriate day care settings, transportation, and access to other services of which the parents may not have any knowledge. The social worker is often involved in home visits.

Needs of families are different at various stages in the child's development. New crises - changes of environment, a new home, a new school, may precipitate feelings of a lack of

security. This may be manifested by sleep disturbances or
regression in behaviour, lessening of communication, or acting out, any and all of which require new adjustments by the
family. A change in environment or handling can also bring
about a positive change in the child once he understands what
is happening.

     The prevalence of behaviour problems in children with
hearing loss and another handicap (e.g. brain damage, language, vision, mental retardation), has been well documented.
It is suggested here that behaviour problems and, in some
cases, language learning, may be exacerbated by the sensory
deprivation which occurs when a child is not diagnosed or
aided until 2 years of age or even older. For that reason,
it is felt that late diagnosis should be treated as an
additional handicapping condition!!

Late Diagnosis

     Table I illustrates the additional handicapping effects
of late diagnosis. Of 28 preschool children with sensorineural hearing loss, aged 3 to 6 years, 5 are from bilingual
families (including 1 with a hearing impaired parent where
American Sign Language is the first language). In 2 of the
bilingual families, there is a hearing impaired sibling.
Language is not a problem in that the children are learning
English easily and well. Bilingual parents, in general,
seem very cognizant of the difficulties children may have in
learning language. Where there are cultural differences, the
greatest problem arises from a reluctance to discipline the
child or to do anything to control behaviour.

     Nine of the 28 children in our group have only one
parent in the home. Single parents are, in general, less
able to participate actively in the program; home books and
telephone are contact vehicles.

     Five of our 28 children have hearing impaired siblings.
Eight have some degree of language learning problems above
that expected from the hearing loss. Twenty were diagnosed
very late. Fourteen have problems of behaviour or tension,
at least 3 have motor involvement disorders, 1 has severe

TABLE I: Children with severe to profound hearing loss late diagnosed or aided, 3-6 years old

Child	Family Characteristics				Additional Problems			
	Single Parent	Bilingual	Sibling H.I.	Twin	Language Learning	Behaviour Attention	Sign	Anomalies
1	x				x	x		
2	x							
3	x		x		x	x		x
4	x		8					
5	x							
6	x				x			x
7	x							
8	x		4			x		x
9	x			x		x		
10	x							
11		x	x					
12p		x						
13	x	x						
14		ASL					x	
15p		x	x		x	x		x
16								
17					x	x		x
18						x		
19						x		x
20						x		
21	x					x		
22								
23p						x		
24p						x	x	
25								
26					x	x		
27p							x	
28p						x	x	

413

visual problems, and another has multiple congenital disorders. Upper respiratory infections and middle ear disease
are rampant in this population. Four primarily communicate
with sign.

From the pattern of the entries on the Table, the
multiple nature of the problems can be seen. In many cases,
earlier assessment and intervention and work with the parents
may have lessened behavioural and attention problems. This
has been demonstrated with other children, where a dramatic
turn-around in behaviour is seen after a short treatment time.
The problems caused by late diagnosis are compounded by
delays in achieving consistent use of a hearing aid, illustrated by Case 27 on Table I, a profoundly deaf, gifted child.
There is a definite influence from the child's earlier
behaviour patterns and the care-giver's lack of understanding
of the problem. Frankly, it is difficult to overcome the
patterns, habits and frustrations of years in just a few
months following identification and treatment.

By the age of 2 or even 3 or later, many of these
children have developed ways of dealing with parents, siblings
and others which are often characterized by tantruming,
screaming, and acting out. These are behaviours which
escalate and feed upon themselves. Eventually, the parents
feel they cannot take the child into a public place. This,
in turn, builds on the resentment already directed toward the
child from the others in the family, and increases the
parents' feelings of inadequacy. The child makes no progress
toward socially acceptable means of environmental control.

After diagnosis, hearing aid fitting, and initiation of
communication, one facet of parent training which becomes
extremely important in combating this devastating cycle is
behavioural management. This should include the importance
of consistent hearing aid use. Learning techniques analyzing
situations for their application and the consistency of their
use become important, not only for the child's development,
but also for parent preservation. "Reinforcement", "ignoring"
and "time out" must be learned. Incidentally, "ignoring" may
be hardest for the parent. Behavioural control is essential
as a prerequisite for giving and maintaining attention to
learning tasks. The child gains security from knowing what
to expect.

A communication system is one of the most crucial needs of the late diagnosed, hearing impaired child. It is the one method of controlling the environment in a positive fashion. Because late diagnosed children are so often frustrated by inability to express wants and emotions, it is often preferable to teach parent and child a brief sign vocabulary as an initial communication method, even in a situation where the child may have good potential for oral language and speech. Total communication is often instituted as the primary method of communication, particularly where the loss is profound. Staff should be alert for problems in language learning which may call for the application of a variety of additional procedures for language development.

Another pattern which is sometimes seen in late diagnosed children and which is, perhaps, more alarming to the teacher, is the child who is pleasant, co-operative and smiling, but who does not seem to have a communicative attitude. This does seem paradoxical, a charming child who is more difficult to teach than a stubborn, tantruming child. One explanation is that the smiling child has been babied and has learned by imitation. He has had everything done for him so he has not needed to communicate. The other child, the behavioural problem, is expressing frustration at not being able to communicate. He knows that something is missing. The key is to teach attention and beginning language as fast as possible to both children.

In at least one 4 year old in our group (number 6 on Table I), a severe language learning problem has been found in addition to that caused by the hearing loss. Initially, the child used jargon and echolalia, and failed to retain vocabulary, even when signed. Progress in any mode was excrutiatingly slow. This was complicated by difficulty with fine motor co-ordination. In this case, with a single working parent and a child who gained communication very slowly, it was necessary to demonstrate some deficits and some skills before the mother could become actively concerned in the child's problems. The mother was led to an awareness of the child's problems and her co-operation increased in proportion to her understanding. A breakthrough was made after it was demonstrated the boy could match printed forms. The association phonemic method was instituted. Of necessity, most of the work falls upon the teaching staff. The child is still progressing slowly, but at least he is progressing.

Another little girl who was not aided until 3 years was
a Rubella child with a severe loss. She readily identified
environmental sounds but did not develop language. Progress
with speech sounds was slow and sporadic. By age 4 1/2,
behaviour was characterized by screaming and tantruming. In
a behaviour modification program at the Glenrose Hospital, it
was determined that, in spite of good aided hearing, speech
had no meaning for her. Sign was instituted and she learned
rapidly. The parents learned sign and reported life to be
easier at home (and in the neighbourhood), as lessened frustration made tantrums and screaming unnecessary. This child was
taught symbol-sound association and began to develop speech.
The program aided reading skills and added meaning to listening. The child was then able to use total communication.

Meadow (1980) has suggested that "...even if we assume
that children who acquire language late can 'catch up', both
linguistically and cognitively, there is still the question
of their need to 'catch up' on the social and emotional tasks
that are gained through symbolic interaction (the use of
language) with their parents". She goes on to say, "Perhaps
one of the ingredients of a successful early education program
is a staff of people trained in coping with the emotional
responses of parents. Some of the most successful preschool
teachers of the deaf are those who are willing to listen week
after week to parents expressing their disappointment, anger,
and sadness. Only then can the speech and language lessons
proceed."

If teachers and parents can begin interactive communication development in infancy, the likelihood of severe behavioural problems by school age should be lessened. Early
assessment and intervention must be viewed as preventative of
some additional problems, as well as habilitative.

The Gifted Hearing Impaired

The final comment in this paper is concerned with a
minority of a minority - the gifted, hearing impaired child.
Today, the opportunities for further education for deaf
students are very limited, particularly in Canada. Post
secondary education has become much more available in the

United States in the last 12 or so years. This is surely an
area where activist parents of deaf children in Canada have
a fertile field for exploration. If it is the case, as
Meadow (1980) suggests, that moving from one community or
subculture to another is desirable for community leaders,
whether hearing or deaf, then education should encourage
communication skills to make such mobility possible. Meadow
has suggested that community leaders of the deaf are apt to be
fluent in their use of spoken and signed English, as well as
ASL. For hearing families, signed English can be a realistic
goal if they wish to aid their gifted deaf child. The child
will probably learn ASL as well.

Quality education for the gifted deaf child should
foster high levels in reading and writing as keys to academic
excellence. This means high levels of achievement in English,
of which speech should be a part.

Discussion

K. MURPHY
When Larchmore School was in existence in England, it
was a school for emotionally disturbed children. We did a
survey at that school. At that time, the approach to
language in English schools was a little confusing. That is
to say, they practiced covert manualism. In that particular
school there was freedom to use manualism, and there were
children who not only were not good speakers, but were not
good signers. We decided to investigate to determine, if we
could, what lay behind this incapacity. We used 3 tests,
one of visual perception, one of visual motor function, and
one of fine motor function. In all 3, 64% had significant
deficits, and those children with the greatest deficits in
all 3 were also the least successful in any language medium –
spoken or signed.

References

Bromwich, R., Working with Parents and Infants (Baltimore:
    University Park Press), 1981.

Cober-Ostby, C., "Introductory Guidelines for Counselors," Model Demonstration Program University of Arizona, 1979.

Kaufman, B.A., "Summary Impressions," Parent-Infant Intervention: Communication Disorders (New York: Grune & Stratton, Inc.), Simmons-Martin, A., & Calvert, D. (Eds.), 1979.

Kershman, S.M., "The Training Needs of Parents of Deaf-Blind Multihandicapped Children - Part One: The Parent Competencies," Education of the Visually Handicapped 13:98-108, 1982.

Luterman, D., Counselling Parents of Hearing-Impaired Children (Boston: Little, Brown & Co.), 1979.

Matkin, N.D., "A Critical Assessment of Current Practices in the Audiologic Management of Preschool Children," Speech Assessment and Speech Improvement for the Hearing Impaired (Washington, D.C.: A.G. Bell Association), J. Subtelny (Ed.), 1980.

McInnes, J.M., and Treffrey, J., Deaf-Blind Infants and Children (Toronto: University of Toronto Press), 1982.

Meadow, K., Deafness and Child Development (Berkeley: University of California Press), 1981.

Moses, K.L., and Van Hecke-Wulatin, M., "The Socio-Emotional Impact of Infant Deafness: A Counselling Model," Early Management of Hearing Loss (New York: Grune & Stratton, Inc.), Mencher, G., & Gerber, S. (Eds.), 1981.

Murphy, A.T., (Ed.), "The Families of Hearing Impaired Children," The Volta Review, Vol. 81, No. 5, 1979.

Schlesinger, H.S., and Meadow, K.P., Sound and Sign (Berkeley: University of California Press), 1972.

Simmons-Martin, A., "Early Management Procedures for the Hearing Impaired Child," Pediatric Audiology (Englewood Cliffs: Prentice-Hall, Inc.), Martin, F.N. (Ed.), 1978.

Simmons-Martin, A., and Calvert, D. R., Parent-Infant Intervention (New York: Grune & Stratton), 1979.

Stream, R.W., and Stream, K.S., "Counselling the Parents of the Hearing Impaired Child," Pediatric Audiology (Englewood Cliffs: Prentice-Hall, Inc.), Martin, F.N. (Ed.), 1978.

Stromer, R., and Miller, J., Severely Handicapped Hearing Impaired Students: Strengthening Service Delivery (Baltimore: P. Brookes), 1982.

BIBLIOGRAPHY

Aase, J.M., Wilson, A.C., and Smith, D.W., "Small Ears in Down's Syndrome: A Helpful Diagnostic Aid," Journal of Pediatrics 82:845-847, 1973.

Achor, L. J. and Starr, A., "Auditory Brainstem Responses in the Cat: I. Intracranial and Extracranial Recordings," Electroencephalography and Clinical Neurophysiology 48:154-173, 1980.

Ajuriaguerra, J. de. and Abensur, J., "Desordres Psychopathologiques Chez l'Enfant Sourd," Psychiatric Enfant, pp. 217-244, 1972.

Altshuler, K.Z., "Personality Traits and Depressive Symptoms in the Deaf," In Wurtis, J. (Ed.), Recent Advances in Biological Psychiatry, Volume VI (New York: Plenum Press), 1964.

Altshuler, K.Z., Deming, W.E., Vollenweider, J., Rainer, J.D., and Tendler, R., "Impulsivity and Profound Early Deafness: A Cross Cultural Inquiry," American Annals of the Deaf 121:331-345, 1976.

ASHA, Joint Committee on Infant Hearing (Position Statement) Asha, 1982.

Anderson, F.W., "Symposium on Cerebral Palsy: Part I. Obstetrical Factors in Cerebral Palsy," Journal of Pediatrics 40:340-375, 1952.

Auletta, K., "A Reporter at Large - The Underclass," New Yorker, Nov. 16, 23, 30, 1981.

Ault, R.L., Children's Cognitive Development (New York: Oxford University Press), 1977.

Bailey, J. and Meyerson, L., "Vibration as a Reinforcer with the Profoundly Retarded Child," Journal of Applied Behavioral Analysis 2:135-137, 1969.

Balkany, T., "Otologic Aspects of Down's Syndrome," Seminars in Speech, Language and Hearing 1:39-48, 1980.

Balkany, T., Downs, M.P., Jafek, B.W., and Krajicek, M.J., "Hearing Loss in Down's Syndrome," Clinical Pediatrics 18:116-118, 1979.

Banik, N.L., Davidson, A.N., Palo, J., and Savolainen, H., "Biochemical Studies of Myelin Isolated from the Brains of Patients with Down's Syndrome," Brain 98:213-218, 1975.

Baratz, S.S. and Baratz, J.C., "Early Childhood Intervention: The Social Science Base of Institutional Racism," Harvard Educational Review 40:29-50, 1970.

Barnard, K.E., "Infant Stimulation," In Koch, R. and de la Cruz, F.F. (Eds.), Down's Syndrome (Mongolism): Research, Prevention and Management (New York: Brunner/Mazel), 1975.

Barnes, G.W. and Kish, G.B., "Reinforcing Effects of Manipulation in Mice," Journal of Comparative and Physiological Psychology 54:713-715, 1961.

Barnet, A.B. and Lodge, A., "Click-evoked Responses in Normal and Developmentally Retarded Infants," Nature 214:252-255, 1967.

Barnet, A.B., Ohlrich, E.S., and Shanks, B.L., "EEG Evoked Responses to Repetitive Auditory Stimulation in Normal and Down's Syndrome Infants," Developmental Medicine and Child Neurology 13:321-329, 1971.

Barnet, A.B., Ohlrich, E.S., Weiss, I.P., and Shanks, B., "Auditory Evoked Potentials During Sleep in Normal Children from Ten Days to Three Years of Age," Electroencephalography and Clinical Neurophysiology 39:29-41, 1975.

Barr, B., "Pure Tone Audiometry for Preschool Children," Acta Oto-laryngologica (Stockholm), Supplement #121, 1953.

Barr, B., Stensland-Junker, K., and Svard, M., "Early Discovery of Hearing Impairment: A Critical Evaluation of the BOEL Test," Audiology 17:62-67, 1978.

Basel, K.E. and Quigley, S.P., "Influence of Certain Language and Communication Environments in Early Childhood on the Development of Language in Deaf Individuals," Journal of Speech and Hearing Research 20:81-94, 1977.

Bayshear, S.R., "The Use of Tympanometry for Screening Developmentally Disabled Childen," Audiology and Hearing Education 2:35-40, 1976.

Bereiter, C. and Engleman, S., Teaching Disadvantaged Children in Preschool (Englewood Cliffs, New Jersey: Prentice-Hall), 1966.

Bernstein, B., "Social Structure, Language, and Learning," In DeCecco, J.P. (Ed.), The Psychology of Language, Thought and Instruction (New York: Holt, Rinehart & Winston), 1967.

Bernstein, B., (Ed.), Class, Codes and Control: Vol. 1, Theoretical Studies Towards a Sociology of Language (London: Routledge & Kegan), 1971.

Biber, B., "A Developmental-Interaction Approach: Bank Street College of Education," In Day, M.C. and Parker, T.K. (Eds.), The Preschool in Action: Exploring Early Childhood Programs (Boston: Allyn & Bacon), Day, M.C., & Parker, T.K. (Eds.), 1977.

Bigum, H.B., Dustman, R.E., and Beck, E.C., "Visual and Somatosensory Evoked Responses from Mongoloid and Normal Children," Electroencephalography and Clinical Neurophysiology 28:576-585, 1970.

Bilovsky, D. and Schare, J., "The ITPA and Down's Syndrome: An Exploratory Study," American Journal of Mental Deficiency 70:78-82, 1965.

Blackwell, P.M., Engen, E., Fischrund, J., and Zarcadoolas, C., Sentences and Other Systems: A Language and Learning Curriculum for Hearing-Impaired Children (Washington, D.C.: A.G. Bell Association), 1978.

Blager, F.B., "Speech and Language Development of Down's Syndrome Children," Seminars in Speech, Language and Hearing 1:63-73, 1980.

Blank, M., "Cognitive Functions of language in the Preschool Years," Developmental Psychology 10:229-245, 1974.

Bloom, L., Language Development: Form and Function in Emerging Grammars (Cambridge, Massachusetts: M.I.T. Press), 1970.

Bloom, L. and Lahey, M., Language Development and Language Disorders (New York: John Wiley & Sons), 1978.

Bloom, L., Lifter, K., and Broughton, J., "What Children Say and What They Know: Exploring the Relations Between Product and Process in the Development of Early Words and Early Concepts," In Stark, R.E. (Ed.), Language Behavior in Infancy and Early Childhood (New York: Elsevier North Holland), 1981.

Booth, L.L., Lasky, E.Z., and Kricos, P.B., "Comparison of the Language Abilities of Deaf Children and Young Deaf Adults," American Annals of the Deaf 15:10-16, 1981.

Boothroyd, A., Hearing Impairments in Young Children (Englewood Cliffs, New Jersey: Prentice-Hall), 1982.

Borbely, A.A. and Hall, R.D., "Effects of Pentobarbitone and Chlorpromazine on Acoustically Evoked Potentials in the Rat," Neuropharmacology 9:575-586, 1970.

Borg, E., "Dynamic Characteristics of the Intra Muscle Reflex," In Feldman, A. and Wilber, L. (Eds.), Acoustic Impedance and Admittance - The Measurement of Middle Ear Effusion (Baltimore: Williams and Wilkins Co.), 1976.

Bowlby, J., _Attachment and Loss: Volume I (Attachment)_ (New York: Basic Books), 1969.

Bows, J., "Acoustic Impedance Measurement with Hard of Hearing Mentally Retarded Children," _Journal of Mental Deficiency Research_ 16:196-202, 1972.

Bradley, R.H. and Caldwell, B.M., "The Relation of Infants' Home Environments to Mental Test Performance at Fifty-Four Months: A Follow-up Study," _Child Development_ 47:81-94, 1976.

Brady, J.V., "Temporal and Emotional Factors Related to Electrical Self Stimulation of the Limbic System," In Jasper, H.H. (Ed.), _Reticular Formation of the Brain_ (Boston: Little, Brown & Co.), 1958.

Branemark, P-I., Breine, U., Adell, R., Hansson, B.D., Lindstrom, J., and Ohlsson, A., "Intraosseous Anchorage of Dental Prosthesis: I. Experimental Studies," _Scandinavian Journal of Plastic and Reconstructive Surgery_ 3:81-100, 1969.

Branemark, P-I., Hansson, B-O., Adell, R., Breine, U., Lindstrom, J., Hallen, O., and Olman, A., "Osseointegrated Implants in the Treatment of the Endentlous Jaw," _Scandinavian Journal of Plastic and Reconstructive Surgery_ (Volume 11, Supplement #16), 1977.

Bricker, D.D. and Bricker, W.A., "A Programmed Approach to Operant Audiology for Low-functioning Children," _Journal of Speech and Hearing Disorders_ 34:312-320, 1969.

Brooks, D.N., Wooley, H., and Kanjilal, G.C., "Hearing Loss and Middle Ear Disorders in Patients with Down's Syndrome (Mongolism)," _Journal of Mental Deficiency Research_ 16:21-29, 1972.

Bromwich, R., _Working with Parents and Infants_ (Baltimore: University Park Press), 1981.

Brown, C., _My Left Foot_ (London: Pan), 1972.

Budden, S.S., Robinson, G.C., MacLean, C.D., and Cambon, K.G., "Deafness in Infants and Preschool Children: An analysis of Etiology and Associated Handicaps," _American Annals of the Deaf_ 119:387-395, 1974.

Burchard, E.M. and Myklebust, H.R., "A Comparison of Congenital and Adventitious Deafness with Respect to its Effect on Intelligence, Personality, and Social Maturity," _American Annals of the Deaf_ 87:140-154, 342-360, 1942.

Byrne, D.J. and Stevens, C.P., "Mentally Handicapped Childen's Response to Vibrotactile and Other Stimuli as Evidence for the Existence of a Sensory Hierarchy," _Apex Journal of the British Institute of Mental Handicaps_ 8:96-98, 1980.

Campbell, C.W., Polomeno, R.C., Elder, J.M., Murray, J., and Altosar, A., "Importance of an Eye Examination in Identifying the Cause of Congenital Hearing Impairment," <u>Journal of Speech and Hearing Disorders</u> 46:258-261, 1981.

Carlson, F., "A Format for Selecting Vocabulary for the Non-Speaking Child," <u>Language, Speech and Hearing Services in the Schools</u> 12:240-245, 1981.

Carr, J., "Mental and Motor Development in Young Mongol Children," <u>Journal of Mental Deficiency Research</u> 14:205-220, 1970.

Cazden, C., <u>Child Language and Education</u> (New York: Holt, Rinehart & Winston), 1972.

Cazden, C.B., Baratz, J.C., Labov, W., and Palmer, F.H., "Language Development in Day Care Programs," In Grotberg, E.H. (Ed.), <u>Day Care: Resources for Decisions</u> (Washington, D.C.: Office of Economic Opportunity, Government Printing Office) 1971.

Chess, S., Korn, S.J., and Fernandez, P.B., <u>Psychiatric Disorders of Children with Congenital Rubella</u> (New York: Brunner/Mazel), 1971.

Chomsky, N., <u>Language and the Mind</u> (New York: Harcourt, Brace, Jovanovich), 1968.

Clark-Stewart, K.A., "Interactions Between Mothers and Their Young Children: Characteristics and Consequences," <u>Monographs of the Society for Research in Child Development</u> 38 (6-7, Serial No. 153), 1973.

Cober-Ostby, C., "Introductory Guidelines for Counselors," <u>Model Demonstration Program</u> University of Arizona, 1979.

Cohen, M.M. and Rapin, I., "Evoked Potential Audiometry in Neurologically Impaired Childen, In Naunton, R. and Zerlin, S. (Eds.), <u>Evoked Electrical Activity in the Auditory Nervous System</u> (New York: Academic Press), 1978.

Coleman, C.L., Cook, A.M., and Myers, L.S., "Assessing Non-Oral Clients for Assistive Communication Devices," <u>Journal of Speech and Hearing Disorders</u> 45:515-526, 1980.

Coleman, M., "Down's Syndrome," <u>Pediatric Annals</u> 7:36-63, 1978.

Coleman, M., Schwartz, R.H., and Schwartz, D.M., "Otologic Manifestations in Down's Syndrome," <u>Down's Syndrome Papers and Abstracts for Professionals</u> 2:1, 1979.

Collins-Ahlgren, M., "Teaching English as a Second Language to Young Deaf Children," <u>Journal of Speech and Hearing Disorders</u> 39:486-500, 1974.

Collins-Ahlgren, M.,   "Language Development of Two Deaf
   Children," American Annals of the Deaf 120:524-539, 1975.

Collins, J.L., Communication Between Deaf Children of Pre-School
   Age and Their Mothers (Unpublished Ph.D. dissertation,
   University of Pittsburgh), 1969.

Connelly, C. and Oviatt, D., "Physiologic Measures in Pediatric
   Audiology," Human Communication 4:299-305, 1979.

Connor, F.P., Williamson, G.C., and Siepp, J.M., Program Guide
   for Infants and Toddlers with Neuromotor and Other
   Developmental Disabilities (New York: Columbia University
   Press), 1978.

Coopersmith, S.,   The Antecedents of Self-Esteem (San Francisco:
   W.H. Freeman), 1967.

Cornett, R.O.,   "Cued Speech," American Annals of the Deaf
   112:3-13, 1967.

Corsaro, W., "The Development of Social Cognition in Preschool
   Children: Implications for Language Learning," Language
   Disorders 2:77-95, 1981.

Creedon, M.P., Appropriate Behavior Through Communication: A
   New Program in Simultaneous Language for Non-Verbal Childen
   (Chicago: Dysfunctioning Child Center Publications), 1973.

Crome, L.and Stern, J., Pathology of Mental Retardation
   (Baltimore: Williams and Wilkins Co.), 1972.

Crome, L., Cowie, W., and Slater, E.,   "A Statistical Note on
   Cerebellar and Brainstem Weight in Mongolism," Journal of
   Mental Deficiency Research 10:69-72, 1966.

Culatta, B. and Culatta, R.,   "Spina Bifida Children's Non-
   Communicative Language: Examples and Identification
   Guidelines," Allied Health and Behavioral Sciences 1:22-29,
   1978.

Curriculum for the Development of Self-Awareness, Survival, and
   Independent Living Skills, California School for the Deaf,
   Fremont.

Dahle, A.J. and Daly, D.A., "Tangible Rewards in Assessing Auditory
   Discrimination Performance of Mentally Retarded Children,"
   American Journal of Mental Deficiency 78-625-630, 1974.

Dahle, A.J., McCollister, F.P., Stagno, S., Reynolds, D.W., and
   Hoffman, H.E., "Progressive Hearing Impairment in Children
   with Congenital Cytomegalovirus Infection," Journal of Speech
   and Hearing Disorders 44:220-229, 1979.

Danella, E.A., "A Study of Tactile Preference in Multiply Handicapped Children," _American Journal of Occupational Therapy_ 27:457-463, 1973.

Davis, G.L., "Clinical Cytomegalovirus and Hearing Loss: Clinical and Experimental Observations," _Laryngoscope_ 89:1681-1688, 1979.

Davis, H., "The Young Deaf Child: Identification and Management," _Acta Otolaryngologica (Supplement 206)_, pp 33-52, 1965.

Davis, H., "Principles of Electric Response Audiometry," _Annals of Otology, Rhinology, and Laryngology_ Volume 85, Supplement #85, 1976.

Davis, H., "Abnormal Hearing and Deafness," In Davis, H. & Silverman, S.R. (Eds.), _Hearing and Deafness_ (4th ed.) (New York: Holt, Rinehart & Winston), 1978.

Davis, H. and Onishi, S., "Maturation of Auditory Evoked Potentials," _International Audiology_ 8:24-33, 1969.

Dee, A., Rapin, I., and Ruben, R.J., "Speech and Language Development in a Parent-Infant Total Communication Program," _Annals of Otology, Rhinology, and Laryngology_, In Press.

Despland, P.A. and Galambos, R., "The Auditory Brainstem Response (ABR) is a Useful Diagnostic Tool in the Intensive Care Nursery," _Pediatric Research_ 14:154-158, 1980.

DiCarlo, L.M., _The Deaf_ (Englewood Cliffs, New Jersey: Prentice-Hall), 1964.

DiCarlo, L. and Bradley, W., "A Simplified Test for Infants and Young Children," _Laryngoscope_ 71:628-646, 1961.

Dicks-Mireaux, M.J., "Mental Development of Infants with Down's Syndrome," _American Journal of Mental Deficiency_ 77:26-32, 1972.

Diebold, A.R., Jr., "The Consequences of Early Bilingualism in Cognitive Development and Personality Formation," Paper prepared for the Symposium, _The Study of Personality: An Interdisciplinary Appraisal_ (Rice University, Houston, Texas), 1966.

DiFrancesca, S., _Academic Achievement Test Results of a National Testing Program for Hearing Impaired Students, United States: Spring, 1971 -Series D, Number 9_ (Washington, D.C.: Office of Demographic Studies, Gallaudet College), 1972.

DiFrancesca, S. and Carey, S., _Item Analysis of an Achievement Testing Program for Hearing Impaired Students, United States: Spring, 1971-Series D, Number 8_ (Washington, D.C.: Office of Demographic Studies, Gallaudet College), 1972.

Dix, M.R. and Hallpike, C.S., "The Peepshow: A New Technique for Pure-tone Audiometry in Young Children," British Medical Journal 2:719-723, 1947.

Dore, J., "A Pragmatic Description of Early Language Development," Journal of Psycholinguistic Research 3:343-350, 1974.

Down, J.L., "Observations on Ethnic Classifications," London Hospital Reports 3:259-262, 1866.

Downs, M.P., "Audiometry in Children," International Audiology 1:268-270, 1947.

Downs, M.P., "The Expanding Imperative of Early Identification," In Bess, F.H. (Ed.), Childhood Deafness: Causation, Assessment and Management (New York: Grune & Stratton, Inc.), 1977.

Downs, M.P., "The Hearing of Down's Individuals," Seminars in Speech, Language & Hearing 1:25-38, 1980.

Downs, M.P. and Sterritt, G.M., "Identification Audiometry for Neonates: A Preliminary Report," Journal of Auditory Research 4:69-80, 1964.

Dublin, W.B., "The Auditory Pathology of Anoxia," Otolaryngology 86:27-39, 1978.

Eilers, R.E., Wilson, W.R., and Moore, J.M., "Developmental Changes in Speech Discrimination in Infants," Journal of Speech and Hearing Research 20:766-780, 1977.

Eilers, R.E. and Oller, D.K., "A Comparative Study of Speech Perception in Young Severely Retarded Children and Normally Developing Infants," Journal of Speech and Hearing Research 23:419-428, 1980.

Eisele, W.A., Berry, R.C., and Shriner, T.H., "Infant Sucking Response Patterns as a Conjugate Function of Changes in Sound Pressure Level of Auditory Stimuli," Journal of Speech and Hearing Research 18:296-307, 1975.

Eppstein, J., No Music By Request (Melbourne: Collins), 1979.

Erickson, E., Childhood and Society (New York: Norton Press), 1963.

Evans, D., "The Development of Language Abilities in Mongols: A Correlational Study," Journal of Mental Deficiency Research 21:103-117, 1977.

Eviatar, L., Miranda, S., Eviatar, A., Freeman, K., and Borkowski, M., "Development of Nystagmus in Response to Vestibular Stimulation in Infants," Annals of Neurology 5:508-514, 1979.

Ewing, I.R. and Ewing, A.W.G., "The Ascertainment of Deafness in Infancy and Early Childhood," _Journal of Laryngology and Otology_ 59:309-333, 1944.

Flathouse, V.E., "Multiply Handicapped Deaf Children and Public Law 94-142," _Exceptional Children_ 45:560-565, 1979.

Foale, M. and Patterson, J.W., "Hearing of Mental Defectives," _American Journal of Mental Deficiency_ 59-264-258, 1954.

Folsom, R.C., Widen, J.E., and Wilson, W.R., "Auditory Brainstem Responses in Down's Syndrome Infants," Work in Progress (1983).

Frailberg, S., _Clinical Studies in Infant Mental Health: The First Year of Life_ (New York: Basic Books, Inc.), 1980.

Fraser, F.C. and Haiai, F., "Frequency of the Brachio-oto-renal (BOR) Syndrome in Children with Profound Hearing Loss," _American Journal of Medical Genetics_ 7:341-349, 1980.

Freeman, R.D., Carbin, C.F., and Boese, R.J., _Can't Your Child Hear? - A Guide for Those Who Care About Deaf Children_ (Baltimore: University Park Press), 1981.

Friedrich, B.W., "Clinical Evaluation of Hearing in Developmentally Disabled Children," _Audiology Journal of Continuing Education-Tapes_ (New York: Grune & Stratton, Inc.), Vol., 5, No. 8, 1980.

Fristoe, M. and Lloyd, L., "A Survey of the Use of Non-Speech Systems with the Severely Communication Impaired," _Mental Retardation_ 16:104-107, 1978.

Fulton, R.T., "Standard Pure Tone and Bekesy Audiometric Measures with the Mentally Retarded," _American Journal of Mental Deficiency_ 72:60-73, 1967.

Fulton, R.T., Gorzycki, P.A., and Hull, W.L., "Hearing Assessment with Young Children," _Journal of Speech and Hearing Disorders_ 40:397-404, 1975.

Fulton, R.T. and Graham, J.D., "Conditioned Orientation Reflex Audiometry with the Mentally Retarded," _American Journal of Mental Deficiency_ 70:703-708, 1966.

Fulton, R.T. and Lamb, L.E., "Acoustic Impedance and Tympanometry with the Retarded: A Normative Study," _Audiology_ 11:199-208, 1972.

Fulton, R.T and Lloyd, L.L., "Hearing Impairment in a Population of Children with Down's Syndrome," _American Journal of Mental Deficiency_ 73:298-302, 1968.

Fulton, R.T. and Lloyd, L.L., _Auditory Assessment of the Difficult-to-Test_ (Baltimore: Williams & Wilkins Co.), 1975.

Fulwiler, R.L. and Fouts, R.S., "Acquisition of American Sign Language by a Noncommunicating Autistic Child," _Journal of Autism and Childhood Schizophrenia_ 6:43-51, 1976.

Furth, H.G., "A Comparison of Reading Test Norms of Deaf and Hearing Children," _American Annals of the Deaf_ 111:461-462, 1966.

Furth, H.G., "A Review and Perspective on the Thinking of Deaf People," In Hellmuth, J. (Ed.), _Cognitive Studies_ (New York: Brunner/Mazel), Hellmuth, J. (Ed.), 1970.

Furth, H., _Deafness and Learning: A Psychological Approach_ (Belmont, California: Wadsworth Press), 1973.

Galambos, R., "Use of ABR in Infant Testing," In Gerber, S.E. and Mencher, G.T. (Eds.), _Early Diagnosis of Hearing Loss_ (New York: Grune & Stratton, Inc.), 1978.

Galambos, R. and Despland, P., "The Auditory Brainstem Responses (ABR) Evaluates Risk Factors for Hearing Loss in the Newborn," _Pediatric Research_ 14:159-163, 1980.

Galambos, R., Hicks, G., and Wilson, J.J., "Hearing Loss in Graduates of a Tertiary Intensive Care Nursery," _Ear and Hearing_ 3:87-90, 1982.

Gelatt, J.P., Cherow, E., Holzhoure, E., and Schultz, J., _Hearing Impaired Developmentally Disabled Children and Adolescents: An Interdisciplinary Look at a Special Population_ (Washington, D.C.: American Speech-Language-Hearing Association), 1982.

Gentile, A. and DeFrancesca, S., _Academic Achievement Test Performance of Hearing Impaired Students, United States: Spring, 1969_ (Washington, D.C.: Office of Demographic Studies, Gallaudet College), 1969.

Gerber, S.E., "Communicative Disorders and Asphyxia Neonatorum," Paper Presented to the XVth International Congress of Audiology, Krakow, Poland, September, 1980.

Gerber, S.E. and Mencher, G.T., _Auditory Dysfunction_ (Houston: College-Hill Press), 1980.

Gerber, S.E. and Mencher, G.T. (Eds.), _Early Diagnosis of Hearing Loss_ (New York: Grune & Stratton, Inc.), 1978.

Giles, S., "The Early Education Program of United Cerebral Palsy of New York City," _Communication Outlook_ 3:8, 1982.

Gladwin, T., Poverty U.S.A. (Boston: Little, Brown & Co.), 1967.

Gleason, J. and Weintraub, S., "The Acquisition of Routines in Child Language," Journal of the Linguistic Society 5:129-136, 1976.

Gliddon, J.B., Busk, J., and Galbraith, J.C., "Visual Evoked Responses as a Function of Light Intensity in Down's Syndrome and Nonretarded Subjects," Psychophysiology 12:416-422, 1975.

Glovsky, L., "Audiological Assessment of a Mongoloid Population," Training School Bulletin 63:27-36, 1966.

Golden, M., Birns, B., Bridger, W., and Moss, A., "Social-Class Differentiation in Cognitive Development Among Black Preschool Children," Child Development 42:37-45, 1971.

Goldin-Meadow, S., The Representation of Semantic Relations in a Manual language Created by Deaf Children of Hearing Parents: A Language You Can't Dismiss out of Hand (Unpublished Doctoral Dissertation, University of Pennsylvania, College Park, Pennsylvania), 1975.

Goodhill, V., Personal Correspondence, 1978.

Goodman, L. and Kroc, R., "A Classroom Sign Communication Program for the Severely Handicapped," Language, Speech and Hearing Services in the Schools 12:233-239, 1981.

Goss, R.N., "Language Used by Mothers of Deaf Children and Mothers of Hearing Children," American Annals of the Deaf 115:93-96, 1970.

Gould, H.J., "Aspects of Hearing in Craniofacial Malformation," Audiology Journal of Continuing Education -Tapes (New York: Grune & Stratton, Inc.), Vol. 4, No. 5, 1978.

Graham, F.K., Ernhart, C.B., Thurston, D.B., and Craft, M., "Development Three Years After Perinatal Anoxia and Other Potentially Damaging Newborn Experiences," Psychological Monographs 76:522, 1962.

Green, D.D., "The Peep-Show: A Simple, Inexpensive Modification of the Peep Show," Journal of Speech and Hearing Disorders 23:118-120, 1958.

Greenberg, D.B., Wilson, W.R., Moore, J.M., and Thompson, G., "Visual Reinforcement Audiometry (VRA) with Young Down's Syndrome Children," Journal of Speech and Hearing Disorders 43:448-458, 1978.

Greenberg, M., "Social Interaction Between Deaf Preschoolers and Their Mothers," Developmental Psychology 16:465-474, 1980.

Greenberg, M. and Marvin, R., "Attachment Patterns in Profoundly Deaf Preschool Children," Merrill-Palmer Quarterly 25:265-279, 1979.

Gregory, S., The Deaf Child and His Family (London: George Allen & Urwin), 1976.

Grey, H.A., D'Asaro, M.J., and Sklar, M., "Auditory Perceptual Thresholds in Brain Injured Childen," Journal of Speech and Hearing Research 8:45-56, 1965.

Guberina, P. and Asp, C., The Verbo-Tonal Method (New York: World Rehabilitation Fund Monographs), 1981.

Haggstrom, W.C., "The Power of the Poor," In Riessman, F., Cohen, J., & Pearl, A. (Eds.), Mental Health of Poor (New York: Free Press), 1964.

Hall, J.W., "Hearing Loss Prediction by the Acoustic Reflex in a Young Population: Comparison of Seven Methods," International Journal of Pediatric Otorhinolaryngology 3:225-243, 1981.

Halliday, M.A., Exploration in the Functions of Grammar (London: Arnold Publishing), 1973.

Hakansson, B., Tjellstrom, A., and Rosenhall, U., "Psychoacoustic Measurements with the Bone-Anchored Hearing Aid," In Preparation, 1983.

Hammarstedt, B. and Amcoff, S., Integration of Hearing Impaired Children in Comprehensive School (In Swedish) (Uppsala: Pedagogic Institution, Uppsala University), 1979.

Hanshaw, J.B., "School Failure and Deafness After 'Silent' Congenital Cytomegalovirus Infection," New England Journal of Medicine 295:468-470, 1976.

Harada, T. and Sando, I., "Temporal Bone Histopathologic Findings in Down's Syndrome," Archives of Otolaryngology 107:96-103, 1981.

Hardy, J.B., Dougherty, A., and Hardy, W.G., "Hearing Responses and Audiologic Screening in Infants," Journal of Pediatrics 55:382-390, 1959.

Hardy, W.G. and Bordley, J.W., "Problems in the Diagnosis and Management of the Multiply Handicapped," Archives of Otolaryngology 98-269-274, 1973.

Harlow, H.F., "Primary Affectional Patterns in Primates," American Journal of Orthopsychiatry 30:676-684, 1960.

Harris, R.I., "Impulse Control in Deaf Children: Research and Clinical Issues," In Liben, L.D. (Ed.), Deaf Children: Developmental Perspectives (New York: Academic Press), 1978.

Hayden, A.H. and Haring, N.G., "The Acceleration and Maintenance of Developmental Gains in Down's Syndrome School-age Children," In Mittler, P. (Ed.), Research to Practice in Mental Retardation: Care and Intervention -Volume 1 (Baltimore: University Park Press), 1977.

Hecox, K. and Galambos, R., "Brainstem Auditory Evoked Responses in Human Infants and Adults," Archives of Otolaryngology 99:30-33, 1974.

Hecox, K.E., Cone, B., and Blair, M.E., "Brainstem Auditory Evoked Response in the Diagnosis of Pediatric Neurology Diseases," Neurology 31:832-840, 1981.

Heider, F. and Heider, G.M., "Studies in the Psychology of the Deaf," Psychological Monographs, Volume 53, No. 242, 1941.

Heider, G.M., "Adjustment Problems of the Deaf Child," Nervous Child 7:38-44, 1948.

Heimer, C.B., Cutler, R., and Freedman, A.M., "Neurological Sequelae of Premature Birth," American Journal of Diseases of Children 108:122-123, 1964.

Henderson, F.W., Collier, A.M., Sanyal, M.A., Watkins, J.M., Fairclough, D.L, Clyde, W.A., and Denny, F.W., "A Longitudinal Study of Respiratory Viruses and Bacteria in the Etiology of Acute Otitis Media with Effusion," The New England Journal of Medicine 306:1377-1383, 1982.

Hermelin, B. and O'Connor, N., "Like and Cross Modality Responses in Normal and Subnormal Children," Quarterly Journal of Experimental Psychology 12:48-53, 1960.

Hess, R.D.and Shipman, V.C., "Early Experience on the Socialization of Cognitive Modes in Children," Child Development 34:869-886, 1965.

Hetherington, J., Uncommon Men (Melbourne: Cheshire), 1965.

Hicks, W.M. and Pfau, G.S., "Deaf-Visually Impaired Persons: Incidence and Services," American Annals of the Deaf 124:76-92, 1979.

Higashi, Y., Yasui, M., Monotani, Y., Kawasaki, H., Asai, T., and Shingyoji, I., "Visually Evoked Potential of Retarded Children," Clinical Electroencephalography 14:541-549, 1972.

Hodgson, K.W., The Deaf and Their Problems, A Study in special Education (London: C.A. Watts & Company, Ltd.), 1953.

Hoemann, H., "The Development of Communication Skills in Deaf
   and Hearing Children," Child Development 43:990-1003, 1972.

Holm, V. and Kunze, L., "Effects of Chronic Otitis Media On
   Language and Speech Development," Pediatrics 43:833-838, 1969.

House, H., Personal Correspondence, 1977.

Hsu, J.R., A Developmenetal Guide to English Syntax: An Aid for
   Teachers in Facilitating the Acquisition of Linguistic
   Competence by Hearing Impaired Children (New York: St.
   Joseph's School for the Deaf), 1977.

Igarashi, M., Takahashi, M., Alford, B.R., and Johnson, P.E.,
   "Inner Ear Morphology in Down's Sydrome," Acta
   Otolaryngologica 83:175-181, 1971.

Jacobson, J.T., Seitz, M.R., Mencher, G.T., and Parrott, V.,
   "Auditory Brainstem Response: A Contribution to Infant
   Assessment and Management," In G.T. Mencher and S.E. Gerber
   (Eds.), Early Management of Hearing Loss (New York: Grune &
   Stratton, Inc.), 1980.

Jaffe, B.F. (Ed.), Hearing Loss in Children (Baltimore:
   University Park Press), 1977.

Jerger, J.F. and Hayes, D., "The Cross-Check Principle in Pediatric
   Audiometry," Archives of Otolaryngology 104:456-461, 1978.

Jerger, J.F., Hayes, D., and Jordon, C., "Clinical Experience
   with Auditory Brainstem Response Audiometry in Pediatric
   Assessment," Ear and Hearing 1:19-25, 1980.

Jerger, J.F. and Mauldin, L., "Prediction of Sensorineural Hearing
   Level from the Brainstem Evoked Response," Archives of
   Otolaryngology 104:456-461, 1978.

Jerger, S., Jerger, J., Mauldin, L., and Segal, P., "Studies in
   Impedance Audiometry: Children Less Than 6 Years Old," In
   Northern, J.L. (Ed.), Selected Readings in Impedance Audiometry
   (Dobbs Ferry, New York: American Electromedics Corp.), 1976.

Jewett, D.L.and Williston, J.S., "Auditory-Evoked Far Fields
   Averaged from the Scalp of Humans," Brain 94:681-696, 1971.

Jilek, L., Travnickova, E., and Trojan, S., "Characteristic
   Metabolic and Functional Responses to Oxygen Deficiency in the
   Central Nervous System," In Stave, U. (Ed.) Physiology of the
   Perinatal Period (Vol. 2) (New York: Appleton-Century-Crofts),
   1970.

Johnson, D., Furth, H., and Davey, G., "Vibration and Praise as
   Reinforcers for Mentally Handicapped People," Mental
   Retardation 16:339-342, 1978.

Joint Committee on Infant Hearing (Position Statement), Pediatrics, 70:496-497, 1982.

Jones, C., "Uses of Mechanical Vibration with the Severely Mentally Handicapped, Part I," Apex Journal of the British Institute of Mental Handicap 7:81-82, 1980.

Jones, C., "Uses of Mechanical Vibration with the Severely Mentally Handicapped, Part II," Apex Journal of the British Institute of Mental Handicap 7:112-114, 1980.

Juenke, D., An application of a Generative-Transformational Model of Lingistic Description of Hearing Impaired Subjects in the Generation and Expansion Stages of Language Development (Unpublished Master's Thesis, University of Cincinnati, Cincinnati, Ohio), 1971.

Kaga, K., Suzuki, J., Marsh, R.R., and Tanaka, Y., "Influence of Labyrinthine Hypoactivity on Gross Motor Development of Infants," Annals of the New York Academy of Science 374:412-420, 1981.

Kamhi, C.K., "An Application of Piaget's Theory to the Conceptualization of a Preschool Curriculum," In Parker, R.K. (Ed.), The Preschool in Action: Exploring Early Childhood Programs (Boston: Allyn & Bacon), 1972.

Kankkunen, A., "Preschool Children with Impaired Hearing," Acta Oto-laryngologica (Stockholm) Supplement #391, 1982.

Kankkunen, A., and Liden, G., "Respiration Audiometry," Scandinavian Audiology 6:81-86, 1977.

Kankkunen, A., and Liden, G., "Early Identification of Hearing Handicapped Children," Acta Oto-laryngologica (Stockholm) Supplement #386, 1982.

Karchmer, M.A., Milone, M.N., and Work, S., "Educational Significance of Hearing Loss at Three Levels of Severity," American Annals of the Deaf 124:97-109, 1979.

Karchmer, M.A., Petersen, L.M., Allen, T.E., and Osborn, T.I., Highlights of the Canadian Survey of Hearing Impaired Children and Youth (Washington, D.C.: Gallaudet College, Office of Demographic Studies), Spring, 1979.

Kaye, K., "Toward the Origin of Dialogue," In Shaffer, H.R. (Ed.) Studies in Mother-Infant Interaction (New York: Academic Press), 1977.

Kaufman, B.A., "Summary Impressions," In Simmons-Martin, A. & Calvert, D. (Eds.), Parent-Infant Intervention: Communication Disorders (New York: Grune & Stratton, Inc.), 1979.

Keith, R., "Impedance Audiometry with Neonates," _Archives of Otolaryngology_ 97:465-467, 1973.

Keith, R., "Middle Ear Function in Neonates," _Archives of Otolaryngology_ 101:376-379, 1975.

Kent, A., "Audiological Assessment and Implications," In Walsh, S.R. and Holaberg, R. (Eds.), _Understanding and Evaluating the Deaf-Blind/Severely and Profoundly Handicapped_ (Springfield, Ill.: Charles C. Thomas), 1981.

Kershman, S.M., "The Training Needs of Parents of Deaf-Blind Multihandicapped Children - Part One: The Parent Competencies," _Education of the Visually Handicapped_ 13:98-108, 1982.

Kevanishvili, Z.Sh., and Von Specht, H., "Human Slow Auditory Evoked Potentials During Natural and Drug-Induced Sleep," _Electroencephalography and Clinical Neurophysiology_ 47-280-288, 1979.

Kiang, N.Y.S., Neame, J.H., and Clark, L.F., "Evoked Cortical Activity from Auditory Cortex in Anesthetized and Unanesthetized Cats," _Science_ 13:1927-1928, 1961.

Kileny, P., "The Frequency Specificity of Tone-Pip Evoked Auditory Brainstem Responses," _Ear and Hearing_ 2:270-275, 1981.

Kileny, P., "Auditory Brainstem Responses as Indicators of Hearing Aid Performance," _Annals of Otology, Rhinology, and Laryngology_ 91:61-64, 1982.

Kileny, P. and Berry, D., "Selective Impairment of Late Vertex or Middle Latency Auditory Evoked Responses in Multiply Handicapped Children," This Volume.

Kileny, P., Connelly, C., and Robertson, C., "Auditory Brainstem Rsponses in Perinatal Asphyxia," Paper Presented to the 1980 Annual Meeting of the Canadian Speech and Hearing Association, Winnipeg, Manitoba.

Kileny, P., Connelly, C., and Robertson, C., "Auditory Brainstem Responses in Perinatal Asphyxia," _International Journal of Pediatric Otorhinolaryngology_ 2:147-159, 1980.

Kileny, P., Dobson, D., and Gelfand, E.T., "Middle Latency Auditory Evoked Responses During Open-Heart Surgery with Hypothermia," In Preparation, 1983.

Kish, G.B., "Learning When the Onset of Illumination is Used as a Reinforcing Stimulus," _Journal of Comparative and Physiological Psychology_ 48:261-264, 1955.

Klein, C., "Variables to Consider in Developing and Selecting
    Services for Deaf-Blind Children, Part 2," American Annals of
    the Deaf 123:430-433, 1978.

Klein, N. and Vernon, M., "Hearing Impaired in the 1980s,"
    Hearing Aid Journal 35:17-19, 1982.

Knight, R. T., Hilyard, S.A., Woods, D. L., and Neville, H.J.,
    "The Effects of Frontal and Temporal-Parietal Lesions on the
    Auditory Evoked Potential in Man," Electroencephalography
    and Clinical Neurophysiology 50:112-124, 1980.

Knoblock, H. and Pasamanick, B., "Syndrome of Minimal Cerebral
    Damage in Infancy," Journal of the American Medical
    Association 170:1384-1387, 1959.

Kodman, F., Powers, T.R., Weller, G.M., and Philip, P.P., "Pure
    Tone Audiometry with the Mentally Retarded," Exceptional
    Children 24:303-305, 1958.

Konigsmark, B.W. and Gorlin, R.J., Genetic and Metabolic Deafness
    (Philadelphia: W.B. Saunders), 1976.

Kretschmer, R.R.and Kretschmer, L., Language Development and
    Intervention with the Hearing-Impaired Child (Baltimore:
    University Park Press), 1978.

Krynski, S., Diament, A.J., Levisky, D.L., and Dominques, W.M.,
    "Perinatal Anoxia and Mental Retardation," Acta
    Paedopsychiatrica 39:347-355, 1973.

Kumar, K.L.and Nankeruis, G.A., "Inapparent Congenital
    Cytomegalovirus Infection," New England Journal of Medicine
    288:1370-1372, 1973.

Labov, W., "Some Sources of Reading Problems for Negro Speakers
    of Nonstandard English" (Champaign, Illinois: National Council
    of Teachers of English), 1967.

Lamb, L. and Norris, T., "Acoustic Impedance Measurement," In
    Fulton, R. and Lloyd, L. (Eds.), Audiometry for the Retarded
    (Baltimore: Williams & Wilkins Co.), 1969.

Lambert, W.E. and Peal, E., "The Relation of Bilingualism to
    Intelligence," Psychological Monographs, Number 76, 1962.

Landthaler, G. and Andrieu-Guitrancourt, J., "Contribution a
    l'etude des Ataxies et des Surdites Secondairs aux Menigites
    Purulents de l'Enfant," Annals of Otolaryngology (Paris)
    91:293-309, 1974.

Lavatelli, C. (Ed.), Language Training in Early Childhood
    Education (Urbana: University of Illinois Press), 1974.

Levine, E.S., <u>Youth in a Soundless World, A Search for Personality</u> (New York: New York University Press), 1956.

Lewis, M.M., <u>Language and Personality in Deaf Children</u> (Slough: National Foundation for Educational Research in England and Wales), 1968.

Lewis, N., "Otitis Media and Linguistic Incompetence," <u>Archives of Otolaryngology</u> 102:387-390, 1976.

Libb, J.W., Myers, G.J., Graham, E., Bell, B., "Correlates of Intelligence and Adaptive Behavior in Down Syndrome," Paper presented at the 104th Annual Meeting of the American Association on Mental Deficiency, San Francisco, May, 1980.

Liden, G. and Kankkunen, A., "Visual Reinforcement Audiometry," <u>Acta Oto-laryngologica</u> 67:281-292, 1969.

Liden, G. and Kankkunen, A., "Methods of Early Identification of Hearing Impaired Children," <u>Proceedings of the First Otolaryngology Congress of the South-East Asian Federation, Thailand</u> (Basel, Switzerland: Karger), 1982.

Light, M.H., Ferrell, C.J., and Sandberg, R.K., "The Effects of Sedation on the Impedance Test Battery," <u>Archives of Otolaryngology</u> 103:235-237, 1977.

Lillie, D.L., Trohanis, P.L., and Goin, K.W. (Eds.), <u>Teaching Parents to Teach</u> (New York: Walker & Co.), 1976.

Lindstrom, J., Branemark, P-I., and Albrektsson, T., "Mandibular Reconstruction Using Preformed Autologous Bone Graft," <u>Scandinavian Journal of Reconstructive Surgery</u> 15:29-39, 1981.

Ling, D., Ling, A.H., and Doehring, D.G., "Stimulus Response and Observer Variables in the Auditory Screening of Newborn Infants," <u>Journal of Speech and Hearing Research</u> 13:9-18, 1970.

Lis, E.F., "Implications of Screening Techniques for Compehensive Care," In Oglesby, A. and Sterling, H. (Eds.), <u>Proceedings Bi-Regional Institute on Earlier Recognition of Handicapping Conditions in Childhood</u> (Berkeley: University of California School of Public Health), 1970.

Litoff, S.G. and Feldman, V.J., "Treatment Issues with Deaf Children: An Eriksonian Perspective," In Stein, L., Mindel, E. & Jabaley, T. (Eds.), <u>Deafness and Mental Health</u> (New York: Grune & Stratton, Inc.), 1981.

Lloyd, L.L., "Use of the Slide Show Audiometric Technique with Mentally Retarded Children," <u>Exceptional Children</u> 32:93-98, 1965.

Lloyd, L.L. (Ed.), Communication Assessment and Intervention Strategies (Baltimore: University Park Press), 1976.

Lloyd, L.L., and Dahle, A.J., "Detection and Diagnosis of a Hearing Impairment in the Child," A Bicentennial Monograph on Hearing Impairment: Trends in the U.S.A. (Washington, D.C.: A.G. Bell Association), Frisina, R., (Ed.), 1976.

Lloyd, L.L., and Frisina, D.R. (Eds.), The Audiologic Assessment of the Mentally Retarded: Proceedings of a National Conference (Parsons, {Kansas} State Hospital and Training Center), 1965.

Lloyd, L.L., Spradlin, J.E., and Reid, M.J., "An Operant Audiometric Procedure for Difficult-to-Test Subjects," Journal of Speech and Hearing Disorders 33:236-245, 1968.

Loban, W., The Language of Elementary School Children: Research Report No. 1 (Champaign, Illinois: National Council of Teachers of English), 1963.

Lyle, J.G., "The Effect of an Institution Environment Upon the Verbal Development of Imbecile Children; II: Speech and Language," Journal of Mental Deficiency Research 4:1-13, 1960.

Lyle, J.G., "Comparison of the Language of Normal and Imbecile Children," Journal of Mental Deficiency Research 5:40-51, 1961.

Mark, H. and Hardy, W., "Orienting Reflex Disturbance in Central Auditory or Language Handicapped Children," Journal of Speech and Hearing Disorders 23:237-242, 1958.

Martin, J.A.M. and Moore, W. J. (Eds.), Childhood Deafness in the European Community (Luxembourg: Office for Official Publications of the European Communities), 1979.

Matkin, N.D., "A Critical Assessment of Current Practices in the Audiologic Management of Preschool Children," In J. Subtelny (Ed.), Speech Assessment and Speech Improvement for the Hearing Impaired (Washington, D.C.: A.G. Bell Association), 1980.

McCandless, G.A. and Allred, P.L., "Tympanometry and Emergence of the Acoustic Reflex in Infants," In Harford, E.R., Bess, F.H., Bluestone, L.D., and Klein, J.O. (Eds.), Impedance Screening for Middle Ear Disease in Children (New York: Grune & Stratton, Inc.), 1978.

McDade, H.L and Adler, S., "Down's Syndrome and Short-term Memory Impairment: A Storage or Retrieval Deficit?" American Journal of Mental Deficiency 84:561-567, 1980.

McDonald, E., "Identification of Children at Risk," In Vanderheiden, G.C. & Grilley, P. (Eds.), Non-Vocal Communication Techniques and Aids for the Severely Physically Handicapped (Baltimore: University Park Press), 1976.

McDonald, E., "Design and Application of Communication Boards," In Vanderheiden, G.C. & Grilley, P. (Eds.), Non-Vocal Communication Techniques and Aids for the Severely Physically Handicapped (Baltimore: University Park Press), 1976.

McInnes, J.M. and Treffrey, J., Deaf-Blind Infants and Children (Toronto: University of Toronto Press), 1982.

Meadow, K., Deafness and Child Development (Berkeley: University of California Press), 1981.

Meier, J., Screening and Assessment of Young Children at Developmental Risk (Washington, D.C.: DHEW Publication #05-73-90), Produced by The President's Committee on Mental Retardation, 1973.

Mencher, G.T, "Prologue: The Way We Were," In Mencher, G.T. and Gerber, S.E. (Eds.), Early Management of Hearing Loss (New York: Grune & Stratton, Inc.), 1981.

Mencher G.T., Baldursson, G., Tell, L., and Levi, C., "Mass Behavioral Screening and Follow-up," Paper presented at the National Research Council-National Academy of Sciences, Assembly of Behavioural and Social Sciences, Meeting of the Committee on Hearing, Bioacoustics, and Biomechanics, Omaha, Nebraska, 1978.

Mendel, M.I., Hosick, E.C., Windman, T.R., Davis, H., Hirsh, S.K, and Dinges, D.F., "Audiometric Comparison of the Middle and Late Components Awake and Asleep," Electroencephalography and Clinical Neurophysiology 38:27-33, 1975.

Mendelson, T. and Salamy, A., "Maturational Effects on the Middle Components of the Averaged Electroencephalic Response," Journal of Speech and Hearing Research 46:140-144, 1981.

Meyerhoff, W.L., "Medical Management of Hearing Loss - The Otolaryngologist's Responsibility," Laryngoscope 88:960-973, 1978.

Meyerson, L., Kerr, N., and Michael, J., In Bijou, S. & Baer, D. (Eds.), "Behaviour Modification in Rehabilitation," Experimental Analysis (New York: Appleton-Century Crofts), 1967.

Michel, F., Peronnet F., and Scott, B., "A Case of Cortical Deafness: Clinical and Electro-physiological Data," Brain and Language 10:367-377, 1980.

Miller, A. and Miller, S., "Cognitive-Developmental Training with Elevated Boards and Sign Language," Journal of Autism and Childhood Schizophrenia 3:65-85, 1973.

Miller, J., Chapman, R.S., Branston, M.B., and Reichle, J., "Language Comprehension in Sensorimotor Stages V and VI," Journal of Speech and Hearing Research 23:284-311, 1980.

Milner, E., "A Study of the Relationship Between Reading Readiness in Grade One School Children and Patterns of Parent-Child Interaction," Child Development 22-95-112, 1951.

Mitchell, O.C. and Richards, G.B., "Effects of Various Anesthetic Agents on Normal and Pathological Middle Ears," ENT Journal 55:36-44, 1976.

Mokotoff, B., Schulman-Galambos, C., and Galambos, R., "Brainstem Auditory Evoked Responses in Children," Archives of Otolaryngology 103:38-43, 1977.

Moller, A.R., Janetta, P., Bennet, M., and Moller, M.B., "Intracranially Recorded Responses from the Human Auditory Nerve: New Insights into the Origin of Brain Stem Evoked Potentials (BSEP)," Electroencephalography and Clinical Neurophysiology 52:18-27, 1981.

Moore, J.M., Thompson, G., and Thompson, M., "Auditory Localization of Infants as a Function of Reinforcement Conditions," Journal of Speech and Hearing Disorders 40:29-34, 1975.

Moore, J.M. and Wilson, W.R., "Visual Reinforcement Audiometry (VRA) With Infants," In Gerber, S.E. & Mencher, G.T. (Eds.), Early Diagnosis of Hearing Loss (New York: Grune & Stratton, Inc.), 1978.

Moore, J.M., Wilson, W.R., and Thompson, G., "Visual Reinforcement of Head-Turn Responses in Infants Under 12 Months of Age," Journal of Speech and Hearing Disorders 42-328-334, 1977.

Moores, D.E., Educating the Deaf: Psychology, Principles and Practices (Boston: Houghton Mifflin Co.), 1978.

Morris, S.E., "Communication/Interaction Development at Mealtimes for the Multiply Handicapped Child: Implications for the Use of Augmentative Communication Systems," Language, Speech and Hearing Services in the Schools 12:216-232, 1981.

Moses, K. and Hecke-Wulatin, M.V., "The Socio-Emotional Impact of Infant Deafness: A Counselling Model," In Mencher, G.T. & Gerber, S.E. (Eds.), Early Management of Hearing Loss (New York: Grune & Stratton, Inc.), 1981.

Moskowitz, H. and Lohmann, W., "Auditory Threshold for Evoking an Orienting Reflex in Mongoloid Patients," Perceptual Motor Skills 31:879-882, 1970.

Murphy, A.T. (Ed.), "The Families of Hearing Impaired Children," The Volta Review, Vol. 81, No. 5, 1979.

Murphy, K.P., "Development of Hearing in Babies -- A Diagnostic System for Detecting Early Signs of Deafness in Infants," Child and Family 1:16-17, 1962.

Murphy, K.P., Investigation of the Incidence of Hearing Loss in the Mentally Retarded, Confidential Report for the R.N.I.D., 1977.

Murphy, K.P., Early Development of Auditory Function, Paper Presented to the National Convention of the American Speech and Hearing Association, San Francisco, 1978.

Murphy, K.P. and Byrne, D.J., "The Blind-Deaf Multiply Disabled Infant," In Mencher, G.T. & Gerber, S.E. (Eds.) Early Management of Hearing Loss (New York: Grune & Stratton, Inc.), 1980.

Musiek, F.E. and Geurkink, N.A., "Auditory Brainstem and Middle Latency Evoked Response Sensitivity Near Threshold," Annals of Otology, Rhinology, and Laryngology 90:236-240, 1981.

Mykelbust, H., The Psychology of Deafness: Sensory Deprivation, Learning, and Adjustment (New York: Grune & Stratton, Inc.), 1960.

National Development Group, Helping Mentally Handicapped People in Hospital, Department of Health and Social Security, 1978.

Northern, J.L. and Downs, M.P., Hearing in Children (1st. ed.), (Baltimore: Williams and Wilkins Co.), 1974.

Northern, J.L. and Downs, M.P., Hearing in Children (2nd ed.), (Baltimore: Williams and Wilkins Co.), 1978.

Ohwaki, S. and Stayton, S.E., "Preference by the Retarded for Vibratory and Stimulation as a Function of Mental Age and Psychotic Reaction," Journal of Abnormal Psychology 85:516-522, 1976.

Olds, J., "Self Stimulation and Differentiated Award Systems," In Jasper, H.H. (Ed.), Reticular Formation of the Brain (Boston: Little, Brown & Co.), 1958.

Olds, J. and Milner, P., "Positive Reinforcement Produced by Electrical Stimulation of Septal and Other Regions of Rat Brain," Journal of Comparative and Physiological Psychology 47:419-427, 1954.

Olds, M.E. and Olds, J., "Approach Avoidance Analysis at Rat Diencephalon," <u>Journal of Comparative Neurology</u> 120:259-295, 1963.

Ozdamar, O., Kraus, N., and Curry, F., "Auditory Brain Stem and Middle Latency Responses in a Patient with Cortical Deafness," <u>Electroencephalography and Clinical Neurophysiology</u> 53:224-230, 1982.

Palo, J. and Savolainen, H., "The Proteins of Human Myelin in Inborn Errors of Metabolism and in Chromosomal Anomalies," <u>Acta Neuropathologica</u> 24:56-61, 1973.

Paparella, M.M., "Differential Diagnosis of Hearing Loss - The Otolaryngologist's Responsibility," <u>Laryngoscope</u> 88:952-959, 1978.

Pappas, D.G. and Mundy, M.R., "Sensorineural Hearing Loss: Infectious Agents," <u>Laryngoscope</u> 92:752-753, 1982.

Paradise, J.L., Smith, C.G., and Bluestone, C.D., "Tympanometric Detection of Middle Ear Effusion in Infants and Young Children," <u>Pediatrics</u> 58:198209, 1976.

Parving, A., Salomon, G., Elberling, C., Larsen, B., and Lassen, N.A., "Middle Components of the Auditory Evoked Response in Bilateral Temporal Lobe Lesions," <u>Scandinavian Audiology</u> 9:161-167, 1980.

Pawlby, S.J., "Initiative Interaction," In Schaffer, H.R. (Ed.), <u>Studies in Mother-Infant Interaction</u> (London: Academic Press), 1977.

Peckham, C.S., Martin, J.A.M., Marshall, W.C., and Dudgeon, J.A., "Congenital Rubella Deafness: A Preventable Disease," <u>Lancet</u> 1:258-261, 1979.

Perier, O., Capouilliz, J.M., and Paulissen, D., "The Relationship Between the Degree of Auditory Deficiency and the Possibility of Succesful Mainstreaming in Schools for Hearing Children," In Hartman, H. (Ed.), <u>First International Congress of the Hard of Hearing</u> (Hamburg: Deutscher Schwerhorigenbund), 1980.

Perry, R.L., "Help for the Handicapped," <u>Owning Your Home Computer</u> (Chicago: Playboy Paperbacks), 1980.

Pfaffman, C. "The Pleasures of Sensation," <u>Psychological Review</u> 67:253-268, 1960.

Piaget, J., <u>The Origins of Intelligence in Children</u> (New York: International University Press), 1952.

Piaget, J. and Inhelder, B, <u>The Child's Conception of Space</u> (London: Routledge & Paul), Langdon, F.J. & Lunzer, J.L. (Translators), 1956.

Piaget, J. and Inhelder, B., The Psychology of the Child (New York: Basic Books), 1969.

Picton, T.W., Hillyard, S.A., Krausz, H.I., and Galambos, R., "Human Auditory Evoked Potentials: I. Evaluation of Components," Electroencephalography and Clinical Neurophysiology 36:179-190, 1974.

Picton, T.W., Quellette, B.A., Hamel, G., and Smith, A.D., "Brainstem Evoked Potentials to Tone Pips in Matched Noise," Journal of Otolaryngology 8:289-314, 1979.

Plumer, D., "A Summary of Environmentalist Views and Some Educational Implications," In Williams, F. (Ed.) Language and Poverty (Chicago: Rand McNally Publishing), 1970.

Poole, P.B., Sheeley, E.C., and Hannah, J.E., "Predicting Hearing Sensitivity and Audiometric Slope for Mentally Retarded Persons," Ear and Hearing 3:77-82, 1982.

Pradhan, S.N. and Galambos, R., "Some Effects of Anesthetics on the Evoked Responses in the Auditory Cortex of Cats," Journal of Pharmacology and Experimental Therapeutics 139:97-106, 1963.

Precechtel, A., "Contribution a l'Etude de la Fonction Statique dans la Periode Foetale et dans la Premiere Periode de la Vie Extrauterine: Syndrome Typique du Defaut Congenital de l'Appareil Otolithique," Acta Otolaryngologica 7:206-226, 1925.

Price, L.L., "Evoked Response Audiometry," In Fulton, R.T. and Lloyd, L.L. (Eds.), Auditory Assessment of the Difficult-to-Test (Baltimore: Williams & Wilkins Co.), 1975.

Pringle, M.L.K., Deprivation and Education (London: Longman's Green), 1965.

Quigley, S.P., Wilbur, R.B., and Montanelli, D.S., "Question Formation in the Language of Deaf Students," Journal of Speech and Hearing Research 17:699-713, 1974.

Rapin, I., "Hypoactive Labyrinths and Motor Development," Clinical Pediatrics 13:922-937, 1974.

Rapin, I., "Effects of Early Blindness and Deafness on Cognition," In Katzman, R. (Ed.), Congenital and Acquired Cognitive Disorders (New York: Raven Press), 1979.

Rapin, I., Children with Brain Dysfunction: Neurology, Cognition, Language, and Behavior (New York: Raven Press), 1982.

Rapin, I. and Ruben, R.J., "Appraisal of Auditory Function in Children," In Lewis, M. and Taft, L.T. (Eds.), Developmental Disabilities in Preschool Children (New York: S. P. Medical and Scientific Books), 1981.

Rasmussen, P., "Neuropediatric Aspects of Seven-Year-Old Children with Perceptual, Motor and Attentional Deficits," In Preparation, 1982.

Rawlins, B. and Gentile, A., Additional Handicapping Conditions, Age at Onset of Hearing Loss, and Other Characteristics of Hearing Impaired Students, United States: 1968-69 (Washington, D.C.: Office of Demographic Studies, Gallaudet College), 1970.

Rehagen, N.J. and Thelen, M.H., "Vibration as Positive Reinforcement for Retarded Children," Journal of Abnormal Psychology 80:162-167, 1972.

Renshaw, S., "The Errors of Cutaneous Localization and the Effect of Practice on the Localizing Movement in Children and Adults," Journal of Genetic Psychology 28:223-238, 1930.

Rice, B., A Comprehensive Facility Program for Multiply Handicapped Deaf Adults (Fayetteville: Arkansas Rehabilitation Research and Training Center), 1973.

Rincover, A., "Sensory Extinction: Procedure for Elimination of Self-Stimulatory Behavior in Developmentally Disabled Children," Journal of Abnormal Child Psychology 6:299-310, 1978.

Rittmanic, P.A., "Hearing Rehabilitation for the Institutionalized Mentally Retarded," American Journal of Mental Deficiency 63:778-783, 1959.

Robertson, C., "Pediatric Assessment of the Infant at Risk for Deafness," In Gerber, S.E. and Mencher, G.T. (Eds.), Early Diagnosis of Hearing Loss (New York: Grune & Stratton, Inc.), 1978.

Robertson, C., Shea, R., and Whyte, L., "Prospective Identification of Infants with Hearing Loss and Multiple Handicaps," This Volume.

Robinson, W.P. and Rackstraw, S.J., "Variations in Mothers' Answers to Children's Questions as a Function of Social Class, Verbal Intelligence Test Scores, and Sex," Sociology 1:259-265, 1967.

Roeser, R. and Downs, M.P. (Eds.), Auditory Disorders In School Children (New York: Thieme-Stratton, Inc.), 1981.

Rohr, A. and Burr, D.B., "Etiological Differences in Patterns of Psycholinguistic Development of Children of IQ 30-60," American Journal of Mental Deficiency 82:549-553, 1978.

Ross, A.E., The Exceptional Child and the Family (New York: Grune & Stratton, Inc.), 1964.

Ross, R.T., Fair View Self Help Scale (California: Fair View State Hospital), 1969.

Rowe, M.J.,   "The Brainstem Auditory Evoked Response in Neurological
    Disease: A Review," Ear and Hearing 2:41-51, 1981.

Ruben, R.J. and Rapin, I.,   "Plasticity of the Developing Auditory
    System," Annals of Otology, Rhinology, and Laryngology 89:303-311,
    1980.

Rubin, M.,   "Serous Otitis Media in Severe-Profound Hearing Impaired
    Children, Age 0-6," Volta Review 80:81-85, 1978.

Rubin, M.,   Unpublished Analysis of Lexington School's Infant Center
    Population, Annual Report of Lexington School (1980-1981), New
    York.

Rynders, J., Behlen, K., and Horrobin, J.,   "Performance
    Characteristics of Preshcool Down's Syndrome Children Receiving
    Augmented or Repetitive Verbal Instruction," American Journal of
    Mental Deficiency 84:67-73, 1979.

Sadock, B.J.,   "Psychiatry and the Urban Setting," In Sadock, B.J.,
    Kaplan, H.I., Freedman, A.M., Suffman, N. (Eds.), Comprehensive
    Text Book of Psychiatry (Baltimore: Williams & Wilkins Co.), 1975.

St.James-Roberts, I.,   The Development of Multi-modality Assessment
    Procedures for use in the Audiological Testing of Children, Ph.D
    Thesis, University of Newcastle, 1972.

St. James-Roberts, I.,   "Cross-modal Facilitation of Response in
    Behavioural Audiometry with Children," Journal of American
    Audiology Society 1:119-125, 1975.

Salamy, A. and McKean, C.M.,   "Postnatal Development of Human
    Brainstem Potentials During the First Year of Life," Electro-
    encephalography and Clinical Neurophysiology 40:418-426, 1976.

Salvin, A., Routh, D.K., Foster, R.E., Jr., and Lovejoy, K.M.,
    "Acquisition of Modified American Sign Language by a Mute Autistic
    Child," Journal of Autism and Childhood Schizophrenia 7:359-371,
    1977.

Sarno, C.N. and Clemis, J.D.,   "A Workable Approach to the
    Identification of Neonatal Hearing Impairment," Laryngoscope
    90:1313-1320, 1980.

Schachtel, E.G.,   "The Development of Focal Attention and the
    Emergence of Reality," Psychiatry 17:309-324, 1954.

Schachtel, E.G.,   Metamorphosis: On the Development of Affect,
    Perception, Attention, and Memory (New York: Basic Books), 1959.

Schachter, F.F.,   Everday Mother-Talk to Toddlers: Early Intervention
    (New York: Academic Press), 1979.

Schaefer, H., "Visual Versus Tactile Receptor Preference in Normal and Schizophrenic Children," Journal of Experimental Analysis of Behavior 3:160, 1960.

Schein, J.D. (Ed.), Education and Rehabilitation of Deaf Persons with Other Disabilities (New York: Deafness Research and Training Center, New York University), 1974.

Schiefelbusch, R.L. (Ed.), Nonspeech Language and Communication (Baltimore: University Park Press), 1980.

Schlanger, B.B., "Effects of Listening Training on Auditory Thresholds of Mentally Retarded Children," Asha 4:273-275, 1962.

Schlesinger, H.S., "Meaning and Enjoyment: Language Acquisition of Deaf Childen," In O'Rourke, T.J. (Ed.) Psycholinguistics and Total Communication: The State of the Art (Washington, D.C.: American Annals of the Deaf) 1972.

Schlesinger, H.S., "The Acquisition of Bimodal Language," In Schlesinger, I.M. and Namir, L. (Eds.), Sign Language of the Deaf (New York: Academic Press), 1978.

Schlesinger, H.S., "The Effects of Deafness on Childhood Development: an Eriksonian Perspective," In Liben, L.S. (Ed.), Deaf Children: Developmental Perspectives (New York: Academic Press), 1978.

Schlesinger, H.S., Early Words, Manuscript In Preparation.

Schlesinger, H.S., Untitled Manuscript In Preparation.

Schlesinger, H.S. and Meadow, K.P., Sound and Sign (Berkeley: University of California Press), 1972.

Schlesinger, H.S. and Meadow, K.P., Studies of Family Interaction, Language Acquisition and Deafness. Final report to the Office of Maternal and Child Health, Grant MC-R-060160 (San Francisco: Langley Porter Neuropsychiatric Institute), 1976.

Schoenberg, B., "Loss and Grief," In Schoenberg, B. (Ed.), Psychological Management in Medical Practice (New York: Columbia University Press), 1970.

Schoggen, M. and Schoggen, P., "Environmental Forces in the Home Lives of Three-Year-Old Children in Three Population Subgroups," JSAS Catalog of Selected Documents in Psychology (No. 1178), 1976.

Schopler, E., "Visual Versus Tactile Receptor Preference in Normal and Schizophrenic Childen," Journal of Abnormal Psychology 71:108-114, 1966.

Schulman-Galambos, C. and Galambos, R., "Brainstem Auditory Evoked Responses in Premature Infants," Journal of Speech and Hearing Research 12:394-401, 1969.

Schwartz, D.M. and Schwartz, R.H., "A Comparison of Tympanometry and Acoustic Reflex Measurements for Detecting Middle Ear Effusion in Infants Below Seven Months of Age," In Harford, E.R, Bess, F.H., Bluestone, C.D., and Klein, J.O. (Eds.), Impedance Screening for Middle Ear Disease in Children (New York: Grune & Stratton, Inc.), 1978.

Schwartz, D.M. and Schwartz, R.H.. "Acoustic Impedance and Otoscopic Findings in Young Children with Down's Syndrome," Archives of Otolaryngology 104:652-656, 1978.

Semel, E.M. and Wiig, E.H., Clinical Evaluation of Language Functions (Columbus: C.E. Merrill Publishing Co.), 1980.

Shane, H.C., "The Value of Toys," Communication Outlook 3:8, 1981.

Shane, H.C and Bashir, A., "Election Criteria for the Adoption of an Augmentative Communication System," Journal of Speech and Hearing Disorders 45:408-414, 1980.

Shea, J., Personal Correspondence, 1977.

Sheeley, E.C., "Audiological Assessment," In Proceedings of the Special Study Institute, Assessment and Education of Deaf-Blind Childen (Sacramento: California State Department of Education), 1978.

Sherrington, C.S., The Integrative Action of the Nervous System (London: Cambridge University Press), 1906.

Silverman, F.H., Communication for the Speechless (Englewood Cliffs, New Jersey: Prentice Hall), 1980.

Simmons, F.B., "Patterns of Deafness in Newborns," Laryngoscope 90:448-453, 1980.

Simmons-Martin, A., "Early Management Procedures for the Hearing Impaired Child," In Martin, F.N. (Ed.), Pediatric Audiology (Englewood Cliffs, New Jersey: Prentice-Hall), 1978.

Simmons-Martin, A. and Calvert, D.R., Parent-Infant Intervention (New York: Grune & Stratton, Inc.), 1979.

Sisco, F.H., Krantz, P.L., Lund, N.L., and Schwartz, G.C., "Developmental and Compensatory Play: A Means of Facilitating Social, Emotional, Cognitive, and Linguistic Growth in Deaf Children," American Annals of the Deaf 124:850-857, 1979.

Skinner, P. and Antinoro, F., "Auditory Evoked Responses In Normal Hearing Adults and Children Before and During Sedation," Journal of Speech and Hearing Research 12:394-401, 1969.

Smith, D.W., "Recognizable Patterns of Human Malformation: Genetic Embryologic and Clinical Aspects," In A. J. Schaffer (Consulting Ed.), Major Problems in Clinical Pediatrics - Volume 7 (New York: A.J. Saunders Co.), 1976.

Smith, D.W. and Wilson, A.A., The Child with Down's Syndrome (Mongolism) (Philadelphia: W.B. Saunders Co.), 1973.

Snow, C.E., "Mother's Speech Research: From Input to Interaction," In Snow, C.E. and Ferguson, C.A. (Eds.), Talking to Children: Language Input and Acquisition (Cambridge: Cambridge University Press), 1977.

Sohmer, H. and Student, M., "Auditory Nerve and Brainstem Evoked Responses in Normal, Autistic, Minimal Brain Dysfunction and Psychomotor Retarded Children," Electroencephalography and Clinical Neurophysiology 44:388-389, 1978.

Squires, N., Aine, C., Buchwald, J., Norman, R., and Galbraith, G., "Auditory Brain Stem Response Abnormalities in Severely and Profoundly Retarded Adults," Electroencephalography and Clinical Neurophysiology 50:172-185, 1980.

Stapells, D.R. and Picton, T.W., "Technical Aspects of Brainstem Evoked Potential Audiometry Using Tones," Ear and Hearing 2:20-29, 1981.

Starr, A., Amlie, R.N., Martin, W.H., and Sanders, S., "Development of Auditory Function in Newborn Infants Revealed by Auditory Brainstem Potentials," Pediatrics 60:831-839, 1977.

Starr, A. and Hamilton, A.E., "Correlation Between Confirmed Sites of Neurological Lesions and Abnormalities of Far-Field Auditory Brainstem Responses," Electroencephalography and Clinical Neurophysiology 41:595-608, 1976.

Stayton, S.E., "Multi-Modality Responding as a Function of Mental Age and Retardation," Journal of Perceptual and Motor Skills 33:1122, 1971.

Stein, L.K., Ozdamor, O., and Schnable, M., "Auditory Brainstem Response (ABR) with Suspected Deaf-Blind Children," Ear and Hearing 2:30-40, 1981.

Stewart, I.F., "Newborn Infant Hearing Screening - A Five Year Pilot Project," Journal of Otolaryngology 6:477-481, 1977.

Stewart, L., "Problems of Severely Handicapped Deaf: Implications for Educational Programs," American Annals of the Deaf 116:362-368, 1971.

Stewart, L.G., "Hearing Impaired/Developmentally Disabled Persons in the United States: Definitions, Causes, Effects, and Prevalence Estimates," The American Annals of the Deaf 123:488-498, 1978.

Stockard, J.J., Stockard, J.E., and Sharbrough, F.W., "Non-pathological Factors Influencing Brainstem Auditory Evoked Potentials," American Journal of EEG Technology 18:177-209, 1978.

Straumanis, J.J., Shagass, C., and Overton, D.A., "Auditory Evoked Responses in Young Adults with Down's Syndrome and Idiopathic Mental Retardation," Biological Psychiatry 6:75-79, 1973.

Straumanis, J.J., Shagass, C., and Overton, D.A., "Auditory Evoked Responses in Down's Syndrome," Archives of General Psychiatry 29:544-546, 1973.

Stream, R.W. and Stream, K.S., "Counselling the Parents of the Hearing Impaired Child," In Martin, F.N. (Ed.), Pediatric Audiology (Englewood Cliffs: Prentice-Hall, Inc.), 1978.

Strome, M., "Down's Syndrome: A Modern Otorhinolaryngological Perspective," Laryngoscope 91:752-753, 1982.

Stromer, R. and Miller, J., Severely Handicapped Hearing Impaired Students: Strengthening Service Delivery (Baltimore: P.Brookes), 1982.

Suzuki, T. and Ogiba, Y., "Conditioned Orientation Reflex Audiometry," Archives of Otolaryngology 74:192-198, 1961.

Tait, C.A., "Hearing and the Deaf-Blind Child," In Lowell, E.L. and Rouin, C.C. (Eds.), State of the Art: Perspectives on Serving Deaf-Blind Childen (Sacramento: California State Department of Education), 1977.

Tarakanov, V.V. and Zinchenke, B.P., "Comparative Analysis of Touch and Vision: Communication VI, Voluntary and Involuntary Learning of Form in Pre-School Age (in Russian)," Doklady Akademiia. Pedagogicheskikh. Nauk. R.S.F.S.R. Volume 5, 1960.

Taylor, I., Neurological Mechanisms of Hearing and Speech in Children (Manchester: University Press), 1964.

Thompson, G. and Weber, B.A., "Responses of Infants and Young Childen to Behavior Observation Audiometry (BOA)," Journal of Speech and Hearing Disorders 39:140-147, 1974.

Thompson, G., Wilson, W.R., and Moore, J.M., "Application of Visual Reinforcement Audiometry (VRA) to Low-functioning Children," Journal of Speech and Hearing Disorders 44:80-90, 1979.

Tjellstrom, A., Hakansson, B., Lindstrom, J., Branemark, P-I, Hallen, O., Rosenhall, U., and Leijon, A., "Analysis of the Mechanical Impedance of Bone-Anchored Hearing Aids," Acta Oto-laryngologic (Stockholm) 89:85-92, 1980.

Tjellstrom, A., Lindstrom, J., Hallen, O., Albrektsson, T., Branemark, P-I., "Osseointegrated Titanium Implants in the Temporal Bone," American Journal of Otology 2:304-310, 1981.

Tjellstrom, A., Lindstrom, J., Nylen, O., Albrektsson, T., Branemark, P-I., Birgersson, B., Nero, H., and Sylven, C., "The Bone-Anchored Auricular Episthesis," The Laryngoscope 91:811-815, 1981.

Tjellstrom, A., Lindstrom, J., Hallen, O., Albrektsson, T., and Branemark, P-I., "Direct Bone Anchorage of External Hearing Aids," In Preparation.

Tjellstrom, A., Lindstrom, J., Nylen, O, Albrektsson, T., and Branemark, P-I., "Direct Bone-Anchored Implants for Fixation of Aural Episthesis," In Preparation.

Tough, J., The Development of Meaning: A Study of Childen's Use of Language (New York: John Wiley), 1977.

Tronick, E., "Infant Communicative Intent: The Infant's Reference to Social Situations," In Stark, R.E. (Ed.) Language Behaviour in Infancy and Early Childhood (New York: Elsevier North Holland), 1981.

Trybus, R., Buchanan, C., and DeFrancesco, S., Studies in Achievement Testing, United States: Spring, 1971, Series D, Number 11 (Washington, D.C.: Office of Demographic Studies, Gallaudet College), 1973.

Tulkin, S.R. and Kagan, T., "Mother-Child Interaction in the First Year of Life," Child Development 43:31-41, 1972.

Vanderheiden, G.C. (Ed.), Non-Vocal Communication Response Book (Baltimore: University Park Press), 1978.

Vanderheiden, G.C., "Vocabulary Studies," Communication Outlook 2:12, 1982.

VanderVeer, B. and Schweid, E., "Infant Assessment: Stability of Mental Functioning in Young Retarded Children," American Journal of Mental Deficiency 79:1-4, 1974.

Van Lieshout, C.F.M., "The Assessment of Stability and Change in Peer Interaction of Normal Hearing and Deaf Preschool Children," Paper presented at the 1973 biennial meeting of the International Scoiety for the Study of Behavioral Development, Ann Arbor, Michigan, August 21-25, 1973.

Van Nort, J.B., "Myelomeningocele: Educational Importance," Division of the Physically Handicapped, Homebound and Hospitalized Journal (Council for Exceptional Children) 3:7-9, 1977.

Vaughn, H.G. and Ritter, W., "The Sources of Auditory Evoked Responses Recorded from the Human Scalp," Electroencephalography and Clinical Neurophysiology 28:306-367, 1970.

Vernon, M. "Relationship of Language to the Thinking Process," Archives of General Psychiatry 16:325-333, 1967.

Vernon, M., "Usher's Syndrome - Deafness and Progressive Blindness: Clinical Cases, Prevention, Theory and Literature Survey," Journal of Chronic Disorders 22:133-151, 1969.

Vernon, M., "Sociological and Psychological Factors Associated with Hearing Loss," Journal of Speech and Hearing Research 12:541-563, 1969.

Vernon, M. and Klein, N., "Hearing Impairment in the 1980's," Hearin Aid Journal 35:17-20, 1982.

Wachs, T., Uzgiris, I. and Hunt, J.McV., "Cognitive Development in Infants of Different Age Levels and from Different Environmental Backgrounds: An Exploratory Investigation," Merrill-Palmer Quarterly 17:283-317, 1971.

Waters, P.D., "Maximization of Minimum Control Function and Increasing Efficiency," Communication Outlook 3:11, 1982.

Watrous, B.S., McConnell, F., Sitton, A.B., and Fleet, W., "Auditory Responses of Infants," Journal of Speech and Hearing Disorders 40:357-367, 1975.

Weber, B.A., "Validation of Observer Judgments in Behavioral Observation Audiometry," Journal of Speech and Hearing Disorders 34:350-355, 1969.

Weber, B.A., "Comparison of Two Approaches to Behavioral Observation Audiometry," Journal of Speech and Hearing Disorders 13:823-825, 1970.

Weber, B.A. and Fujikawa, S.M., "Brainstem Evoked Response (BER) Audiometry at Various Stimulus Presentation Rates," Journal of the American Audiology Society 3:59-62, 1977.

Wethered, C.E., "Teacher-Made Response-Contingent Materials," In Anderson, R., Greer, J. & Odel, S. (Eds.), Strategies for Helping Severely and Multiply Handicapped Citizens (Baltimore: Univesity Park Press), 1982.

White, B.L, Kaban, B., Shapiro, B., and Attanucci, J., "Competence and Experience," In Uzgiris, I.C. & Weizmann, F. (Eds.), The Structuring of Experience (New York: Plenum Press), 1967.

Widen, J.E., The Effects of Intensity on the Auditory Brainstem Response in Down's Syndrome. Unpublished Doctoral Dissertation University of Washington, 1982.

Wilbur, R.B., American Sign Language and Sign Systems (Baltimore: University park Press), 1979.

Williams, R. and Naremore, R., "Social Class Differences in Children's Syntactic Performance: A Quantitative Analysis of Field Study Data," Journal of Speech and Hearing Research 12:778-793, 1969.

Williamson, D.G., Ross, R., and Woodrow, S., "A Comparison of Two Response-Reinforcement Mehtods in Pure-tone Testing of the Retarded," Journal of the American Audiology Society 4:36-38, 1978.

Wilson, J.J., Rapin, I., Wilson, B.C., and VanDenburgh, F.V., "Neuropsychologic Function of Children with Severe Hearing Impairment," Journal of Speech and Hearing Research 18:634-652, 1975.

Wilson, W.R., "Behavioral Assessment of Auditory Function in Infants," In Minifie, F.D. and Lloyd, L.L. (Eds.), Communicative and Cognitive Abilities - Early Behavioral Assessment (Baltimore: University Park Press), 1978.

Wilson, W.R., Lee, K.H., Owen, G., and Moore, J.M., Instrumentation for Operant Infant Auditory Assessment (Seattle: Child Development and Mental Retardation Center), 1976.

Wilson, W.R., Moore, J.M., and Thompson, G., "Sound-field Auditory Thresholds of Infants Utilizing Visual Reinforcement Audiometry (VRA)," paper presented at the 1976 American Speech and Hearing Association Convention, Houston, Texas.

Wood, M.H., Seitz, M.R., and Jacobson, J.T., "Brainstem Electrical Responses from Selected Tone Pip Stimuli," Journal of the American Audiology Society 5:156-162, 1979.

Woods, G.E., "Visual Problems in the Handicapped Child," Child: Care, Health and Development 5:303-322, 1979.

Worthington, D.W. and Peters, J.F., "Quantifiable Hearing and No ABR: Paradox or Error?" Ear and Hearing 1:281-285, 1980.

Wright, D., Deafness - A Personal Account (New York: Penguin Press), 1969.

Wrightstone, J.W., Arownow, M.S., and Moskowitz, S., "Developing Reading Test Norms for Deaf Children," American Annals of the Deaf 108:311-316, 1963.

Yamamoto, K., "Bilingualism: A Brief Review," Mental Hygiene 48:468-477, 1964.

Yellin, A.M., Lodwig, A.K., and Jerison, H.J., "Effects of Rate of
    Repetitive Stimulus Presentation on the Visual Evoked Brain
    Potentials of Young Adults with Down's Syndrome," _Biological
    Psychiatry_ 14:913-924, 1979.

Yellin, A.M., Lodwig, A.K., and Jerison, H.J., "Auditory Evoked Brain
    Potentials as a Function of Interstimulus Interval in Adults with
    Down's Syndrome," _Audiology_ 19:255-262, 1980.

Zaporozhets, A.V., "The Origin and Development of the Conscious
    Control of Movements in Man," In O'Connor, N. (Ed.), _Recent
    Soviet Psychology_ (New York: Liveright), 1961.

Zekulin, X.Y., Gibson, D., Mosely, J.L., and Brown, R.I., "Auditory-
    Motor Channeling in Down's Syndrome Subjects," _American Journal
    of Mental Deficiency_ 78:571-577, 1974.

Zigler, E. and Trickett, P.K., "I.Q., Social Competence and
    Evaluation of Early Childhood Intervention Programs," _American
    Psychologist_ 33:789-798, 1978.

Author Index

Aase, J. M., 261, 294
Abensur, J., 163, 169
Achor, L. J., 233, 256
Adell, R., 80
Adler, S., 263, 297
Aine, C., 298
Ajuriaguerra, J. De., 163, 169
Albrektsson, T., 81
Alford, B. R., 296
Allen, T. E., 64
Allred, P. L., 187, 202
Altosar, A., 198
Altshuler, K. Z., 85, 107
Amcoff, S., 67, 80
Amlie, R. N., 204
Anderson, F. W., 317, 330
Andrieu-Guitrancourt, J., 152
Antinoro, F., 234, 258
Aronow, M. S., 84, 114
Asai, T., 296
Asp, C., 170
Attanucci, J., 114
Auletta, K., 89, 107
Ault, R. L., 336, 351

Bailey, J., 362, 366, 391
Baldursson, G., 331
Balkany, T. J., 51, 64, 173, 197, 260,
    261, 262, 294, 307, 315
Banik, N. L., 262, 294

Baratz, J. C., 92, 107, 109
Baratz, S. S., 92, 107
Barnard, K. E., 259, 294
Barnes, G. W., 362, 391
Barnet A. B., 252, 253, 256, 263, 294
Barr, B., 68, 80, 151
Basel, K. E., 87, 108
Bashir, A., 342, 353
Bayshore, S. R., 186, 197
Beck, E. C., 264, 294
Behlen, K., 263, 297
Bell, B., 201
Bereiter, C., 104, 107
Bergstrom, L., 207, 226
Bernstein, B., 93, 99, 102, 107
Berry, D. A., 233–258, 334, 352
Berry, R. C., 176, 199
Bess, F. H., 306, 315
Biber, B., 104, 108
Bigum, H. B., 264, 294
Bilovsky, D., 263, 294
Birgersson, B., 81
Birns, B., 110
Blackwell, P. M., 118, 135
Blager, F. B., 261, 294
Blair, M. E., 190, 200
Blank, M., 100, 108
Bloom, L., 118, 123, 135, 136, 348,
    351
Bluestone, C. D., 203

Bochner-Wuidar, A., 155–170
Boese, R. J., 45, 46, 49
Boothe, L. L., 103, 108
Boothroyd, A., 117–137, 220, 226
Borbely, A. A., 253, 256
Bordley, J. W., 363, 392
Borg, E., 188, 197
Borkowski, M.,152
Bowlby, J., 118, 136
Bows, J., 186, 197
Bradley, R. H., 91, 108
Bradley, W., 172, 198
Brady, J. V., 360, 391
Branemark, P-I, 76, 80, 81
Branston, M. B., 353
Breine, U., 80
Bricker, D. D., 181, 198
Bricker, W. A., 181, 198
Bridger, W., 110
Bromwich, R., 410, 417
Brooks, D. N., 260, 295
Broughton, J., 123, 136
Brown, C., 25
Brown, R. I., 299
Buchanan, C., 84, 114
Buchwald, J., 298
Budden, S. S., 46, 49
Burchard, E. M., 85, 108
Burr, D. B., 263, 297
Busk, J., 264, 296
Byrne, D. J., 15, 26, 355, 359, 366, 372, 391, 393

Caldwell, B. M., 91, 108
Calvert, D. R., 410, 418
Cambon, K. G., 49
Campbell, C. W., 174, 198
Capouilliz, J. M., 170
Carbin, C. F., 45, 46, 49
Carey, S., 109
Carlson, F., 334, 343, 352
Carr, J., 259, 295
Cazden, C. B., 94, 104, 108
Chapman, R. S., 353
Cherow, E., 199
Chess, S., 47, 49, 85, 108, 141, 151
Chomsky, N., 118, 136
Clark, L. F., 256
Clarke-Stewart, K. A., 91, 109

Clemis, J. D., 52, 62, 65
Clyde, W. A., 200
Cober-Ostby, C., 407, 418
Cohen, M. M., 192, 198, 233, 251, 256
Coleman, C. L., 342, 352
Coleman, M., 259, 260, 262, 295, 301
Collier, A. M., 200
Collins, J. L., 100, 109
Collins-Ahlgren, M., 86, 108, 109
Cone, B., 190, 200
Connelly, C., 257, 317, 330, 334, 352
Connor, F. P., 220, 227
Cook, A. M., 352
Coppersmith, S., 88, 109
Cornett, R. O., 157, 169
Corsaro, W., 118, 136
Cowie, W., 262, 295
Craft, M., 330
Creedon, M. P., 163, 169
Crome, L., 262, 295
Culatta, B., 213, 227
Culatta, R., 213, 227
Curry, F., 257
Cutler, R., 318, 330

D'Asaro, M. J., 181, 200
Dahle, A., 171–205
Daly, D. A., 181, 198
Danella, E. A., 365, 392
Davey, G., 366, 367, 392
Davis, G. L., 52, 53, 62
Davis, H., 172, 189, 198, 252, 253, 256, 257, 262, 295
Davison, A. N., 294
Dee, A., 147, 152
Deming, W. E., 107
Denny, F. W, 200
Despland, P. A., 189, 199, 207, 224, 227, 233, 256
Diament, A. J., 331
Dicarlo, L. M., 85, 109, 172, 198
Dicks-Mireaux, M. J., 259, 295
Diebold, Jr., A. R., 102, 109
Difrancesca, S., 84, 109, 110, 114
Dinges, D. F., 257
Dix, M. R., 172, 198
Dobson, D., 257
Doehring, D. G., 267, 296

Dominques, W. M., 331
Dore, J., 105, 109, 118, 136
Dougherty, A., 171, 200
Down, L., 260, 295
Downs, M. P., 51, 52, 64, 65, 171,
  172, 176, 188, 198, 203, 213,
  227, 261, 294, 301–316
Dublin, W. B., 326, 330
Dudgeon, J. A., 50
Dustman, R. E., 264, 294

Eilers, R. E.,178, 199, 277, 281, 295
Eisele, W. A., 176, 199
Elberling, C., 258
Elder, J. M., 198
Engen, E., 135
Engleman, S., 104, 107
Eppstein, J., 25
Erikson, E., 118, 136
Ernhart, C. B., 330
Evans, D., 261, 295
Eviatar, A., 152
Eviatar, L., 143, 152
Ewing, A. W. G., 171, 199
Ewng, I. R., 171, 199

Fairclough, D. L., 200
Feldman, V. J., 118, 136
Fernandez, P. B., 47, 49, 85, 108, 151
Ferrell, C. J., 188, 202
Fishchrund, J., 135
Flathouse, V. E., 53, 64
Fleet, W., 205
Foale, M., 392
Folsom, R. C., 259–299
Foster, Jr., R. E., 170
Fouts, R. S., 163, 169
Fraiberg, S., 104, 109
Fraser, F. C., 213, 227
Freedman, A. M., 318, 330
Freeman, K., 152
Freeman, R. D., 45, 46, 47, 49
Friedrich, B. W., 227
Frisina, D. R., 172, 202
Fristoe, M., 333, 352
Fujikawa, S. M., 190, 205
Fulton, R. T., 172, 177, 181, 186, 199,
  260, 296

Fulwiler, R. L., 163, 169
Furth, H. G., 84, 109, 110, 118, 136,
  366, 367, 392

Galambos, R., 189, 190, 199, 200,
  203, 207, 208, 224, 227, 233,
  234, 253, 256, 257, 258
Galbraith, G., 298
Galbraith, J. C., 264, 296
Gelatt, J. P., 171, 199
Gelfand, E. T., 257
Gentile, A., 46, 50, 84, 110
Gerber, S. E., 15, 173, 199, 317–331
Gibson, D., 299
Giles, S., 338, 352
Gladwin, T., 88, 110
Gleason, J., 118, 136
Gliddon, J. B., 264, 296
Glovsky, L., 260, 296
Goin, K. W., 104, 112
Golden, M., 91, 92, 110
Goldin-Meadow, S., 85, 110
Goodhill, V., 307, 315
Goodman, L., 333, 352
Gorlin, R. J., 152, 213, 227
Gorzycki, P. A., 181, 199
Goss, R. N., 100, 110
Gould, H. J., 213, 227
Graham, E., 201
Graham, F. K., 318, 326, 330
Graham, J. D., 172, 199
Green, D. D., 172, 200
Greenberg, D. B., 179, 200, 260, 262,
  271, 275, 279, 281, 282, 296
Greenberg, M., 100, 110, 118, 136
Gregory, S., 86, 110
Grey, H. A., 181, 200
Guberina, P., 155, 170, 359
Guerkink, N. A., 255, 257

Haggstrom, W. C., 88, 100
Haiai, F., 213, 227
Hakansson, B., 77, 78, 80, 81
Hall, J. W., 188, 200
Hall, R. D., 253, 256
Hallen, O., 81
Halliday, M. A., 105, 110
Hallpike, C. S., 172, 198
Hamel, G., 203

Hamilton, A. E., 233, 258
Hammarstedt, B., 67, 80
Hannah, J. E., 186, 203
Hanshaw, J. B., 53, 64
Hansson, B. D., 80
Harada, T., 262, 290, 296, 315
Hardy, J. B., 171, 200
Hardy, W. G., 171, 200, 358, 363, 392
Haring, N. G., 259, 296
Harlow, H. F., 362, 392
Harris, R. I., 87, 110
Hayden, A. H., 259, 296
Hayes, D., 190, 191, 192, 200
Heaton, E. M., 333–353
Hecke-Wulatin, M. V., 89, 112
Hecox, K. E., 190, 200
Heider, F., 85, 111
Heider, G. M., 85, 94, 111
Heimer, C. B., 318, 330
Henderson, F. W., 187, 200
Hermelin, B., 369, 392
Hess, R. D., 86, 94, 111
Hetherington, J., 25
Hicks, G., 208, 224, 227
Hicks, W. M., 47, 50
Higashi, Y., 264, 296
Hillyard, S. A., 257, 258
Hirsch, S. K., 257
Hodgson, K. W., 85, 111
Hoemann, H., 100, 111
Hoffman, H. E., 198
Holm, V., 51, 64
Holzhoure, E., 199
Horrobin, J., 263, 297
Hosick, E. C., 257
House, H., 307, 315
Hsu, J. R., 144, 152
Hull, W. L., 181, 199
Hunt, J. M. V., 91, 114

Igarashi, M., 262, 290, 296
Inhelder, B., 118, 137, 365, 394

Jacobson, J. T., 189, 190, 200, 205
Jafek, B. W., 64, 294
Jaffe, B. F., 48, 50
Janetta, P., 257
Jenner, M., 337
Jerger, J. F., 188, 190, 191, 192, 200,
    201, 227

Jerger, S., 216, 227
Jerison, H. J., 263, 264, 299
Jewett, D. L., 189, 201
Jilek, L., 317, 326, 330
Johnson, D., 366, 367, 392
Johnson, P. E., 296
Jones, C., 366, 392
Jordon, C., 191, 192, 200
Juenke, D., 86, 111

Kaban, B., 114
Kaga, K., 140, 152
Kagan, T., 91, 114
Kamil, C. K., 104, 111
Kanjilal, G. C., 260, 295
Kankkunen, A., 67–81, 177, 201
Karchmer, M. A., 52, 62, 64, 171, 201
Kaufman, B. A., 410, 418
Kawasaki, H., 296
Kaye, K., 98, 111
Keet, S., 6
Keith, R., 186, 201
Kent, A., 175, 201
Kerr, N., 362, 393
Kershman, S. M., 411, 418
Kevanishvili, Z. Sh., 234, 252, 256
Kiang, N. Y. S., 253, 256
Kileny, P., 190, 201, 233–258, 317,
    330, 334, 352
Kish, G. B., 361, 362, 366, 368, 391,
    392
Klein, C., 49, 50
Klein, N., 65, 403, 407
Knight, R. T., 234, 253, 257
Knobloch, H., 317, 331
Kodeman, F., 172, 201
Konigsmark, B. W., 152, 213, 227
Korn, S. J., 47, 49, 85, 108, 151
Krajicek, M. J., 64, 294, 302, 316
Krantz, P. L., 137
Kraus, N., 257
Krausz, H. I., 258
Kretschmer, L., 118, 136
Kretschmer, R. R., 118, 136
Kricos, P. B., 103, 108
Kroc, R., 333, 352
Krynski, S., 326, 331
Kumar, K. L., 53, 64
Kunreuther, G., 207–231
Kunze, L., 51, 64

La Cosse, E., 397–407
Labov, W., 92, 102, 108, 111
Lahey, M., 348, 351
Lamb, L. E., 186, 199, 201
Lambert, W. E. 102, 111
Landthaler, G., 141, 152
Larsen, B., 258
Lasky, E. Z., 103, 108
Lassen, N. A., 258
Lavatelli, C., 96, 111
Lee, K. H., 299
Levi, C., 331
Levine, E. S., 84, 112
Levisky, D. L., 331
Lewis, M. M., 384, 392
Lewis, N., 304, 316
Libb, J. W., 188, 201
Liden, G., 67–81, 177, 201
Lifter, K., 123, 136
Light, M. H., 188, 202
Lillie, D. L., 104, 112
Lindstrom, J., 81
Ling, A. H., 267, 296
Ling, D., 267, 296
Lis, E. F., 6, 8, 11
Litoff, S. G., 118, 136
Lloyd, L. L., 172, 174, 175, 177, 181,
    199, 202, 260, 296, 333, 352
Loban, W., 94, 112
Lodge, A., 263, 294
Lodwig, A. K., 263, 264, 299
Lohmann, W., 276, 277, 297
Lombardi, N., 207–231
Lovejoy, K. M., 170
Lund, N. L., 137
Luterman, D., 410, 418
Lyle, J. G., 261, 296, 297

MacDonald, E., 342, 343, 352
MacLean, C. D., 49
Mahood, J. A., 337
Mark, H., 358, 392
Marsh, R. R., 152
Marshall, W. C., 50
Martin, J. A. M., 11, 50
Martin, W. H., 204
Marvin, R., 118, 136
Matkin, N. D., 409, 418
Mauldin, L., 190, 201
McCandless, G. A., 187, 202

McClain, S. C., 409–419
McCollister, F. P., 171–205
McConnell, F., 205
McDade, H. L., 263, 297
McInnes, J. M., 410, 418
McKean, C. M., 233, 258
Meadow, K. P., 83, 86, 87, 89, 90,
    100, 112, 113, 163, 170, 416, 418
Meier, J., 8, 11
Mencher, G. T., 5–14, 15, 173, 199,
    200, 317, 318, 319, 330, 331
Mendel, M. I., 234–257
Mendelson, T., 237, 257, 317, 331
Meyerhoff, W. L., 54, 55, 57, 58, 64
Meyerson, L., 362, 366, 391, 393
Michael, J., 362, 393
Michel, F., 234, 257
Miller, A., 163, 170
Miller, J., 336, 353, 410, 419
Miller, S., 163, 170
Milner, E., 94, 112
Milner, P., 360, 393
Milone, M. N., 171, 201
Miranda, S., 152
Mitchell, O. C., 188, 202
Mokotoff, B., 253, 257
Moller, A. R., 233, 257
Moller, M. B., 257
Monotani, Y., 296
Montanelli, D. S., 152
Moore, J. M., 172, 178, 179, 200, 202,
    204, 260, 267, 269, 274, 275,
    277, 295, 296, 297, 298, 299
Moore, W. J., 11
Moores, D., 83, 112, 171, 202
Morris, S. E., 336, 353
Mosley, J. L., 299
Moses, K. L., 89, 112, 409, 418
Moskowitz, H., 276, 277, 297
Moskowitz, S., 84, 114
Moss, A., 110
Mundy, M. R., 54, 65
Murphy, A. T., 418
Murphy, K. P., 13–26, 175, 202, 355–
    395
Murray, J., 198
Musiek, F. E., 255, 257
Myers, G. J., 201
Myers, L. S., 352
Myklebust, H., 84, 85, 108, 112

Nankeruis, G. A., 53, 64
Naremore, R., 94, 114
Neame, J. H., 256
Nero, H., 81
Neville, H. J., 257
Norman, R., 298
Norris, T. W., 186, 201
Northern, J. L., 52, 65, 176, 203, 213, 227
Nylen, O., 81

O'Connor, N., 369, 392
Ogiba, Y., 172, 177, 204
Ohlrich, E. S., 256, 263, 294
Ohwaki, S., 365, 393
Olds, J., 360, 393
Olds, M. E., 360, 393
Oller, D. K., 178, 199
Onishi, S., 252, 256
Osborn, T. I., 64
Overton, D. A., 263, 264, 298
Oviatt, D., 334, 352
Owen, G., 299
Ozdamar, O., 192, 204, 228, 234, 254, 257

Palmer, F. H., 108
Palo, J., 262, 294, 297
Paparella, M. M., 52, 65
Pappas, D. G., 54, 65
Paradise, J. L., 186, 187, 203
Parrott, V., 200
Parving, A., 234, 254, 258
Pasamanick, B., 317, 331
Patterson, J. W., 392
Paulissen, D., 170
Pawlby, S. J., 98, 112
Peal, E., 102, 111
Peckham, C. S., 47, 50
Perier, O., 155–170
Peronnet, F., 257
Perry, R. L., 346, 353
Peters, J. F., 192, 205, 234, 251, 258
Petersen, L. M., 64
Pfaffman, C., 361, 362, 363
Pfau, G. S., 47, 50
Philip, P. P., 201

Piaget, J., 118, 137, 363, 365, 393, 394
Picton, T. W., 190, 203, 204, 234, 252, 253, 258
Plumer, D., 90, 112
Polomeno, R. C., 198
Poole, P. B., 186, 203
Powers, T. R., 201
Pradhan, S. N., 234, 253, 258
Precechtel, A., 140, 152
Price, L. L., 189, 203
Pringle, M. L. K., 94, 112
Prutting, C. A., 317–331

Quellette, B. A., 203
Quigley, S. P., 87, 108, 144, 152

Rackstraw, S. J., 94, 113
Rainer, J. D., 107
Rapin, I., 139–153, 192, 198, 234, 251, 256
Rasmussen, P., 74, 81
Rawlings, B., 46, 50
Rehagen, N. J., 362, 394
Reichle, J., 353
Reid, M. J., 181, 202
Renshaw, S., 363, 394
Reynolds, D. W., 198
Rice, B., 84, 112
Richards, G. B., 188, 202
Rincover, A., 394
Ritter, W., 253, 258
Rittmanic, P. A., 359, 394
Robertson, C., 27–43, 45, 46, 208, 224, 228, 257, 317, 319, 330, 331, 333, 353
Robinson, G. C., 49
Robinson, W. P., 94, 113
Roeser, R., 304, 316
Rohr, A., 263, 297
Rosenhall, U., 80
Ross, A. E., 89, 113
Ross, R., 182, 205
Ross, R. T., 366, 372, 394
Routh, D. K., 170
Rowe, M. J., 190, 203
Ruben, R. J., 140, 145, 152, 153
Rubin, M., 207–231
Rynders, J., 263, 297

Sadock, B. J., 88, 113
Salamy, A., 233, 237, 257, 258, 317, 331
Salomon, G., 258
Salvin, A., 163, 170
Sandberg, R. K., 188, 202
Sanders, S., 204
Sando, I., 262, 290, 296, 315
Sanyal, M. A., 200
Sarno, C. N., 52, 62, 65
Savolainen, H., 262, 294, 297
Schachtel, E. G., 363, 365, 394
Schachter, F. F., 92, 93, 95, 98, 102, 105, 113
Schaefer, H., 362, 366, 394
Schare, J., 294
Schein, J. D., 46, 50
Schiefelbusch, R. L., 348, 353
Schlanger, B. B., 172, 181, 203
Schlesinger, H. S., 83–115, 137, 157, 163, 170, 418
Schnable, M., 192, 204, 228
Schoenberg, B., 26
Schoggen, M., 91, 113
Schoggen, P., 91, 113
Schopler, E., 365, 394
Schott, B., 257
Schulman-Galambos, C., 189, 203, 233, 257, 258
Schultz, J., 199
Schwartz, D. M., 187, 203, 260, 261, 262, 295, 297
Schwartz, G. C., 137
Schwartz, R. H., 187, 203, 260, 261, 262, 295, 297
Schweid, E., 259, 298
Seitz, M. R., 190, 200, 205
Semel, E. M., 320, 331
Shagass, C., 263, 264, 298
Shane, H. C., 338, 342, 353
Shanks, B. L., 256, 263, 294
Shapiro, B., 114
Sharbrough, F. W., 189, 204
Share, J., 263
Shea, J., 312
Shea, R., 9, 45–50, 353
Sheeley, E. C., 175, 186, 203
Sherrington, C. S., 363, 394
Shingyoji, I., 296

Shipman, V. C., 94, 111
Shriner, T. H., 176, 199
Siepp, J. M., 227
Silverman, F. H., 333, 348, 353
Simmons, F. B., 208, 219, 224, 228
Simmons-Martin, A., 118, 137, 410, 418
Sisco, F. H., 118, 137
Sitton, A. B., 205
Skinner, P., 234, 258
Skylar, M., 181, 200
Slater, E., 262, 295
Smith, A. D., 203
Smith, C. G., 203
Smith, D. W., 52, 65, 260, 261, 294, 298
Snow, C. E., 98, 113
Sohmer, H., 189, 192, 204
Spradlin, J. E., 181, 202
Squires, N., 264, 286, 291, 298
St. James-Roberts, I., 182, 204, 369, 394
Stagno, S., 198
Stapells, D. R., 190, 204
Starr, A., 189, 204, 233, 256, 258
Stayton, S. E., 365, 393, 395
Stein, L. K., 192, 204, 226, 228
Stensland-Junker, K., 151
Stern, J., 262, 295
Sterritt, G. M., 172, 198
Stevens, C. P., 366, 391
Stewart, I. F., 51–65
Stewart, L. G., 52, 62, 65, 84, 114
Stockard, J. E., 189, 204
Stockard, J. J., 189, 204
Straumanis, J. J., 263, 264, 298
Stream, K. S., 407, 418
Stream, R. W. 407, 418
Strohbach, B. L., 333–353
Strome, M., 57, 65
Stromer, R., 410, 419
Student, M., 189, 192, 204
Suzuki, J., 152
Suzuki, T., 172, 177, 204
Svard, M., 151
Sylven, C., 81

Tait, C. A., 175, 176, 181, 204
Takahashi, M., 296

Tanaka, Y., 152
Tarakanov, V. V., 363, 395
Taylor, I., 364, 367, 395
Tell, L., 331
Tendler, R., 107
Thelen, M. H., 362, 394
Thompson, G., 172, 175, 178, 180,
    200, 202, 204, 260, 262, 267,
    271, 274, 275, 277, 281, 282,
    296, 297, 298, 299
Thompson, M., 267, 297
Thurston, D. B., 330
Tjellström, A., 67–81
Tough, J., 96, 97, 114
Travnickova, E., 317, 326, 330
Treffrey, J. A., 410, 418
Trickett, P. K., 96, 115
Trohanis, P. L., 104, 112
Trojan, S., 317, 326, 330
Tronick, E., 123, 137
Trybus, R., 84, 114
Tulkin, S. R., 91, 114

Uben, R. J., 144
Uzgiris, I., 91, 114

Van Hecke-Wulatin, M., 89, 112, 418
Van Lieshout, C. F. M., 85, 114
Van Nort, J. B., 213, 228
Vandenburgh, F. V., 153
Vanderheiden, G. C., 342, 348, 353
Vanderveer, B., 259, 298
Vaughn, H. G., 253, 258
Vernon, M., 83, 114, 141, 146, 153,
    403, 407
Vollenweider, J., 107
Von Specht, H., 234, 252, 256

Wachs, T., 91, 114
Waters, P. D., 345, 353
Watkins, J. M., 200
Watrous, B. S., 176, 205

Weber, B. A., 175, 190, 204, 205,
    267, 271, 298
Weintraub, S., 118, 136
Weiss, I. P., 256
Weller, G. M., 201
Wethered, C. E., 339, 341, 353
White, B. L., 91, 114
Whyte, L., 27–43, 353
Widen, J. E., 259–299
Wiig, E. H., 320, 331
Wilbur, R. B., 152, 333, 353
Wile, E., 317–331
Williams, R., 94, 114
Williamson, D. G., 182, 205, 227
Williston, J. S., 189, 201
Wilson, A. A., 260, 298
Wilson, A. C., 261, 294
Wilson, B. C., 153
Wilson, J. J., 146, 153, 208, 224, 227
Wilson, W. R., 172, 178, 179, 200,
    202, 204, 236, 258, 259–299
Windman, T. R., 257
Wolk, S., 171, 201
Wood, M. H., 190, 205
Woodrow, S., 182, 205
Woods, D. L., 257
Woods, G. E., 65
Wooley, H., 260, 295
Worthington, D. W., 192, 205, 234,
    251, 258
Wright, D., 26
Wrightstone, J. W., 84, 114

Yamamoto, K., 115
Yasui, M., 296
Yellin, A. M., 263, 264, 299

Zaporozhets, A. V., 363, 395
Zarcadoolas, C., 135
Zekulin, X. Y., 263, 299
Zigler, E., 96, 115
Zinchenke, B. P., 363, 395

Subject Index

Ability, 14
Abnormality, 46, 51, 229, 230, 261, 301
  of pinna, 212, 229
Abuse, 8
Access devices, 339, 340
Accident, 5
Accountability, 3
Achievement, 9, 17
  academic, 96
  scores, 84
  tests, 398
Acoustic analysis, 267
Acoustic environment, 131, 220
Acoustic immitance measurements, 231
Acoustic neuroma, 58
Acoustic reflexes, 31, 185, 186, 187, 188
Acoustic signal, 269
Acoustic testing, 229
Acquisition, 279
Acuity, 359, 378
Adenovirus, 58
Adults, 104
Advocacy, 6
AEP. See Auditory evoked potentials
AER. See Auditory evoked response
Age, 273
Agencies, 3

Aggression, 13, 402
Air–bone gap, 188
Air conduction
  audiogram, 217
  threshold, 314
Albers-Schonberg disease, 57. See
  also Osteopetrosis
Allergies, 37
Allocentricity, 363, 365
Alport's syndrome, 54, 58
Alstrom's syndrome, 58
Amblyopia, 42
American Sign Language, 412, 417
Aminoglycocides, 34, 37, 43
Amniocentesis, 52
Amplification, 15, 21, 86, 98, 99, 125, 207, 208, 220, 222, 309, 311, 334, 360, 370
Amplitude ratio, 252
Amygdaloid nucleus, 360
Anesthesia, 253
Anomalies, 188, 248
Anoxia, 71, 208, 235, 317
Antibiotics, 53
Anticonvulsant, 253
Apert syndrome, 55
Apgar, 34, 37, 43, 212, 230, 240, 249
Aplasia, 57, 67
Apnea, 29, 35, 240
Articulation, 33, 250

Asphyxia, 29, 34, 43, 212, 230, 235,
    240, 249, 254, 317, 322, 324, 328
  of babies, 317
  of children, 333
  of group, 323
Assessment, 1, 30, 31, 46, 117, 118,
    128, 129, 134, 182
  descriptive, 127
  interdisciplinary, 46
  team, 129
  tools of, 128, 404
Assets, 355
  appraisal of, 19
  identification of, 3, 16
Assignments, 347
Association phonemic method, 415
Asthma, 213, 219
Astrocytosis, 240
Attitude, 23, 47
Ataxia, 58
Atresia, 194
  meatal, 72, 75, 79
Atrophy, 236
Attention, 143, 390
  centering, 358
  span, 341
Audiograms, 141, 144
Audiologists, 7, 21, 30, 38, 139, 147,
    172, 209, 220, 221, 230, 255,
    267, 290, 312, 326, 334, 409
Audiology, 10, 48, 240, 242, 248
  assessment in, 195, 409
  equipment and, 225
  evaluation in, 173, 183, 208, 223,
    229
  intrauterine, 52
  investigation in, 46, 54
  management in, 220, 231
  mobile unit and, 208
  screening tests in, 363
  services of, 398
  suite and, 225
  team, 210
  testing in, 6, 210, 215
Audiometer, 209
Audiometric assessment, 370
Audiometric findings, 217
Audiometric procedures, 171

Audiometric results, 218
Audiometric tests, 274
Audiometry, 31, 68, 148, 172, 189,
    302
  baseline, 209
  behavioral, 173, 174, 175, 182, 190,
    194, 215, 231, 236, 239, 243,
    244, 259, 265, 267
  identification, 209
  mobile, 209
  play, 181, 182, 183
  visual reinforcement, 128. See also
    Visual reinforcement
    audiometry
Audition, 222, 367
Auditory acuity, 359
Auditory agnosia, 254
Auditory attention, 126
Auditory brainstem
  evoked response, 38, 39, 62, 144,
    190, 233
  pathway, 265
  response, 185, 189, 233, 236, 242,
    243, 259, 265, 269, 317, 328
  audiometry, 190, 207, 223, 270
  latencies, 282, 291
  threshold, 290
Auditory central processing, 1
Auditory channel, 360
Auditory cortex, 234, 252, 261, 326
Auditory cues, 276
Auditory deficits, 2
Auditory evoked response, 234, 235,
    238, 244, 255, 263
  cortical, 140, 144
Auditory evoked potentials, 231, 248,
    254, 264
Auditory function, 247, 254, 265, 391
Auditory impairments, 367
Auditory inputs, 364, 369
Auditory intensity, 375
Auditory nerve, 233
Auditory nervous system, 269
Auditory modality, 358
Auditory oral, 48
Auditory pathway, 234
Auditory problems, 185
Auditory reflex, 358

Auditory reinforcement, 362
Auditory reinforcer, 379
Auditory sensitivity, 21, 182
Auditory sense, 389
Auditory skills, 281
Auditory stimulation, 370
Auditory stimulus, 179, 358, 370, 376
Auditory system, 226, 261
Auditory thresholds, 359
Auditory training, 15, 155, 312, 359
Augmentative communication aids,
   346
Augmentative communication system,
   335, 336, 340, 341, 342, 348, 349
Aural habilitation, 398
Auricle, 54
   epithesis of, 67
   malformation of, 75
Autism, 51, 52, 63, 139, 163, 192,
   356, 368, 369, 379, 402
Autocentricity, 363, 365
Autonomy, 95
Autopsy, 240
Avoidance, 107

Baby talk, 93
Barbituate, 253
Basilar membrane, 190, 262
Behavior, 13, 21, 99, 100, 122, 165,
   357, 358, 383, 409
   aggressive, 402
   age and, 366
   assessment of, 265, 266, 271
   audiometry of, 173, 174, 182, 190,
      194
   change in, 355
   management of, 414
   modification of, 132, 133, 397, 400
   performance, 28
   problems, 52, 106, 374, 416
   procedures, 181
   quotient, 374, 376
      scores, 378
   responses, 175, 176, 230, 245, 247
Behavioral observation audiometry,
   175, 178, 183, 215, 217, 218,
   221, 231, 236, 243, 259, 265,
   267, 268, 271, 292

Bilingualism, 101, 102, 104
   families and, 412
   pathology of, 102
Bilirubin, 34, 37, 43
   encephalopathy, 33
Bimodal input, 103
Bioelectrical correlates, 269
Birth defects, 209
Birth history, 212, 213, 219
Birthweight, 29, 39, 43, 53, 80, 212,
   229, 240, 333
Blindness, 5, 6, 10, 22, 30, 31, 33, 34,
   36, 38, 366, 377
   in children, 139, 358
   and deafness, 333, 401, 410
   and learning, 355
Body language, 336
Boller-Herold syndromes, 214
Bone anchored hearing aid, 76, 77, 78
Bone conduction, 314
   hearing aid, 67, 75, 78
   thresholds of, 314
Brain, 262
   damage of, 51, 52, 140, 181, 317,
      359, 412
   dysfunction of, 139, 141, 148
   function of, 140, 142
   lesions, 192, 234, 253
   systems, 146
Brainstem, 140, 233, 234, 238, 245,
   262, 269, 291, 328, 359
   lesions in, 233
   potentials of, 189
   responses of, 248
Brainstem audiometry, 190. See also
   Auditory brainstem evoked
   response
Broadband,
   click stimuli, 190
   noise and, 267
Broncho-pulmonary dysplasia, 214

Canon communication, 345, 346
Cardiopulmonary handicap, 214
Care, 14
   continuum of, 23
Caregivers, 1, 409
Case history, 173

Cataracts, 6
Caudal regression syndrome, 248
Causality, 336, 342
Causative factor, 386
Centers, special, 23
Central auditory brainstem pathway
    functioning, 190
Central auditory dysfunction, 235, 255
Central auditory processing, 1
Central auditory system, 357
Central nervous system, 29, 33, 34,
    35, 38, 39, 47, 53, 192, 259, 265,
    282, 317
  abnormality in, 318
  dysfunction in, 141
  lesions of, 235
  pathology of, 253
Central processing
  disorders, 265
  dysfunction, 250
Cerebellum, 262
  blood flow in, 327
  cortex and, 240, 326
  damage of, 358
  dysfunction of, 10
  hemisphere and, 328
  lesion in, 326
Cerebral palsy, 5, 6, 31, 33, 34, 36,
    45, 47, 52, 58, 67, 70, 213, 214,
    317, 318
Cerumen, 261
Cheilo-palatoschisis, 72
Cholesteatomas, 307
Chorioretinitis, 142, 145
Chromosome, 260
  defects of, 309
Chronological age, 266, 272, 274,
    276, 286
Circumvention, 131, 132
  intervention, 131
Classification, 16
Cleft palate, 67, 213, 214, 215, 219,
    229, 248
  teams, 7
Click(s), 236, 237, 264, 265
Club foot, 215
CMV. See Cytomegalovirus
CNS. See Central nervous system

Cochlea, 194, 290, 291, 370
  abnormality of, 290
  function of, 140, 286, 293
  impairment of, 190, 194
  mechanics of, 314
  partition of, 314
  pathology of, 291
  spirals of, 262
  turns of, 308
Codes, 383
Cognition, 19, 28, 144, 387
  abilities and, 343, 388
  capacity for, 388
  competence of, 140
  deficits of, 1, 149, 217, 335
  development of, 105, 118, 121, 259
  functioning of, 371, 402
  impairment of, 45, 117
Cohesion, 15
Communication
  bimodal, 157, 158, 161, 162
  competence and, 99, 100, 101
  deficits in, 335
  disorders in, 317, 325
  handicaps of, 327
  interpersonal, 3
  manual, 48, 87, 333. See also Sign
    language
  method of, 415
  signs, 381
  skills, 49, 84, 100, 101, 229, 334,
    342, 379, 380, 383, 402
    evaluation of, 231
    teacher of, 398
  system of, 415
  training and, 15
Community, 22, 23
Compensation, 131, 132
Competence, 91, 122, 145
  positive, 16
  primary, 3
Complex noise stimulus, 278
Compliance, 271, 357, 376
Computer, 236, 346, 347
Computerized tomography scan, 54,
    63, 145, 235, 236, 242, 245, 248,
    249, 253, 254
Conceptual development, 122, 123

Conceptual function, 377
Conceptual skills, 356
Conditioned orientation reflex
    audiometry, 177
Conductive losses, 260, 304, 306,
    308, 313
    of hearing, 6, 35, 36, 37, 38, 54,
        55, 301, 313
    bilateral, 36
Confidence, 14, 95
Congenital deafness, 317, 403
Congenital disabilities, 13
Congenital diseases, 52
Congenital disorders, 414
Congenital handicap, 214
Congenital hearing loss, 55
Congenital heart disease, 214
Congenital rubella, 140
Consequences, secondary, 1, 125
Consistency, in care, 21
Consultation, 22
Control, 127
  internal, 401
Convulsions, 29, 33, 34, 42, 245
Convulsive disorders, 31, 235, 240,
    254
Cooperation, professional, 7
COR. See Conditioned orientation
    reflex audiometry
Cornea, 42
Cornelia de Lange syndrome, 214,
    219
Corrective intervention, 130, 132
Cortical nerve cells, 326
Cortical potentials, 263
Cost effectiveness, 6
Counselling, 310, 311, 410
  genetic, 2
Cranial self-stimulatory activity,
    360
Cranio-facial anomaly, 40
Crib-O-Gram, 208
Critical age, 124, 125, 126
Cross modal conditioning, 369
Cross modal transfer, 388
CT scan. See Computerized
    tomography
Cued speech, 156–161

Culture, 3
  of poverty, 93
Curiosity, 21
Custodial care, 403
Cyanosis, 29, 215, 219
  congenital heart disease and, 221
Cytomegalovirus, 53, 57, 71, 173,
    183, 229

Damaged children, 14
Day care, 411
Deafness
  in blind children, 410
  congenital, 403
  and learning, 355
  and the multihandicapped child,
    404
  profound, 414
Decision-making, 3
Dedication, 17
Deficit, 355
  attentional, 74
  auditory, 2
  cognitive, 1
  educational, 7
  emotional, 1
  intellectual, 21
  language, 1
  motor deaf, 74
  ophthalmological, 6
  perceptual, 74
  sensory, 1
  social, 1
  of speech, 1
  visual deaf, 47
Delay
  developmental, 6, 38
  language, 49
  motor, 49
Demand
  response arc, 384
  symbol, 384
Dependency, 8
Depression, 156
Deprivation
  cognitive, 93
  therapy and, 22
Detection, 2, 229

Development
    language, 1, 125
    problems, 29
    stage of, 372
Developmental age, 266, 276, 281,
    282
Developmental approach, 118, 134,
    411
Developmental asynchrony, 125, 131
Developmental delay, 6, 47, 48, 51,
    207, 217
Developmental disabled, 52, 62, 184,
    225
    deafness, 106
    in children, 209
    in the hearing impaired, 409
Developmental examination, 33
Developmental history, 174
Developmental interactions, 125
Developmental milestones, 142
Developmental process, 118, 129
Developmental progress, 125
Developmental shift, 365
Developmental stage, 364
Developmental synchrony, 126, 132
Dexterity, manual, 333, 338
Diabetes, 247
Diagnosis, 1, 2, 6, 10, 15, 19, 21, 51,
    63, 130, 301, 368
    audiometric equipment and, 209
    evaluation of, 231
    information and, 220, 411
    intervention and, 2
    medical, 139
    procedure, 53
    process of, 9
    tests and, 398
    therapy of, 3, 14, 19
Dialect switching, 102
Didacticism, 104
Direct selection mode, 345
Disability, 9, 17, 23, 46, 47, 48
    multiple, 19
    physical, 49
Disadvantaged community, 88, 98
    child in, 91, 97
Discipline, 8, 10
Discomfort, 20, 127

Discrimination, 178, 277, 282, 303,
    386
    tests in, 215
Disease, 5, 318
    complicating, 7
Disorder, 9
    secondary, 7
    integration and, 10
Distance receptors, 366, 373
Distortion, 261
Distress in neonates, 363
Divorce, 8
Down's Syndrome, 16, 40, 57, 70,
    173, 179, 188, 213, 214, 219,
    259–293, 301–315
Drugs, 234
Dysphasia, 139, 141

Ear
    canal, 261, 271, 291, 314
        volume of, 287
    infections in, 126
    malformations of, 68, 72, 74
    molds, 309, 310, 311, 370
        fittings of, 314
Echolalia, 415
Economic restraints, 404
Educability, 42, 99
Education, 2, 10, 14, 15, 18, 83, 147,
    364, 409, 417
    deficits and, 7
    funding for, 7
    programming and, 7, 416
    services for, 9
Educational care, 25
Educational development, 334, 374
Educational growth, 13
Educational inputs, 146
Educational intervention, 229
Educational model, 5
Educational progress, 400
Educational skills, 17
Educational staff, 23
Educational training program, 265
Educator, 22, 48, 88, 123, 326, 334
    deaf therapist, 14, 15, 21, 22, 23,
        25
EEG, 145, 235, 240, 242, 245, 248

Egocentrism, 96
Electric response, audiometric, 269
Electrical activity, 189
Electroacoustic impedance bridge, 271
Electrocardiogram, 54
Electrocochleography, 164, 269
Electrode, 189, 270
  configuration of, 236
Electroencephalogram, 63, 145
Electronic communication, 345
Electronystagmography, 143, 149, 221
Electrophysiological approach, 259
Electrophysiological assessment, 233, 265
Electrophysiological factors, 263
Electrophysiological indicators, 247
Electrophysiological procedures, 269
Electrophysiological response, 231
Electrophysiological studies, 282
Electrowriter, 348
Emotions
  adjustment of, 106
    deficits, 1
    differences, 3
    support, 2, 409
  behavior and, 402
  development of, 8, 49, 105, 122
  disturbance of, 359
  issues of, 123
  problems of, 52
  relationships and, 13
  responses of parents to, 416
  status and, 127
Empathy, 15
Employment, 399
End organ, 359
Endocrine system, 54
Endotrachial intubation, 319
Energy, 356, 357
English, 104, 412
Enrichment, 131
Environment, 1, 126, 127, 128, 129, 336, 338, 339, 383, 384
  aids and, 347
  control of, 414
  cues of, 341
  deprivation of, 104

external, 361
home, 91
language learning, 91
sounds of, 416
verbal, 92
Epilepsy, 52, 160
Epileptiform activity, 236, 245
Episthesis, 79
Epithelium, 262
Epitympanum, 308
Equipment, 18, 344, 346
Erythroblastosis fetalis, 58
Ethics, 14
Ethnocentric bias, 103
Etiology, 264, 334
Eustachian tube, 262
  dysfunction of, 57, 60
Evoked potential, 240, 247, 251, 252, 255
Evoked response, 148
  audiometry, 334
  battery, 250
  records, 141
Evolution, 129, 179
  comprehensive, 5
  multi-disciplinary, 2, 30
  of school, 29
Exclusion, 90
Experimental procedures, 372
Exploration, 127, 372
Expression, 384
Expressive language, 250, 313
  skills of, 174
    signing in, 398
External auditory canal, 54
  walls of, 187
Eye pointing, 345
  chart, 344

Facial asymmetry, 326
Facial canal, 308
Facial deformaties, 60
Facial genu, 308
Facial nerve, 226, 306
  canal of, 307, 308
Facio-digito-vertebro-costal
  dysmorphic syndrome, 167
Faith, 14, 22, 23

Family, 15, 16, 19, 336
  history of, 212, 230, 318
  stress and, 3
  support of, 2
  team, 22
Fathers, 19
Feedback, 124
Feelings, 13
Fetal alcohol syndrome, 214
Fetal periods, 318
Fetoscopy, 52
Fine motor
  areas, 384
  coordination, 222, 415
  function, 417
  skills, 369, 389, 390, 402
Finger spelling, 333
First arch syndrome, 309
Fluid, amniotic, 239
Follow-up, 27, 28, 38, 45, 46, 195
Frequency response, 309
Frustration, 89, 356
Fulfillment, 25
Function, 359, 378, 379
  affective, 1
  independence and, 399
  intellectual, 1
  motor, 1
  visual, 1
Functional age, 281, 302
Functional language, 399
Functional level, 339
Functional skills, 334, 397
Funding, 7

Gait, 143
Gastroenteritis, 245
Genetic counselling, 2, 147, 209
Genetic deafness syndrome, 142
Genetic defects, 219
Genitalia, 143
Genitourinary system, 54, 143
  malfunctions of, 145
Gestation, 34, 37, 43
Gesture, 3, 144
Gifted hearing impaired child, 416
Glia, 326
Glomerulonephritis, 58

Goals, 3, 18, 25, 29, 92, 129
Goldenhar syndrome, 72
Government, 7
Grammar, 104, 122
Grief, 22, 89, 409
Gross motor skills, 369, 390, 402
Growth, 22, 30
  affective, 1
  cognitive, 1
  intrauterine, retardation of, 240
  normal, 10
Guilt, 7, 8
Gustatory reinforcer, 379

Habilitation, 2, 45, 47, 49, 75, 139,
    148, 155, 156, 164, 194, 225, 231
  plan of, 141, 259
Habilitative methods, 3
Habituation, 267
Half-way houses, 405
Handivoice, 345
Hard copy, 345
Hardship, financial, 8
Head
  position trainer, 341
  trauma, 29, 35
Head-turn response, 277
Health
  model, 5
  service, 9
Hearing aid, 6, 68, 130, 220, 250,
    309, 310, 311, 360, 370, 409,
    411, 414
  amplification of, 313
  dealer of, 311
  efficacy of, 232
  fitting for, 155, 414
  maintenance of, 310
  therapy and, 312
  use of, 312, 315
Hearing levels, 286
Hearing rehabilitation, 359
Hearing screening, 229
Hearing sensitivity, 177, 189, 259,
    290, 292
Hearing test, 215
Hearing therapists, 315
Hemorrhage, intracranial, 29, 34, 226

Hepatosplenomegaly, 53
Heredity, 70, 71, 320
Herpes, 183, 229, 403
  simplex virus, 53
  zoster virus, 58
High renin hypertension, 240
High risk, 224, 326
  children, 318
  mothers, 27
  neonates, 27
  registers, 51, 208, 213, 318
History
  intrauterine, 54
  medical, 216
  peripartum, 54
Holophrasis, 99
Home demonstration, 410
Hormonal influences, 361
Human services, 9
Humiliation, 24
Hurler's syndrome, 57
Hyaline membrane disease, 214
Hydrocephalus, 213, 214, 318
Hydrocephaly, 33, 42, 43
Hyperbilirubinemia, 212, 229, 318
Hyperkinesis, 13
Hypoparathyroid, 248
Hypoplasia, 308
Hypoplastic mandible, 248
Hypothalamus, 360
Hypotonia, 212, 230, 235, 240, 242,
  245, 261
Hypoxia, 58, 235, 240, 317, 318, 326
Hypoxic-ischemic encephalopathy, 29,
  33, 36
Hypsarhythmia, 236, 240

Identification, 1, 3, 6, 9, 10, 27, 40,
  53, 118, 126, 188, 301, 368
  audiometry, 207, 209
  skills, 356
Illnesses, intercurrent, 142
Imagination, 97
Immaturity, 84
Immunization, 6
Impairments, 46, 47, 129, 260
  cognitive, 45
  hearing, 45

linguistic, 172
mental, 172
motor, 172
motor development, 45
primary, 107, 131
secondary, 107, 130, 131
visual, 45, 172
Impedance, 31, 77, 186, 219, 231
  audiometry, 190, 215, 216, 217, 271
  bridge, 209
  results, 187, 191
  tympanometry, 306
Impedance matched hearing aid, 77,
  78
Incus, 307
Independence, 23, 87, 130, 366
Infant stimulation program, 209
Infection, 229
  bacterial, 58
  intrauterine, 141, 144, 230
  transplacental, 53
Inflammation, 307
Influence, home, 91
Influenza, 230
Infrastructure, 358
Injury, 5
Inner ear conductive losses, 262, 309
  of hearing, 307
Insight, 15
Intellect, 7, 15, 46, 240
  capacity of, 16, 401
  deficits of, 21
  development of, 8
  function of, 1, 20, 23
  potential of, 83
  status of, 364
Intelligence, 42. See also IQ
  groupings, 34
  testing, 30, 320, 398
Intelligibility, 78
Intensity, 270
Interaction, 105, 127, 128
Interactive communication
    development, 416
Interdisciplinary assessment, 38, 46
Interdisciplinary evaluation, 30
Internal auditory canal films, 54
Intersensory development, 364, 365

Intervention, 1, 21, 83, 104, 117, 118,
    123, 128, 129, 130, 131, 132,
    134, 155, 333, 334, 335, 416
  diagnostic, 2
  early, 105
  medico-surgical, 15
  program, 2, 14
Intrinsic drives, 124
Intubated babies, 41
IQ
  scores of, 33, 34, 35, 36, 87, 101,
    145

Jargon, 415
Jaundice, 47, 53
Jervell and Lange-Nielsen syndrome,
    54, 57
Jugular bulb, 308

Kanamycin, 36. *See also*
    Aminoglycocides
Kidney, 240
Kinesthetically distracted, 364

Labelling, 98
Labial sounds, 222
Labyrinth, 54, 151
Laminograms, 145
Language, 83, 94, 96, 97, 104, 105,
    144, 155, 260, 317, 318, 358, 416
  acquisition, 99, 101, 147
  in deaf children, 328
  deficiency in, 156, 397
  deficits in, 1, 33, 35, 117
  delays of, 31, 125, 241, 244, 317
  development of, 1, 83, 118, 123,
    155, 252, 261, 301, 318
  disorders of, 317, 318, 319, 326,
    327
  environment and, 98
  expression of, 33, 100, 398
  functional, 399
  impairment of, 327
  intervention in, 348
  learning of, 412, 415
    environment, 91
    problem, 415
  processing of, 140

  progress in, 162
  reception of, 33, 120, 398
  retardation and, 412
  skills of, 103
  spoken, 117
  spontaneous, 97
  system of, 122
  use of, 99
Late vertex auditory evoked
    responses, 233–255
Latency, 190, 243, 250, 252, 264,
    265, 286, 287, 291, 292, 293
  intensity function of, 290, 293
  norms of, 286
  of response, 190
Leadership, 22
Learning, 13, 20, 21, 36, 103, 105,
    129, 347, 355, 357, 358, 366,
    383, 389, 396
  disabilities of, 52, 63
  disorders in, 53
  environment and, 338
  experiences in, 18
  process of, 360
  programs for, 347
  skills of, 387, 388, 390
Lesion, 234, 253
  of central nervous system, 235
  site of, 54, 255
Lexicon, 122
Life-style, 23
Limbic system, 360, 361
Limitations, 16, 411
  of professionals, 8
Linguistics
  abilities of, 343
  acculturation and, 102
  codes of, 94
  communication and, 1
  competence in, 96
  complexity of, 343
  concepts of, 320
  development of, 8, 147
  environment of, 98, 131
  feedback of, 101
  impairments of, 172
  input of, 93, 99
  skills of, 104

spurts of, 103
status of, 127
structure of, 96, 371
Lip reading, 161
Liver function, 54
Localization, 172, 259, 262, 265, 275, 292
Locomotive deficits, 335
Locomotive skills, 334
Loudness recruitment, 188
LVAER *See* Late vertex auditory evoked response

Macrophages, 326
Macula, 42
Mainstreaming, 83, 155
Maladaptation, 88
Malformations, 52, 67, 70, 78, 212, 229, 313
  of ear, 68, 72, 74
Malleus, 307
Manometer, 271
Manualism, 417
Masking signal, 267
Mastoid, 236, 270
  films and, 54
  process of, 76
Maternal age, 34, 37
Maternal verbal responsiveness, 91
Maturation, 129, 190, 282
Maturity, 87, 363, 366
Measles, 58
Meatus, external, 79
Meconium, 240
Medical management, 231
Medication, 10, 188
Medico-surgical intervention, 15
Memory, 143, 390
  unit of, 345
Memowriter, 346
Menière's disease, 291
Meningitis, 29, 33, 47, 53, 71, 140, 141, 212, 230, 320
  bacterial, 214
  meningococcal, 58
Mental age, 301, 365
Mental age equivalent, 274, 276
Mental deficiency, 139

Mental handicap, 364, 365, 366, 367
Mental impairments, 172
Mental retardation, 5, 6, 10, 13, 31, 33, 36, 38, 42, 45, 51, 52, 62, 67, 70, 72, 171, 186, 259, 260, 261, 263, 264, 277, 282, 301, 333, 359, 385, 386, 391, 412
Mental subnormality, 387, 388
  in children, 390
  hospital for, 16
Mesenchymal tissue, 308
Metabolic disorders, 57, 58
Microcomputer, 345, 347, 348
Microelectronics, 345
Microprocessors, 344
Microsomia, 72
Microtia, 72, 79
Middle components, 245
Middle ear, 72, 188, 261, 308
  cavity of, 308
  disease of, 260
  disorder of, 217, 414
  effusion in, 186, 306
  infection of, 130
  pathology of, 54, 217, 279
  problems in, 173
Middle evoked potentials, 317
Middle latency, 233, 238
Minimal brain dysfunction, 74, 192
Middle latency auditory evoked responses, 233–255
Mixed hearing loss, 32, 34, 36, 38, 54, 55
Mobile audiological unit, 208
Mobile audiometry, 209, 224, 225
Mobility patterns, 401
Möbius syndrome, 55
Moral standards, 94
Mortality, infant, 53
Mothers, 100, 105, 310, 338, 409
  educated, 95
  speech and, 92
Motivation, 14, 96, 356
Motor activity, 164
Motor capacities, 124
Motor coordination, 46
Motor deficits, 117, 143, 217
Motor development, 30, 174, 259

Motor disorders, 207
Motor dysfunctions, 213
Motor function, 387
Motor impairment, 45, 117, 172
Motor integration, 1
Motor mechanisms, central,
    peripheral, 127
Motor pattern, 385
Motor performance, 28
Motor skills, 128, 368, 379, 380, 383
Motor status, 127
Motor systems, 119, 121
Multidisciplinary committees, 7
Multidisciplinary evaluation, 2
Multiple sclerosis, 328
Mumps, 58
Muscular structures, 119
Musculoskeletal system, 54
Myelination, 262
Myelomeningocele, 213, 214
Myoelectric switches, 345
Myringotomy, 6, 37, 218

Near receptors, 373
Near senses, 365
Necrosis, 326
Neonate, 29, 33, 187
    asphyxia of, 318, 319, 320, 325,
        326, 327
    clinic for, 333
    follow-up of, 28
    illness and, 27
    meningitis in, 318
Nerve
    VIIIth, 262, 269
    fiber, 360
Nervous system, 327, 361
Neural centers, 326
Neural development, 286
Neural generators, 233
Neural messages, 361
Neural responses, 263
Neural structures, 282
Neural systems, 119
Neuroelectrical activity, 234, 236
Neuroelectrical potentials, 269
Neurological capacities, 124
Neurological deficits, 117, 140, 142,
    226, 333

Neurological disorders, 207
Neurological exam, 33, 54, 193, 318
Neurological impairments, 133
Neurological involvement, 235
Neurological mechanics, 127
Neurological systems, 124
Neurologically impaired multiply
    handicapped children, 234
Neurologists, 139, 162
    pediatric, 140, 141, 147, 148
Neurology, pediatric, 6, 142
Neuroma, acoustic, 58
Neuromotor problems, 326
Neuromotor skills, 379
Neuronal depletion, 240
Neuronal growth, 262
Neurons, 360
Neurophysiological research, 360
Neuropsychological test profiles,
    146
Neuropsychology, 162
Neurosensory handicaps, 318
Neurosensory problems, 326
Newborn, 51, 189
Nonverbal communication, 144, 156
Normative latency, 189
Nystagmus, 143, 149

Object permanence, 336
Observation audiometry, 68
Observer bias, 267
Ocular system, 54
Occupational therapy, 22, 38, 220,
    222, 333, 411
Odor, 356
Onset, latent, 8
Operant conditioning, 32, 33, 175,
    180, 366, 368, 369
Ophthalmologic deficits, 6
Ophthalmologic evaluation, 145
Ophthalmologic examination, 174
Ophthalmologists, 334
Optic atrophy, 42, 58, 240
Optimal intervention program, 14
Organics
    disturbance of, 318
    internal, 361
Orienting reflex threshold, 276
Orthopedic surgery, 6

Ossicle(s), 262, 308
    abnormalities of, 308
    chain, 306
    disarticulations of, 188
Osseointegrated implants, 76
Osteogensis imperfecta, 57
Osteopetrosis, 57. *See also* Albers-
    Schönberg disease
Otic capsule, 144, 308
Otitis, 139
    media, 6, 41, 57, 60, 71, 222, 241,
        260, 261, 262, 306, 307
Otolaryngologist, 7, 54, 139, 306, 334
Otological chair, 210
Otological examination, 216, 218
Otologist, 57, 62, 147
Otomicroscopy, 230
Otosclerosis, 57
Otoscopy, 186, 187, 230
Ototoxic drugs, 57, 142. *See also*
    Kanamycin; Aminoglycocides
Outer ear, 188
Output format, 345

Paget's disease, 57
Palatal deformities, 60
Paralysis, 10
Parents
    child programs and, 409
    counselling of, 129, 139, 194
    deaf, 106
    education of, 411
    groups of, 411
    infant interaction with, 125, 410
    infant program and, 48
    single, 413
    training of, 48, 410
Passivity, 357
Patent ductus arteriosis, 214
Pathologist, speech, 7, 30, 38, 139,
    312, 326, 333
Pathology, speech, 10, 22, 48
Patience, 15
PB–K discrimination lists, 303
Pediatricians, 139, 147, 334
Pedopsychiatric consultation, 157
Peers, 96
Pendred's syndrome, 54, 57
Perceptive hearing loss, 167

Perceptual motor organization, 123
Perceptual motor program, 399
Perceptual status
Performance, 91
    levels of, 403
Perilymphatic spaces, 308
Perinatal asphyxia, 233
Perinatal infections, 230
Perinatal periods, 318
Peripheral auditory dysfunction, 325
Peripheral auditory pathway, 233
Peripheral hearing loss, 235, 251
Peripheral hearing sensitivity, 189,
    234, 242, 245
Peripheral impairment, 192
Peripheral loss, 193
Peripheral processing disorders, 265
Peripheral sensory sensitivity, 3
Peripheral visual function, 1
Periventricular lucomalacia, 328
Periventricular white matter, 327
Personality, 118
Personnel, 129, 134
Pessimism, 15
Petechiae, 53
Phocomelia, 214
Phonological dysfunction, 317
Physical development, 8
Physical examination, 142
Physical handicap, 334, 335, 338,
    341, 342, 347
Physical health, 266
Physical skills, 49
Physical strength, 356
Physical therapists, 140, 220, 334
Physically handicapped hearing
    impaired, mentally retarded, 348
Physiotherapy, 22, 38, 411
Piagetian theory, 104, 363
Pierre-Robin syndrome, 55, 213, 214,
    215, 219
Pinna, 72, 261, 291
    abnormalities of, 229
    deformities of, 60
Placenta, insufficiency of, 43
Plastic surgeons, 7
Play, 339
    audiometry and, 68, 181, 182, 183,
        217, 236

Pleasure, 360–363, 372
Pneumatic otoscopy, 302
Pointing response, 344
Polarity reversal, 253
Polytomography, 54, 63
Population, subject, 8
Postnatal maturation, 282
Poverty, 88, 90
Power, 88, 89, 96, 105
Preauricular pits, 72
Predictability, 356
Pregnancy, 142
Prematurity, 34, 37, 43, 71, 80 141
Prenatal care, 53
Prenatal disease, 318
Preparatory skills, 340
Pride, 372
Primary auditory cortex, 253
Primitive exploration, 20
Processing, 261
  central auditory, 1
  oral directions, 320
Professional competence, 14, 15
Professional cooperation, 7
Profound deafness, 414
Prognostications, 16, 17
Program
  immunization, 6
  intervention, 2
  special, 6
Programming, 3, 5, 23, 410
Proprioceptive cues, 370
Prosody, 155
Prostheses, 359
Prosthodontist, 7
Psychiatric disturbance, 31
Psychiatric team, 164
Psychiatric therapy, 156
Psychiatric treatment, 403
Psychiatric work, 169
Psychiatrist, 157, 333
  child, 146
  consulting, 398
Psychoeducational management, 231
Psychological advantages, 9
Psychological concomitants, 101
Psychological problems, 75, 83, 156
Psychologists, 139, 320, 334, 398

Psychology, 10, 48
Psychomotor
  age equivalent, 274
  development, 301
  retardation, 192
Psychopathology, 99
Psychosis, 156, 163
  infantile, 162
Psychotic children, 164, 166, 168,
  169
Punishers, 133
Pure tones, 178, 195, 221
  audiometric techniques of, 215
  average, 73, 304
  thresholds of, 287
Purpura, 53

Quadraplegia, 38

Ratiocination, 20
Reading ability, 94, 95
Receptive language skills, 174, 398
Reciprocity, 336
Referral, 216
Reflexes, 143, 218, 220, 221, 226
  acoustic, 31, 185, 186, 187, 188
Regression, 412
Rehabilitation, 221
  engineer of, 346
  medicine for, 209
  plans for, 225
Reinforcement, 133, 277, 356, 366,
  367, 373, 381
Rejection, 90
Remediation, 131, 132
Renal disease, 213, 214
Renal function, 54
Residual hearing, 86, 98, 161, 358,
  359
Residual sensory function, 358
Residual visual function, 358
Resource center, 6
Respiration audiometry, 68
Respiratory distress, 213, 219, 319
  syndrome of, 214
Respiratory infections, upper, 261
Response measurement, 364
Responsiveness, maternal verbal, 91

Retardation, 47, 181, 222, 241, 265
    academic, 88, 98, 286, 334, 338,
        358, 364
    in children, 267, 313, 358, 360, 362,
        380
    moderate, 6
    and motor function, 215
Retinal degeneration, 58
Retinitis pigmentosa, 142
Retinoblastoma, 214, 219
Retinopathy, 47, 160
Rh incompatibility, 47
Round window, 54, 308, 314
Rubella, 53, 57, 74, 141, 173, 174,
        183, 229, 313, 320, 363, 403, 416
    congenital, 140
    deaf children, 47
    epidemic, 6
    pregnancies and, 6
    vaccine for, 53

Saccular spaces, 308
Scanning mode, 344
School
    districts, 266
    for the deaf, 157
    environment, 103
    performance, 95
Screening, 45, 51, 62, 224, 230
Second arch syndrome, 309
Secondary auditory projections, 253
Seizures, 214, 221, 240, 242
    disorder and, 219
Self confidence, 93, 96, 105
Self exploration, 21
Self help, 368, 384
    skills of, 372, 373, 379, 383
Self manipulation, 21
Self mutilation, 13
Self occupation, 382
Self regard, 389
Self stimulation, 20, 356, 361, 365
Semantic structure, 86, 99, 104, 105
Semicircular canals, 308
Senses
    dominance of, 367
    functioning of, 21
    organs, 119, 121, 379

    of smell, 367
    of touch, 367
Sensorineural hearing loss, 6, 32, 34,
        35, 36, 38, 54, 55, 58, 220, 221,
        290, 412
Sensory-motor deficits, 207
Sensory-motor development, 364
Sensory-motor function, 378
Sensory-motor learning, 371
Sensory-motor organization, 123
Sensory-motor period, 363
Sensory-motor skills, 123
Septal areas, 360
Serial play audiometry, 215
Sex
    differences, 291
    distribution, 34, 37
Signal/noise ratio, 78
Sign language, 87, 98, 102, 131, 144,
        156, 163, 165, 414, 416
    acquisition of, 86
    American, 412, 417
    English, 158, 417
    French, 159, 160, 161, 164
Signs, 99, 105, 147, 168, 385, 386,
        415
Single parent, 413
Skeletal structure, 119
Skills, 14, 23, 122, 125, 349, 357, 383
    development of, 378, 387
    maturation of, 378
    methodological, 24
    personal, 22
    readiness of, 130
    self-help, 23
Sleep, 234
    disturbance of, 412
Smoking
    in the home, 35, 39, 43
Social behaviour, 402
Social class, 91, 92, 102
    deficits of, 1
    development of, 8, 122, 174
    differences in, 3
Social cognition, 123
Social competencies, 101
Social disruption, 15
Social emotional development, 121

Social issues, 123
Social problems, 83
Social reinforcement, 133
Social restriction, 23
Social skills, 49, 89
Social status, 127
Social system, 9
Social worker, 146, 334, 411
Somatosensory evoked potentials,
   264
Sound field, 216, 248
   testing, 215
Spasms, infantile, 53
Spastic quadriplegia, 240, 254
Spasticity, 235, 242
Speech
   acts of, 92
   audiometry of, 215
   audiometry threshold of, 241
   awareness of, 31
   comprehension of, 390
   deficits of, 1
   delays of, 31, 317
   development of, 54, 75, 261, 318
   discrimination of, 78
   disorders of, 53, 326, 327
   frequency range of, 195
   information of, 131
   of the mother, 92
   reading, 84, 144, 156, 158
   reception thresholds, 303
   sound discrimination, 259, 262,
      269
   stimulus, 269
   therapy, 398
Spina bifida, 17, 213, 214
Spondaic words, 215
SRT. See Speech, reception
   thresholds
Stapedectomies, 307
Stapedial artery, 308
Stapedial reflexes, 193
Stapedius muscle reflexes, 215
Stapes, 306, 307, 308
   fixation of, 262, 313
   footplate of, 306
   malformation of, 313
Stereotypic behaviour, 389

Stimulation, 1, 377, 388, 389
   extra-personal, 21
   sensory, 3
Strabismus, 58
Stress, 24
Structure
   semantic, 86
   syntactic, 86
Student/teacher ratio, 397
Subarachnoid hemorrhage, 236
Subskills, 124
Subject population, 8
Success rate, 276
Surgery, 1, 3, 37, 147
Sylvian fissure, 253
Synaptogenesis, 262
Syntactic structure, 86
Syntactical dysfunction, 317
Syntax, 104, 105, 160
Syphilis, 53, 229
Systematic communication patterns,
   389

Tactile dominance, 363, 369
Tactile inputs, 371
Tactile kinesthetic localization, 363
Tangible reinforcement operant
   conditioning audiometry, 181
Tantrums, 13, 125
Tape recorder, 342, 347
Teacher, 13, 16, 19, 220, 321, 409,
   411, 416
Teacher-therapist, 129, 130, 132, 134
Team
   approach, 23, 400
   cleft palate, 7
   multi-disciplinary, 7
Technical advances, 348
Technical aid, 334
Tectorial membrane, 262
Telecommunication
   aids, 335
   systems, 348
Television set, 342
Temporal bone, 76, 79, 262, 290, 291,
   307, 313
   investigation of, 306
   study of, 308

Temporal lobe
 cerebral infarcts of, 242
 lesions of, 234, 254
Temporal parietal cortex, 234
Temporo-parietal lesions, 253
Tensor veli palatini, 262
Testing, 62
 acoustic, 229
Thalamus, 234, 253, 360
Therapeutic approach, 18
Therapeutic armamentum, 18
Therapeutic care, 25
Therapeutic management, 3
Therapeutic model, 22
Therapeutic program, 385
Therapeutic progress, 18
Therapeutic regime, 3, 18, 365
Therapeutic situation, 24
Therapeutic skills, 17
Therapeutic staff, 23
Therapeutic team, 19
Therapeutic theme, 24
Therapist, 13, 16, 20, 24
 educator, 15, 19, 355
 teacher dedication, 17
Therapy, 3, 14, 15, 18, 19, 21, 22,
 146, 310, 357, 359, 371
Thresholds, 192, 268, 274, 278, 281,
 282
 measurement of, 215
Thyroid, 54
 function of, 145
Time, 10, 14, 23
 differences, 324
 sampling, 383
Toxoplasmosis, 53, 174, 183,
 229
Toys, 342
 adapted, 338
Tracheotomy tubes, 213, 218
Transdisciplinary approach, 220
Trauma, 318
Treacher Collins' syndrome, 55, 72,
 75
21Trisomy, 260, 266
TROCA. See Tangible reinforcement
 operant conditioning audiometry
TTY, 348

Tubes, 6
 drainage, 279
 ventilation, 188, 218
Tympanic membrane, 54, 188
Tympanograms, 184, 185, 187, 188,
 194, 248, 279, 287
Tympanometry, 54, 144, 186, 188,
 215, 217, 221, 225, 279, 281,
 287, 302
 findings of, 218
 measurements of, 271
 results of, 186
Typewriter, 345

Ultra-sound, 52
Upper respiratory infections, 414
Urinalysis, 230
Usher's syndrome, 47, 52, 58, 141,
 150
Utricular spaces, 308

Ventilation, 29, 34, 35, 37, 43, 319,
 320
Ventricles, 247, 248, 253
 dilation of, 236
Verbal auditory abilities, 263
Verbal mediation, 101
Verbo-tonal method, 155
Vestibular aqueduct, 308
Vestibular dysfunction, 140, 148
Vestibular function, 141, 145, 150
Vestibular impairment, 151
Vestibular tests, 141, 149
Vibration stimulus, 378
Vibro-tactile condition, 377
Vibro-tactile input, 383
Vibro-tactile perception, 155
Vibro-tactile reinforcement, 373,
 379
Vibro-tactile sensory modality, 362
Vibro-tactile stimulation, 182, 362,
 365, 379, 382, 383, 389
Video games, 347
Viral studies, 54
Viremia, 52
Viruria, 53
Virus, 57

Vision, 42, 143, 341, 359, 361, 363, 367, 373
  acuity of, 128, 359
  central, 1
  defect of, 266
  deficit of, 47
  difficulties in, 52
  disorder of, 67
  evoked response, 242, 244
  function of, 377
  handicaps of, 385
  impairment, 30, 31, 33, 34, 36, 45, 171, 172, 333, 335
    in children, 182
  inputs, 369, 383
  localization of, 363
  modality of, 334, 366, 376
  motor channels of, 263
  motor function of, 417
  perception and, 417
  reference to, 100
  reinforcement of, 275, 368
  reinforcer of, 268, 269, 379
  retardation of, 412
  stimulation of, 364, 365, 375
  stimulus of, 180, 182, 367

Visual reinforcement audiometry, 68, 128, 171, 177, 178, 179, 183, 215, 217, 218, 236, 259, 265, 268, 271, 274, 276, 277, 281, 282, 292
Vitamin A, 262
Vocabulary, 343
  deficits in, 33
  studies of, 348
Vocal habits, 155
Vocal praise, 367
Vocational rehabilitation, 405
Vocational teacher, 398
Von Recklinghausen's syndrome, 58
VRA. See Visual reinforcement audiometry

Waardenburg's syndrome, 33, 52, 58
Wavepeaks, 189
Weyer's syndrome, 214
Wheelchair, 342
White matter, 240, 328
White noise, 248, 367, 374
Word
  and sentence structure, 320
Workshops, sheltered, 405

a
b
3 c
4 d
5 e
6 f
7 g
8 h
9 i
8 0 j